THE WORLD BIBLIOGRAPHICAL SERIES

This series, which is principally designed for the English speaker, will eventually cover every country (and many of the world's principal regions), each in a separate volume comprising annotated entries on works dealing with its history, geography, economy and politics; and with its people, their culture, customs, religion and social organization. Attention will also be paid to current living conditions – housing, education, newspapers, clothing, etc. – that are all too often ignored in standard bibliographies; and to those particular aspects relevant to individual countries. Each volume seeks to achieve, by use of careful selectivity and critical assessment of the literature, an expression of the country and an appreciation of its nature and national aspirations, to guide the reader towards an understanding of its importance. The keynote of the series is to provide, in a uniform format, an interpretation of each country that will express its culture, its place in the world, and the qualities and background that make it unique. The views expressed in individual volumes, however, are not necessarily those of the publisher.

VOLUMES IN THE SERIES

Please renew/return items by last date shown. Please call the number below:

Renewals and enquiries: 0300 123 4049

Textphone for hearing or speech impaired users: 0300 123 4041

www.hertsdirect.org/librarycatalogue
L32

India

WORLD BIBLIOGRAPHICAL SERIES

General Editors:

Robert G. Neville (Executive Editor)

John J. Horton

Robert A. Myers   Hans H. Wellisch

Ian Wallace   Ralph Lee Woodward, Jr.

John J. Horton is Deputy Librarian of the University of Bradford and currently Chairman of its Academic Board of Studies in Social Sciences. He has maintained a longstanding interest in the discipline of area studies and its associated bibliographical problems, with special reference to European Studies. In particular he has published in the field of Icelandic and of Yugoslav studies, including the two relevant volumes in the World Bibliographical Series.

Robert A. Myers is Associate Professor of Anthropology in the Division of Social Sciences and Director of Study Abroad Programs at Alfred University, Alfred, New York. He has studied post-colonial island nations of the Caribbean and has spent two years in Nigeria on a Fulbright Lectureship. His interests include international public health, historical anthropology and developing societies. In addition to *Amerindians of the Lesser Antilles: a bibliography* (1981), *A Resource Guide to Dominica, 1493-1986* (1987) and numerous articles, he has compiled the World Bibliographical Series volumes on *Dominica* (1987), *Nigeria* (1989) and *Ghana* (1991).

Ian Wallace is Professor of German at the University of Bath. A graduate of Oxford in French and German, he also studied in Tübingen, Heidelberg and Lausanne before taking teaching posts at universities in the USA, Scotland and England. He specializes in contemporary German affairs, especially literature and culture, on which he has published numerous articles and books. In 1979 he founded the journal *GDR Monitor*, which he continues to edit under its new title *German Monitor*.

Hans H. Wellisch is Professor emeritus at the College of Library and Information Services, University of Maryland. He was President of the American Society of Indexers and was a member of the International Federation for Documentation. He is the author of numerous articles and several books on indexing and abstracting, and has published *The Conversion of Scripts and Indexing and Abstracting: an International Bibliography*, and *Indexing from A to Z*. He also contributes frequently to *Journal of the American Society for Information Science*, *The Indexer* and other professional journals.

Ralph Lee Woodward, Jr. is Professor of History at Tulane University, New Orleans. He is the author of *Central America, a Nation Divided*, 2nd ed. (1985), as well as several monographs and more than seventy scholarly articles on modern Latin America. He has also compiled volumes in the World Bibliographical Series on *Belize* (1980), *El Salvador* (1988), *Guatemala* (Rev. Ed.) (1992) and *Nicaragua* (Rev. Ed.) (1994). Dr. Woodward edited the Central American section of the *Research Guide to Central America and the Caribbean* (1985) and is currently associate editor of Scribner's *Encyclopedia of Latin American History*.

VOLUME 26

India

Revised Edition

Ian D. Derbyshire

Compiler

CLIO PRESS
OXFORD, ENGLAND · SANTA BARBARA, CALIFORNIA
DENVER, COLORADO

British Library Cataloguing in Publication Data

India, Rev. ed. – (World Bibliographical Series;
Vol. 26)
I. Derbyshire, Ian D.
II. Series
016.945

ISBN 1–85109–200–5

ABC-CLIO Ltd.,
Old Clarendon Ironworks,
35A Great Clarendon Street,
Oxford OX2 6AT, England.

———

ABC-CLIO Inc.,
130 Cremona Drive,
Santa Barbara,
CA 93116, USA

Designed by Bernard Crossland.
Typeset by Columns Design and Production Services Ltd., Reading, England.
Printed and bound in Great Britain by Bookcraft (Bath) Ltd., Midsomer Norton.

Contents

Contents

Contents

Contents

Contents

Introduction

India's place in the world

In terms of its impact on global civilization, India stands alongside China, Greece, Italy, Japan, Britain, France, Russia, Germany, Spain and the United States as one of the world's most significant nations. In the length and breadth of its historical and cultural impact, only China can truly compare. The subcontinent has been the cradle of two of the great religions of the modern world, Buddhism and Hinduism, as well as many related faiths, notably Jainism and Sikhism. Four and a half thousand years ago it was the site of one of the great early urban civilizations, the Harappan, and an early centre of cotton textile production. Across the centuries it has produced many great philosophers, writers, artists, and sculptors; a unique social system, the caste system; the *ayurvedic* system of alternative medicine; a distinctive cuisine, style of dress and music; and has given the world its greatest intellectual game, chess.

One explanation for India's global influence is the sheer size of the country and the vitality of its population. The contemporary Indian Union covers an area of 1.2 million square miles and has a population of more than 890 million. It is the world's seventh largest nation-state, comparable in size to Western Europe, and the second most populous. Nearly a fifth of the world's population reside in India: a proportion which has remained broadly constant over the past five millennia. Many millions of Indians also now reside overseas, in Asia, Africa, Europe, the Middle East, Oceania and the Americas, in a diaspora which, again, only has a Chinese parallel.

The other explanation of India's significance is its strategic location, between East and West, and its openness, by land and sea, to external conquest and influences. In prehistoric and ancient times, there were invasions by the Aryans, Alexander of Macedon, the Shakas (Scythians) and visits by Chinese Buddhist pilgrims. From the early medieval period, there were Arab, Turk and Persian conquests from the West, bringing the influence of a new great religion, Islam. Since early modern times, first coastal and then interior parts of the subcontinent came into contact, through Portuguese, Dutch, French and British traders and missionaries, with Christian teachings and from the later 18th century much of the subcontinent came under the overarching control of the British Imperial Raj.

These contacts with other civilizations have been mutually enriching. New ways of thinking and new technologies have been added to the fabric of Indian life. However, changes have been incremental rather than fundamental, and at its core Indian civilization has retained its own distinctive values and modes of social organization: the 'Indian tradition'. External influences have been, perhaps, greatest in the north, where Islamic control was significant during the medieval and early modern periods. The south, in contrast, linguistically and geographically distinguishable from the north, has been subject to different historical rhythms until it was finally united with the rest of the subcontinent under the British Raj during the 19th century.

Characterized by the great British novelist E. M. Forster as 'a mystery and a muddle' and by the distinguished writer V. S. Naipaul, an Indian by descent, as 'a country of a million little mutinies', India is a complex nation for the outsider to comprehend. With its regional diversity – with fifteen recognized regional languages, each with a well developed literary tradition – it defies simplistic generalization. As a distinct nation state, the Indian Union is less than fifty years old, having been created through the partition of the subcontinent on substantially communal lines in 1947. Previously India, or Hindustan ('land of the Hindus'), had been a general term applied to the Indian subcontinent, bounded to the north by the Himalayan mountain range, and comprising the contemporary states of Pakistan and Bangladesh. For this reason, while for the post-independence era, bibliographic coverage in this guide is confined exclusively to the Indian Union, for earlier periods entries are included which cover areas, for example the Indus Valley Civilization, geographically now part of Pakistan.

Historical background

More than a fifth of the entries in this bibliographic guide are devoted to India's historical development, embracing archaeology and protohistory (83-106), early, medieval and modern history and related travellers' accounts (107-227), biographies and autobiographies of famous historical figures (228-70), the history of Indian urbanization

(287-308), economic history (662-77), and the history of science and technology (798-803). This reflects the depth and richness of the Indian historical heritage.

There is evidence as far back as 40,000 BC, from parts of Punjab and Central India of the existence of mesolithic communities using flint tools and leaving behind, in rock shelters, primitive paintings of animals. By ca. 5000 BC animals had been domesticated, wheat and barley were being cultivated, and pottery produced, at first in the Indus Valley Basin and then, from 3000 BC, further to the east. At Harappa and Mohenjo-Daro in the Indus Valley, from ca. 2500 BC, the Indian subcontinent's first real urban centres were developed, with populations of more than 30,000 according to some accounts. The Harappan civilization, which lasted until ca. 1800 BC, was characterized by extensive commerce and a distinctive script and language. India's 'second urbanization' occurred from ca. 600 BC in the Ganges valley region of north India, the setting for the great historical epics, the *Mahabharata* (822) and *Ramayana* (820). It was stimulated by the growing use of iron technology, developing long-distance commerce, and the migration after 1500 BC of Indo-Aryan pastoralist tribes from Iran. It was during this period that the *varna* order of caste hierarchy became established in northern India.

Under the Mauryan dynasty (ca. 321-185 BC), the first great territorial empire was established across northern and central India, with its capital at Pataliputra, in Bihar, at that time the world's largest city. Buddhism also flourished under the patronage of emperor Asoka (reign ca. 268-31 BC). Under the Guptas (ca. 320-480 AD), another great northern Indian empire was established, with great achievements in the arts. The succeeding centuries were characterized by a decentralization of both the polity and economy, termed by some writers an 'Indian feudalism', with the rise of Rajput dynasties in the north and Pallava, Pandya and Chola kingdoms in the south. Already around forty million at the end of the Gupta era, the Indian population had reached roughly seventy million by the time the Delhi Sultanate was established in northern India by a corps of Turkish slaves (Mamluks) and military officers who had invaded from the northwest. The Delhi Sultanate remained the dominant force in northern India for three centuries until it was replaced by the Mughals, also Muslim rulers, in 1526. A new infusion of ideas and technologies enabled the all-India population to expand to nearly 150 million by the mid-18th century, with expansion also registered in the south where the magnificent Vijayanagara empire dominated for nearly three centuries from 1336.

The Mughal and Vijayanagara eras were characterized by tremendous opulence at the centre, which greatly impressed Western

living being is subject). Two of the greatest early Indian philosophers were Sankara (ca. 788-820), a proponent of *Advaita* ('nondualistic') *Vedanta*, or the belief that there is nothing real except the pure consciousness that is Brahman, and Ramanuja (ca. 1025-1137), of the *Vishishtadvaita* ('qualified nondualistic') *Vedanta* school, which interpreted the Brahman of the *Upanishads* (455) as a personal god and thus prepared the way for the devotional *bhakti* strain of Hinduism. During the present century India has produced three truly great philosophers who have laid typical emphasis on the importance of spiritual values: Mahatma Gandhi (460), Aurobindo Ghose (459), and Sarvepalli Radhakrishnan (467).

Language, along with religion, has been a divisive force in recent Indian political life. Since 1956, when the administrative map was redrawn, India's states have been based on the unilingual principle. The chief contemporary languages are shown in Table 1. They follow two broad divisions: Indo-Aryan languages, which are found in the north, centre and west of the Union; and Dravidian, which predominate in the south. The Dravidian languages have a totally different root from Hindi, the main language of the Ganges Valley heartland of northern India and which, along with the valuable, élite-spoken 'link-language' of English, is recognized as the official language of India.

Table 1: Religion and Language Groups ca. 1991

Religion	Millions	% of Population
Hindu	703.0	82.7
Muslim	95.2	11.2
Christian	22.1	2.6
Sikh	16.2	1.9
Buddhist	6.0	0.7
Jain	4.3	0.5
Other	3.4	0.4
Total	850.2	100.0

Language Group	Millions	% of Population
INDO-ARYAN		
Hindi	258.4	30.4
Bengali	65.5	7.7
Marathi	64.6	7.6
Gujarati	39.1	4.6
Oriya	30.6	3.6
Punjabi	21.3	2.5
Assamese	13.6	1.6

DRAVIDIAN

Telegu	73.1	8.6
Tamil	59.5	7.0
Kannada	34.0	4.0
Malayalam	33.2	3.9

OTHER

English	21.3	2.5
Urdu	45.0	5.3

As Table 1 shows, India is overwhelmingly a Hindu nation. Nevertheless its Muslim community is one of the world's largest and comparable to those of neighbouring Pakistan and Bangladesh. The community is strongest in the Ganges valley area of the north, while in the state of Punjab the Sikhs form a majority of the population. The Hindu community itself is by no means monolithic. It is divided between two levels of tradition: a great Sanskritic tradition of Brahminical Hinduism, related to the ancient great texts, the holy cities (*tirthas*), and the three great deities, Vishnu, Shiva and Brahma; and, within each cultural-linguistic area, a 'little tradition' of local gods and practices by which most villagers live their religious lives.

India has produced some of the world's greatest early literature in the forms of the *Rigveda-samhita*, a collection of more than 1,000 hymns to the Aryans' gods written from ca. 12000 BC, and the Vedic historical-religious epics, the *Mahabharata*, which contains the Hindu holy-book the *Bhagavad Gita* (456), and the *Ramayana*. Written around 300 BC, the latter works stand comparison with the great Greek epics written by Homer during the 8th century BC, the *Iliad* and *Odyssey*. Indians have continued to produce fine works in regional languages across the centuries (809-33), while the Indian experience inspired during the British Raj era some fine works of Western fiction (834-38), notably by E. M. Forster (835) and Rudyard Kipling (837). But what has been particularly striking has been the skill with which Indians have used the English language to highlight aspects of the Indian condition and experience (839-52). In 1913 Rabindranath Tagore (856), a prolific, multi-talented poet, dramatist, novelist and composer, became the first Asian to win the Nobel prize for literature. During more recent years, R. K. Narayan (846, 858), Salman Rushdie (848), and Vikram Seth (850) have established themselves as both popular and highly respected novelists, while Indian poetry in English flourishes through such exponents as Nissim Ezekiel and Keki Daruwalla (825).

Introduction

The arts – painting (893-98), sculpture and architecture (899-914), decorative arts and crafts (915-20), dance and theatre (921-29), and music (930-39) – have flourished in India since Vedic times. Each period of history, through the Guptas, Cholas, Vijayanagara, Rajputs, Mughals, and British Raj, has produced its own wonders, sponsored by political and religious patronage (886) and which reflected related themes. There has coexisted with this 'high art', a popular folk art and culture (944-62), which has survived through performance, oral recitation and through living rituals. Over the course of the last century new activities, in the spheres of photography (940-43), sports (963-69), and film, radio and television (970-76), have been added to popular culture and new artistic, literary, and musical schools and movements have emerged.

Post-independence political and economic developments

At the centre of power for all but five years since independence in 1947 (see Table 2), the Indian Union has been dominated to such a degree by the Congress Party that the term 'one-party democracy' was coined. Furthermore, as in the other states of South Asia, India's democracy has been quasi-dynastic. One north India-based Kashmiri Brahmin family, the Nehru-Gandhis, has provided three of the country's longest-serving prime ministers, holding power for thirty-seven years in aggregate.

Table 2 : Prime Ministers of the Indian Union

Leader	Party	Term
Jawaharlal Nehru	Congress	1947-64
Lal Bahadur Shastri	Congress	1964-66
Indira Gandhi	Congress	1966-77
Morarji Desai	Janata	1977-79
Charan Singh	Janata	1979-80
Indira Gandhi	Congress	1980-84
Rajiv Gandhi	Congress	1984-89
V. P. Singh	Janata Dal	1989-90
Chandra Shekhar	Samajvadi Janata Party	1990-91
P. V. Narasimha Rao	Congress	1991-

Post-independence politics in India have been characterized by mounting levels of caste and communal based violence, culminating, during the 1980s and early 1990s, in the Punjab and Ayodhya crises and the assassinations of Indira Gandhi and her son Rajiv, in 1984 and 1991 respectively. This has led to increasing concerns that the nation of 'a million mutinies' may be becoming ungovernable and that key political institutions, notably the weak, inherited federal political structure (606-13, 615, 623) and the nation's political parties, have been increasingly unable to perform a national cementing role. Such concerns are expressed in many of the entries 543-70. Yet despite these anxieties, with the exception of the brief Emergency of 1975-77, the recent periods of quasi-military control imposed over Punjab and Jammu and Kashmir, and insurgencies in the northeastern hill states, democratic traditions have survived in India with far greater success than in its neighbours – Pakistan, Bangladesh, and Sri Lanka. The military (626) have obeyed the commands of democratic politicians, the Indian Civil Service (610, 612) has continued to act as a unifying 'steel frame', the press has remained free and articulate, and the judiciary, notably the Supreme Court (616, 620), referred to by Nehru as the 'third House of Parliament', has acted as an important political check.

The policies pursued by successive administrations have exhibited a substantial degree of continuity. In defence and foreign affairs (625-54) priority has been given to the preservation of India's independence, avoiding dominance by any single 'great power', the promotion of the non-aligned movement as a force for world peace, and the maintenance of a dominant position, both militarily and diplomatically, in the South Asia region. This has involved India in border-war conflicts with Pakistan and China and periodic interventions in Sri Lanka and the Maldives during recent years. Domestically, a mildly left-of-centre, mixed-economy policy programme has been pursued by both Congress and Janata governments, involving a measure of state planning and regulation of the economy and the launching of poverty reduction and, in recent years, affirmative action (positive discrimination/job quota) programmes in an effort to improve the position of depressed social groups.

The party system (571-95) of the Indian Union has been dominated by the Congress Party, the catch-all, mass-party heir to the Indian National Congress (estd. 1885), which spearheaded the drive for Indian independence during the British Raj. Congress split in 1969 and 1978, to form the Congress (I), comprising members loyal to Indira Gandhi. Congress has traditionally formed a cross-caste and cross-religion secular coalition, uniting land-controlling Hindu élites, Muslims, and low-caste, poor, and disadvantaged Hindus. Though strongest in the northern 'Hindi-belt', it has been the only truly national political force in terms of both its organizational structure and levels of support. Nevertheless, Congress has never polled more than 49 per cent of the national vote, the level attained by Rajiv Gandhi in 1984, in elections to the federal parliament (*Lok Sabha*) and its success in establishing a 'one-party dominance' has been as much the result of the disunity of opposition forces as of its own electoral appeal. Only twice, after the Emergency of 1975-77 and in the late 1980s after the reputation of prime minister Rajiv Gandhi was tarnished by the Bofors arms scandal, have the opposition forces temporarily united in electoral coalitions which succeeded in removing Congress from office. However, on both occasions the coalitions, comprising parties drawn from the socialist left, the centre and the conservative right, have proved too fractious to survive in office for as long as two years.

At the level of India's twenty-five self-governing states, Congress has been less dominant. In elections to the state assemblies (*Vidhan Sabhas*) regionally based parties, such as the Telugu Desam (estd. 1982) in Andhra Pradesh, the Dravida Munnetra Kazhagam (DMK) and its offshoot, the All-India Anna DMK, in Tamil Nadu, the Asom Gana Parishad in Assam, the Jammu and Kashmir National Conference Party in Jammu and Kashmir, and the Akali Dal in Punjab, have tasted electoral success, while ideological parties, such as the Communists in West Bengal and Kerala and the Hinduchauvinist Bharatiya Janata Party (BJP) in northern India, have also been successful (596-605).

Since independence the population of the Indian Union has advanced from 340 million to more than 890 million by the early 1990s, a rate of annual increase averaging 2.2 per cent. In short, a population almost the size of Western Europe and the United States combined has been added to that inherited from the British Raj. Fortunately the economic growth rate has, averaging 3.9 per cent per annum, more than kept pace with the fast-growing population, enabling per capita incomes to improve by roughly 1.7 per cent per annum. Despite this growth achievement, made possible by a combination of industrial development, urbanization and a green revolution in agriculture which has significantly raised yields and productivity and has brought about self-sufficiency in foodstuffs, poverty remains acute in many parts and for many people in India. With improvements in the system of food distribution, there have been no serious famines during recent decades. However, in parts of the Union, particularly eastern states such as Bihar and east Uttar Pradesh, growth has lagged behind that registered in more dynamic states such as Punjab, Haryana, Gujarat, Maharashtra and Andhra Pradesh. Differentials between regions and social groups threatened to widen during the 1990s as the administration of Narasimha Rao, impelled by a fiscal crisis, pragmatically adopted a more liberal economic strategy, dismantling much of the industrial-licensing system and encouraging the private sector and foreign inward investment. By the mid-1990s it was claimed that India had a consumerist middle class numbering 250 million. Despite this average per capita GDP remained as low as $310 and overall GDP was the same as Belgium, a country with a population of just ten million. Barely half the Indian population could read, forty per cent of the people lived below the official poverty line, and, according to the World Bank, sixty-three per cent of the country's under-five-year-olds were malnourished. Indeed, it has been estimated that perhaps forty per cent of the world's desperately poor live in India. A country with a nuclear capability, the second largest pool of scientists and technicians in the world, including Nobel laureates in medicine (H. G. Khorana: 1968) and physics (S. Chandrasekhar: 1983), and which has launched its own satellites and rockets since 1980, India remains as much a land of contrasts as during the Mughal and Vijayanagara eras.

The purpose of this bibliographic guide

In accordance with the aims of the Clio *World Bibliographical Series*, this guide provides a selective, annotated bibliography which aims to provide an interpretation of India, expressing its culture, place in the world, and background and qualities that make it unique. The work is intended for an audience ranging from the informed general reader to the scholar who wishes to obtain background information in a field other than his own. The entries included have been restricted to English language works and have excluded articles. For readers seeking to extend their bibliograpic searches, entries 1019-39 provide a wealth of additional references, with entries 1031 (Patterson and Alspaugh) and 1033 (Gidwani and Navalani), though now well over a decade old, listing over 28,000 books and articles and 20,000 items respectively.

This edition builds on an earlier volume compiled by Brijen K. Gupta and Datta S. Kharbas, with the assistance of Judith N. Kharbas and Arthur D. Lopatin, and published in 1984. Classic works have been retained, but this edition has been rearranged in structure. New sections have been included on archaeology, biography and environmental concerns and important works produced over the last decade have been added. Particular assistance has been accorded by colleagues in the British Association of South Asian Studies, the staff of the Cambridge University and India Office libraries, Nicholas

Introduction

Morgan of the bibliographic department of W. H. Heffers, Susan Gole of Jaya Books, and Lionel Carter, librarian at the Centre for South Asian Studies, Cambridge, J. Denis Derbyshire and Luciana Santos. To those concerned, sincere thanks are extended.

Cambridge, England
28 January 1995

Chronology

ca. 2500-1500 BC	Harappan (Indus Valley) culture
ca. 1500-1200 BC	Migration of the Aryans to India, settlement of Ganges valley and development of Brahmanism and the caste system.
ca. 1300-1000 BC	Composition of *Rig Veda*
ca. 900 BC	The great Bharata War
ca. 900-500 BC	Composition of the *Samhitas, Brahmanas* and early *Upanishads*
ca. 599-527 BC	Vardhamana Mahavira establishes the Jain religion
ca. 563-483 BC	Gautama Buddha establishes the Buddhist faith
ca. 500-300 BC	Composition of the *Mahabharata, Ramayana* and *Bhagavad Gita*
ca. 325 BC	Alexander the Great in Punjab
ca. 322-298 BC	Reign of Chandragupta of Magadha, founder of the Mauryan dynasty; composition of Kautilya's *Arthasastra*
ca. 268-231 BC	Reign of Asoka, Mauryan emperor of northern India
ca. 1st century AD	Roman trade with south India
ca. 78 AD	Accession of Kanishka, Kusana king of the northwest
320-480	Imperial Guptas reunite north India in a 'golden age'
405-11	Fa Hsien visits India
629-45	Hsuan Tsang visits India during the reign of king Harsha of Kanauj
712	Arabs in western India
ca. 788-820	Life of the philosopher Sankara
ca. 800-1250	Chola dynasty in Tamil Nadu

Chronology

999-1026	Mahmud of Ghazni repeatedly raids northwest India
ca. 1025-1137	Life of the philosopher Ramanuja
ca. 1100	Buddhism becomes virtually extinct in India
1206	Establishment of Islamic hegemony over northern India under the Delhi Sultanate Slave dynasty
1288, 1293	Marco Polo visits south India
1333-42	Travels of Ibn Batuta in India
1336	Founding in south India of Vijayanagara, the last great Hindu empire in India, extending to Malaysia, Indonesia and the Philippines
1421, 1431	Chinese naval forces visit Bengal
1440-1518	Life of Kabir, the great *bhakti* saint-poet
1469-1539	Life of Guru Nanak, founder of Sikhism
1498	Vasco de Gama, having rounded the Cape of Good Hope, lands on the Malabar coast
1510	Portuguese occupy Goa
1526	Commencement of the age of the Great Mughals, dominant across northern India after the battle of Panipat
1556-1605	Reign of emperor Akbar, who pacifies northern India
1631	Death of Mumtaz, in whose honour emperor Shah Jahan (reign 1627-58) built the remarkable Taj Mahal at Agra
1651	The English East India Company opens its first factory in Bengal
1658-1707	Reign of the last great Mughal emperor, Aurangzeb.
1661	Bombay becomes a British possession
1664	Shivaji declares himself king of Maharashtra
1757	At Plassey, Robert Clive subdues Bengal to become master of northern India
1764	English East India Company decisively defeats coalition of Mughal imperial forces at Buxar to secure the *diwani* of Bengal
1813	Trading monopoly of English East Company abolished
1818	The British defeat the last Maratha Peshwa
1853	First railway is opened in India
1857-58	Following an Indian Rebellion, the British Crown takes over the administration of India from the East India Company

1877	Queen Victoria is proclaimed Empress of India
1885	The Indian National Congress is founded in Bombay as a focus for nationalism
1896-1900	Seven million die in a series of famines across India
1906	Foundation of Muslim League
1911	The capital of British India is transferred from Calcutta to New Delhi
1918	Seventeen million Indians die in an influenza epidemic
1919	Montagu-Chelmsford reforms provide for dyarchy, granting Indians increased political powers, particularly at the provincial level
1920-22	Mahatma Gandhi's non-violent non-cooperation campaigns
1935	Indian control over the federal legislature is increased by the Government of India Act
1943-44	More than a million die in the Bengal famine
1947	Independence and partition of India, with the creation of the Indian Union and Pakistan; Nehru becomes prime minister.
1948	Assassination of Mahatma Gandhi
1956	Reorganization of the states on linguistic lines
1962	Chinese attack on India
1964	Death of Jawaharlal Nehru
1965	Conflict with Pakistan
1966	Indira Gandhi becomes prime minister
1971	Conflict with West Pakistan over the East Bengal issue, culminating in the creation of Bangladesh
1975-77	State of National Emergency is declared, with many civil rights suspended
1977	Janata coalition, led by Morarji Desai, replaces Indira Gandhi in power
1980	Landslide electoral victory for Indira Gandhi's Congress (I)
1984	Storming of Golden Temple at Amritsar, occupied by Sikh extremists, provokes assassination of Indira Gandhi by her Sikh bodyguards; Rajiv Gandhi is elected prime minister by a landslide margin.
1989	Janata Dal coalition, led by V. P. Singh, removes Congress (I) from power

1991   Assassination of Rajiv Gandhi during election campaign; Congress (I), led by Narasimha Rao, returns to power and embarks on a more liberal economic programme.

1992   Over 1,200, mainly Muslims, are killed in communal violence, following the destruction of a mosque in Ayodhya, north India, by Hindu extremists.

The Country and Its People

1 **Sociology of 'developing societies': South Asia.**
Edited by Hamza Alavi, John Harris.   London: Macmillan, 1989. 324p.
bibliog.

Part of a series of regional volumes, this collection of twenty-four readings covers a
wide range of historical and contemporary topics related to the broad theme of the
development of South Asia's political economy and society. The volume is arranged
in five broad sections: 'the colonial transformation', 'the political economy of South
Asia', 'ideologies and realities of inequality', 'regionalism and ethnicity', and
'classes and popular struggles'. Each section contains an editor's introduction. As the
section titles might suggest, the editors and individual authors approach the subject
matter from a radical, often Marxian, perspective. Topics covered include Indian
industrialization, the relationship between business and politics, the position of
women, peasant resistance, and ecology movements. Several readings relate to
Bangladesh, Pakistan and Sri Lanka.

2 **Sources of Indian tradition.**
Edited by William Theodore de Bary (and others).   New Delhi: Motilal
Banarsidass, 1988. rev. ed. 961p. maps. bibliog.

India's intellectual tradition from the *Rig Veda* to the Nehru era is represented almost
in its entirety in this standard and widely recommended work, which was first
published in 1958. The contents consist mainly of translations of Indian-language
materials into English, with each section prefaced by an authoritative essay. The
selections are judicious and seldom longer than a few pages. The reader should be
aware that in emphasizing the literary and the 'great tradition', i.e. those elements of
the culture which are widespread and long-lasting, the book largely omits the day-to-
day living traditions of India. Thus the quality of Indian life is not pictured as a
whole.

3   **The continent of Circe: being an essay on the peoples of India.**
Nirad Chandra Chaudhuri.   London: Chatto & Windus, 1967; Bombay:
Jaico, 1983. 320p. bibliog.

An eminently readable, highly controversial, immensely opinionated, sweeping essay
on the peoples and cultures of India. The book is an attack on Indian spirituality and
the Indian penchant for glorifying such contradictions as the maintenance of both
tradition and modernity in the body-politic. Chaudhuri argues that Hindus and
Europeans share common Indo-Aryan traits, but that the Hindus have been corrupted
by the baleful influence of India's geographical environment. Until the people of
India conquer their environment and recover their Indo-Aryan spirit, the nation
cannot hope to get out of its present socio-economic morass.

4   **Encylopaedia of India.**
Edited by P. N. Chopra.   New Delhi: Rima, 1992-94. 32 vols. bibliogs.

This work comprises individual volumes, each ranging in length from between 150 to
400 pages, on the states and Union territories of contemporary India. Within each
regional volume there are individual sections on physical conditions, history, people,
political structure, agriculture, education, culture, languages, economic life, and
places of interest. The text is complemented by colour and monochrome plates and
there are chronologies and bibliographies.

5   **An anthropologist among the historians, and other essays.**
Bernard S. Cohn.   New Delhi: Oxford University Press India, 1987.
682p.

This book represents a combination of historical and anthropological approaches to
the study of Indian society and culture. Excellent essays deal with the problem of land
tenure under the Mughals and the British, town and village differences, the census in
British India, the recruitment and training of civil servants, and the presence of
traditional as well as modern elements in urban behaviour.

6   **An introduction to South Asia.**
Bertram Hughes Farmer.   London: Methuen & Co., 1993. 2nd ed. 197p.
maps. bibliog.

A clearly-written and concise introduction to the subcontinent's political and
economic development and its current problems. The author, an emeritus Cambridge
University geographer, is an authority on the green revolution and agricultural
colonization. The work is divided into five parts: environment/geography, history,
political developments since independence, international relations, and economic
developments. Intended as a basic introductory textbook for students taking
interdisciplinary courses on South Asia for the first time, and for the general reader,
developments in Pakistan, Sri Lanka, Bangladesh, and Nepal are dealt with, as well as
those in India.

7   **India file: inside the subcontinent.**
Trevor Fishlock.   London: John Murray, 1987. 2nd ed. 189p. map.

In this short, highly readable book, Fishlock, South Asia correspondent for *The Times*
of London between 1980-83, provides an insightful picture of life in modern India.
Drawing upon the experience of his travels and his interviews with politicians,

administrators, police officers, doctors, businessmen, and educationalists, from the mainstream; and astrologers, bandits, and godmen, from the fringes, he vividly depicts the 'functioning anarchy' of the contemporary Indian state and its painful and confusing social contradictions. There are chapters covering such topics as the Indian press and film industry; love and marriage; 'gods and the guru business'; the Indian countryside; and the three metropolises, Bombay, Calcutta, and New Delhi.

8   **India: A Reference Annual.**
     New Delhi: Ministry of Information and Broadcasting, Research and Reference Division, 1953- . annual.
This standard reference annual is based on official sources and carries information on the political, constitutional, educational, cultural, scientific, and financial aspects of the country. Each chapter includes a selective bibliography which directs the user to further reading on the subject. A very useful source for ready reference.

9   **Imagining India.**
     Ronald B. Inden.   Oxford: Basil Blackwell, 1990. 299p. bibliog.
Inspired by Edward Said's *Orientalism* (1978), this revisionist work is a stong attack on Indian historiography and anthropology, particularly the late 19th and early 20th-century colonialist obsession with pigeon-holing the Indian population on crude caste lines. Inden argues that the dominant Western interpretation of India has deprived its inhabitants of their own agency and rationality and made them prisoners of such essences as caste, the 'Hindu mind', village India, and divine kingship.

10   **India: rebellion to republic – selected writings, 1857-1990.**
     Edited by Robin Jeffrey and others.   New Delhi: Sterling, for the Asian Studies Association of Australia, 1990. 510p. 5 maps.
Designed as a university course-book on modern India, this volume comprises an eclectic selection of previously published articles on various facets of Indian colonial and post-colonial history, politics, economic affairs, and society. The historical section includes papers by Eric Stokes on the 1857 great revolt, Richard Cashman on Tilak, Gail Omvedt, Shahid Amin and Ashis Nandy on Gandhi, and Robin Moore on Jinnah. The government, economy and society section includes chapters by W. H. Morris-Jones on Indian political institutions, Robin Jeffrey and Peter Mayer on the Punjab troubles and Indira Gandhi's 1975-77 Emergency, V. M. Dandekar on the impact of state policies on poverty, Barbara Joshi on the persistence of social discrimination and the need for reservation policies, and articles from the news-magazine *India Today* on the green revolution, the 'new middle class', and small businesses.

11   **The inner world: a psychoanalytic study of childhood and society in India.**
     Sudhir Kakar.   New Delhi: Oxford University Press India, 1989. new ed. 250p. bibliog.
An incisive analysis of Indian culture from the viewpoint of contemporary psychoanalytic theory. Kakar examines the Hindu world view, including such key concepts as *dharma* (righteousness) and *moksha* (liberation), relations between mothers and infants, the extended Indian family, and major Indian myths. His thesis

that Indian children have a much longer relationship with their mothers than their Western counterparts, and that Indians do not place great emphasis on individualism and self-sufficiency, is very well argued.

12 The speaking tree: a study of Indian culture and society.
Richard Lannoy. London: Oxford University Press, 1974. 466p. bibliog.

An influential, yet controversial, study of the major themes in the Indian ethos. Lannoy deals with the aesthetic, social, and religious content of Indian art; examines the family system, particularly child-rearing, sexual relationships, and recent changes in family structure; and analyses patterns of Indian philosophical concepts, political organization, and Gandhi's influence on Indian history. There is an excellent discussion of the 'compartmentalization' habit of modern intellectuals who are caught between tradition and modernity and are unable to synthesize the two.

13 Peoples of South Asia.
Clarence Maloney. New York: Holt, Rinehart & Winston, 1974. 584p. 8 maps. bibliog.

This work has become a basic American college textbook on South Asian society. Clearly written, it covers a wide range of topics, from social structure to socio-linguistics.

14 India: a million mutinies now.
Vidiadhar Surajprasad Naipaul. London: Minerva, 1991. 521p.

A perceptive and elegantly written analysis of the changing state of India as perceived by the celebrated, Trinidad-born, but now England-based, novelist and travel writer during his (third) extended visit to his country of origin during 1989. Naipaul depicts a vital, but unstable and uncertain new India – a nation characterized on the one hand by economic progress, particularly for the expanding urban middle class, but also by dangerously increasing sectarian and inter-caste tensions as *dalits* (the ex-untouchables), Muslims, Sikhs, the lower castes, and women rebel against traditional identities and injustices. During his journey, Naipaul encounters a rich array of characters, including Shiv Sena chauvinists, ex-Naxalites, and Sikh terrorists. Indispensable for visitors anxious to penetrate India's external veil. It is interesting to contrast Naipaul's impressions in this work with those presented in his earlier *India: a wounded civilization* (Harmondsworth, England: Penguin, 1979. 175p.).

15 India: a country study.
Edited by Richard F. Nyrop. Washington, DC: American University, Foreign Area Studies, 1985. 4th ed. 686p. maps. bibliog.

A comprehensive introductory survey of historical, geographic, religious, ethnic, political, economic, and security facets of contemporary India and its evolution. The ten analytical chapters are written by seven academics. Particularly strong is the coverage of foreign relations and national security issues. The volume is part of a series of Area Handbooks produced by The American University, Washington, DC.

16 **The soul of India.**
Amaury de Riencourt. London: Honeyglen, 1986. 416p. bibliog.
A loosely structured philosophical study of Indian culture, civilization and history from Harappan to modern times. First published in 1960, for this edition the French writer has added an additional chapter covering the era of Indira Gandhi. The approach of de Riencourt, author of a companion volume, *The soul of China* (1958), is in the continental Hegelian tradition.

17 **The people of India.**
Herbert Risley, edited by William Crooke. New Delhi: Oriental Books Reprint Corp., 1969. 2nd ed. 472p. maps. bibliog.
A pioneering classification of the people of India, undertaken following the 1901 census, on the basis of anthropometry. Part one of the book deals with the physical types; part two with social types; and the remaining five parts with the origin of caste and its relationship to religion, social institutions, folk tradition, and nationality. Risley's book has been criticized for assuming that the process of physical and social amalgamation has not been pervasive in India, and that various caste, linguistic, and tribal groups have continued to coexist without much interaction with each other. Criticism has also been levelled against some of Risley's theories on the origin of several ethnic groups. In spite of these shortcomings, Risley's anthropometric classifications continue to be of use to scholars.

18 **The Cambridge encyclopedia of India, Pakistan, Bangladesh, Sri Lanka, Nepal, Bhutan and the Maldives.**
Edited by Francis C. R. Robinson. Cambridge: Cambridge University Press, 1989. 520p. maps. bibliog.
An authoritative and up-to-date volume written by sixty-nine expert contributors. The work is arranged analytically in nine sections: land, peoples, history to independence, politics, foreign relations, economies, religions, societies, and culture. Books for further reading are suggested at the end of smaller sub-sections written by each contributor. This volume is attractively illustrated with colour and black-and-white photographs, drawings and maps, and it is wide-ranging in its coverage. It is recommended as a starting point and reference guide to Indian affairs.

19 **Encyclopedia Indica.**
Jagdish Saran Sharma. New Delhi: Chand, 1981. 2nd rev. ed. 2 vols.
Designed to provide 'correct and exhaustive' information on 'all subjects relating to India', this encyclopaedia falls far short of its goal. It has good biographical sketches, satisfactory geographical descriptions, and cogent information on a variety of miscellaneous topics. The encyclopaedia is not altogether satisfactory, but quite useful. A similar work is P. N. Chopra and Prabha Chopra's *Encyclopaedia of India* (New Delhi: Agam Prakashan, 1988. 2 vols.).

20 **An exploration of India: geographical perspectives on society and culture.**
Edited by David Edward Sopher. Ithaca, New York: Cornell University Press, 1980. 334p. maps. bibliog.

A lively collection of essays examining the social dimensions of Indian social order and cultural regions. Statistical results are displayed in maps, graphs, diagrams, charts, and tables. Included is a useful paper by Charles J. Bennett on language boundaries within the subcontinent.

21 **Changing India: bourgeois revolution on the subcontinent.**
Robert W. Stern. Cambridge: Cambridge University Press, 1993. 251p. maps. bibliog.

A very readable and, at times, provocative description and analysis of modern India, its polity, economy, and social institutions. Part one focuses on the Indian countryside and includes chapters on caste, class, and 'linguistic and tribal states'. Part two, 'Change from above', comprises an historical chapter on India's political development since the time of the British Raj and a chapter on political, diplomatic, and economic developments. Stern's central thesis is that changes in India's traditional and modern institutions have been considerable during recent years, but have been adaptive, rather than disruptive, to the remarkable continuity and vitality of the country's underlying social systems. This the author ascribes to India's 'bourgeois revolution', entailing the simultaneous development of capitalism and parliamentary democracy. A stimulating general work.

22 **The Times of India Directory and Yearbook Including Who's Who.**
Bombay: Bennett, Coleman, 1914- . annual.

The title of this useful annual compendium has varied in past years: 1914-47, *The Indian Yearbook*; 1948-52/53, *The Indian and Pakistan Yearbook*. Its very extensive coverage of Indian economic, political, and social information includes several maps and statistical tables on various aspects of life in India. The who's who section contains biographical data on distinguished persons in various walks of life. A separate section is devoted to states of the Union and the Union territories. Listings of Indian diplomatic representatives abroad, foreign diplomatic representatives in India, and membership of legislative assemblies and legislative councils of states are included. This is unquestionably one of the most useful yearbooks published in India.

23 **No full stops in India.**
Mark Tully. New Delhi: Viking, 1991; Harmondsworth, England: Penguin, 1992. 336p.

Reflections on life in contemporary India by the BBC's Delhi correspondent for the last two and a half decades. Tully narrates ten unrelated stories, unmasking the vitality of the 'real India' and its deep, complex cultural roots and social linkages. The work exhibits a natural empathy for the poor and deprived and includes a description and analysis of the *Kumbh Mela* religious gathering. Tully is particularly concerned that increasing Westernization, individualism, and materialism are gradually undermining India's creative genius and the support systems so crucial to the poor and deprived.

Geography and Travel

General

24 **The Ganges in myth and history.**
Steven G. Darian. Honolulu, Hawaii: University of Hawaii Press, 1978. 219p. bibliog.
This book presents a comprehensive picture of the great river's cultural importance. Using materials from archaeology, art history, comparative religion, mythology, Sanskrit and Bengali literature, classical and medieval European texts, and folklore, the author explains how and why the Ganges has come to occupy a central position in Hindu life and institutions. There is also some analysis of Ganges river commerce over the centuries.

25 **Monsoons.**
Edited by Jay S. Fein, Pamela L. Stephens. New York: John Wiley, 1987. 632p.
A multifaceted review of the monsoon through India's history and at the present day. This work comprises nineteen interdisciplinary essays by meteorologists, historians, anthropologists, and journalists. Of particular interest are the chapters by Khushwant Singh on the Indian monsoon in literature, Brian J. Murton on the monsoon in agricultural proverbs in Tamilnadu, and the descriptions of the various predictive models used to forecast future monsoons and analyse monsoon variability.

26 **The Himalaya: aspects of change.**
Edited by J. S. Lall, A. D. Moddie. New Delhi: Oxford University Press India, 1981. 481p. bibliog.
A collection of papers, intended for both general and specialist readers, which cover both the Indian and Nepal Himalaya. The essays are arranged in three sections: 'Nature', 'Man', and 'Interrelationships'. The topics discussed include climate,

wildlife, water resource potential, and geology. The basic facts of physical and human geography are well presented and current ecological and economic problems are highlighted.

27 Historical geography of ancient India.

Bimala Churn Law. New Delhi: Munshiram Manoharlal, 1984. reprint of 1920 ed. 354p. maps. bibliog.

Based largely on epigraphic data, the author gives the location of places and regions mentioned in ancient Indian and foreign texts. A complementary work, covering all geographical matters mentioned in *Puranic* and inscriptional place names, is Dinesh Chandra Sircar's *Studies in the geography of ancient and medieval India* (New Delhi: Motilal Banarsidass, 1971. 2nd ed. 401p.). More wide-ranging and provocative is *Geographical factors in Indian history* (Bombay: Bharatiya Vidya Bhavan, 1959, 3rd. ed. 128p.), by the distinguished historian and diplomat Kavalam Madhava Panikkar.

28 India: a regional geography.

Edited by R. L. Singh. Varanasi, India: National Geographical Society of India, 1971. 992p. maps. bibliog.

A comprehensive volume which comprises twenty-eight regional chapters written by Indian geographers, each including details of the historical background, physical setting, climate, natural resources, demographic structure, economy, and culture. A particular feature is the attention given to the analysis of settlement patterns. More than 600 cartographic illustrations accompany the text. A briefer complementary work, covering the economic and social landscape in sixty-five short essays, is *India: an area study* (New Delhi: Vikas, 1977. 237p.), by Surendra Nath Chopra.

29 India and Pakistan: a general and regional geography.

Oskar H. K. Spate, Andrew T. A. Learmonth. London: Methuen, 1972. 3rd ed. 878p. maps. bibliog.

This volume constitutes the most complete geographical treatment of South Asia, including Sri Lanka. Written in superlative prose, the work is broadly conceived and full of illustrative anecdotes and useful maps and diagrams. The land, the people, and the economy make up the first three parts of the book, and these are particularly recommended to the general reader. Part four, 'The face of the land', covers the individual regions of the subcontinent and, although packed with an abundance of useful material, is likely to be too detailed and technical for the purposes of most non-specialists.

30 Asia, east by south: a cultural geography.

J. E. Spencer, William L. Thomas. New York: John Wiley, 1971. 2nd ed. 669p. maps. bibliog.

This comprehensive cultural geography of monsoon Asia is divided into two main sections: systematic geography, and the regional expression of cultures. The chapters in the first section, dealing with the region as a unit, contain substantial information on the society and culture of India. The second part of the book has two chapters on India, one dealing with cultural history and the other with recent economic and social developments.

Economic

31 **India, resources and development.**
Basil Leonard Clyde Johnson. London: Heinemann, 1983. 2nd ed.
212p. maps. bibliog.

A careful analysis of India's human and physical resources. Johnson discusses such key issues as drought and water scarcity, patterns of crops, population growth, industry and urbanization, and small-scale manufacturing, and their place in modern India's economic development. The final chapter provides vignettes of eight Indian cities: Pilibhit, Kolhapur, Madurai, Bangalore, Delhi, Bombay, Calcutta and Chandigarh. Concise and well illustrated, with maps, photographs and tables, an introductory work, this second edition incorporates data from the 1981 census. Johnson is also author of *South Asia: selective studies of the essential geography of India, Pakistan, Bangladesh, Sri Lanka and Nepal* (London: Heinemann, 1981. 240p.), which includes a number of useful sample studies of village agriculture.

32 **Economic and commercial geography of India.**
C. B. Mamoria. New Delhi: Shiva Lal Agarwala, 1980. 523p. maps. bibliog.

A comprehensive survey of India's physical features and economic resources. Each chapter includes up-to-date economic statistics on the production of the relevant economic item. Chapters dealing with the industrial sector provide an historical outline of the development of each particular industry. An indispensable almanac for students of Indian economics.

Maps, atlases and gazetteers

33 **An historical atlas of Islam.**
Edited by William Charles Brice. Leiden, the Netherlands: E. J. Brill, 1981. 71p. 57 maps. bibliog.

A companion to the *Encyclopedia of Islam* (Leiden, The Netherlands: E. J. Brill, 1960.), this work contains ten maps illustrating Islamic penetration of India and the areas ruled by Muslim dynasties. A similar work is Francis Robinson's *Atlas of the Islamic world since 1500* (Oxford: Phaidon, 1982. 238p.).

34 **Fully annotated atlas of South Asia.**
Ashok K. Dutt, M. Margaret Geib. Boulder, Colorado; London: Westview Press, 1987. 231p. maps. bibliog.

This work contains numerous illuminating charts and tables and ninety-five pages of double-column text, making it more a descriptive geography than a pure atlas. A graphic representation of South Asia's political, physical, economic, historic, cultural, and social characteristics.

35 Gazetteer of India: Indian Union.

New Delhi: Ministry of Education and Social Welfare, 1965-78. 4 vols.
maps. bibliog.

Since 1882 the government of India has periodically issued the *Imperial Gazetteer of India*, containing an exhaustive account of the country and its people. The 1907-09 edition of the *Imperial Gazetteer,* edited by William W. Hunter, was published in twenty-five volumes, with the first four volumes devoted to a discussion of the general features of Indian society, culture, environment, history, economy, and the administrative system. The remaining volumes are arranged alphabetically, with details on towns and regions, and were last reprinted by Messrs Today & Tomorrow Printers & Publishers in 1974. A provincial series of gazetteers was published at the same time. While the entire 1907-09 edition has not been brought up to date, the first four volumes have now been thoroughly revised and rewritten by distinguished scholars.

36 Early maps of India.

Susan Gole. New Delhi: Sanskriti, Arnold-Heinemann, 1976. 126p.
maps. bibliog.

An illustrated history of the early European maps of India (16th-18th centuries) together with a comprehensive catalogue of the maps of India printed between 1513 and 1795. This work is complemented by two separate volumes of reproductions compiled by the author: *A series of early printed maps of India in facsimile* (London: J. Potter, 1986. 64p.); and *Indian maps and plans, from earliest times to the advent of European surveys* (New Delhi: Manohar, 1989. 207p.). The second volume contains a wide range of Indian maps – religious, topographical, military, town plans, and sea charts – ranging in date from a mesolithic cave painting to the present day.

37 An atlas of the Mughal empire.

Irfan Habib. New York: Oxford University Press USA, 1982. 120p.
maps. bibliog.

This atlas provides detailed regional and national maps of the Mughal empire between 1556 and 1857. Each region of the empire is covered by separate political and economic sheets. The political maps show district and state boundaries, forts and administrative centres, including more than 4,000 place names. The economic maps show geographical features, including the extent of the forested area, and economic resources and activities, for example the types of cash crops produced and centres of textile, metal, and mineral production. Detailed bibliographic and explanatory notes accompany each map.

38 A social and economic atlas of India.

Edited by Subbiah Muthiah. New Delhi: Oxford University Press
India, 1987. 254p. maps.

This volume contains 240 attractively coloured maps, with supplementary texts and 370 charts, to provide a detailed picture of India's environment, society, and economy during the 1980s. Subjects covered include demographic and climatic data; natural resources; infrastructure for health, education, transportation, communications, irrigation, power, and banking; animal, agricultural, and industrial production; tourism; development indicators and government outlays; imports and exports; and Indian foreign aid outlays. Sources include the 1981 census of India and documents from the Planning Commission, government ministries, and non-governmental data. A very useful, up-to-date reference work.

39   Census of India: census atlas, national volume, 1981.
Produced under the direction of B. K. Roy.   New Delhi: Controller of Publications, Government of India for the Registrar General and Census Commissioner, 1989. 212p.

Continuing the tradition first set by the 1961 Census, atlases were produced at both the national and state levels to accompany the 1981 Census. This volume contains administrative plates (showing boundary changes since 1971), demographic maps and plates (on population distribution, density, growth patterns, age and sex structure, rural house-types, urbanization etc), economic and socio-cultural maps and plates (covering occupational patterns, migration, literacy, religion, scheduled castes, tribes etc), and maps of physiographic regions. The maps are accompanied by text, tables and histograms. There are also detailed appendices. The volume is supplemented by twenty-nine additional census atlases covering each of the states and Union territories of India as of 1981.

40   District gazetteers of British India: a bibliography.
Henry Scholberg.   Zug, Switzerland: Inter Documentation Co., 1970. 131p.

This book lists 1,344 district and state gazetteers which were produced by the British Indian government during the period between the early 19th century and independence in 1947. A useful reference work for research scholars.

41   A historical atlas of South Asia.
Edited by Joseph E. Schwartzberg.   Oxford: Oxford University Press, 1993. 2nd ed. 420p. 650 maps. bibliog.

A comprehensive, justly acclaimed, cartographic record of the history and culture of South Asia from prehistoric times to the present. Maps and plates are divided into fourteen principal sections followed by a similarly arranged explanatory text. The maps and full-colour plates, totalling 650 and 158 respectively, cover everything from the routes taken by Chinese Buddhist pilgrims between AD 400 and 700, to the plans of various kinds of Indian villages of today. There are also numerous tables, charts and photographs. The main bibliography, listing some 4,000 items, and classified, is a substantial reference source in itself.

42   People of India: an anthropological atlas.
Edited by K. S. Singh.   New Delhi: Oxford University Press India, 1994. 160p. 149 maps. bibliog. (People of India, Vol. XI).

An offshoot of the 'People of India' project, this volume uses the information generated to provide a cartographical representation of the distribution of cultural, biological and linguistic traits, anthropometry, and demographic features. A useful reference work.

Tourist guides

43   *Hippocrene* **companion guide to southern India.**
Jack Adler.   New York: Hippocrene, 1992. 301p.

An informative companion guide for visitors to south India written by a travel writer for the *Los Angeles Times*. The work is divided into two parts. Part one comprises sixteen general chapters on such themes as south Indian history, religion, temples, arts and culture, politics, and cuisine. Part two contains seventeen short chapters on towns, regions, and places to visit. The book needs to be supplemented by a map.

44   *Fodor's* **India: the complete guide to the subcontinent with expanded coverage of Nepal.**
Edited by Andrew E. Beresky.   New York: Fodor's Travel, 1993 (annual). 27th ed. 590p. maps.

One of the best short tourist guides, this volume provides information on the most popular sites and major cities of India. For the uninitiated, there is a short history of India, its architecture, music, dance, painting, sculpture, literature, food, hotels, and inter-city and intra-city transportation. Brief information on weather, customs regulations, foreign exchange, and health conditions is also given.

45   **South Asian handbook, 1992: India, Pakistan, Nepal, Bangladesh, Sri Lanka, Bhutan, the Maldives.**
Edited by Robert Bradnock, William Whittaker, Roma Bradnock.
New York: Prentice Hall General Reference, 1991. 1,528p. maps.

An informative, well-written travel guide which combines historical facts, places of interest and practical information on such matters as climate and transport links for each city covered. This handbook offers travellers a wider variety of accommodations than the *Fodor's* guide.

46   **India: a travel survival kit.**
Edited by Geoff Crowther, Tony Wheeler, Prakash A. Ray, Bryn Thomas, Hugh Finlay, Tony Graham.   Hawthorn, Australia: Lonely Planet Publications, 1993. 5th ed. 1,099p. maps.

Designed for the low-budget, back-packing independent traveller, this established guide provides a mixture of background historical and sightseeing information and practical, personally researched, recommendations concerning travel, food and budget accommodation. It also contains many city maps. In addition, there is a companion volume, *Trekking in the Indian Himalaya,* and a slim, inexpensive *Hindi/Urdu phrasebook* (South Yarra, Australia: Lonely Planet Publications, 1988. 106p.). A work similar in scope, linked to a British television series and targeted at the younger traveller, is *India: the rough guide* (London: Penguin, 1994. 1163p.), by David Abram, Harriet Podger, Devdan Sen, and Gareth John Williams.

47   Insider's guide to India.
Kirsten Ellis.   Hong Kong: CFW, 1990. 358p. maps.

Sumptuously illustrated with striking colour photographs, this guide contains interesting historical and sightseeing information, arranged in a regional format, as well as travel advice. Similar in layout and pictoral presentation is *Insight guides: India* (Singapore: APA, 1992. 4th ed. 359p.), edited by Samuel Israel and Bikram Grewal. Short, illustrated chapters are contributed by twenty-six specialists, covering such topics as Indian religions, history, music, festivals, wildlife, and handicrafts. There is also a thirty page 'travel tips' section. There are also more detailed single-volume Insight guides on *Rajasthan* (1989), *South India* (1993), and *Delhi, Jaipur, Agra* (1993). *Cadogan guides: India, Kathmandu Valley – Nepal* (London: Cadogan Books, 1993. 3rd ed. 530p.), edited by Frank Kusy, contains similar sightseeing information and includes rail fares and timetables for the principal routes.

48   India by rail.
Royston Ellis.   Chalfont St. Peter, England: Bradt Publications UK, 1993. 2nd ed. 244p. maps. bibliog.

Designed for both the general tourist intending to journey around the subcontinent by rail as well as for the rail enthusiast, this work provides valuable general travel information and detailed descriptions of rail routes. The author is himself a rail enthusiast and an experienced writer and traveller in India. The work is usefully supplemented by Bill Aitken's *Exploring Indian railways* (New Delhi: Oxford University Press India, 1994. 272p.). An amusing, but also informative, travellers' account, it covers a wide range of aspects of current railway practices, from station bookshops and bureaucracy to locomotive types and the workings of the various gauges.

Twentieth-century travellers' accounts

49   Hindoo holiday: an Indian journal.
Joe R. Ackerley.   Harmondsworth, England: Penguin, 1983. 276p.

A beautifully written and hugely entertaining account of a five-month sojourn in India in 1923 as private secretary and tutor to the Maharaja of Chhokrapur. Ackerley, a friend of E. M. Forster, provides here a kaleidoscopic picture of Indian customs and culture, mixing subtle irony with scenes of pure farce. A classic work.

50   Seven sacred rivers.
Bill Aitken.   New Delhi: Penguin India, 1992. 196p.

A sensitive and informed travel journal written by a professional Scottish traveller. As well as the Ganges, Aitken explores the Kosi, Chambal, Hooghly and Brahmaputra rivers in north India, the Narmada, Tapti and Mahanadi in the Deccan, and the Cauvery, Krishna and Tungabhadra in the far south, meeting conservationists, pilgrims and devotees en route.

51 **A walk along the Ganges.**
Dennison Berwick. London: Century Hutchinson, 1986. 234p. map.
bibliog.

This lively and graphic travelogue describes the seven-month-long journey undertaken by the author alone and on foot from the mouth of the Ganges to its source, 12,000 feet up in the Himalayas. The excursion was undertaken for charity (the Save the Children Fund) during 1983-84. The work relates adventures en route and includes digressions on Indian history, religion, art, society, and politics.

52 **Arrow of the blue-skinned god: a journey through India.**
Jonah Blank. London: Simon & Schuster, 1994. new ed. 496p. map.

An account of a journey through India during which the author, a young American journalist, retraces Rama's legendary trek from Ayodhya in north India to Sri Lanka, and his spiritual voyage from Man to God as set out in the epic *Ramayana* (see item no. 820). En route, Blank encounters a vivid cast of characters. He joined the Maharajah of Jaipur and conversed with terrorists in the Punjab, guerrillas in Trincomalee, and the commander of a Sri Lankan death squad.

53 **Indian summer.**
James Cameron. London: Macmillan, 1974. 224p.

A sparkling account of India during the late 1960s and early 1970s by a renowned English journalist. The author, a frequent traveller to the subcontinent during the previous twenty-five years and married to an Indian, was an acute observer of the Indian scene and he shares the joys and sorrows of his experiences with the reader. This book was written at the time of the Indo-Pakistan conflict over the creation of Bangladesh.

54 **City of Djinns: a year in Delhi.**
William Dalrymple, with illustrations by Olivia Fraser. London:
Harper Collins, 1993. 351p.

The travel writer William Dalrymple devoted a year to observing Delhi and in this work he skilfully interlaces stories connecting present-day Delhi with its past cities and histories. There are tales of the city's founding and the creation myth contained in the epic *Mahabharata* (see item no. 822). The years under Muslim rule and the British Raj are recounted, along with the effect of partition in 1947. Through the words of an assortment of 'Delhi wallahs' - a taxi driver, a eunuch, a Mughal princess now fallen on hard times – the past is illuminated.

55 **A journey in Ladakh.**
Andrew Harvey. London: Picador, 1994. 256p.

Situated high up on the remote Indian borders with Tibet, China and Pakistan, beyond the Kashmir Valley, is the rugged, arid, mountainous district of Ladakh. Peopled by sheep-rearing nomadic tribes, it is one of the last places where a Tibetan Buddhist community survives. This work recounts the author's 1981 travels through the region.

56 In Clive's footsteps.

Peter Holt.   London: Arrow, 1991. new ed. 209p. map. bibliog.

The author, a direct descendant of Robert Clive of India, describes his adventures during 1988-89 as he retraced his ancestor's journeys around eastern and southeastern India. The work interweaves a biography of Clive and the East India Company with Holt's own, often amusing, experiences, related with frankness and charm.

57 The city of joy.

Dominique Lapierre.   London: Arrow, 1987. new ed. 528p.

Immensely popular, sales of this book exceed seven million. There have been fifteen translations and the work has also been the subject of a film directed by Roland Joffe. The title of the work refers to 'Anand Nagar', a chronically poor and overpopulated slum neighbourhood of the teeming metropolis of Calcutta. Here the author, a French writer, stayed for several months and was uplifted by the simple heroism, joy and hope of so many of its inhabitants.

58 Om: an Indian pilgrimage.

Geoffrey Moorhouse.   London: Hodder & Stoughton, 1993. 255p.

An absorbing and typically well-written account of a tour of famous south Indian pilgrimage and worship centres by the author, who has written extensively on colonial and post-colonial India (see items no. 194, 301), during 1992. Moorhouse recounts his conversations with pilgrims, temple functionaries and others he met during his visit and acutely observes the practises of devotees.

59 Slowly down the Ganges.

Eric Newby.   London: Pan Books, 1983. 298p. maps.

An engaging account of a 1,200 mile journey made by the travel writer Eric Newby and his wife down the sacred Ganges river during 1963-4. The journey commenced at the holy city of Hardwar, where *Ganga Ma* (Mother Ganges) enters the great plain of Hindustan, and was undertaken in a wide variety of boats. En route, staying at night sometimes on sandbanks, in the manner of European travellers of the early 19th century, the Newbys came into contact with a colourful assortment of characters.

60 India: a literary companion.

Bruce Palling.   London: John Murray, 1992. 264p. bibliog.

Written by a seasoned Asia correspondent and, latterly, travel editor of *Tatler*, this work colourfully weaves together the accounts of European travellers to India – conquerors, traders, missionaries and artists. Particular prominence is given to the impressions and 'encounters' of 20th-century travellers. The ten chapters cover the topics: arrival, departure, climate, religion, travel, village India, the great cities, maharajas, the rulers, and Mutiny and Partition.

61 The great railway bazaar: by train through Asia.

Paul Theroux.   London: Hamish Hamilton, 1975. 342p.

A hugely entertaining account of an epic series of railway journeys from London, via Iran, Pakistan, India, Myanmar (Burma), Malaysia and Vietnam, to Japan, by the renowned American novelist and travel writer. Eleven of the chapters concern Theroux's train journeys across South Asia and his encounters with a colourful array of fellow travellers. This book is complemented by Theroux's sumptuously illustrated *The Imperial Way: by rail from Peshawar to Chittagong* (Boston: Houghton Mifflin, 1985. 143p. photographs by Steve McCurry), which records Theroux's impressions during a subsequent visit to the subcontinent.

Flora, Fauna and Conservation

Flora and fauna

62 **Forests in India: environmental and production frontiers.**
V. P. Agrawala.   New Delhi: Oxford & IBH, 1985. 344p.
A descriptive review of the land-use and forest area in India by an author with experience of the forestry profession. The work includes a history of forestry in India and considers economic – wood and non-wood production and employment – and ecological and environmental aspects of India's forests.

63 **Handbook of the birds of India and Pakistan together with those of Bangladesh, Nepal, Bhutan and Sri Lanka.**
Salim A. Ali, Sidney Dillon Ripley.   New Delhi: Oxford University Press India, 1987. 2nd ed. 10 vols. maps. bibliog.
These volumes provide a definitive account of the life history, behaviour, and biogeography of the birds of South Asia. The principal author, Salim Ali (1896-1987), was a celebrated conservationist and ornithologist who became a nominated member of the Rajya Sabha, the upper house of the Indian Parliament. For shorter accounts, see Ali's *The book of Indian birds* (New Delhi: Oxford University Press India, 1979. 11th ed. 187p.); and S. A. Ali and S. D. Ripley's *Compact handbook of the birds of India and Pakistan* (New Delhi: Oxford University Press India, 1987. 2nd ed. 737p.).

64 **Indian wildlife.**
Ramesh Bedi, photographs by Rajesh Bedi.   London: William Collins, 1984. 312p.
This book describes animals and birds from all parts of India and the national parks. The information is arranged in regional chapters and is accompanied by dramatic colour photographs. A non-academic work designed for the general reader.

65   A textbook of the plant geography of India.

F. R. Bharucha.   Bombay: Oxford University Press India, 1983. 179p. maps. bibliog.

Intended, as its title suggests, as a textbook for students, this work, divided into 13 chapters, provides a detailed account of the climatic conditions, soils, and flora of the various regions of India. It explains why India's forests, grasslands, and deserts are situated where they are and considers related climatic, edaphic and biotic factors.

66   Field guide to the common trees of India.

P. V. Bole, Yogini Vaghani.   New Delhi: Oxford University Press India, for World Wildlife Fund, 1986. 125p.

An illustrated paperback guide, produced in conjunction with the World Wildlife Fund. For each tree, there is a description of its common, scientific, and vernacular names, and also its origin, characteristics, fruit, flower, and uses.

67   The book of Indian reptiles.

J. C. Daniel.   Bombay: Oxford University Press India, for the Bombay Natural History Society, 1983. 141p. bibliog.

Illustrated with black-and-white pictures and line drawings, this work describes the common reptiles found in India – crocodiles, turtles, snakes, and lizards.

68   Useful plants of India and Pakistan.

Jehangir Fardunji Dastur.   Bombay: Taraporevala, 1977. 2nd ed. 185p. bibliog.

A comprehensive survey of native plants and trees of industrial, economic, and commercial value. The local names of these plants are given and the use of each is fully covered. A classified list of the plants according to their uses is given in an appendix. There is a companion volume, *Medicinal plants of India and Pakistan* (Bombay: Taraporevala, 1962. 2nd ed. 212p.), which provides equivalent information on plants used for drugs and remedies according to the *Ayurvedic*, *Unani*, and *Tibbi* systems of India.

69   Encyclopedia of Indian natural history: centenary publication of the Bombay Natural History Society 1883-1983.

Edited by R. E. Hawkins, illustrations editors Doris Norden, Bittu Sahgal.   New Delhi: Oxford University Press India, for the Bombay Natural History Society, 1986. 620p. map.

This handsomely illustrated work, covering the plant and animal life of the subcontinent, comprises over 500 entries, contributed by ninety-six scholars. Published at an attractively low, subsidized price, it forms an invaluable, clearly-written handbook for reference within the field, as well as for travellers to India. Numerous well-produced drawings, photographs and colour plates are included. An interesting, related, historical work is *The European discovery of the Indian flora* (Kew, England: The Royal Botanical Gardens, 1992. 355p.), by Ray G. C. Desmond.

70   **Jim Corbett's India: stories from** *Man-eaters of Kumaun, My India, Jungle love,* **and others.**
Selected by R. E. Hawkins.   Oxford: Oxford University Press, 1986.
272p. map. bibliog.

A paperback selection of popular and evocative natural history tales by Jim Corbett, renowned for his tiger exploits and after whom a National Park is named. Corbett's life story is recounted in *Carpet sahib: a life of Jim Corbett* (Oxford: Oxford University Press, 1991. new ed. 278p.), by Martin Booth.

71   *Insight* **guide: Indian wildlife.**
Edited by Samuel Israel, Toby Sinclair.   Singapore: APA, 1992.
2nd ed. 380p. 19 maps.

A comprehensive guidebook to Indian, Nepalese, and Sri Lankan wildlife parks and sanctuaries and their inhabitants, intended for the interested amateur and wildlife specialist. The volume includes essays on such topics as wildlife in Indian mythology and folklore, and observing wildlife. There are also separate chapters on individual animals, including the Asian elephant, the Indian rhinoceros, tiger, reptiles, and birds, as well as on wildlife in the Himalayas and Indian desert, marine life, and each national park. The text, written by experts, is accompanied by colour photographs. Addresses of the wildlife parks are provided in the appendix, along with recommended times for visits.

72   **The freshwater fishes of India, Pakistan, Bangladesh, Burma and Sri Lanka: a handbook.**
K. C. Jayaram.   Calcutta: Zoological Survey of India, 1981. 475p.
bibliog.

A study of 742 species and 64 families of the fish to be found in South Asian inland waters. The habitat of each species and its distinguishing physical characteristics are included in the entries.

73   **Flowers of the Himalaya.**
Oleg Polunin, Adam Stainton.   Oxford; New York: Oxford University Press, 1984. 580p. maps. bibliog.

A comprehensive field guide which identifies all common species of Himalayan flora. There are 1,495 entries, each annotated with a full scientific description, 689 colour photographs, and 316 line drawings. A concise edition of the work was published in 1988.

74   *Collins* **handguide to the birds of the Indian sub-continent.**
Martin Woodcock.   London: Collins, 1990. reprint. 176p.

A brief and inexpensive pocket guide designed for non-specialist visitors to India. The guide covers 545 of the 1,250 species found in South Asia, each accompanied by a colour illustration. A similar work is, *Birds of India: Odyssey guide* (London: Odyssey, 1994.).

Environmental concerns and conservation

75   **Conservation of the Indian heritage.**
     Edited by Bridget Allchin, F. Raymond Allchin, B. K. Thapar.   New
     Delhi: Cosmo, 1989. 275p.

This volume, the outgrowth of a seminar held at the 1983 British Festival of India
which was attended by Indian and British scholars, provides an overview of the
conservation movement in India as it existed in the early 1980s. The articles are
concerned with the conservation of India's natural and architectural heritage, and
recognize the complexity of conservation issues and the pressures imposed by a
growing population and the capability to exploit natural resources. It is argued that
education – of villagers, industrialists, and the forestry service – is critical to the
success of the conservation movement, combined with legislative measures and
targeted projects on the 'Project Tiger' model.

76   **Indian environment: crises and responses.**
     Edited by Jayanta Bandyopadhyay and others.   Dehra Dun, India:
     Natraj, 1985. 309p.

The chief editor of this volume is a crusading environmentalist who, along with
research partner Vandana Shiva, exposed how plantation forestry in Karnataka was
turning scarce food crop lands into capitalist tree farms and has headed the Ganga-
Yamuna Watershed Project. This book comprises twenty-one short reports presented
by natural resource analysts and managers, covering a wide range of regions. Topics
reported on include professional forestry practices, water resource systems, industrial
pollution, environmental law, and environmental action campaigns. The book
includes an article by Sunderlal Bahuguna, leader of the Chipko rural tree-
preservation movement in the Garhwal Himalayas. Bandyopadhyay has edited a
subsequent volume with Vandana Shiva, *Ecology and the politics of survival:
conflicts over natural resources in India* (New Delhi, London: Sage Publications,
1991. 365p.).

77   **Conservation in developing countries: problems and prospects.**
     Edited by J. C. Daniel, J. S. Serrao.   Bombay: Oxford University Press
     India, for the Bombay Natural History Society, 1990. 656p. maps.
     bibliog.

A collection of sixty-one specialist papers on Indian conservation matters which were
presented at the centenary seminar of the Bombay Natural History Society. The topics
covered include wildlife trade, post-1800 forest policy, environmental education, the
environmental impact of hydroelectric power projects, and the conservation of
individual species, for example sea turtles, crocodiles, black buck, and vultures.
Abstracts of seventeen papers are also reproduced.

78 **The unquiet woods: ecological change and peasant resistance in the Himalaya.**
Ramachandra Guha. New Delhi: Oxford University Press India, 1989. 214p. map. bibliog.

A study of Indian forests, their people, and state-peasant protest, focusing on developments in Uttarakhand, the eight hill districts of the north Indian state of Uttar Pradesh, since the 19th century. The author shows that the peasant Chipko movement against commercial forestry which swept the region during the 1970s was part of a much longer history of resistance and protest. Guha also stresses that Chipko is primarily a movement in defence of traditional peasant rights in the forest and only secondarily, if at all, an 'environmental' or 'feminist' movement. With Madhav Gadgil, Guha has written a wide-ranging work, *The fissured land: an ecological history of India* (New Delhi: Oxford University Press India, 1992. 274p.).

79 **The Himalayan dilemma: reconciling development and conservation.**
John D. Ives, Bruno Messerli. London, New York: The United Nations University, Routledge, 1989. 295p. maps. bibliog.

Drawing on the work of experts from several nations, this volume considers the problems of the Himalayan region as a whole. The authors are critical of over-alarmist interpretations of the situation and suggest that large-scale technological solutions carry the danger of making matters worse. The bibliography is particularly useful.

80 **The political economy of forest use and management.**
M. V. Nadkarni, S. A. Pasha, L. S. Prabhakar. New Delhi: Sage Publications, 1989. 182p. map. bibliog.

The central argument of this work is that the state, concerned with 'common good', has played the prominent role in forestry planning, conservation and regeneration, whereas local people have shown little or no awareness of the need to conserve the forests, but, instead, have exploited their resources, often in an indiscriminate manner. The authors' conclude that an increased level of state intervention is desirable in order to bring wasteland and degraded areas under effective institutional control and use them for tree-planting. The analysis is controversial since it inadequately addresses the interrelated reasons – for example insecurity of harvest rights in wasteland areas, and discouraging private planting – which may explain why local communities take little interest in forest protection and regeneration. However, the work contains a good historical and class analysis of the problem.

81 **Indigenous vision: peoples of India attitudes to the environment.**
Edited by Geeti Sen. New Delhi, London: Sage Publications and Indian International Centre, 1992. 304p.

This UNDP-supported volume contains twenty-four essays on current and past Indian attitudes towards the environment. Papers range from literary and academic discussions of Hindu myths and earth gods and goddesses to the more polemical views of Medha Patkar, an anti-Narmada Dam activist.

82 **Elephant days and nights: ten years with the Indian elephant.**
    Raman Sukumar. New Delhi: Oxford University Press India, 1994.
    186p.

This work is an account of the author's experiences during ten years of research on the Indian elephant. Sukumar, a leading naturalist, has been a key member of 'Project Elephant', an Indian government-funded scheme set up, along the lines of 'Project Tiger', to protect the elephant. Sukumar is also author of the complementary volume, *The asian elephant: ecology and management* (Cambridge: Cambridge University Press, 1993. 263p.), which examines human interaction and its impact on the conservation of South Asian elephants.

Archaeology and Prehistory

83 The archaeology of India.

D. P. Agrawal. London: Curzon Press, 1982. 294p. map. bibliog. (Scandinavian Institute of Asian Studies Monograph Series, no. 46).

An excellent, up-to-date archaeological synthesis written from a multi-disciplinary perspective and covering a vast time-span from the Lower Palaeolithic (early Stone Age) era, via the Chalcolithic (Copper Age) period, to the beginning of the Iron Age. Intended for both scholar and general reader and richly illustrated, there is information on the history of Indian archaeology, the ecological background, prehistoric art, and the Indus civilization.

84 Essays in Indian protohistory.

Edited by D. P. Agrawal, Dilip Kumar Chakrabarti. New Delhi: BR Publishing, 1979. 392p.

A collection of essays by some of India's leading archaeologists, including the editors, B. B. Lal, M. K. Dhavalikar, K. N. Dikshit, and A. Ghosh, covering various facets of Indian prehistory from the beginning of food production to the use of iron. The work is arranged in six sections, including the Harappan period, Neolithic-chalcolithic, iron, and radiocarbon chronology, and reflects advances in archaeological methodologies and new emphases on the ecological and anthropological approach. Chakrabarti is author of *The early use of iron in India* (New Delhi: Oxford University Press India, 1992. 200p.).

85 The rise of civilization in India and Pakistan.

F. Raymond Allchin, Bridget Allchin. Cambridge: Cambridge University Press, 1982. 379p. maps. bibliog. (Cambridge World Archaeology).

Using ethnographic, linguistic, and historical evidence, as well as archaeological records, the authors trace the origins and development of Indian culture in the subcontinent from its roots in the palaeolithic era, through the rise, efflorescence, and disintegration of the Indus civilization. The emergence of regional cultures in the Indo-Gangetic plains and in the Deccan, and the spread of Indo-Aryans throughout India are discussed in admirable fashion. The volume concludes with an examination of the appearance of city states in the early Buddhist period. Excellent illustrations accompany the text. Available in paperback, this is the pre-eminent introductory text on Indian archaeology.

86 A sourcebook of Indian archaeology.

F. Raymond Allchin, Dilip Kumar Chakrabarti. New Delhi: Munshiram Manoharlal, 1979. 354p. maps. bibliog.

These readings, the first of a projected three-volume sourcebook, show the development of Indian archaeology from its late 18th-century beginnings to the present. Excerpts from the most important of older as well as the best of contemporary research on each topic are included. The first volume includes materials grouped under four headings: historical background to Indian archaeology; earliest researches; geography, climate, and early man; and domestication of plants and animals.

87 *Bharatvarsha* (an account of early India with special emphasis on social and economic aspects).

Arun Bhattacharjee. New Delhi: Ashish, 1988. 212p. maps. bibliog.

An introductory overview of early South Asian civilizations, from the Harappas to the Kusanas. There are individual chapters on the position of women, education, seafaring, slavery, the caste system, literature, and political organization. There are also useful reviews of the progress of archaeology in India and non-Indian approaches to Indology.

88 A history of Indian archaeology: from the beginning to 1947.

Dilip Kumar Chakrabarti. New Delhi: Munshiram Manoharlal, 1988. 262p. bibliog.

A clearly-written overview, based on secondary sources, of the basic pattern of Indian archaeological discoveries and writings till 1947. It begins by examining the 17th- and 18th-century writings on Indian monuments by European travellers. However, the bulk of the work is concerned with archaeological activity during the colonial period carried out by British officers. Chakrabarti reviews the pioneering surveys of Alexander Cunningham, who was appointed as the first archaeological surveyor to the Government of India in 1861 and remained in post until 1885; the impetus given to epigraphy, conservation and research by Lord Curzon, viceroy between 1899-1905; and the famous 1944-48 excavations at Harappa overseen by Sir Mortimer Wheeler.

89 Harappan bibliography.

R. N. Dandekar. Poona, India: Bhandarkar Oriental Research Institute, 1987. 495p.

Books, articles, monographs and allied studies of Harappan civilization are included in this useful volume arranged in nine sections: general studies; script, language, and seals; arts; flora and fauna; people; religion; Harappan and Vedic Aryan; external relations; and miscellaneous. Many entries are annotated to indicate arguments, conclusions and cross references, and a wide range of periodicals, exceeding 400 in different languages, has been consulted. There is an author index, but not, unfortunately, a subject index.

90   **The roots of ancient India: the archaeology of early Indian civilization.**
Walter A. Fairservis, Jr., drawings by Jan Fairservis.   London: George Allen & Unwin, 1971. 482p. 28 maps. bibliog.

A significant work of synthesis and analysis of Indian archaeological evidence by a prominent American scholar. The author begins with the earliest evidence from the stone age, dating back more than a quarter of a million years. Fairservis analyses the transition to settled habitation and then discusses the Harappan era.

91   **An encyclopaedia of Indian archaeology.**
Edited by Amalananda Ghosh.   New Delhi: Munshiram Manorharlal; Leiden, the Netherlands: E. J. Brill, 1990. 2 vols. bibliog.

An authoritative reference work edited by the late Amalananda Ghosh (1910-81), former Director-General of the Archaeological Survey of India. The first volume is arranged in twenty subject chapters, dealing with such topics as archaeobotany, environmental archaeology, pottery, rock art, writing, and weapons. Each chapter is alphabetically arranged and contains a bibliography. The second volume is a gazetteer which contains data on all the explored and excavated sites in India, as well as references to published reports on each.

92   **Studies in the archaeology of India and Pakistan.**
Edited by Jerome Jacobson.   Warminster, England: Aris & Phillips; New Delhi: Oxford & IBH, 1987. 327p. maps. bibliog.

This collection of twelve scholarly papers gives an indication of the range and interests of American archaeologists working on South Asia in the 1980s. The papers on the Harappan civilization cover both the material culture, and social and cultural life. One revisionist article on cultural continuity in eastern Punjab sites questions whether there ever was an Aryan invasion from Central Asia and suggests, instead, that change came from the Gangetic valley.

93   **The archaeology of Indian trade routes up to c. 200 BC: resource use, resource access and lines of communication.**
Nayanjot Lahiri.   New Delhi: Oxford University Press India, 1992. 461p. 46 maps. bibliog.

This study of protohistoric and early historic trade routes is based on an analysis of settlement and literary evidence, but also, most significantly, of material cultures and uses and sources of raw materials. The author shows that two major trans-regional trade routes existed – the *Uttarapatha* (northern grand route) and *Dakshinapatha* (southern grand route) – and that there were also inter-regional routes, but that shifts occurred over time. Chapter two looks at Harappan trade routes. Numerous charts and maps accompany the text.

94 Frontiers of the Indus civilization.

Edited by B. B. Lal, S. P. Gupta. New Delhi: Books & Books, 1984. 545p.

A comprehensive, impressive, richly illustrated work produced by the Indian Archaeological Society in commemoration of Sir Mortimer Wheeler (1890-1976) who first excavated Mohenjo-Daro and Harappa in the Indus Valley. It comprises fifty-three chapters contributed by leading Indian and Western archaeologists including D. P. Agrawal, F. R. and B. Allchin, D. K. Chakrabarti, K. N. Dikshit, W. A. Fairservis, B. B. Lal, and B. K. Thapar. All aspects of Harappan civilization are covered: climate, culture, disease, environment, language, political life, social stratification, trade, and urbanization. A definitive dating for the early and mature Harappan periods is suggested in the appendix at between 3200-2200 BC and 2700-2100 BC respectively.

95 Settlement history and the rise of civilization in Ganga-Yamuna *doab* (from 1500 BC – 300 AD).

Makkhan Lal. New Delhi: B. R. Publishing, 1984. 363p. maps. bibliog.

A specialized, but innovative, work from the new discipline of 'settlement/spatial archaeology'. Drawing on a painstaking survey of more than 150 sites in the vicinity of Kanpur in Uttar Pradesh, Lal presents a fascinating picture of changing settlement patterns and sizes between the second half of the second millennium BC and the beginnings of the Christian era. The picture painted is one of population growth, agricultural development and incipient urbanization.

96 The people of South Asia: the biological anthropology of India, Pakistan, and Nepal.

Edited by John R. Lukacs. New York, London: Plenum, 1984. 465p. map. bibliog.

A collection of specialist papers in the field of physical anthropology. The essays are arranged in two sections: palaeoanthropology and the biological anthropology of the contemporary population. Included are two chapters on Harappa by Pratap C. Dutta and Jim G. Shaffer. Palaeoanthropology is also covered in *Studies in the archaeology and palaeoanthropology of South Asia*, edited by Kenneth A. R. Kennedy and Gregory L. Possehl (New Delhi: Oxford & IBH, 1984.).

97 Artifacts as categories: a study of ceramic variability in central India.

Daniel Miller. Cambridge: Cambridge University Press, 1985. 253p. bibliog.

A case-study of the village of Dangwara in the Malwa region of central India which employs the new approach of contextual, or structural, archaeology in which archaeological analysis is grounded in contemporary social theory. In particular, the author uses the implicit categorizations of pottery objects to provide evidence concerning the structural relations that underline cultural groups.

98   **Protohistoric India.**
     K. P. Nautiyal.   New Delhi: Agam Kala Prakashan, 1989. 209p. maps.
     bibliog.

A concise overview of India's earliest history from pastoralism, via the Harappan civilization, to the iron age and Ganges valley urban development. The period covered is from the 7th-6th millennium BC to ca. 1000 BC. There are eighty-five plates.

99   **Harappan civilization: a contemporary perspective.**
     Edited by Gregory L. Possehl.   Warminster, England: Aris & Philips,
     1982. 440p. maps. bibliog.

A useful collection of papers by Indian and American archaeologists presented to a 1979 conference. The essays are arranged in sections dealing with the following topics: Harappan urbanization, ecology, technology and trade, biological anthropology, recent fieldwork results, and the history of research on Harappan civilization. There is also a paper on the Indus script and on modern interpretations which emphasises the complexity of the processes of cultural change during the Harappan era. The editor, Gregory Possehl, has written extensively on Harappan civilization and urbanization and is also the author of an important work, *Kulli: an exploration of an ancient civilization in South Asia* (Durham, North Carolina: Carolina Academic Press, 1986. 168p.), which describes archaeological remains found in southeastern Baluchistan. An earlier classic account of Harappa is, Mortimer Wheeler *The Indus civilization* (London: Cambridge University Press, 1968. 3rd. ed. 144p.).

100   *Puratattva*: **Bulletin of the Indian Archaeological Society.**
      New Delhi: Indian Archaeological Society, 1967-68- . annual.

An annual collection of articles and book reviews by India's leading archaeologists.

101   **Historical archaeology of India: a dialogue between archaeologists**
      and historians.
      Edited by Amita Ray, Samir Mukherjee.   New Delhi: Books &
      Books, 1990. 376p.

An up-to-date collection of thirty-four papers presented at an interdisciplinary seminar at Calcutta University. Topics covered include early urbanization (six papers), technology, religion, and the emergence of art. A useful earlier collection of thirty-eight papers presented to the 1980 congress of the Indian Archaeological Society is *Indian archaeology: new perspectives* (New Delhi: Agam Kala Prakashan, 1982. 319p.), edited by R. K. Sharma.

102   **The Ganges civilization (a critical archaeological study of the**
      Painted Grey Ware and Northern Black Polished Ware periods of
      the Ganga plains of India).
      T. N. Roy.   New Delhi: Ramanand Vidya Bhawan, 1983. 293p. maps.
      bibliog.

This work covers the period between ca. 800 BC and ca. 100 BC and looks at the beginning, dating and diffusion of the Painted Grey Ware and Northern Black

Polished Ware periods of culture in the Ganges valley region. Based on the critical survey of nearly sixty sites, Roy provides chronologies and describes settlement patterns and technologies associated with these iron age cultures which provided the basis for urban development.

103 Prehistory of India.

Hasmukh Dhirajlal Sankalia. New Delhi: Munshiram Manoharlal, 1977. 211p. maps. bibliog.

A clear, general exposition of Indian prehistory, covering the period until written records became available, written by the late H. D. Sankalia (1908-89), the doyen of Indian archaeologists who was preeminent in palaeolithic research. The opening chapters sets Indian developments in the context of world prehistory. Subsequent chapters cover such topics as Harappan culture, the iron age in south India, and the copper hoard culture. The work is attractively illustrated.

104 Palaeo-environments and prehistory of the middle Son valley.

Edited by G. R. Sharma, J. D. Clark. Allahabad, India: Abinash Prakashan, 1983. 320p. bibliog.

This volume sets out the results of multi-disciplinary investigations into the history of earliest human settlements and the palaeo-environment of part of the Son valley in Madhya Pradesh in north-central India. Working on the project during 1980-81 were scholars from India, the United States, Australia and New Zealand. They have reconstructed the evolution of the sub-region's climate, environment and human adaptations during a period from more than 100,000 years to about 2,000 years ago.

105 Archaeology of north-eastern India.

Edited by Jai Prakash Singh, Gautam Sengupta. New Delhi: Vikas, 1991. 372p. bibliog.

This volume contains essays contributed by specialists from a wide variety of disciplines: geographers, geologists, ecologists, linguists, cultural historians, and anthropologists. Hitherto, this region has been little studied, but here new light is cast on its early coinage, inscriptions and physical structures.

106 From lineage to state: social formation in the mid-first millennium BC in the Ganga valley.

Romila Thapar. New Delhi: Oxford University Press India, 1984. 189p. bibliog.

A pioneering study of change in ancient India from lineage-based social formations to those dominated by a state system and the formation of a caste-class society in the first millennium BC. The author relates Indian developments to comparative studies of ancient societies and draws upon a range of archaeological, sociolinguistic and anthropological evidence. There is acute analysis of the lineage-based Vedic societies of upper Sind, Punjab, and the western Ganges valley, and the growth in commerce which later triggered urbanization, and related socio-political changes, in the middle Ganges valley. An impressive, stimulating work.

History

General

107 A cultural history of India.
Edited by Arthur Llewellyn Basham.   New Delhi: Oxford University
Press India, 1983. 585p. maps. bibliog.

Containing thirty-five essays from twenty-eight specialists, and originally published
in 1975, this volume is the successor to the 1937 *Legacy of India*, edited by G. T.
Garratt. It contains excellent essays on ancient, early, medieval and Islamic history,
literature and art. The fourth section of the book dealing with India's contacts with
Europe is reliable and informative. Essays on Hindu devotionalism and Mughal-
British relations, however, are less impressive.

108 Situating Indian history: for Sarvepalli Gopal.
Edited by Sabyasachi Bhattacharya, Romila Thapar.   New Delhi:
Oxford University Press India, 1986. 463p.

This *festschrift* volume, to honour a great Indian historian, comprises thirteen essays
by members of the Centre for Historical Studies at Delhi's Jawaharlal Nehru
University. A wide range of topics and periods are covered in an interdisciplinary
manner. Particularly significant are the revisionist contributions by R.
Champakalakshmi and B. D. Chattopadhyaya on urban centres and urbanization in
early medieval south India, which implicity criticizes the thesis of 'Indian feudalism',
and by Muzzafar Alam, who views the agrarian uprisings in early 18th-century
northern India as indications of economic buoyancy rather than decline. There are
also chapters by Bhattacharya, Bipan Chandra, Aditya Mukherjee, and Bhagwan Josh
on nationalist opposition to the colonial state.

109 **Dictionary of Indian history.**
Sachchidananda Bhattacharya. Westport, Connecticut: Greenwood, 1977. 963p.

This dictionary covers the ancient, medieval and modern period of Indian history. Approximately 3,000 entries include persons, places, works, and institutions, and are arranged alphabetically. A dictionary of this size covering more than 2,500 years of Indian history cannot be exhaustive, comprehensive, or without error, but in the absence of anything similar it is of great value.

110 **Imagining India: essays on Indian history.**
Ainslie T. Embree, edited by Mark Juergensmeyer. New Delhi: Oxford University Press India, 1989. 220p.

A collection of fifteen essays written between 1963 and 1987 by the distinguished Canadian historian, editor of the *Encyclopaedia of Asian history* (New York: Scribner, 1988. 4 vols.). The papers are arranged in three thematic sections: 'Perceptions of India'; 'The making of British India'; and 'Nationalism and the contemporary state'. Particularly noteworthy are the essays on the views of al-Biruni, the 1857 revolt, and religion and politics in the 1980s. In this work Embree focuses on elements of change and continuity.

111 **The new Cambridge history of India.**
Gordon Johnson (general editor), Christopher Alan Bayly, John F. Richards (associate editors). Cambridge: Cambridge University Press, 1988- . 28 vols. maps. bibliog.

Written, in the *Cambridge history* tradition, by distinguished scholars, this new series comprises twenty-eight projected volumes covering Indian history from the Mughal era to the present day. Unlike the original *Cambridge history of India,* published between 1922 and 1953, each volume is a short (200-350 page) , self-contained work, dealing with a separate theme and written by a single specialist. The monographs take full account of recent scholarship and each contains a useful annotated bibliographic essay. By 1994, thirteen volumes had been published, with several available in a paperback format. (See items no. 161, 162, 164, 169, 185, 213, 214, 365, 556, 677, 744, 896, 899). The original *Cambridge history of India,* which comprised five published volumes and a supplementary volume on *The Indus civilization* is now dated by its overly imperialist and Eurocentric interpretations, but it does include two volumes on the pre-Mughal period.

112 **A history of India.**
Hermann Kulke, Dietmar Rothermund. London: Croom Helm, 1986. 409p. maps. bibliog

This volume is intended to serve as an introductory undergraduate textbook. It is written by two German scholars from the University of Heidelberg's South Asia Institute. Kulke is a specialist in the medieval history of south India, notably the history of temples, and has a keen interest in Southeast Asian and Orissan history. Rothermund has written extensively on agrarian and land revenue systems during the colonial period and on the nationalist movement. The book is divided almost equally between pre-Mughal and post-Mughal times and coverage extends up to the present day. Though dry stylistically, the treatment is balanced and reliable and there are twelve useful maps, a chronology and a seventeen page bibliography. Rothermund has written a separate companion volume on Indian economic history (see item no. 673).

113 The history and culture of the Indian people.
Ramesh Chandra Majumdar (general editor).   Bombay: Bharatiya Vidya Bhavan, 1951-77. 11 vols. maps. bibliog.

Conceived in 1937 by Jadunath Sarkar, the then doyen of Indian historians, and Rajendra Prasad, later the first president of independent India, as the definitive Indian response to the *Cambridge history of India*. Originally twenty-one volumes were conceived, to be written primarily by Indian scholars. After the death of Jadunath Sarkar, R. C. Majumdar took over as general editor and K. M. Munshi, later governor of Bombay, became patron and producer of the series. The subtitles of the volumes are: 1. *Vedic age (up to 600 BC)*; 2. *Age of imperial unity (600 BC-320 AD)*; 3. *Classical age (320-730)*; 4. *Age of imperial Kanauj (730-1000)*; 5. *Struggle for empire (1000-1300)*; 6. *Delhi sultanate (1300-1526)*; 7. *The Mughal empire*; 8. *The Maratha supremacy*; 9 & 10. *British paramountcy and Indian renaissance (1818-1905), Parts 1 and 2*; 11. *Struggle for freedom (1905-1947)*. Volumes six and seven are marred by an anti-Muslim bias.

114 The discovery of India.
Jawaharlal Nehru.   Bombay: Asia, 1969. 582p. maps. bibliog.

Written during Nehru's last imprisonment, this is a rich but subjective interpretative essay on India's history, written from the Indian nationalist point of view. Nehru is at his best discussing movements like Buddhism, Indo-Muslim syncretism under Akbar, and the failure of the British to extend the fruits of the Industrial Revolution. The book also marks Nehru's emergence as a leader of liberal nationalism and reflects a corresponding moderation of the socialist emphasis found in his earlier writings, *Toward freedom* and *Glimpses of world history*.

115 The cultural heritage of India.
Ramakrishna Mission, Institute of Culture.   Calcutta: Advaita Ashram; Bourne End, England: Ramakrishna Vedanta Centre, 1958-86. 2nd rev. ed. 5 vols. bibliog.

A detailed, topical, encyclopaedic survey of Indian history, social customs, philosophies, religion, and languages and literatures, written by foremost Indian scholars. Volume subtitles are: 1. *The early phases: prehistoric, Vedic and Upanisadic, Jaina, and Buddhist*; 2. *Itihasas, Puranas, Dharma and other 'sastras'*; 3. *The philosophies*; 4. *The religions*; 5. *Languages and literatures*.

116 A history of the Indian people.
D. P. Singhal.   London: Methuen, 1983. 481p. 12 maps. bibliog.

A comprehensive, single-volume narrative survey of Indian history from prehistoric times to the 1980s. The classical and medieval periods are well covered.

117   The Oxford history of India.

Edited by Vincent Arthur Smith, T. G. Percival Spear.   London:
Oxford University Press, 1981. 4th ed. 945p. maps. bibliog.

The first edition of this book, published in 1920, originated the now standard division
of textbooks on Indian history into ancient, medieval, and modern sections. Originally
written by Smith himself, the latest edition was revised by four leading British
specialists: Mortimer Wheeler, A. L. Basham, J. Harrison, and T. G. P. Spear. Except
for the prehistory section by Wheeler and the modern section by Spear, there is very
little revision of the original text. The section by Spear is outstanding.

118   A history of India.

Romila Thapar, T. G. Percival Spear.   Harmondsworth, England:
Penguin, 1965-66. 2 vols. maps. bibliogs.

Available as *Penguin* paperbacks, these two volumes are popular and elegantly-
written introductory historical surveys which have been reprinted at almost annual
intervals. The first volume (381p.), written by Thapar, an expert on the Mauryan and
pre-Mauryan eras, covers the period up to Babur's victory at the battle of Panipat
(1526) and the consequent establishment of the Mughal empire. There are separate
chapters on divergent developments in northern and southern India and also
discussions of the arts, economic changes, and social, intellectual and religious
history. The second volume (284p.), written by Spear, covers the Mughal, British
colonial and post-independence eras. Here, the focus is more narrowly on political
and military history. A new single volume *Penguin* history, *A history of Indian
civilization* (Harmondsworth, England: Penguin Books, 1994. 304p.), written by
Ravinder Kumar and covering developments since 800 BC, is now also available.

119   South Asia: a short history.

Hugh Tinker.   Basingstoke, England: Macmillan, 1989. 2nd ed. 290p.
12 maps. bibliog.

A concise and imaginative historical synthesis covering the states of South Asia:
India, Pakistan, Sri Lanka, Bangladesh, Nepal, and Myanmar (Burma). The approach
is part thematic and part chronological. Developments up to 1988 are covered, with
half the text devoted to the events of the last century-and-a-half.

120   A new history of India.

Stanley A. Wolpert.   Oxford; New York: Oxford University Press,
1992. 4th. ed. 512p.10 maps. bibliog.

This clearly-written introductory survey is intended for the general reader and stands
as the best single-volume history of India. The most detailed coverage is given to the
Mughal empire, British rule, and India's independence and partition. Concluding
chapters provide an adequate and balanced summary of the achievements of post-
independence governments. An annotated but graded (in importance) bibliography is
reasonably comprehensive. The fourth edition provides coverage up to and including
the assassination of Rajiv Gandhi.

Travellers' accounts and official manuals

121 **The *A'in-i Akbari*.**
Abu'l Fazl Allami, translated by H. Blochmann, H. S. Jarrett, revised by D. C. Phillott, Jadunath Sarkar. New Delhi: Atlantic, 1989. reprint. 3 vols.

The single most important source for the study of Indian history in the Mughal period, this classic work is a treasure trove of details concerning the mode of government of the Mughal empire during the reign of its greatest emperor, Akbar. The official compiler, Abu'l Fazl, was Akbar's principal administrator. The volume, first published in English translation in 1873-96, is divided into three sections. The first details the royal household and military affairs; the second, the revenues of the empire; the third, social conditions. The sayings and observations of the emperor are also listed. An equally useful companion volume is Abu'l Fazl's *The Akbarnama* (New Delhi: Atlantic, 1989. reprint. 3 vols.), translated by H. Beveridge, which is the official court biography of the life of emperor Akbar.

122 ***Babur-nama* (Memoirs of Babur).**
Babur, translated by A. S. Beveridge. New Delhi: Atlantic, 1989. reprint. 2 vols.

The memoirs of Babur, a direct descendant of Tamerlane (Timur) and the founder of the Mughal empire in India in the early 16th century. The volume describes in rich detail Babur's successful military campaigns and also the Indian countryside and Babur's interest in the arts. Originally written in Turki, they were translated first into Persian and later into English. A valuable and very readable sourcebook.

123 **Travels in the Mogul empire, AD 1656-1668.**
François Bernier, translated by Archibald Constable, second rev. ed. by Vincent A. Smith, based on the version by Irving Brock. New Delhi: Oriental Books Reprint Corp., 1983. 497p. maps. bibliog.

Descriptions of Surat, Agra, Gwalior, Golconda, Gujarat, Mathura, Lahore, Assam, and Chittagong by a 17th-century French traveller, the physician François Bernier (1620–88). In this important sourcebook for the condition of India during the Great Mughal era, Bernier also includes the history of the reign of emperor Shah Jahan and notes on Mughal administration, Hindu social customs, and Indian military organization. The original translation of Bernier's *Histoire de la dernièré revolution des états du Gran Mogul* was made by Irving Brock in 1891 and subsequently improved and annotated by Constable. In 1916, Smith revised the Constable-Brock version. The current edition is a reprint of the Smith edition published by the Oxford University Press in 1934.

124 **Alberuni's India: an account of the religion, philosophy, literature, geography, chronology, astronomy, customs, laws, and astrology of India about AD 1030.**
al-Biruni, translated by Edward C. Sachau. New Delhi: Atlantic, 1989. reprint of 1887 ed. 431p. maps. bibliog.

An invaluable source for the study of 11th-century India, Hindu religion and customs, mathematical, astronomical and other sciences, and general political history. The 11th century marks the beginning of the medieval period in Indian history, with the decline of the Hindu hegemony and gradual Islamic domination. There is an abridged version edited by Qeyamuddin Ahmad, *India by Al-Biruni* (New Delhi: National Book Trust, 1988. rev. ed. 306p.).

125 **Up the country: letters written to her sister from the Upper Provinces of India.**
Emily Eden, with notes by Edward Thompson and an introduction by Elizabeth Claridge. London: Virago, 1984. 410p. map.

A collection of letters written by Emily Eden (1797-1869), sister of Lord Auckland, governor-general of India between 1836 and 1842. Written in delightful prose, these letters provide a vivid account of the governor-general's two-and-a-half year tour 'up the country' between 1837 and 1840, travelling in the pre-railway era in quasi-regal cavalcade from Calcutta to Simla via Banaras, Kanpur and Delhi and meeting nawabs and maharajas en route. The tour was conducted at a time of severe famine, but provides a picture of the subcontinent seen from the perspective of the privileged ruling élite. A companion volume, *Golden interlude: the Edens in India, 1836-1842* (Gloucester: Alan Sutton, 1985. 239p.), has been edited by Janet Dunbar, drawing upon the unpublished letter-journals of Emily's youngest sister, Fanny. Emily Eden's experience of India is also described, along with those of Charlotte Canning, Edith Lytton, and Mary Curzon, wives of 19th-century viceroys, in Marian Fowler's *Below the peacock fan: first ladies of the Raj* (New York: Viking, 1987. 337p.).

126 **Travels of Fa Hsien (399-414 AD), or record of the Buddhist kingdoms.**
Fa Hsien, translated by Herbert Allen Giles. Westport, Connecticut: Greenwood, 1981. 96p. maps.

A description of the Buddhist centres in South Asia, such as Ladakh, Taxila, Peshawar, Mathura, Kanauj, Kosala, Kapilvastu, Vaisali, Gaya, Patna, Banaras, Champa, and Magadha, by the Chinese traveller Fa Hsien. The description is valuable for the Gupta period of Indian history. Complementary works are: *Si-Yu-ki: Buddhist records of the Western world* (London, 1894, New Delhi: Oriental Books Reprint Corp., 1983. reprint. multi-pagination.), translated by Samuel Beal; and *A record of Buddhistic kingdoms, being an account by the Chinese monk Fa-Hsien of his travels in India and Ceylon (AD 399-414) in search of the Buddhist books of discipline* (New Delhi: AES, 1993. reprint. multi-pagination.), translated by James Legge.

127 **Early travels in India, 1583-1619.**
William Foster. New Delhi: Munshiram Manoharlal, 1985. reprint of
1921 ed. 351p. maps. bibliog.
This volume includes travel accounts by the pioneering Ralph Fitch (1583-91); John
Mildenhall (1599-1606), the self-styled ambassador from Queen Elizabeth to Akbar;
the merchants William Finch (1608-11), William Hawkins (1608-13) and Nicholas
Withington (1612-16); Thomas Coryat (1612-17), a courtier of James I; and the
chaplain Edward Terry (1616-19). Taken together they form an excellent picture of
India from the foothills of the Himalayas to Cape Comorin in the south, and from
Ahmedabad in the west to Chittagong in the east.

128 **The political theory of the Delhi Sultanate (including a translation
of Ziauddin Barani's *Fatawa-i-Jahandari*, circa 1358-9 AD).**
Mohammad Habib, Afsar Umar Salim Khan. Allahabad, India: Kitab
Mahal, 1960. 172p.
The chief section of this work comprises an English translation of Barani's *Fatawa-i-
Jahandari*, the most important political text produced in the medieval period.
Barani's thoughts are also analysed.

129 **Narrative of a journey through the Upper Provinces of India.**
Reginald Heber. New Delhi: B.R. Publications, 1985. reprint. 3 vols.
Originally published by John Murray in 1828, this work comprises the reprinted daily
travel journals kept during 1823-24 by Reverend Reginald Heber (1783-1826), the
Bishop of Calcutta. Heber's tour of northern India included visits to Banaras,
Allahabad, Agra and Lucknow. These journals describe the people and culture of the
region in a respectful, non-didactic manner.

130 **The travels of Ibn Batuta, AD 1325-1354.**
Ibn Batuta, translated with revisions by Hamilton A. R. Gibb, from the
Arabic text, edited by C. Defremery, B. R. Sanguinetti. New Delhi:
Munshiram Manoharlal, 1993. reprint. 771p.
The travelogue of the Moorish traveller, Ibn Batuta, who was born in Tangier in 1304
and arrived in the Indian subcontinent in 1333. He left Delhi for China in 1342 in the
role of ambassador to the Delhi Sultanate ruler Muhammad bin Tughluq. This
account, originally written in Arabic and previously published by the Hakluyt Society
in four volumes between 1958-71, throws important light on India's society and
economy during the 14th century. There are discussions on the Indian postal service,
the custom of widow-burning (*sati*), the fort of Gwalior, Delhi and other historical
places.

131 **The *Shah Jahan Nama* of 'Inayat Khan: an abridged history of the
Mughal emperor Shah Jahan, compiled by his royal librarian.**
'Inayat Khan, translated by Abraham Richard Fuller, edited by Wayne
Edison Begley, Ziauddin Ahmed Desai. New Delhi: Oxford
University Press India, 1990. reprint. 624p. maps. bibliog.
The contemporary court chronicle of the Great Mughal emperor Shah Jahan (1592-
1666), whose exalted title translates as 'King of the World'. Obsessed with his place

in history, Shah Jahan ensured that his every deed was officially recorded. Despite its hyperbolic excesses, this official record of the emperor's thirty-year reign (1627-58) provides a fascinating insight into court life, military campaigns, audiences with foreign travellers, and imperial architectural projects, including the construction of Shahjahanabad and the famed Taj Mahal. The editor has also written a useful introduction and an epilogue on the final years of Shah Jahan after he fell ill and was eventually replaced on the throne by his third son, Aurangzeb.

132   Kautilya's *Arthasastra.*

Kautilya, translated by R. P. Kangle.   New Delhi: Motilal Banarsidass, 1986. reprint. 2nd ed. 3 vols.

A work on political philosophy, written in the 4th century BC, and of the highest importance for the study of Indian law and public administration. The author, Kautilya, is beleved to have been political adviser to India's first emperor, Chandragupta Maurya. The duties of kings, ministers, and other officials are explained in detail. An ideal form of government, a centralized benevolent monarchy is advocated by Kautilya. The *Arthasastra* is comparable in importance to Machiavelli's *The Prince* and has greatly influenced subsequent treatises on not only politics, but such disparate subjects as erotics, ethics, and poetics.

133   India in the fifteenth century: being a collection of narratives of voyages to India.

Edited by Richard Henry Major.   New Delhi: Manohar, 1974. reprint of 1857 edition. 297p. maps. bibliog.

Narratives of the travels of Abdul Razzak (Arab), Nicolo Conti (Italian), Athanasius Nikitin (Russian), and Hieronimo di Santo Stefano (Portuguese) in the century preceding the discovery in 1498 of the Portuguese Cape route to India by Vasco de Gama. These accounts fuelled European interest in India and Indian opulence.

134   The classical accounts of India: the Greek and Roman accounts of ancient India.

Edited by Ramesh Chandra Majumdar.   Calcutta: Firma KLM, 1981. 504p. maps.

Since the ancient Indians themselves wrote no history, the writings of foreign travellers and historians are an important source for the study of India. The present collection, originally published in 1960, includes all the classical texts having a bearing on India. Subjects covered include political administration, trade and commerce, military science, geography, religious beliefs, and social practices. Authors include Arrian, Strabo, Pliny, Ptolemy, Priaulx, and others.

135   Travels of Fray Sebastien Manrique, 1629-1643.

Sebastien Manrique, translated by C. Eckford Luard.   Oxford: Hakluyt Society, 1927. 2 vols. 19 maps. bibliog.

Manrique, a Portuguese missionary, travelled widely in Asia during the 17th century, recording his impressions in a travelogue which he wrote in Spanish. These have been translated into English by C. E. Luard. His visit to India in 1640-41 is recounted in volume two and makes interesting reading.

136 *Storia do Mogor*, **or Mogul India, 1653-1708.**
Niccolao Manucci, translated by William Irvine. New Delhi,
Oriental Books Reprint Corp., 1981. reprint of 1907-08 ed. 4 vols.
maps. bibliog.

A fascinating account of the Indian career of an Italian adventurer, Manucci, who ran
away from his native Venice in 1653 at the tender age of thirteen, reached Surat in
western India three years later, and died in Madras in 1717. In between the author
served as an artilleryman in the army of Dara Shukoh, the son of emperor Shah Jahan
who was executed by Aurangzeb in 1659, and as a quack doctor, ambassador and
interpreter. Written originally in a mixture of Italian, French and Portuguese, before
being translated into English, the *Storia* is a mine of information on 17th-century
India. It is particularly rich in descriptions of south India, a region generally ignored
by other European travellers, and in its accounts of Hindu religion, manners and
customs.

137 **Jahangir's India: the** *Remonstrantie* **of Francisco Pelsaert.**
Francisco Pelsaert, translated from Dutch by William Harrison
Moreland, Peter Geyl. Cambridge: W. Heffers, 1925. 88p.

Pelsaert, a factor with the Dutch East India Company, was sent to Agra in north India
to make commercial contacts between 1620-27. This account, first published in 1629,
is of particular value in giving an insight into Indian commerce during the 'high
Mughal' era, highlighting the flourishing trade along the routes between Surat,
Ahmedabad, Agra and Lahore.

138 **Glimpses of India: an annotated bibliography of published
personal writings by Englishmen, 1583-1947.**
Compiled by John F. Riddick. New York: Greenwood, 1989. 195p.

A useful reference work, containing 580 annotated entries on foreign observers who
visited the subcontinent between 1583 and 1947 and have left published records of
their impressions. The entries are arranged alphabetically in seven chronological
chapters. The title of the volume is misleading since there are entries on non-English
and female travellers. The work can be usefully read alongside H. K. Kaul's
Travellers' India: an anthology (New Delhi: Oxford University Press India, 1979.
535p.), which contains nearly 400 selections from 170 travel accounts, many from the
19th century; and H. K. Kaul's *Travels in South Asia: a selected and annotated
bibliography of guide books and travel books on South Asia* (New Delhi: Arnold-
Heinemann, 1979. 215p.), which contains 1,016 entries in English covering the
ancient to modern periods.

139 **Travels in India by Jean-Baptiste Tavernier, Baron of Aubonne.**
Jean-Baptiste Tavernier, translated by V. Ball, edited by William
Crooke. New Delhi: Oriental Books Reprint Corp., 1977. reprint.
2 vols.

The author, a Frenchman, visited India on three occasions: 1640, 1645-47, and 1665-
67. On his last visit he had an audience with emperor Aurangzeb. His impressions are
recorded in some detail and the notes on cotton cloth, indigo, and diamonds are
particularly valuable.

140 **Annals and antiquities of Rajasthan.**
James Tod.   New Delhi: M. N. Publishers, 1978. reprint of 1914 ed.
2 vols.

This classic work is both a personal narrative of travels through Rajputana betweer
1819 and 1822 by Colonel Tod (1782-1835) and a mine of social, cultural anc
historical information. Tod, the son of a Mirzapur indigo planter, describes the
desolate harshness of the countryside of central India, his own rough, horseback
based style of living, and the people of the region.

141 **On Yuan Chwang's travels in India, A. D. 629-645.**
Thomas Watters.   San Francisco: Chinese Materials Center, 1975.
reprint of 1904-05 ed. 2 vols. maps. bibliog.

A reprint of the 1904-05 edition, edited by T. W. Rhys Davids and S. W. Bushell, thi
account is valuable for understanding the political and economic transformation o
India between the 5th century AD (as reported by Fa Hsien, see item no. 126) and the
final Hindu hegemony under Harsha in the 7th century. Yuan Chwang (ca. 600-64)
more commonly known as Hsuan/Hiuen Tsang, was a Chinese Buddhist monk an
acute observer of Indian customs and conditions. He travelled 40,000 miles throug
China and India during the years covered by this account and while in north Indi
emperor Harsha became his patron. The work is useful in discussing the Hindu
Buddhist synthesis during the resurgence of Hinduism under Gupta patronage.

Early history (ca. 320 BC-ca. 1192 AD)

142 **The wonder that was India: a survey of the history and culture of
the Indian subcontinent before the coming of the Muslims.**
Arthur Llewellyn Basham.   London: Sidgwick & Jackson, 1985.
reprint of 1979 3rd rev. ed. 568p. maps. bibliog.

A comprehensive and scholarly magisterial survey of pre-Muslim India. Written i
brilliant prose by the late A. L. Basham (1914-86), one of the foremost authorities o
ancient India, and designed primarily for readers with little or no background i
Indian history, the book is used widely in schools and colleges. The approach i
topical: history; political life and thought; religion and philosophy; everyday life
language and literature; the arts; social order; and India's contributions to the science
and technology. Over 200 plates and illustrations and a topical bibliography ad
substantially to the book's value. A minor classic which should be acquired b
everyone interested in India.

143 **Ancient Indian history and civilization: trends and perspectives.**
Narendra Nath Bhattacharyya.   New Delhi: Manohar, 1988. 330p.
bibliog.

Written by the Calcutta University cultural historian, this work provides a wide
ranging overview of Indian history from prehistoric to early medieval times (ca

1000-1300 AD). A feature of the volume is the ample space that has been afforded to the history of ideas, literature and religions, with four of the eleven chapters being devoted to these topics.

144 Mauryan India.
G. M. Bongard-Levin.   New Delhi: Sterling, 1985. 428p. bibliog.

A critical examination and synthesis of accepted theories of the Mauryan polity, society and economy by a prominent Russian Marxist scholar. The range of topics covered includes political history, economic and social developments, the administrative system, and religious and philosophical trends. The bulk of the evidence presented pertains to the Mauryan empire's Ganges valley (Magadha) metropolitan core rather than its outlying peripheral regions. This text can be usefully read in conjunction with *The Mauryas revisited* (Calcutta: Bagchi, 1987. 60p.), an important lecture by Romila Thapar which reassesses the degree to which the Mauryan state can be characterized as an empire and its duration as such.

145 Feudal social formation in early India.
Edited by D. N. Jha.   New Delhi: Chanakya, 1987. 427p. bibliog.

An anthology of fifteen articles published during the last two decades by the principal contributors to the debate over whether a feudal social formation was established in the Indian subcontinent during the early centuries of the Christian era. The work is divided into three parts: 'Transition to feudalism', which contains two general theoretical articles by R. S. Sharma and B. N. S. Yadava and regional case studies of Assam (A. Guha), Kashmir (D. D. Kosambi) and Tamil Nadu (N. Karashima); 'Feudal society and economy'; and 'Feudal ideology', which considers the *bhakti* movement, Tantricism, and art. Jha contributes a useful, up-to-date introductory chapter, which reviews the present state of research on 'Indian feudalism'. By and large, the volume seeks to restate the Marxist position that a feudal formation was gradually established through Gupta and post-Gupta land grants to Brahmans, temples, monasteries and, later, to military vassals. Sharma, author of three essays in this volume, sets out this interpretation in more detail in Ram Sharan Sharma, *Indian feudalism, c. AD 300-1200* (New Delhi: Macmillan, 1980. 2nd ed. 265p.). However, it has recently been challenged by B. D. Chattopadhyaya in *The making of early medieval India* (New Delhi: Oxford University Press India, 1994. 300p.).

146 The culture and civilization of ancient India in historical outline.
Damodar Dharmanand Kosambi.   New Delhi: Vikas, 1981. new ed. 243p. maps. bibliog.

A striking, thought-provoking and influential study of Indian history until 500 AD. The author, a mathematician by training, utilizes a neo-Marxian and functionalist approach, combining history, archaeology and anthropology to provide a first-rate analysis of the formative period of India's civilization. This volume, the author's last published work, can be usefully read in conjunction with Kosambi's wider ranging *An introduction to the study of Indian history* (London, New Delhi: Sangam Books, 1985. 2nd ed. 415p.), a classic work on ancient and early medieval history which was first published in 1956.

147 The imperial Guptas and their times, c. AD 300-550.

Sachindra Kumar Maity.　New Delhi: Munshiram Manoharlal, 1975.
286p. bibliog.

The period of the Gupta rulers has been popularly known as the 'golden age' of Indian history, rivalling the Periclean era in Greece. Maity's comprehensive summary takes into account recent discoveries of inscriptions, coins, and archaeological materials. The chapters in this volume are topical and, in addition to political history, deal with public administration, social and economic life, education, and literary, artistic, and cultural achievements. The work is now complemented by a short volume by D. K. Ganguly, carrying the same title (New Delhi: Bagchi, 179p.), and by Parmeshwari Lal Gupta's comprehensive, *The imperial Guptas* (Varanasi, India: Vishwavidyalaya Prakashan, 1974-79. 2 vols.).

148 A concise history of ancient India.

Asoke Kumar Majumdar.　New Delhi: Munshiram Manoharlal, 1980.
3 vols. maps. bibliog.

A three-volume set dealing with the history and culture of history. The first volume covers political history; the second, political theories, administration, and economic life; and the third, society, religion and philosophy. Majumdar rejects 650 or 1200 AD – the most widely accepted dates – as the terminal date for the 'ancient' period, and in these volumes covers Indian history up to ca. 1500. In the first volume there is an excellent discussion of the principal sources of ancient Indian history.

149 Temple economy under the Colas (c. AD 850-1070).

B. K. Pandeya.　New Delhi: Bahri, 1984. 186p. bibliog.

A fascinating exposition of the multifaceted role of the temple in the social, political and economic life of early medieval south India. In return for providing legitimizing spiritual services, temples received land grants from local rulers on such occasions as the coronation of crown princes and at the outset of military expeditions. Pandeya shows how this land wealth was used, with chapters on temples as employers, money-lenders, and consumers of rural goods and services. There are seven appendices filled with data on wage rates, land tax levels, and interest rates in the Chola era. This work can be usefully read alongside *Trade and statecraft in the age of the Colas* (New Delhi: Abhinav, 1980. 238p), by Kenneth R. Hall, which focuses on political elements.

150 Interpreting early India.

Romila Thapar.　New Delhi: Oxford University Press India, 1992.
181p.

A collection of six lectures delivered by the eminent scholar, Romila Thapar, during the 1970s and 1980s. Topics covered include the historiography and changing interpretations of early Indian history and society, and the contribution of D. D. Kosambi to Indology.

Period of Islamic dominance (ca. 1192-ca. 1757)

151   **The crisis of empire in Mughal north India: Awadh and the Punjab, 1707-1748.**
Muzaffar Alam.   New Delhi: Oxford University Press India, 1992. new ed. 332p. 7 maps. bibliog.

A revisionist scholarly work which moves beyond existing 'dark period' interpretations of the 18th century by emphasizing that, while the Mughal empire collapsed and declined at its centre, there was significant new growth at the provincial level as 'liberated' rulers invested retained revenues and made accommodations with local commercial and service groups. Developments in the *subahs* (imperial provinces) of Awadh (Oudh) and Punjab, which progressively became new 'successor states', are presented as case studies. The volume complements another key revisionist work, Christopher A. Bayly's *Rulers, townsmen and bazaars: north Indian society in the age of British expansion, 1770-1870* (New Delhi: Oxford University Press India, 1992. new ed. 516p.), which covers a later period.

152   **The apparatus of empire: awards of ranks, offices and titles to the Mughal nobility (1573-1658).**
Muhammad Athar Ali.   New Delhi: Oxford University Press India, 1985. 378p. maps. bibliog.

This specialist volume, the product of more than two decades of research, is a study of the ethnic components of the Mughal ruling class. All grants of official rank (*mansab*), promotions, appointments to offices, and awards of titles from 1573 to the end of Shah Jahan's reign in 1658 are listed here and analysed by ethnic categories. Comprising 300 pages of tables but only 13 pages of text, it is designed to serve as a reference work to enable scholars to trace the entire career of Mughal officers mentioned in the major sources.

153   **Aspects of Rajput state and society.**
Anil Chandra Banerjee.   New Delhi: Rajesh, 1986. 208p.

This work, based on a series of public lectures, analyses a wide range of facets of the culture and history of Rajputs and Rajasthan. The author explains the origins of the Rajputs as a Hindu martial caste, their resistance to Muslim invasions during the medieval period, the structure of the pre-British Rajput polities and society, and Rajput decline. Banerjee is also author of *The Rajput states and British paramountcy* (New Delhi: Rajesh, 1980. 245p.), which describes the integration of the Rajput states of Mewar, Jaipur, and Marwar into the British India empire during the 19th century.

154   **The state and society in northern India 1206-1526.**
Anil Chandra Banerjee.   Calcutta: Bagchi, 1982. 378p. bibliog.

An excellent study of the administrative, economic and cultural history of the Delhi Sultanate, setting out the ideas and institutions which shaped life in northern India where the Sultanate held sway. Separate chapters are devoted to the agrarian system, architecture, the economy, language and literature, the machinery of government, the monarchy, religion, society, and the theocratic state. The appendix contains notes on five eminent historians of the period, including Ziauddin Barani.

155 Medieval India: society, the *jagirdari* crisis and the village.
Satish Chandra.   New Delhi: Macmillan, 1982. 192p. bibliog.

A selection of papers on medieval Indian society and institutions written over a period of two decades. Destroying the myth of the 'unchanging Orient', the essays deal with processes of growth in medieval Indian society and economy, analyse the structure and stratification of village society in eastern Rajasthan, and consider the factors which created the crisis of the late 17th century which led to the gradual disintegration of the Mughal empire. Chandra is also author of the important paper, *The eighteenth century in India: its economy and the role of the Marathas, the Jats, the Sikhs and the Afghans* (Calcutta: Centre for Studies in Social Sciences, 1986. 40p), an insightful survey.

156 The Jats: their role in the Mughal empire.
Girish Chandra Dwivedi.   Bangalore, India: Arnold, 1989. 259p. bibliog.

An intensive study of the Jats, a Hindu warrior-agriculturist community based in northern India who played a dynamic role in the later phase of the Mughal empire. In 1669 they rose up against the oppressive anti-Hindu regime of Aurangzeb and in the early 18th century, under the leadership of Surajmal, an extensive Jat state was established. Centred around the fort-city of Bharatpur, it extended over substantial portions of Haryana, east Rajasthan and northwestern Uttar Pradesh. A neighbouring 18th-century 'successor state' regime is analysed in *The Ruhela chieftaincies: the rise and fall of Ruhela power in India in the eighteenth century* (New Delhi: Oxford University Press India, 1994. 253p.), by Iqbal Husain.

157 The medieval Deccan: peasants, social system and states, sixteenth to eighteenth centuries.
Hiroshi Fukazawa.   New Delhi: Oxford University Press India, 1991. 252p. map. bibliog.

This volume comprises a collection of studies by the late Hiroshi Fukazawa, Japan's foremost historian of India, who died in 1986. Many of the pieces are articles drawn from the *Hitotsubashi Journal of Economics* and a number have been previously only available in Japanese. The principal focus is the political, agrarian and social history of Maharashtra and its Maratha state during the 18th century. Fukazawa's work is characterized by careful scholarship and skilled use of Persian and Marathi primary sources, including a pioneering use of local materials.

158 The great Moghuls.
Bamber Gascoigne, with photographs by Christina Gascoigne.
London: Jonathan Cape, 1987. new ed. 264p. maps. bibliog.

A magnificently illustrated digest of the contributions of the first six Mughal emperors of the 16th and 17th centuries: Babur, Humayun, Akbar, Jahangir, Shah Jahan, and Aurangzeb. Gascoigne tells a great deal about the personal lives of these emperors, their contributions to arts and letters, architecture and city buildings, and above all their religious attitudes. The section on Akbar's religious synthesis is particularly illuminating. Much of the book's worth lies in its readability and its beautiful monochrome photographs. It was first published in 1971.

159 The agrarian system of eastern Rajasthan.

Satya Prakash Gupta.   New Delhi: Manohar, 1986. 352p. 2 maps. bibliog.

Drawing upon the rich archival material held at the State Archives, Bikaner, the author has meticulously employed village and *pargana* (local revenue division) level records to significantly advance understanding of the working of the Mughal system of land revenue administration and agrarian trends over time. The volume includes chapters on agrarian trade, the structure of land rights and agrarian society, the system of rural taxation, and the working of the *jagir* (revenue assignment) and revenue farming (*ijara*) systems. This detailed regional study reveals the complexities and differential character of the Mughal agrarian system.

160 Medieval India: researches in the history of India, 1200-1750.

Edited by Irfan Habib.   New Delhi: Oxford University Press India, 1992- . 224p.

The 1992 volume was envisaged as the first of an annual series. As such, it is intended to constitute the successor to the earlier *Medieval India Quarterly* (5 vols. 1950-63) and *Medieval India – a miscellany* (4 vols., 1969-75), issued successively under the editorship of Professors S. A. Rashid, S. Nurul Hasan, K. A. Nizami and Irfan Habib. Each volume contains between eight and ten essays, the fruits of recent research on medieval India conducted at Indian universities, primarily Aligarh Muslim University. Relevant historical documents are also reproduced and books reviewed. Irfan Habib is author of *The agrarian system of Mughal India* (Bombay: Asia Publishing House, 1963. 453p.), the seminal work on the political-economy of the Mughal state, although its interpretation of the factors behind Mughal decline in the 18th century is now contested.

161 The Portuguese in India (Vol. I:1 in the New Cambridge History of India).

M. N. Pearson.   Cambridge: Cambridge University Press, 1988. 178p. bibliog.

A balanced appraisal of the Portuguese lodgement in India, from Vasco da Gama's arrival at Calicut in 1498 to their enforced departure from Goa and the small island of Diu in 1961. The author describes how Goa and Diu, made Portuguese in 1510 and 1535 respectively, formed, as the *Estado da India*, the centre of the Portuguese maritime empire during the 16th century, and also analyses the work of the Catholic missions which came from the 1540s to convert and save souls. Despite attempted rebellions by Ranes (Rajputs) in the New Conquests territory between the 18th and 20th centuries, Portuguese rule continued and from 1822 Goa sent two representatives to the Portuguese parliament.

162 **The Mughal empire (Vol. I:5 in The New Cambridge History of India).**
John F. Richards.   Cambridge: Cambridge University Press, 1993.
320p. maps. bibliog.

An excellent, clearly presented synthesis of the current state of research on the Mughal polity and economy written by an experienced American Mughal-specialist. The first eight chapters describe the Mughal empire's formation and operation during its heyday between 1526 and 1689. Key political and military events are delineated in a conventional narrative history format. In chapter nine there is a brief overview of economic and social developments and international commercial connections. The closing three chapters focus on Mughal decline and the empire's effective collapse between 1707-20. The work contains a useful annotated bibliography. Richards is the author of the local study *Mughal administration in Golconda* (Oxford: Clarendon Press, 1975. 350p.), and editor of a useful work on the Mughal monetary system (see item no. 708).

163 **The wonder that was India: Vol. II, a survey of the history and culture of the Indian sub-continent from the coming of the Muslims to the British conquest, 1200-1700.**
Saiyid Athar Abbas Rizvi.   London: Sidgwick & Jackson, 1987.
416p. maps. bibliog.

Designed to complement A. L. Basham's classic *Wonder that was* volume on the pre-Muslim era (see item no. 142), this sumptuously-illustrated work broadly covers the period between the 10th and 18th centuries. The first three chapters focus on the political history of the successive Arab, Turk, Afghan, and Mughal regimes. The closing four chapters are analytical, dealing with the state, including theories of kingship and military and administrative institutions, social and economic conditions, religion, and the fine arts, revealing the influence of ancient Indian motifs on Islamic architecture. There is a valuable appendix on medieval Indian literature and the *bhakti* movement, and excellent notes on available historical sources, including travellers' accounts.

164 **Vijayanagara (Vol. I:2 in The New Cambridge History of India).**
Burton Stein.   Cambridge: Cambridge University Press, 1989.
156p. 2 maps. bibliog.

A sophisticated analysis of the Vijayanagara kingdom which was dominant over a large part of south-central India for three centuries from the mid-14th century. At the empire's zenith, Vijayanagara's kings were among the greatest historical rulers in India having reduced to subjugation numerous chiefly lineages. The capital Vijayanagara, 'city of victory', became a great centre of power and wealth, society was martialized, and the economy was transformed by urbanization, commercialization and monetization. However, beyond the immediate heartland of Vijayanagara, Stein shows that kingship and sovereignty was largely ritual, the central rulers being content with homage and occasional tribute. Stein is also author of *Peasant state and society in medieval south India* (New Delhi: Oxford University Press India, 1980. 533p.).

165 **The formation of the Mughal empire.**
Douglas E. Streusand. New Delhi: Oxford University Press India, 1989. 206p. bibliog.

This work is concerned with the process of the Mughal empire's establishment and expansion under Babur, Humayun and Akbar and with administrative and ritual organization under emperor Akbar. Streusand analyses the 'gunpowder empire thesis', propounded by the military historians Marshall G. S. Hodgson and William H. McNeill, which asserts that it was the diffusion of firearms, notably siege artillery, that made possible the establishment of such a large new empire. He also looks afresh at such institutions as the *jagir* (revenue assignment) and *mansabdar* (military service) system. Streusand's new interpretations remain tentative.

166 *Al-Hind*: **the making of the Indo-Islamic World. Vol. 1: early medieval India and the expansion of Islam, 7th-11th centuries.**
André Wink. Leiden, the Netherlands: E. J. Brill, 1991. 396p. maps. bibliog.

This is the first volume of an ambitious, projected five-volume *longue duree* analysis of the Islamization of the regions which the Arabs termed *Al-Hind*, that is India and large parts of its Indianized hinterland stretching into Southeast Asia. Wink, a Dutch academic, is the author of a revisionist work on 18th-century Maharashtrian political and economic and social history, *Land and sovereignty in India: agrarian society and politics under the eighteenth-century Maratha Svarajya* (Cambridge: Cambridge University Press, 1986. 419p.). In the opening volume, he looks at the growing commercial connections between the Mediterranean and Indian Ocean during the early medieval period (7th-11th centuries), at the Muslim, Jew and Parsee trading diasporas, and at early Muslim conquests in Sind and Hindustan. Critical of existing interpretations of medieval Indian history, especially the 'Indian feudalism' thesis, the author also surveys the regional Hindu polities which held sway during this period. The subsequent volumes in this series will cover, respectively, the 11th-13th, 14th-15th, 16th-17th and the 18th centuries.

Period of British dominance (ca. 1757-1947)

167 **Lives of the Indian princes.**
Charles Allen, Sharada Dwivedi, with photographs by Aditya Patankar. London: Arena, 1986. new ed. 278p. map.

A sumptuously-illustrated work, containing over 200 paintings and photographs, many from private collections, this volume provides a vivid account of the history and lives of the rulers of the 562 states of Princely India during the days of the British Raj. Until 1948 these princes had formal control over two-fifths of the population of the Indian subcontinent and many enjoyed an extraordinary and opulent lifestyle. Based on more than 300 hours of taped interviews, Allen and Dwivedi shed light on the curious customs and deeply rooted superstitions that characterized the princely states. Two useful, complementary scholarly studies are: Ian Copland, *The British Raj and the Indian princes: paramountcy in western India, 1857-1930* (New Delhi: Sangam Books, 1987. 345p.); and Robin Jeffrey (editor), *People, princes and paramount power: society and politics in the Indian princely states* (New Delhi: Oxford University Press India, 1978. 396p.).

168   **Race, sex and class under the Raj: imperial attitudes and policies and their critics, 1793-1905.**
       Kenneth Ballhatchet.   London: Weidenfeld & Nicolson, 1980. 299p.
       bibliog.

An innovative study of imperial social attitudes and policies in 19th-century India which emphasizes the British rulers' overriding concern to maintain social distance between Europeans and Indians. There are case studies of such imperial institutions as the 'lock hospital', a place where diseased women who served the empire as licensed prostitutes were taken for treatment in an effort to control the spread of venereal disease, and organized army prostitution. There is also a discussion of attitudes towards unattached European women and mixed marriages. A less academic related work is Michael Edwardes' *The sahibs and the lotus: the British in India* (London: Constable, 1988. 285p.).

169   **Indian society and the making of the British empire (Vol. II:1 in the New Cambridge History of India).**
       Christopher Alan Bayly.   Cambridge: Cambridge University Press,
       1988. 230p. maps. bibliog.

This volume covers the period between 1700 and the 1860s, focusing on the process by which the British imperial control over the Indian subcontinent became established. Professor Bayly emphasizes the indigenous Indian input into the colonization process and the interconnections of politics, finance and commerce. This revisionist work attributes the decline of the Mughal empire to the growing assertiveness of merchants, bankers and 'yeoman farmers' who had prospered under the Pax Mughalica and were to become powerful elements within the regional successor states of the immediate pre-British era. It also reveals 'threads of continuity' between the pre-colonial age and the Company Raj. It should be read with *The politics of the British annexation of India, 1757-1857* (New Delhi: Oxford University Press India, 1994. 330p.), a volume edited by Michael H. Fisher which explores a range of perspectives on the process of British imperial expansion during the century between the battle of Plassey (1757) and the Indian Mutiny (1857) when more than sixty per cent of the Indian subcontinent was annexed.

170   **Modern India: the origins of an Asian democracy.**
       Judith M. Brown.   Oxford: Oxford University Press, 1994. 2nd ed.
       459p. maps. bibliog. (The Short Oxford History of the Modern World).

A clearly-written and authoritative survey of 19th- and 20th-century Indian history. The interaction of Indian traditions and the British colonial presence is examined with insight by Professor Brown, a specialist on the life, political career and philosophy of Mahatma Gandhi (see item no. 252). The book includes many useful tables of economic and political statistics, and a fine bibliography. The sections covering the nationalist movement are especially illuminating. The best introductory textbook for this period.

171 The Raj syndrome: a study in imperial perceptions.

Suhash Chakravarty. New Delhi: Penguin India, 1991. 325p. bibliog.
A study in social and intellectual history, analysing the ruling nation's imperialist psychology. The author cites more than a hundred authors, including historians, novelists and poets, in an efforts to understand the 'average Englishman's' mind and perception of the Raj. Chakravarty describes the myths, legends and stereotypes of imperial culture, and reveals the linkages between ideology and empire building.

172 India's struggle for independence.

Bipan Chandra, Mridula Mukherjee, Aditya Mukherjee, K. N. Panikkar, Sucheta Mahajan. New Delhi: Penguin India, 1989. 600p. bibliog.
A history of the independence struggle from the abortive Revolt of 1857 to the transfer of power in 1947, written by an experienced team of Indian historians. The volume draws upon latest research findings, as well as the oral testimony of more than 1,500 freedom fighters who were specially interviewed. Emphasis is given to ideological aspects of the nationalist movement. As well as documenting the central role played by the Indian National Congress and its major leaders, the contributions of Revolutionary Terrorists, Socialist, Communists, States' People's movements, peasants, workers and tribals are analysed.

173 Freedom at midnight.

Larry Collins, Dominique Lapierre. New York: Simon & Schuster, 1975. 572p. maps. bibliog.
A dramatic book about the eclipse of British rule and the birth of independent India. The emphasis is on the period from New Year's Day, 1947, when Lord Mountbatten was chosen to be the last Crown proconsul in India, to February 1948, when Mahatma Gandhi's ashes were dispersed in the Ganges – thirteen months of tumultuous transformation in India. The authors have added several introductory chapters to discuss politics and life in India before 1947. The portraits of Nehru, Gandhi, Jinnah, Mountbatten, and princely life are outstanding. The book is flawed, however, by its open partisanship for Mountbatten.

174 Peasant struggles in India.

Edited by Akshayakumar Ramanlal Desai. Bombay: Oxford University Press India, 1979. 722p. bibliog.
India's nationalist movement, unlike China's, was not a peasant-based one, yet the Indian peasantry played a crucial, if not decisive, role in shaping the politics of India. In this volume, thirty-nine articles examine tribal and peasant struggles in India both before and after independence. The book's strength lies in bringing to light movements and events that are important but likely to be ignored as not meriting a full-length monograph. Two useful supplements are: D. N. Dhanagare, *Peasant movements in India, 1920-1950* (New Delhi: Oxford University Press India, 1986. 254p.); and David Hardiman (editor), *Peasant resistance in India, 1858-1914* (New Delhi: Oxford University Press India, 1992. 304p.).

175 India's search for national identity.

Ainslie T. Embree.   New Delhi: Chanakya, 1980. Indian ed. 144p. bibliog.

This is a skilful analysis of the relationship of the pattern of British administration to the evolution of India's national identity. The author suggests that the use of Hindu values and symbols by the Indian National Congress was responsible for the growth of Islamic separatism. Besides being one of the best introductions to the study of modern South Asia, this is an excellent book for those studying nationalist movements from a comparative perspective.

176 A clash of cultures: Awadh, the British, and the Mughals.

Michael H. Fisher.   London: Sangam Books, 1988. 284p. maps. bibliog.

A very readable history of the north Indian kingdom of Awadh (Oudh), a large Mughal successor state, from its foundation in 1722 by the Persian nobleman, Saadat Khan, a servant of the Mughal court, until its annexation by the British in 1856. The author describes the workings of the Awadh regime, the cultural glory of its court, and, in particular, relations with the English East India Company's Resident, stationed at its capital, Lucknow, from 1772. Fisher's volume can be read alongside two complementary volumes: Richard B. Barnett's, *North India between empires: Awadh, the Mughals, and the British, 1720-1801* (Berkeley, California: University of California Press, 1980. 276p.), which contains a brilliant analysis of the motivations behind Saadat Khan's breakaway from his Mughal superiors; and *Indirect rule in India: residents and the residency system, 1764-1858* (New Delhi: Oxford University Press India, 1991. 516p.), a more general work by Fisher.

177 Land control and social structure in Indian history.

Edited by Robert Eric Frykenberg.   New Delhi: Manohar, 1979. 1st rev. Indian ed. 277p. bibliog.

Indian land-tenures and related socio-political structures, dominated by caste groups, have been vastly different from those encountered in the West. This volume describes and analyses the diverse landholding and social structures in various parts of India prior to the British conquest and the changes introduced by the British in the 19th century. Frykenberg's masterly introduction is followed by three case studies from north India, three from south India, and four broad-based essays.

178 Empire and Islam: Punjab and the making of Pakistan.

David Gilmartin.   Berkeley, California: University of California Press, 1988. 258p. map. bibliog. (Comparative Studies on Muslim Societies, no. 7).

This monograph examines the evolution of support for the Pakistan movement in terms of the Muslim community's search for ideological identity and the severe contradictions established by the colonial state. According to the author, the Pakistan movement amalgamated millenarian tendencies, Islamic revivalism, and political objectives. A complementary work is David Page's *Prelude to partitition: the Indian Muslims and the imperial state system of control, 1920-1932* (New Delhi: Oxford University Press India, 1982. 288p.), which examines the divisive impact of the Montagu-Chelmsford 'dyarchy' reforms of 1919 on provincial politics, leading to a consolidation of communal interests.

179   **Subaltern studies: writings on South Asian history and society.**
       Edited by Ranajit Guha, Partha Chatterjee, Gyanendra Pandey.
       Oxford; New York; New Delhi: Oxford University Press, 1982-92.
       7 vols.

These volumes are collections of revisionist essays by radical Indian and Western social and political historians who, influenced by the ideas of Gramsci, seek to break away from colonialist and bourgeois nationalist élitism and portray Indian historical developments from an autonomous bottom-up perspective. The first six volumes were produced under the general editorship of Guha and volume seven by Chatterjee and Pandey, with the assistance of a collective editorial board comprising Shahid Amin, David Arnold, Gautam Bhadra, Dipesh Chakrabarty, David Hardiman, and Sumit Sarkar. A particular 'Subaltern' concern has been popular ideologies, which draw upon non-official oral testimonies and folk literature. Topics covered have included tribal movements, peasant revolts, Hindu revivalism, famine and disease, and deindustrialization. *Selected Subaltern Studies* (New York; Oxford: Oxford University Press, 1988. 434p.), edited by Ranajit Guha and Gayatri Chakravorty Spivak, reproduces some of the most important essays from the first five volumes.

180   **India's partition: process, strategy and mobilization.**
       Edited by Mushirul Hasan.   New Delhi: Oxford University Press
       India, 1993. 426p. map. bibliog. (Oxford in India Readings: Themes in
       Indian History).

Designed for students, this volume comprises a careful selection of essays and book extracts which enable the reader to critically assess the 'state of the art' on India's partition and chart the key historiographical shifts. There is an annotated bibliography and useful introduction. Reproduced are extracts from the works of Mahatma Gandhi and Jawaharlal Nehru, as well as 1940 Muslim League and Congress addresses by M. A. Jinnah and Abul Kalam Azad. The essays by historians focus on the background to partition in individual regions. The work supersedes *The partition of India: policies and perspectives, 1935-1947* (London: George Allen & Unwin, 1970. 607p.), edited by Cyril Henry Philips and Mary Doreen Wainwright, which is outmoded in places.

181   **Nationalism and communal politics in India, 1885-1930.**
       Mushirul Hasan.   New Delhi: Manohar, 1991. rev. ed. 338p. bibliog.

An ably-researched study of the alliance between Muslim organizations and the Indian nationalist movement, and the eventual disintegration of the alliance between 1916 and 1928. The monograph focuses on three provinces – Bengal, Punjab, and the United Provinces (Uttar Pradesh) – and shows that the Muslim response to nationalism differed regionally according to socio-economic conditions. Hasan finds the all-India nationalist leadership to be élitist and unconcerned with local and provincial issues. Hasan is also editor of two important collections of essays: *Communal and pan-Islamic trends in colonial India* (New Delhi: Manohar, 1985. new ed. 444p.); and *Islam and Indian nationalism: reflections on Abul Kalam Azad* (New Delhi: Manohar, 1992. 196p.).

182 **The great divide: Britain, India, Pakistan**.
Henry Vincent Hodson. Karachi: Oxford University Press Pakistan, 1985. 590p. maps. bibliog.

A study of the simultaneous breach between Britain and its Indian empire, and between Pakistan and India. It was first published in 1969. Much of this book is devoted to the five-year period 1942-1947, and is based on the private papers of leading British participants in the drama of independence and partition such as Sir Stafford Cripps, Lord Mountbatten, Lord Ismay and V. P. Menon. A detailed, authoritative work which can be usefully read in conjunction with the more sensationalist 'historical novel' *Freedom at midnight* (see item no. 173).

183 **Essays in the social history of modern India.**
Ravinder Kumar. New Delhi: Oxford University Press India, 1987. new ed. 306p.

A collection of eleven essays written between 1969 and 1980 by one of India's foremost social historians. The writings focus upon two regions, Bombay and Punjab, and are concerned with such themes as the nature of communalism, patterns of socio-political change, the links between rural and urban classes, and Mahatma Gandhi's role in shaping political and religious dialogue. Particularly outstanding are the essays on the Rowlatt Satyagraha in Lahore, the Bombay textile strike of 1919, and nationalist politics in Bombay city between 1920 and 1932.

184 **The Indian National Congress: centenary highlights.**
Edited by Donald Anthony Low. New Delhi: Oxford University Press India, 1988. 275p.

A collection of ten papers presented to a 1985 conference held at Oxford University to commemorate the centenary of the Indian National Congress and to review the current state of the debate on Indian nationalism. Various facets of the nationalist movement are examined, including its agrarian base, its commercial sponsors, and comparisons with the Italian Risorgimento are made. This volume updates an excellent earlier collection of essays edited by D. A. Low on Congress's operations at the regional and local level: *Congress and the Raj: facets of the Indian struggle, 1917-47* (New Delhi: South Asia Books, 1977. 513p.).

185 **Bengal: the British bridgehead, eastern India 1740-1828 (Vol. II:2 in the New Cambridge History of India).**
Peter James Marshall. Cambridge: Cambridge University Press, 1987. 195p. maps. bibliog.

An exploration of the process by which British rule became established in eastern India during the later 18th and early 19th century. The interplay of social, cultural, economic and political changes is delineated with particular skill. This work builds upon Marshall's earlier monograph, *East Indian fortunes: the British in Bengal in the eighteenth century* (Oxford: Clarendon Press, 1976. 284p.), but ranges more widely in scope.

186 Indian tales of the Raj.

Zareer Masani.   London: BBC Books, 1987. 165p. map. bibliog.

A spin-off from a BBC radio series broadcast in 1986, this book presents the first-hand memories and personal experiences of more than fifty Indian men and women who worked under the British, made friends with them, and later fought, during the nationalist struggle, to overthrow the colonial rulers. There are fascinating and, at times, humorous insights into the complex racial barriers which divided rulers from the ruled. The volume concludes with the reflections of a younger generation of Indians who take a critical look at such colonial legacies as the English language, assessing their relevance in modern independent India. The radio series was inspired by the earlier broadcast reminiscences of the Raj's British ruling class, published in *Plain tales from the Raj: images of British India in the twentieth century* (London: BBC Books, 1985. 2nd ed. 240p.), edited by Charles Allen.

187 Struggling and ruling: the Indian National Congress 1885-1985.

Edited by Jim Masselos.   London: Oriental University Press, 1987. 224p.

A varied collection of papers by Western and Indian scholars published to mark the centenary of the Indian National Congress. They examine the intersection of Congress with Indian society and include essays reassessing the relationship between Allan Octavian Hume and Congress (E. C. Moulton), Congress and princely India 1920-40 (I. Copland), Congress and the Muslim community 1928-34 (M. Hasan), and the abolition of *zamindari* (landed estates) in Uttar Pradesh (P. Reeves).

188 Indian nationalism and the early Congress.

John R. McLane.   Princeton, New Jersey: Princeton University Press, 1977. 404p. map. bibliog.

A survey of the first two decades of the Indian National Congress, from its founding in 1885. The movement's relationship with wider Indian society is examined, along with the attempts made by its English-educated élite leadership to reach broader sections of the Indian population. Particularly strong are the analyses of the related Hindu revivalist cow-protection movement in north India and of divisions within Congress leadership.

189 A dictionary of modern Indian history 1707-1947.

Parshotam Mehra.   New Delhi: Oxford University Press India, 1985. 823p. 31 maps. bibliog.

A very useful and sound reference work intended for students, teachers, journalists and general readers. It comprises nearly 400 alphabetically arranged entries on significant events, people, movements, wars and acts. Each entry is self-contained and averages two pages in length, synthesizing modern research and including a brief bibliography. Topics range from *sati* (widow burning), the *ryotwari* (direct with individual land holders) settlement, and the East India Company, to Indian railways and biographies of political leaders. There is also an accompanying chronology and list of viceroys.

190   **The aftermath of revolt: India 1857-1870.**
       Thomas R. Metcalf.   New Delhi: Manohar, 1990. 2nd ed. 352p.
       bibliog.

First published in 1964, this popular work details the responses of India's British
ruling élite to the shock of the revolt of 1857 and the measures taken to prevent a
further rebellion. These included, in parts of north India, the attempt to secure new
allies among the landed aristocracy – a policy which Metcalf analyses in greater
detail in *Land, landlords and the British Raj: northern India in the nineteenth century*
(Berkeley, California: University of California Press, 1979. 436p.). This edition
includes a new introduction which discusses the validity of the arguments put forward
in 1964, and reviews later research.

191   **The Khilafat movement: religious symbolism and political
       mobilization in India.**
       Gail Minault.   New York: Columbia University Press, 1982. 294p.
       bibliog. (Studies in Oriental Culture, no. 16).

An excellent scholarly study of the 1919-21 Khilafat (Caliphate) movement in India
which was designed to pressurize the British government into supporting the
preservation of the Ottoman ruler's position as Caliph of the Islamic world, despite
the Ottoman empire's defeat after the First World War. The author examines the
different meanings the Caliphate had for various groups in the Muslim community
and concludes that, although it was characterized by remarkable Hindu-Muslim
cooperation, its key symbolic value was in the creation of a sense of a distinct Muslim
identity within the broader Indian population.

192   **The British conquest and dominion of India.**
       Penderel Moon.   London: Duckworth, 1989. 1,235p. maps. bibliog.

This monumental volume surveys in detail the history of the two centuries of British
involvement in India – from the battle of Plassey (1757) to independence and
partition (1947). Its author, the late Sir Penderel Moon, was a veteran India-hand who
served in the Indian Civil Service (ICS) and the new post-independence government.
While ready to chronicle the 'numerous glaring misdeeds' of the British ruling élite
and some of the sordid aspects of the 'Company Raj' of the later 18th century,
Moon's broad theme here is that, 'from start to finish, Britain's Indian empire was far
more a joint Anglo-Indian enterprise and partnership than either party has usually
been inclined to admit'. Particularly strong are the analyses of military affairs,
internal security, and the policies and characters of successive British viceroys and
secretaries of state. Moon's 'compassionate imperialist' interpretation can be
contrasted usefully with the 'committed nationalist' analysis of Chandra (see item no.
172).

193   **Endgames of empire: studies of Britain's India problem.**
       R. J. Moore.   New Delhi: Oxford University Press India, 1988. 230p.
       bibliog.

A collection of seven articles written between 1970 and 1983 by the author, an expert
on British and Indian politics during the 1930s and 1940s, in particular, the transfer of
power. The first three articles assess British policy towards and within India before
the Second World War, and Moore argues that between 1917 and 1945 British
constitutional strategies aimed at consolidating the imperial system of governance

based on intermediary structures of collaboration. The remaining papers include studies of Jinnah and the demand for Pakistan, Lord Mountbatten's viceroyalty and the 'endgame'.

194 India Britannica.
Geoffrey Moorhouse.   London: Paladin, Granada Publishing, 1984.
239p. 2 maps.

A very readable account of the two centuries of British involvement in India as, initially, conquerors and then rulers, before independence was granted in 1947. The author, a non-academic, long fascinated by India's impact on Britain and the British impact on India, presents a highly individual and vivid portrayal of this unique 'love-hate relationship' for the general reader.

195 A centenary history of the Indian National Congress (1885-1985).
Edited by B. N. Pande.   New Delhi: Vikas, 1985. 5 vols.

Sponsored by the All India Congress Committee (I), this project, which was initiated by Prime Minister Indira Gandhi, has resulted in the publication of five chronologically based volumes which set out the role of Congress in the freedom struggle and in governing independent India. The periods covered by the individual volumes are: 1885-1919, 1919-35, 1935-47, 1947-64, and 1964-85. Volumes range in length from between 600 and 900 pages.

196 Hyderabad and British paramountcy, 1858-1883.
Bharati Ray.   New Delhi: Oxford University Press India, 1988. 232p.
bibliog.

A well-written and carefully documented account of the development of imperial policy towards Indian princely states, based on a case study of Hyderabad during the late 19th century. A central figure in this story is the *diwan* (chief minister) Salar Jang (d. 1883), whose career was characterized by both cooperation and conflict with the paramount power. There are vivid portraits of the residents and viceroys and interesting sections on railway development in the princely state. An excellent study of relations between the British Raj and the smaller north-central Indian Princely State of Jaipur is Robert W. Stern's *The cat and the lion* (Leiden, the Netherlands: E. J. Brill, 1988. 331p.).

197 Social conflict and political unrest in Bengal, 1875-1927.
Rajat Kanta Ray.   New Delhi: Oxford University Press India, 1984.
398p.

An excellent study of Bengali politics over five decades which examines the structural bases of political behaviour. The author analyses Bengal's economic and social structure during the age of 'high imperialism', when three-fifths of British capital in India was based in Calcutta, and notes that, with the import-export sector dominated by British managing agencies, educated Bengalis were confined to the government service and professions. As a consequence, they were socially isolated from the larger society, and the region's agriculture was left unmodernized. Ray attributes Muslim communalism to British success in exploiting differences in material interests between high-caste Hindu nationalists and Muslims rather that to agararian tensions between Hindu landlords and Muslim tenants.

198 **The non-official British in India to 1920.**
Raymond K. Renford.   New Delhi: Oxford University Press India, 1987. 468p. map. bibliog.

A well-researched and interesting account of the activities of British non-officials in India. Renford provides analytical chapters describing the growth of the Eurasian and domiciled European community between the late 18th and later 19th centuries and their involvement in such activities as planting, industry, commerce, the professions and missionary activity. The principal focus of the work is on how the community came to organize itself and operate as a pressure group between the 1880s and 1920s, the period which saw the birth and growth of the Indian National Congress and the Muslim League.

199 **Separatism among Indian Muslims: the politics of the United Provinces' Muslims, 1860-1923.**
Francis C. R. Robinson.   Cambridge: Cambridge University Press, 1974. 469p. 4 maps. bibliog. (Cambridge South Asian Studies, no. 16).

A classic study of the development of Muslim politics in north India during the late 19th and early 20th centuries, focusing on the emergence of demands for separate political representation. The author examines the position of the Muslim community and its Urdu-speaking élite in Uttar Pradesh, where it was well entrenched but faced new challenges from British rule. He traces the emergence of the so-called 'old' and 'young' parties among the Muslim élite and their struggle for leadership of the Muslim movement. This volume should be read with Farzana Shaikh's *Community and consensus in Islam: Muslim representation in colonial India, 1860-1947* (Cambridge: Cambridge University Press, 1989. 257p.), which gives greater prominence to the role of ideas.

200 **The last days of the Raj.**
Trevor Royle.   London: Michael Joseph, 1989. 291p. map. bibliog.

A social history of the closing days of British power in India presented in the format of an historical narrative. Royle's work builds upon the insights gained from scores of interviews with both Indians and British expatriates who lived through this turbulent period. He depicts the way of life of the white *sahibs* during the 1930s, the growth in Indian nationalist consciousness and the far-reaching impact that the Second World War and the Japanese threat had on Indian society.

201 **Modern India, 1885-1947.**
Sumit Sarkar.   Basingstoke, England: Macmillan, 1989. 2nd ed. 489p. bibliog.

Sarkar skilfully synthesizes modern scholarship to provide a comprehensive account of political and associated economic, social, and ideological, developments in India during the British Raj's 'high noon' era. A member of the 'Subaltern school' of historians (see item no. 179), Sarkar presents an interpretation which, through emphasizing popular mentalities and non-élite themes, is a useful corrective to traditional Indian nationalist interpretations and to the 'Cambridge school' (see item no. 203) of top-down history. For Sarkar, the popular movements during this period had a measure of autonomy which is sometimes denied by Western historians. A useful college text.

202 **Bengal 1928-1934: the politics of protest.**
Tanika Sarkar. New Delhi: Oxford University Press India, 1987.
183p. bibliog.

A well-researched analysis of a tumultous period in Bengal's history. These years were characterized by a revival of nationalist agitation after the lull of the mid-1920s, a spate of revolutionary terrorism, new forms of struggle in rural areas and among subordinated groups (including tribals and women), and a militant mass upsurge during Civil Disobedience. The economic context was the world depression. The author is critical of the provincial Congress leadership, noting its failure to explore the new possibilities and options presented by the new popular protest movements. Covering the period up to independence *Bengal divided: Hindu communalism and partition, 1932-1947* (Cambridge: Cambridge University Press, 1995. 303p.), by Joya Chatterji, is a complementary work which argues that it was the development of Hindu, rather than Muslim, separatism that was the main impetus behind partition in 1947.

203 **The emergence of Indian nationalism: competition and collaboration in the later nineteenth century.**
Anil Seal. London: Cambridge University Press, 1968. 416p. maps. bibliog.

A classic study of the embryonic phase of Indian nationalism which established a distinctive high politics 'Cambridge school' interpretation of Indian political developments during the late 19th and early 20th centuries . Examining the divisions inside the presidencies of Bengal, Bombay and Madras in terms of caste, community and language, the author concludes that the clear force making for political development were Indians who had been educated in the Western style and that their personal grievances, material and social, drove the early nationalist movement. The work downplays the significance of ideology and of grassroots political activism.

204 **The origins of the partition of India, 1936-1947.**
Anita Inder Singh. New Delhi: Oxford University Press India, 1987.
271p. bibliog.

An up-to-date, meticulously researched analysis of the final decade of the British Raj and the background to partition. The author writes from a pro-Congress standpoint and rejects recent suggestions (see item no. 260) that M. A. Jinnah used the demand for 'Pakistan' merely as a bargaining counter to obtain better conditions for Muslims within an all-India Federation. Singh argues that Jinnah was in part promoted by the British as a counterpoise to Congress, but also suggests that partition did not become inevitable until the 'breaking point' of communal riots during 1946-47.

205 **Congress and Indian nationalism: the pre-independence phase.**
Edited by Richard Sisson, Stanley A. Wolpert. Berkeley, California: University of California Press, 1988. 420p.

A collection of seventeen excellent essays on issues of ideology, mass participation, and class and caste mobilizations at various times and in different regions during the history of the Indian National Congress movement in the pre-independence period. Contributors include John McLane, Rajat Kanta Ray, Gyanendra Pandey, Anthony Low, Zoya Hasan, Claude Markovits, and Mushirul Hasan. Topics include Congress leadership's attitude towards peasant movements, Bombay millworkers, the untouchables, and the Indian business community.

206   The peasant armed: the Indian rebellion of 1857.
Eric T. Stokes, edited by Christopher A. Bayly.   Oxford: Clarendon Press, 1986. 261p. maps. bibliog.

This work is the product of detailed local-level research by a leading authority on the Mutiny of 1857. The author's untimely death in 1981, with the manuscript unfinished, has meant that the editor has had to fill in many key gaps. For Stokes the seed-bed of resistance to the British in 1857 was provided by a complex mixture of old proprietary groups of high-caste Brahmins and Rajputs and semi-nomadic, cattle keeping communities whose future was becoming imperilled by the British Raj. This volume can be complemented by related essays in Stokes' *The peasant and the Raj: studies in agrarian society and peasant rebellion in colonial India* (Cambridge: Cambridge University Press, 1980. 308p.). The contrasting nationalist interpretation of India's so-called 'first war of independence' is presented in S. N. Sen's, *Eighteen fifty-seven* (New Delhi: Publications Division, Ministry of Information and Broadcasting, 1958. 468p.). A very readable narrative history of the Rebellion is Christopher Hibbert's *The Great Mutiny: India 1857* (London: Allen Lane, Penguin, 1978. 472p.).

207   Indian nationalism: an historical analysis.
R. Suntharalingam.   New Delhi: Vikas, 1983. 471p. bibliog.

A popular narrative study of the history of Indian nationalism from its origins in the later 19th century to independence in 1947. This work can be read usefully alongside two more specialist regional monographs, focusing on western and southern India respectively: Gordon Johnson, *Provincial politics and Indian nationalism: Bombay and the Indian National Congress 1880-1915* (Cambridge: Cambridge University Press, 1973. 207p.); and David A. Washbrook, *The emergence of provincial politics: the Madras presidency, 1870-1920* (Cambridge: Cambridge University Press, 1976. 358p.).

208   The French in India: from diamond traders to Sanskrit scholars.
Rose Vincent.   London: Sangam Books, 1990. 165p.

Analyses France's changing perspections of India over a span of three centuries. The early French mercenaries were attracted to India in the late Mughal era by the lure of wealth and adventure. For later French scientists, historians and men of letters the relationship has been marked by curiosity and understanding.

209   Two monsoons: the life and death of Europeans in India.
Theon Wilkinson, with drawings by Bill Smith.   London: Duckworth, 1987. 2nd ed. 240p. map. bibliog.

An original, ingenious work which draws upon records left on gravestones in Indian cemeteries to throw light on the lives led by European traders, artisans, soldiers, missionaries, doctors and adventurers who came to India to live and work during the pre-colonial and colonial periods. Organized into six thematic chapters, the book includes many interesting anecdotes – some sad, some amusing.

210   **The limited Raj: agrarian relations in colonial India, Saran district, 1793-1920.**
Anand A. Yang.   Berkeley, California: University of California Press, 1990. 271p. bibliog.

An innovative monograph which depicts north Indian rural society from below and views the British Raj as an overlordship in which considerable *de facto* local power was devolved to substantial landlords. In this sense, it was a 'limited Raj'. Yang bases this analysis on a case study of the Hathwa Raj estate, which rose to prominence in the late 18th century with British support. There are perceptive analyses of popular mentalities and an evocative reading of the great annual Sonepur fair which Indians celebrated at the confluence of the Ganges and Gandak rivers, to which became appended sporting and social events for the British community.

Regional histories

211   **Lions of the Punjab: culture in the making.**
Richard Gabriel Fox.   Berkeley, California: University of California Press, 1985. 259p. maps. bibliog.

A study of cultural changes within the Sikh community of Punjab between the mid-19th century and 1920s and also of Sikh relations with other Punjabis and the British. The term 'lions' is ascribed to the Sikhs since the author views the community as martial, courageous and stalwart, but also as mastered and used by the British. Fox examines the development of rural and urban classes in Punjab, the rise of religious identity, and the shift of Sikh society by segments from loyalty to rejection of their British overlords. The work culminates with the 1920s struggles to gain control over Sikh shrines, termed by Fox the 'Third Sikh War'.

212   **Cultural history of Rajasthan.**
Kalyan Kumar Ganguli.   New Delhi: Sundeep Prakashan, 1983. 286p. bibliog.

An overview of the long flowing traditions and rich cultural heritage of the north-central Indian region of Rajasthan. Separate chapters consider the geography of the region, Rajasthan's formation as an historical entity, the development of the Rajput tradition, the cult of Krishna, and painting.

213   **The Marathas 1600-1818 (Vol. II:4 in the New Cambridge History of India).**
Stewart Gordon.   Cambridge: Cambridge University Press, 1993. 202p. maps. bibliog.

A succinct overview of the rise of the Maratha polity in western and central India between the 17th and 19th centuries. This work synthesizes Gordon's extensive and innovative writings on the Maratha Hindu quasi-confederacy which challenged the Mughals and then the British as India's dominant supra-regional force. Gordon provides a new, complex understanding of the workings and internal dynamics of the

Maratha polity, describing patterns of authority and personal loyalty, systems of revenue collecting, patronage of Hindu temples and places of pilgrimage, and changing military strategies. Gordon is also author of *Marathas, marauders, and state formation in eighteenth-century India* (New Delhi: Oxford University Press India, 1994. 223p.).

214 The Sikhs in the Punjab (Vol. II:3 in The New Cambridge History of India).
J. S. Grewal.   Cambridge: Cambridge University Press, 1990. 264p. maps. bibliog.

A concise, yet comprehensive, history of the Punjab and its Sikh peoples from Mughal times to the present day. The volume takes full account of the latest research and contains five appendices, including a chronology of events between 1708 and 1849, and a nine-page annotated bibliographic essay. The author's own specialism is 16th-17th century Sikh history, having written separate monographs on Guru Nanak, Guru Tegh Bahadur, and Guru Gobind Singh.

215 South Indian history and society: studies from inscriptions, A.D. 850-1800.
Noboru Karashima.   New Delhi: Oxford University Press India, 1984. 217p. bibliog.

Despite its title, this work focuses chiefly on the Chola period, particularly the 10th-13th centuries, examining socio-economic developments. Karashima argues that, whereas communal landholdings prevailed during early Indian history, private holdings had become common by the last stage of Chola rule. In his later volume, *Towards a new formation: south Indian society under Vijayanagar rule* (New Delhi: Oxford University Press India, 1992. 294p.), Karashima analyses developments during the succeeding Vijayanagara era (14th-16th centuries). He describes the new feudalistic social formation which, characterized by strong state control over *nayakas* (military commanders), had similarities to Tokugawa feudalism in Japan. Karashima's work has superseded K. A. A. Nilakanta Sastri's classic *A history of south India from prehistoric times to the fall of Vijayanagara* (New Delhi: Oxford University Press India, 1976. 4th ed. 521p.).

216 Peasant history in south India.
David Ludden.   Princeton, New Jersey: Princeton University Press, 1985. 310p. maps. bibliog.

An excellent, broad-ranging monograph about the structures of the peasant past over the course of a millennium of south India's history based on a case study of Tirunelveli district in Tamil Nadu. In the first half of the book, the author analyses the period between 900 and 1900 AD, describing the progressive innovations and changes which occurred in both agricultural practices, notably in water control, and in social relations and ritual. The remainder of the book reviews the impact of British colonial rule, stressing the dynamic historical background and the active collaboration of local peasant leaders. Ludden emphasizes the primacy of peasant initiative.

217 History of modern Bengal.
R. C. Majumdar.   Calcutta: G. Bharadwaj, 1978 and 1981. 2 vols.
A detailed history of Bengal between the mid-18th century and mid-20th century. The format is chiefly chronological, but there are also separate chapters on agriculture and industry, culture, education, literature, religion, and society. Volume one covers the period between 1765 and 1905 and volume two covers developments to independence in 1947.

218 Nineteenth century history of Maharashtra. Volume 1.
B. R. Sunthankar.   Pune, India: Shubhada-Saraswar Prakashan, 1988.
688p.
This work had its origins in the Maharashtra State Gazetteers project, when the author was commissioned to write a historical volume on Maharashtra covering the period from the British conquest to 1920. This volume covers the period 1818-57, cataloguing events, persons, activities and institutions in great detail and presenting a largely orthodox nationalist interpretation of the disruptive early impact of British imperial rule. Particularly strong is the section on the Maharashtran 'renaissance' in politics, education and social reform which culminated in the events of 1857.

Historians and historiography

219 Mughals in India: a bibliographical survey of manuscripts.
D. N. Marshall.   London, New York: Mansell, 1985. 634p.
Comprises 2,105 annotated entries, covering all manuscripts, regardless of language, which are relevant to the study of political, economic, and social conditions during the Mughal period. Major works, such as the *A'in-i Akbari* (see item no. 121), are included, as well as minor works relevant to the study of a specific area or topic. This volume should be supplemented with Sri Ram Sharma, *A bibliography of Mughal India (1526-1707 AD)* (Philadelphia: Porcupine Press, 1977. reprint of 1938 ed. 206p.), which surveys a wide range of official and non-official original Mughal sources.

220 On history and historians in medieval India.
Khaliq Ahmad Nizami.   New Delhi: Munshiram Manoharlal, 1983.
267p. bibliog.
An excellent survey of medieval Persian historiography which reviews the works of six prominent historians, including Abu'l Fazl, Barani, and Nizami, and the different types of medieval literature.

221 Historians of India, Pakistan and Ceylon.
Edited by Cyril Henry Philips.   New York: Oxford University Press,
1961. 504p. bibliog.
A comprehensive and critical assessment of the various historical writings that have been published since antiquity, but especially during the last four centuries. There are

essays on historians of different nationalities such as Portuguese, Dutch, and Danish. Other essays deal with such principal authorities as Kalhana, Mill, Elphinstone, and Moreland. There are four essays on regional language materials in Hindi, Urdu, Bengali, and Marathi, and at least one essay examines Western and Indian historians writing on ancient India.

222 Historians and historiography in modern India.

Edited by Siba Pada Sen. Calcutta: Institute of Historical Studies, 1973. 464p. bibliog.

Forty essays assessing the work of eminent historians of India – thirty-three Indian and seven European – give a full account of the development of Indian historiography from the mid-19th to the mid-20th century. Special emphasis is placed on the work of the 19th-century pioneers and their influence on 20th-century historians. Papers are grouped in four categories: ancient, medieval, modern, and regional (Maharashtra, Gujarat, Rajasthan, and Punjab). An admirable survey.

223 Sources of the history of India.

Edited by Siba Pada Sen. Calcutta: Institute of Historical Studies, 1978-80. 3 vols. bibliog.

A thorough description and analysis of archaeological, epigraphic, numismatic, and written records covering ancient, medieval, and modern periods of regional and national Indian history, with contributions by distinguished historians. The first volume covers Karnataka, Andhra Pradesh, Maharashtra, and Goa; the second, Rajasthan, Haryana, Meghalaya, Uttar Pradesh, and Jammu and Kashmir; and the third, Assam, Sikkim, and Tamil Nadu. Each section deals with the extent and dependability of the different categories of source materials and the extent to which they have been utilized.

Professional journals

224 The Indian Historical Review.

New Delhi: Motilal Banarsidass, 1974- . biannual.

Produced for the Indian Council of Historical Research and edited by a board of Indian scholars, this journal, though described as biannual, has been produced in one combined annual issue during recent years. Each issue carries around a dozen articles and more than eighty book reviews. Particular strengths of the journal are early, medieval and Mughal history, though all historical periods are covered.

225 Journal of Indian History.

Trivandrum, India: University of Kerala, 1921- . thrice-yearly.

Though often delayed in publication, this is India's foremost journal covering all aspects of Indian history. Most of the contributions are from scholars teaching in Indian universities. A reasonably good book review section is also included.

226   **South Asian Studies.**
London: Society for South Asian Studies, 1985- . annual.
This journal contains essays on Indian antiquities, art and history. It is particularly strong on early history.

227   **Studies in History.**
New Delhi: Sage Publications, 1979- . biannual.
Edited by S. Gopal of New Delhi's Jawaharlal Nehru University, this biannual journal includes articles reflecting new interdisciplinary developments in Indian historical research. A new series began in 1985.

Political Biographies and Autobiographies

General

228   **India: Who's Who.**
New Delhi: INFA, 1969- . annual.

This annual reference publication provides basic biographical information on over 2,500 eminent Indians. The work, arranged by profession, is divided into eight main sections: business, government, humanities, public affairs, sciences, applied sciences, social sciences and law, and miscellaneous. Each section is further divided into subsections. An appendix at the end gives addresses of various associations, organizations, research institutes and universities.

229   **Dictionary of national biography (supplement).**
Edited by N. R. Ray.   Calcutta: Institute of Historical Studies, 1986.
4 vols.

A supplement to item no. 230, these four volumes, arranged alphabetically, cover the first twenty-five years after independence (1947-72). The volumes are arranged in alphabetical order and include only persons living in what is now India. A selected bibliography is included at the end of each entry.

230   **Dictionary of national biography.**
Edited by Siba Pada Sen.   Calcutta: Institute of Historical Studies, 1972-74. 4 vols.

This dictionary covers the period 1800-1947, and includes over 1,300 biographical sketches of persons from various walks of life, written by 350 contributors. Persons from areas that are now part of Pakistan and Bangladesh have also been included. At the end of each entry is a select bibliography for further research. The most commonly used English spelling for a given surname determines the alphabetical order of the entries – the 'rational manner' in the view of the editor.

Ancient and medieval Indian rulers

231 **Akbar: the greatest Mogul.**
S. M. Burke. New Delhi: Munshiram Manoharlal, 1989. 249p.
bibliog.

A conventional account of Akbar's life (1542-1605) and reign. There are analytical chapters on the emperor's syncretic religious beliefs, military campaigns, the system of government, and Akbar and the arts. A more vividly written, older account of Akbar's extraordinary life, bringing out the contradictions in the emperor's personality, is Laurence Binyon's *Akbar* (New York: Nelson, 1939. 165p.).

232 **Harsha: a political study.**
D. Devahuti. New Delhi: Oxford University Press India, 1983.
2nd ed. 362p. map. bibliog.

An important study of the last great Hindu emperor of India, who died in 647 AD. Utilizing records of Chinese Buddhist pilgrims as well as Sanskrit textual evidence, Devahuti greatly improves the earlier monograph on Harsha by R. K. Mookerji, *Harsha* (New Delhi: Motilal Banarsidass, 1926. 3rd ed. 203p.). Her narrative and analysis includes an examination of the sources for this study, Harsha's political, social, economic, and religious achievements, and Harsha as a great Sanskrit dramatist.

233 **Shah Jahan.**
Muni Lal. New Delhi: Vikas, 1986. 452p. bibliog.

A clearly-written study of the life of the great emperor Shah Jahan (1592-1666), whose reign between 1627-58 saw the Mughal empire at its zenith. The son of Jahangir, Shah Jahan consolidated Mughal power in the Deccan and was an unrivalled patron of the arts, best remembered for the Taj Mahal, the tomb he had constructed for the empress Mumtaz Mahal. Muni Lal has also produced biographies of other Mughal rulers: *Babur: life and times* (New Delhi: Vikas, 1977. 126p); *Humayun* (New Delhi: Vikas, 1978. 242p.); and *Jahangir* (New Delhi: Vikas, 1983. 346p.).

234 **Shivaji: the great patriot.**
Lajpat Rai, translated from Urdu and edited by R. C. Puri. New
Delhi: Metropolitan, 1980. 254p.

A biography of the Maratha warrior-leader Shivaji (1627-80), who carved out an impressive empire in western India during the late 17th century and was a great foe of the Mughal emperor Aurangzeb. Written from a Hindu nationalist perspective, Shivaji is portrayed as a staunch defender of the Hindu faith against Muslim challenges, and as a proto-nationalist.

235 **A short history of Aurangzib, 1618-1707.**
Jadunath Sarkar. New Delhi: Orient Longman, 1979. 426p.

Based on Sarkar's five-volume (1912-24) definitive study of the last of the Great Mughals, Aurangzeb (1618-1707), this abridged volume covers the campaigns that enabled the emperor to extend the frontiers of the empire to its largest extent on the one hand, but which sowed the seeds of rebellion and regional uprisings on the other. Three of the twenty chapters deal with Aurangzeb's personality, character traits, economic system and policies, and attitude towards the arts. The volume was first published in 1930. A more recent study of the life and career of this complex, influential ruler is Muni Lāl's, *Aurangzeb* (New Delhi: Vikas, 1988. 423p.).

236 **The legend of King Asoka: a study and translation of the**
Asokavadana.
John S. Strong.   Princeton, New Jersey: Princeton University Press, 1983. 336p.

A biographical account of India's first great imperial ruler, King Asoka (reign ca. 268-231 BC), who became a convert to Buddhism. The narrative draws upon the ancient *Asokavadana.*

British military and political leaders

237 **Memoirs of a Bengal civilian: John Beames, the lively narrative of a Victorian district officer.**
John Beames, with an introduction by Philip Mason.   London: Eland Books, 1984. 312p. map.

Written between 1875 and 1893 for 'family amusement', this posthumously published volume presents a fascinating and truthful picture of the typical life led by a British district officer in India during the mid- and late-19th century. The author, John Beames (1837-1902), after training at the East India Company's College at Haileybury in England, arrived in Calcutta in 1858 soon after the Mutiny and held posts in the Punjab, Bihar, Orissa, and Chittagong. His comments on and descriptions of some of the British leaders in India, notably John Lawrence and Sir Richard Temple, are characteristically frank. Beames' personal account can be usefully read alongside *The district officer in India, 1930-1947* (London: Scolar Press, 1980. 255p.), written by Roland Hunt and John Harrison, which draws together the 20th-century reminiscences of seventy-three British and Indian district officers.

238 **Clive of India.**
Mark Bence-Jones.   London: Constable, 1987. 393p.

A very readable biography of Robert Clive (1725-74), the adventurous soldier-politician whose victories at Arcot (1751) and Plassey (1757) laid the foundations for British supremacy in the subcontinent. First published in 1974, this volume was reissued in 1987. The author's *Viceroys of India* (London: Constable, 1986. 361p.) is an accessible general work.

239   Anglo-Indian attitudes: the mind of the Indian civil service.

Clive J. Dewey.   London: The Hambledon Press, 1993. 292p. 2 maps bibliog.

This fascinating book comprises both a biography of the lives of two prominen British Indian provincial administrators, Frank Lugard Brayne (1882-1952) and Sir Malcolm Lyall Darling (1880-1969), and an exploration of the ideologies that underpinned British colonialism. Drawing upon family papers, Dewey relates the beliefs of Brayne and Darling to their upbringing in England and describes how they put their contrasting convictions, described as 'the Gospel of Uplift' and 'the Cult of Friendship', into practice as administrators in India.

240   Curzon in India.

David Dilks.   New York: Taplinger, 1970. 2 vols. maps. bibliog.

A vivid and well-written biography of Lord George Nathaniel Curzon (1859-1925), one of the greatest viceroys of India. Dilks brings out the complexities and dichotomies of Curzon's character: a person who loved India immensely, yet criticized its classical literature as useless; one who suppressed Indian nationalists, yet counselled the British government to extend to Indians the right to self-government; one who loved the company of Indian princes, yet considered them irrelevant to India's political future. The contribution of Curzon to archaeological investigations in India, the growth of Indian education, and other socio-economic measures is carefully documented. A more recent biography is *Lord Curzon: the last of the British Moghuls* (New Delhi: Oxford University Press India, 1993. 309p.), by Nayana Goradia.

241   The men who ruled India.

Philip Mason.   London: Pan Books, 1987. 429p. maps. bibliog.

This paperback volume is an abridged edition of Mason's *The founders* and *The guardians*, published originally in 1953 and 1954 respectively under the pseudonym Philip Woodruff. It chronicles vividly the lives and changing perceptions of the British ruling élite who fought, built bridges and railways, administered paternal justice in villages, held missions, and waged war with neighbouring states. Included are useful thumbnail sketches of Warren Hastings, Thomas Munro (see item no. 246), John Malcolm, Charles Metcalfe, Henry and John Lawrence, and Alfred Lyall. In writing this work, Mason drew upon twenty years of personal experience of service in the Indian Civil Service (ICS).

242   The administration of India under Lord Lansdowne (1884-1894).

J. P. Misra.   New Delhi: Sterling, 1975. 260p. bibliog.

A traditional-style account of the long viceregal administration of the 5th Marquis of Lansdowne (1845-1927), which draws on a wide range of private papers. The chief preoccupations of the administration were Northwest Frontier issues and land and constitutional reforms. A Liberal Unionist, who had previously been governor-general of Canada, Lansdowne, in contrast to his predecessor Lord Ripon (1880-84), was an essentially cautious figure.

243 **Sir William Jones: a study on eighteenth-century British attitudes to India.**
S. N. Mukherjee. London: Sangam Books, 1987. 175p. bibliog.

A reliable biography of the great Sanskritist and Orientalist, Sir William Jones (1746-94), who founded the Asiatic Society of Bengal in 1784 and restored Hindu confidence in their ancient culture through the translation of a series of classic texts. The author also describes the political views of Jones, a Whig who believed that Indians must be protected under an enlightened despotism, and the support he received for his encouragement of Asiatic studies from governor-general Warren Hastings.

244 **Mayo: Disraeli's viceroy.**
George Pottinger. Salisbury, England: Michael Russell, 1990. 224p. map. bibliog.

A straightforward, succinct and up-to-date account of the life and Indian career of the Irish-born Lord Mayo (1822-72), who was appointed governor-general of India by the British Conservative Prime Minister, Benjamin Disraeli, in 1869. He served three years as viceroy before being assassinated in 1872 by a Pathan convict during a visit to the Andaman Islands. Pottinger sets out the policies and achievements of the Mayo viceroyalty and describes Mayo's relations with the Indian princes and Sher Ali, the prickly Amir of Afghanistan.

245 **Lord William Bentinck: the making of a liberal imperialist, 1774-1839.**
John Rosselli. London: Chatto & Windus, 1974. 384p. map.

An authoritative account of the life and ideas of Lord William Cavendish Bentinck (1774-1839), a Whig imperialist who served as governor of Madras between 1803-07, provoking the Vellore massacre through his prohibition of *sepoy* beards and turbans. Bentinck returned to India as governor-general of Bengal from 1827 and became the first governor-general of India from 1833. His administration saw significant improvements in internal communications, educational reforms, the substitution of English for Persian and Sanskrit, and the prohibition of *sati* (widow-burning).

246 **Thomas Munro: the origins of the colonial state and his vision of empire.**
Burton Stein. New Delhi: Oxford University Press India, 1989. 374p. bibliog.

An outstanding account of the life, ideas and achievements of Sir Thomas Munro (1761-1827), a military officer who, following the defeat at Seringapatam and deposition of Tipu Sultan in 1799, played a key role in establishing the new British Indian administrative structure in southern India. Munro was renowned for his frequent tours of the Indian countryside, which enabled him to get close to cultivators and local leaders. He was instrumental in the decision to choose a *ryotwari* land settlement directly with cultivators in the the south rather than a permanent settlement with large landlord intermediaries, as had been established by Cornwallis in Bengal.

247 Earl Wavell: the viceroy's journal.

Archibald Percival Wavell, edited by Penderel Moon.   London:
Oxford University Press, 1973. 528p.

The fascinating private journal of Earl Wavell (1883-1950), who served as
commander-in-chief and supreme commander of Allied forces in the Southwest
Pacific from 1941 and as viceroy of India between 1943 and 1947. Wavell held power
at a difficult time of economic problems and rising political tensions as Indians
prepared for the transfer of power. A conventional historical biography covering
Wavell's career during this period, focusing particularly on military matters, is *The
chief: Field Marshall Lord Wavell, commander-in-chief and viceroy 1939-1947.*
(London: Hutchinson, 1980. 282p.), by Ronald Lewin.

248 Cornwallis: the imperial years.

Franklin Wickwire, Mary Wickwire.   Chapel Hill, North Carolina:
University of North Carolina Press, 1980. 340p. 2 maps. bibliog.

Renowned as the British military commander who surrendered to the American
colonists at Yorktown in 1781 during the American War of Independence, Charles
Cornwallis (1738-1805) came to India in 1786 and served as governor-general and
commander-in-chief for seven years. He returned again as governor-general in 1804.
His 'watch' was distinguished by a strengthening of British authority in southern
India, following successes in conflicts with Tipu Sultan of Mysore, and a Permanent
Settlement (1793) with large landcontrollers in Bengal. The Wickwires, who have
written an earlier volume charting Cornwallis's career in America, ably recount his
Indian achievements and failures.

249 Mountbatten: the official biography.

Philip Ziegler.   London: Fontana; New York: Alfred A. Knopf, 1985.
maps. bibliog. 786p.

Ziegler is the first biographer to have been granted full access to the Mountbatten
archive at Broadlands and makes full use of this additional material in this definitive
work. Earl Louis Mountbatten (1900-79), the dashing, flamboyant, sometimes
arrogant, great-grandson of Queen Victoria, enjoyed a remarkable career as both
statesman and military commander. Between 1943-45 he was supreme allied
commander in Southeast Asia, overseeing the successful drive against the Japanese
towards the close of the Second World War. Subsequently, he assumed responsibility
for managing the crumbling British empire, serving nine months as India's final
viceroy (1947). Criticized by some at home as an impetuous bungler, he won the love
and repect of many Indians for his stewardship of the transfer of power. Ten chapters
of this work, covering more than 130 pages, review Mountbatten's India years
(1946-48).

Nationalist and post-independence politicians

250 **Nehru: the making of India.**

M. J. Akbar. New York: Viking; Harmondsworth, England: Penguin, 1989. 624p. bibliog.

A richly detailed, though at times not sufficiently critical, account of the career of India's pre-eminent 20th-century statesman. Akbar writes perceptively about Jawaharlal Nehru's (1889-1964) youth, particularly his relationship with his politician father, Motilal (1861-1931), and his gentlemanly education at Harrow and Cambridge in England. During the nationalist struggle Nehru became a faithful disciple of M. K. Gandhi and passionate opponent of communalism. As prime minister from 1947, he set India on a new course of planned development and industrialization at home and promoted, via the Non-Aligned Movement, neutralism and peace-making abroad.

251 **India wins freedom – the complete version.**

Maulana Abul Kalam Azad. London: Sangam Books, 1988. rev. ed. 283p.

Memoirs of a nationalist Muslim who was the president of the Indian National Congress during the crucial years between 1939 and 1946. Azad (1888-1958), a pragmatist, criticizes Mahatma Gandhi for being so preoccupied with moral objectives as to be blind to political realities. He is equally critical of Jawaharlal Nehru for acting on impulse or being too theoretical and vain. The memoir was first published in 1959 with thirty pages of largely personal comment being excluded from the text at Azad's request. These sections are published for the first time in this revised edition. An excellent biography of Azad is *Abul Kalam Azad: an intellectual and religious biography* (New Delhi: Oxford University Press India, 1988. 358p.), by Ian Henderson Douglas, which is edited by Gail Minault and Christian W. Troll.

252 **Gandhi: prisoner of hope.**

Judith M. Brown. New Haven, Connecticut: Yale University Press, 1990. 440p. bibliog.

An excellent, comprehensive biography of the complex, charismatic figure of Mohandas Karamchand 'Mahatma' Gandhi (1869-1948) by an historian who is the author of two more specialized works on Gandhi's rise to power between 1915 and 1922, and his leadership of the Civil Disobedience Campaigns of the early 1930s. The author presents Gandhi as a fearless, spiritual and optimistic figure who believed that 'people and therefore situations can radically change'. Nevertheless, despite his leadership and tactical skills, Brown argues that the Indian nationalist movement would have reached its goal without the Mahatma since far deeper economic and political forces were at work loosening Indo-British links. Another fine biography of Gandhi, written by a personal acquaintance, is Louis Fischer's *The life of Mahatma Gandhi* (London: Grafton, 1986. rev. ed. 671p.).

253 Gandhi: against the tide.

Anthony Copley.   Oxford: Basil Blackwell, 1987. 118p. map. bibliog.

Part of the 'Historical Association Studies' series of pamphlets, this slim volume is an incisive, critical summary of recent research on the life and political career of Mahatma Gandhi. Students at school and university constitute its target market. The work is arranged in seven analytical chapters dealing with the influences on Gandhi's evolving philosophy, his views on the Indian economy and society, and the legacy of his thinking both within and beyond India. There is a useful bibliography. The author has also written a detailed monograph on the life and career of C. Rajagopalachari, Gandhi's key ally in southern India who later became a founder of the conservative Swatantra Party, *Rajagopalachari: Gandhi's southern commander* (London: Indo-British Historical Society, 1987. 254p.).

254 The story of my life.

Morarji Ranchodji Desai.   New York: Pergamon, 1978. 2 vols.

This two-volume autobiography of India's fourth prime minister is characteristically honest and self-righteous. Desai's differences with Indira Gandhi led to the split in the ruling Congress Party in 1969, and in 1977 a loose coalition led by him ousted Mrs. Gandhi from political power – albeit briefly. This work contains a wealth of material on the inner workings of the Indian political élite.

255 An autobiography: or the story of my experiments with the truth.

Mohandas Karamchand Gandhi, translated from the original Gujarati by Mahadev Desai.   Harmondsworth, England: Penguin, 1982. rev. ed. 454p.

Written by Gandhi during his imprisonment by the British in the 1920s, this extraordinary autobiography first appeared serially in Gandhi's weekly news magazine. Though the autobiography does not cover the last twenty-five years of his life, when Gandhi stood at his political zenith, this is a remarkable book of personal confessions that contain a frank discussion of Gandhi's human weaknesses. Ved Mehta's finely written study of the life and work of Gandhi and of some of his disciples, *Mahatma Gandhi and his apostles* (New York: Viking, 1976. 260p.), provides a useful assessment of the destiny of Gandhism in India. B. R. Nanda's *Gandhi and his critics* (New Delhi: Oxford University Press India, 1985. 178p.), examines issues critics have raised.

256 Krishna Menon: a biography.

T. J. S. George.   London: Jonathan Cape, 1964. 272p.

A solid biography of V. K. Krishna Menon (1896-1974), a leading nationalist politician from south India, who became secretary of the India League in 1929 and the mouthpiece of the Indian National Congress in England. On independence in 1947, Krishna Menon became India's high commissioner in London and between 1957-62 served under Jawaharlal Nehru as defence minister.

Political Biographies and Autobiographies. Nationalist and post-independence politicians

257 Jawaharlal Nehru: a biography.
Sarvepalli Gopal. New Delhi: Oxford University Press India, 1989. Abridged ed. 503p. maps.

This volume is an abridged version of Gopal's monumental official trilogy chronicling the life and achievements of India's first prime minister. The work, reflecting the individual volumes, is divided into three parts broken chronologically between 1889-1947, 1947-56, and 1956-64. The first part clearly sets out Nehru's position and key role within the Indian freedom movement. The second and third parts include reasoned discussions of Nehru's achievements and failures in foreign policy. As an official biography, the account is understandably partisan. The three volume full-length study was published by Harvard University Press between 1976 and 1984. Nehru's own *Autobiography* was published in London by Bodley Head in 1936.

258 Brothers against the Raj: a biography of Indian nationalists Sarat and Subhas Chandra Bose.
Leonard A. Gordon. New York: Columbia University Press, 1990. 807p. bibliog.

A definitive account of the lives of Subhas Chandra Bose (1897-1945) and his elder brother Sarat Bose (1889-1950), controversial Bengali leaders at the centre of the nationalist struggle between the 1920s and 1940s. Frequently imprisoned, Subhas Chandra Bose called for complete Indian independence and during the Second World War supported the Axis powers against the British. He became commander-in-chief of the Japanese-sponsored Indian National Army and was reportedly killed in a plane crash on Taiwan in August 1945.

259 A nationalist conscience: M. A. Ansari, the Congress and the Raj.
Mushirul Hasan. New Delhi: Manohar, 1987. 277p. bibliog.

Dr. Mukhtar Ahmed Ansari (1890-1936), a Muslim from Uttar Pradesh, was one of the foremost 'nationalist Muslims' within the Indian National Congress movement during the freedom struggle. Dr. Ansari remained committed throughout his life to a unified Hindu-Muslim struggle against British colonial rule and, unlike Jinnah of the Muslim League and later Nehru of Congress, refused to inherit a free country at the cost of its integrity. The author shows the difficult task faced by Dr. Ansari in attempting to persuade fellow Muslims to reject the two-nation theory and at the same time justify his existence in the Congress as a true representative of the Muslim community. Ansari suffered virtual elimination from his own community for his secularist views and as a last-ditch effort attempted to launch an All-India Nationalist Party.

260 The sole spokesman: Jinnah, the Muslim League and the demand for Pakistan.
Ayesha Jalal. Cambridge: Cambridge University Press, 1985. 310p. bibliog. (Cambridge South Asian Studies, no. 31).

A controversial reassessment of the career and aims of Mohammed Ali Jinnah (1876-1948), the Muslim League leader and creator and first governor-general of Pakistan. The author argues that there was a deliberate imprecision in the way that Jinnah formulated his demand for Pakistan since it was a goal which he did not really want. Instead, he favoured a loose union between a Pakistan and a Hindustan which would be joined in defence and foreign policy matters and would guarantee Muslims access to political power. However, according to the author, Jinnah was outmanoeuvred in the 'end game' of empire by an alliance of Congress leaders and the last viceroy, Mountbatten. Not surprisingly, this work has been strongly criticized in Pakistan.

261   **Dr. Ambedkar: life and mission.**
Dhananjay Keer.   Bombay: Popular Prakashan, 1990. rev. ed. 541p. bibliog.

An unusually detailed and sympathetic biography of Bhimrao Ranji Ambedkar (1893-1956), the leader of India's untouchables. Keer carefully examines the debate between Mahatma Gandhi and Ambedkar on the position and future role of the untouchables in Indian politics. He also provides an excellent analysis of Ambedkar's contribution to the framing and enactment of independent India's constitution. A major study of one of 20th-century India's most important statesmen.

262   **Indira Gandhi: a personal and political biography.**
Inder Malhotra.   London: Hodder & Stoughton, 1989. 363p. bibliog.

As Malhotra notes in his foreword, more books have been written on Indira Gandhi (1917-84) than her illustrious father, Jawaharlal Nehru. This is explained by the high drama of her life: her phenomenal rise to power in 1966 on the death of Lal Bahadur Shastri (1904-66) and to popularity in the wake of the 1971 general election and victory in the war with Pakistan which led to the creation of Bangladesh; her controversial declaration of a quasi-dictatorial State of Emergency in 1975 and subsequent loss of power in the 1977 general election; her sweeping return as prime minister in January 1980; the untimely death of her beloved younger son and political protégé, Sanjay, in June 1980; and her brutal assassination by her Sikh bodyguard in October 1984. This life story is skilfully and intelligently related by Malhotra, a prominent journalist able to draw upon numerous off-the-record conversations. Additional insight into Indira Gandhi's complex character, combining a deep-seated sense of insecurity with a *realpolitik* expertise in political manoeuvre, is provided in the biographies written by Pupul Jayakar, India's cultural czarina, *Indira Gandhi* (New Delhi: Viking India/Penguin, 1992. 535p.), and by the journalist Pranay Gupte, *Mother India: a political biography of Indira Gandhi* (New York: Charles Scribner's Sons, 1992. 593p.).

263   **Sir Sayyid Ahmad Khan and Muslim modernization in India and Pakistan.**
Hafeez Malik.   New York: Columbia University Press, 1980. 340p. bibliog. (Studies in Oriental Culture, no. 15).

Sir Sayyid Ahmad Khan (1817-98) was a key figure in Muslim modernist thought in South Asia. A member of a Delhi-based Muslim service gentry family which had served the Mughal court, he worked as a judicial officer for the English East India Company and sheltered British officers during the 1857 Indian rebellion. He founded the Western-style Muhammadan Anglo-Oriental College at Aligarh in north India in 1875 and was committed throughout his life to rapprochement between British and Muslims. This work ably considers his views on education and politics.

264 Gokhale: the Indian moderates and the British Raj.

Bal Ram Nanda.   Princeton, New Jersey: Princeton University Press, 1977. 520p. bibliog.

The biography of India's pre-eminent moderate nationalist, Gopal Krishna Gokhale (1866-1915), who believed in using constitutional means to gain political rights from the British. Nanda carefully follows Gokhale from his years as a poor student in late 19th-century Bombay province into nationalist politics and his various social reform and political activities. Written for the specialist, the book includes several rare photographs.

265 Rajiv Gandhi: son of a dynasty.

Nicholas Nugent.   London: BBC Books, 1990. 223p.

A competent biography of Rajiv Gandhi (1944-91), the eldest son of Indira Gandhi, who was reluctantly thrust into a political career after the assassination of his mother in October 1984. The author, a BBC correspondent in South Asia, describes Rajiv Gandhi's personality, evolving political philosophy, and the rise and fall in his fortunes during his period as Indian prime minister between 1984 and 1989. The book was written before its subject's assassination in May 1991 as he seemed poised for a return to high office. Covering Rajiv Gandhi's full career, *Rajiv Gandhi: the end of a dream* (New Delhi: Viking, 1992. 371p.), by Minhaz Merchant is a useful supplement.

266 Gandhi, Nehru, and J. P.: studies in leadership.

Bimal Prasad.   New Delhi: Chanakya, 1985. 294p. bibliog.

A study of three contrasting styles of political leadership and philosophy. The author sees Mahatma Gandhi's political significance resting, not in his role as a conciliator, but rather in his commitment to struggle, even if non-violent. Nehru's political ideology is portrayed as a synthesis of Western liberalism, Marxism, and Gandhi's teachings. Prasad is most penetrating in his analysis of J. P. Narayan (1902-79), drawing upon his earlier edited volume, *Jayaprakash Narayan: a revolutionary's quest: selected writings of Jayaprakash Narayan* (New Delhi: Oxford University Press India, 1980. 406p.).

267 Vallabhbhai Patel: power and organisation in Indian politics.

Rani Dhavan Shankardass.   London: Sangam Books, 1988. 325p. bibliog.

Sardar Vallabhbhai Patel (1875-1950), the Gujarat Patidar leader and first deputy prime minister of independent India, stood at the hub of the Indian National Congress for a quarter of a century. This work, rather than being a conventional biography, focuses on Patel's 'distinctive contribution to political organization and activity', for which he gained a reputation for ruthlessness in his pursuit of power. Much of the book is concerned with Patel's early political years and his close relationship with Mahatma Gandhi during the inter-war years.

268 My presidential years.

Ramaswami Venkataraman.   New Delhi: Indus, 1994. 671p.

In this, the first account of a period in office written by an Indian head of state, Ramaswami Venkataraman describes political events during his tenure of the largely ceremonial position of Indian president between 1987 and 1992. The period was one of crisis and controversy and Venkataraman was forced to deal with four prime ministers – Rajiv Gandhi, V. P. Singh, Chandra Shekhar, and P. V. Narasimha Rao. The book includes a revelation that a senior Congress Party member promised the president 240 MPs if he he would agree to replace Rajiv Gandhi as premier – an offer Venkataraman declined.

269 **Jinnah of Pakistan.**
    Stanley A. Wolpert.   Oxford; New York: Oxford University Press, 1984. 421p. 2 maps. bibliog.

A solid biography of the Karachi-born Muslim League leader and creator of Pakistan, M. A. Jinnah, which is more conventional in its analysis than the work of Jalal (see item no. 260). The author takes the reader through Jinnah's personal and political life, from his early days as a successful London-trained lawyer in Bombay, through the years of relative isolation between 1921 and 1934, to the final decades of intense activity. Roughly half the book is devoted to the period between the Muslim League's passing of the Pakistan Resolution in Lahore in March 1940 and Jinnah's death in 1948, when governor-general of the newly created Pakistan.

270 **Tilak and Gokhale: revolution and reform in the making of modern India.**
    Stanley A. Wolpert.   New Delhi: Oxford University Press India, 1989. 370p. bibliog.

A study of the contributions of India's two chief nationalist leaders before Mahatma Gandhi's post-First World War emergence. Gopal Krishna Gokhale (1866-1915) was a moderate who believed in using constitutional methods to gain Indian independence. Bal Gangadhar Tilak (1864-1920), on the other hand, chose the confrontational path. Wolpert carefully and objectively examines the motives and actions of both these leaders, both drawn from western India. The work was first published by the University of California Press in 1977.

Population and Urban India

General population and family planning

271 The census in British India: new perspectives.
Edited by N. Gerald Barrier.   New Delhi: Manohar, 1981. 234p.

A collection of eight scholarly essays on the uses and weaknesses of the decennial censuses undertaken in British India from the 1860s onwards. The editor provides a valuable introductory overview and Richard Martin a bibliographic chapter. In other excellent papers, the geographer, Joseph Schwartzberg, outlines types of census error; Frank Conlon discusses the value of census data as a source for histories of religion and caste; and Daniel Moore analyses the migration movements of Mysore plantation labourers between 1871 and 1941.

272 India: population, economy, society.
Robert H. Cassen.   London: Macmillan, 1978. 419p. bibliog.

A fascinating and comprehensive survey of India's population and its impact on the nation's economy and society. Following a brief introductory chapter, the second chapter looks at present and future characteristics of India's population – fertility, mortality and migration; the third deals with current and projected family planning programmes. In chapter four there is a lively discussion of the interrelationship between economic development and population change. The closing chapter includes reflections on the problems associated with population growth both in India and China. A useful glossary of demographic terms is provided. This volume is available in paperback.

273 **India's demography: essays on the contemporary population.**
Edited by Nigel Crook, Tim Dyson. New Delhi: South Asian
Publishers, 1984. 235p.

An outstanding collection of papers which had been presented by leading Indian and
Western demographers to an Oxford University symposium held to consider the
Indian population situation at the time of the 1981 census. The essays are arranged in
five sections concerned with the following topics: mortality and fertility levels and
trends; the results of regional sample surveys carried out in Bihar, Kerala and
Rajasthan; health policy; family planning; and village-level demography. At the time
of this volume's publication, India's population had already climbed to 700 million.
However, there were encouraging indications of declining infant mortality, and
fertility levels, and of a rise in life expectancy to around fifty years.

274 **India's historical demography: studies in famine, disease and
society.**
Edited by Tim Dyson. London: Curzon Press, 1989. 296p.

A collection of well-researched papers which reveal new trends and increasing
sophistication in the study of India's demographic history. The editor, in excellent
opening and closing chapters, delineates broad phases in India's population history
since the late 18th century and draws comparisons with Europe, China and Japan.
Topics covered in the remaining eight chapters include a detailed statistical analysis
of the devastating influenza epidemic of 1918-19 (Ian D. Mills), which claimed an
estimated seventeen million lives; cholera between 1817 and 1947 (David Arnold);
depopulation in rural Tamil Nadu between ca.1780 and ca.1830 (Roland Lardinois);
mortality, fertility, and the status of women between 1881 and 1931 (Alice W. Clark);
and the historical demography of Berar since 1881 (Tim Dyson). The work shows that
the long-held view that India has generally been characterized by high fertility is no
longer tenable: there is mounting evidence of conscious fertility choice. The foreword
to the volume is written by Kingsley Davis whose classic *The population of India and
Pakistan* (Princeton, New Jersey: Princeton University Press, 1951. 263p.), remains
an essential reference work.

275 **India's population policy: critical issues for the future.**
Edited by Sheo Kumar Lal, Ambika Chandani. Meerut, India:
Twenty-first Century Publishers, 1987. 189p.

An interdisciplinary collection of papers by Indian scholars presented to a seminar
held at the University of Jodhpur in 1985 and sponsored by the Family Planning
Association of India. The papers are arranged in four sections: national population
policy; family planning; population education; and population dynamics and national
development. A useful related work is *Marital power structure, fertility and family
planning in India* (London: Sangam Books, 1991. 174p.), by S. L. Sud.

276 **India's population: aspects of quality and control.**
Asok Mitra. New Delhi: Abhinav, 1978. 2 vols. bibliog.

The work's central thesis is that effective population control requires commitment to
an enhanced quality of life rather than high economic growth rates or great material
prosperity. Low infant mortality, female literacy, and employment opportunities
outside the home can all be accomplished within prevailing economic constraints.
However, it is imperative that there be a concerted effort to mount effective land

reforms so that gross inequalities are eliminated and scarce capital is freed for necessary investments in social overheads. Mitra blames both the bureaucracy and the intelligentsia for thwarting the required democratic decentralization along socialist lines. The work is a mine of information.

277   Population Review.
Madras: Indian Institute of Population Studies, 1957- . biannual.

Edited by the famous Indian demographer S. Chandrasekhar, this biannual contains articles on population problems, family planning, birth control, and other demographic issues in non-technical language for the informed public. The main emphasis of the articles is on India and Asia.

278   Population growth and poverty in rural South Asia.
Edited by Gerry Rodgers.   New Delhi: Sage Publications, 1989. 249p.

Specially prepared for the International Labour Office, this volume comprises five carefully researched empirical essays which study the relationship between population growth and rural poverty in the countries of South Asia. The demographic components of poverty are examined at both the macro and micro levels, including a household-level analysis in Bihar. The authors conclude that 'population growth is both a cause and a consequence of poverty', but also show that the poor have relatively low fertility and that large family-size is associated with less poverty.

279   Demographic challenge: a study of four large Indian states.
Edited by J. K. Satia, Shireen J. Jejeebhoy.   Bombay: Oxford University Press India, 1991. 268p. bibliog.

The four states of Bihar, Madhya Pradesh, Rajasthan and Uttar Pradesh, situated in northern and central India, are home to forty per cent of the population of all-India. During the last half century they have lagged behind the rest of the country in terms of such socio-economic and demographic criteria as levels of per capita GDP, rates of literacy, life expectancy, and the pace of fertility decline. This excellent study, which comprises papers by India's leading demographers, analyses research findings on recent demographic developments in the states. It concludes that trends have become more encouraging. Crude birth rates have declined since 1981, couple protection rates have increased, and the service delivery infrastructure has improved greatly.

Internal migration

280   Of peasants, migrants and paupers: rural labour circulation and capitalist production in west India.
Jan Breman.   New Delhi: Oxford University Press India, 1985. 472p. bibliog.

An impressive historical-anthropological study of rural labour relations and labour circulation in Gujarat which brings out the domination of labour by the owners of land and capital. The chief focus is the relationship between Patidar farmers and Halpati landless labourers in the central plain of Surat district, and the impact of migrant labour from the tribal hinterland to the east. Breman expertly delineates the agrarian social structure and its dynamics. He discusses changes in the *hali* system of tied agricultural labour, and the process of differentiation within tribal society, and analyses the push and pull factors which impel migration. Breman is also author of the brief *Labour migration and rural transformation in colonial Asia* (Amsterdam, the Netherlands: Free University Press, 1990. 82p.), which reviews international labour migration in 19th-century Asia.

281   **Internal migration in India: a case study of Bengal.**
Haraprasad Chattopadhyaya.   Calcutta: Bagchi, 1987. 551p. bibliog.
An example of the use of census reports for the study of internal migration in India with special reference to Bengal from the later 19th century to 1931. The author provides a careful analysis, distinguishing between different types of internal migration – casual, temporary, periodic, semi-permanent, and permanent, which is often marriage-related – the ages and sexes of those involved, and the various causes. A weakness of the work is the author's uncritical reliance on census data and categorizations.

282   **Men to Bombay, women at home: urban influence on Sugao village, Deccan Maharashtra, 1943-1982.**
Hemalata C. Dandekar.   Ann Arbor, Michigan: University of Michigan Press, 1986. 325p. maps. bibliog.
A vivid and sympathetic study of Sugao, a Deccani village, and its linkages, via migration, to the outside world, specifically to Bombay city. The analysis is based on fieldwork conducted between 1976 and 1982. The author shows that in 1977, with population pressure on agricultural holdings acute, nearly half of the village's adult males earned their livings outside. In Bombay migrants from the village live together in distinct neighbourhoods and use family connections in their quest for employment – hence better off villagers are able to secure better paid city jobs. Residence in the city is conceived as a temporary expedient, although it may continue for thirty years. The absence of menfolk has impacted upon the role played within village society by women. This is also noted in *In the absence of their men: the impact of male migration on women* (New Delhi: Sage Publications, 1993. 174p.), by Leela Gulati.

283   **Causes and consequences of internal migration: a study in the Indian Punjab.**
A. S. Oberai, H. K. Manmohan Singh.   New Delhi: Oxford University Press India, 1983. 434p. maps. bibliog.
A detailed study of the determinants and socio-economic implications of internal migration in contemporary India written by an economist and an econometrician. The work is based on primary data generated in household surveys which were conducted during 1977 in the green revolution belt of the Indian Punjab, specifically in the city of Ludhiana and twenty-six of the district's villages. The authors provide migrant profiles, analyse the perceptions, expectations and experiences of migrants, study remittance flows, and look at the effects of migration on agricultural production, population growth and rural-urban income distribution.

284 **Determinants and consequences of internal migration in India: studies in Bihar, Kerala and Uttar Pradesh.**
A. S. Oberai, Pradhan H. Prasad, M. G. Sardhana. New Delhi: Oxford University Press India, 1989. 156p. bibliog.

This study, prepared for the International Labour Organization, complements item no. 283 by examining the processes and consequences of internal migration in three states which are less developed than Punjab. The findings reinforce those of the authors' 1977 Ludhiana study, demonstrating that migration can generate benefits for migrants and for both their areas of origin and destination. However, an important fresh finding is that the lower the level of rural and infrastructural development the smaller are the gains which accrue from migration. The authors advocate programmes to reduce urban-rural differentials in order to stem the flow of cityward migration.

285 **Studies in migration: internal and international migration in India.**
Edited by M. S. A. Rao. New Delhi: Manohar, 1986. 400p.

A collection of twelve interdisciplinary conference papers, three by the late M. S. A. Rao, on various facets of migration within and from India in the past and contemporary world. All-India migration patterns and motivations are examined by M. K. Premi, K. L. Narayan and K. Sundaram, utilizing 1971 census and 1973-74 National Sample Survey data. There are also chapters on rural-rural migration in Karnataka; migration by the tribal peoples of Chota Nagpur and the Santal Parganas to the Assam tea plantations and West Bengal; and Indian emigration to South Africa (T. R. Metcalf) and southern England (A. W. Helweg).

286 **Sons of the soil: migration and ethnic conflict in India.**
Myron Weiner. Princeton, New Jersey: Princeton University Press, 1978. 383p. maps. bibliog.

This book examines a fundamental problem facing many multi-ethnic federal states of the third world: the right of free interstate migration versus the rights of the local population. Three case studies, of Assam, of the Chota Nagpur region of Bihar, and of Hyderabad, are the context for a brilliant analysis of the rise of 'nativist' movements, the costs and benefits of free migration, and the impact of ethnic conflicts on national identity.

Urbanization

287 **The city in South Asia.**
Edited by Kenneth Ballhatchet, John Harrison. London: Curzon Press, 1980. 342p. map.

This edited volume comprises thirteen published seminar papers by Western and Indian historians and demographers. A wide range of topics are covered, but the primary emphasis is on the 19th and 20th centuries. There are papers on colonialism and the development of the modern Asian city (Anthony D. King), Delhi (Percival

Spear), a north Indian small Islamic gentry town (Christopher A. Bayly), Allahabad (J. Harrison), Calcutta (J. McGuire), Lucknow (S. Ganju and R. Llewellyn-Jones), and Murshidabad (K. M. Mohsin). A complementary volume of sixteen essays is *The city in Indian history: urban demography, society and politics* (New Delhi: Manohar, 1991. 300p.), edited by Indu Banga.

288   Simla: a hill station in British India.
Patt Barr, Ray G. C. Desmond.   London: The Scholar Press, 1978. 108p. map.

The story of Simla, the hill station perched on a 7,000 feet spur of the lower Himalayas north of Delhi, which served as the summer capital of British India between 1864 and 1947. Here, in an alien setting, the English spa concept was implanted and the values and customs of the colonial community were reinforced at official ceremonies and social events attended by the European élite.

289   India's urbanization, 1901-2001.
Ashish Bose.   New Delhi: Tata McGraw-Hill, 1978. 567p. maps. bibliog.

A reliable and comprehensive analysis of trends in Indian urbanization between 1901 and 1971 and projected developments for the period to 2000. The author, India's most accomplished urban demographer, provides plentiful data on divergent trends in urban growth at the state level, and in terms of size categories of urban centres.

290   Urbanisation in India.
Robert W. Bradnock.   London: John Murray, 1984. 58p. maps. (Case Studies in the Developing World).

A succinct college text which sets out the historical pattern, causes and future prospects for urbanization in India and includes case studies of Madras and Hyderabad.

291   India's industrial cities: essays in economy and demography.
Nigel Crook.   New Delhi: Oxford University Press India, 1993. 181p. bibliog. (SOAS Studies on South Asia).

An informed analysis of recent urbanization in India which focuses on newer cities which have a predominantly industrial character, notably steel cities such as Bhilainagar and Durgapur. Crook reviews patterns of recruitment and migration to these centres, utilizing data from the 1961 census, and looks at population, health and housing policies.

292   Urbanisation in early historic India.
George Erdosy.   Oxford: BAR International, 1988. 211p. maps. bibliog. (BAR International Series, no. 430).

An important study of the rise of urbanism in the Gangetic Valley region of north India, focusing on the Allahabad region in eastern Uttar Pradesh. The author shows Ganges urbanism to have been a gradual indigenous development beginning around 1000 BC, with city formations emerging between 600-350 BC. Drawing upon both archaeological and literary data, Erdosy traces the development of settlement hierarchies, charting the spread of locations from the river bank to the interior. He ascribes urbanization to the change from relatively primitive chiefdoms to centralized polities with complex administrative and economic functions as tensions developed between the indigenous inhabitants of the region and the incoming Indo-Aryans.

293   The Indian metropolis: a view towards the West.

Norma Evenson.   New Haven, Connecticut: Yale University Press, 1989. 294p. bibliog.

A survey of the urban and architectural histories of the cities of Madras, Calcutta, Bombay and New Delhi over the last three centuries, focusing on urban space and planning, and economic, social and cultural conditions. The author provides brief histories of the indigenous older cities and then describes how new planned Western-influenced cities were constructed during the colonial period. Particularly interesting are Evenson's discussions of the construction process, of Western architecture as an acculturating device, and of urban planning philosophies.

294   Delhi through the ages: essays in urban history, culture and society.

Edited by Robert Eric Frykenberg.   New Delhi: Oxford University Press India, 1986. 524p. maps. bibliog.

A collection of excellent essays, some of which originated as 1979 conference papers, covering various facets of Delhi's architectural, political, social, cultural, and economic history. A. K. Narain's opening paper relates Delhi's protohistory, and the remaining essays cover a seven century span from the emergence of the Sultanate in the early 13th century to the mid-20th century late British Raj. Particularly interesting are the papers by Stephen Blake on Shahjahanabad, Percival Spear on Delhi as a 'stop-go' capital, Satish Chandra on Delhi's political and cultural role, and M. Athar Ali on Delhi during the Sultanate era.

295   Cities of Mughal India: Delhi, Agra and Fatehpur Sikri.

Gavin Hambly, photographs by Wim Swaan.   New Delhi: Vikas, 1977. 168p. maps. bibliog.

During the 16th and 17th centuries, standing at the zenith of their political and economic power, the Mughal emperors rebuilt the cities of Delhi, Agra, Fatehpur Sikri, and Lahore, to provide the setting for a brilliant court life, the envy of Europe. Hambly's lavishly illustrated volume delineates urban and court life and shows the extent to which the Mughals were great patrons of the arts. The author's text also sheds considerable light on the daily life of the Mughal emperors and the members of their court. It can be complemented by the more detailed works of Stephen P. Blake, *Shahjahanabad: the sovereign city in Mughal India, 1639-1739* (Cambridge: Cambridge University Press, 1991. 226p.), Ishwar Prakash Gupta, *Urban glimpses of Mughal India: Agra, the imperial capital (16th & 17th centuries)* (New Delhi: Discovery Publishing House, 1986. 159p.), and the volume edited by Michael Brand and Glenn D. Lowry, *Fatehpur Sikri* (Bombay: Marg Publications, 1987. 204p.).

296 **Rhetoric and ritual in colonial India: the shaping of a public culture in Surat city, 1852-1928.**
Douglas E. Haynes.   Berkeley, California: University of California Press, 1991. 363p. bibliog.

An innovative work which applies the perspective of ethnohistory to the emergence of Surat's political culture during the colonial period. The author shows how the city's Indian élite assimilated and mastered the discourse of liberal representation in their interactions with the British and how a public culture took shape which excluded the underclasses from genuine participation. The work should be read in conjunction with Anthony D. King's more general, classic work, *Colonial urban development: culture, social power and the environment* (London: Routledge & Kegan Paul, 1976. 328p.).

297 **Bombay in transition: the growth and social ecology of a colonial city, 1880-1980.**
Meera Kosambi.   Stockholm: Almqvist & Wiksell International, 1986. 204p.

A case study of Bombay's spatial growth and social development during the period from 1880 to 1980, examining population changes and also ethnic and linguistic groups and the location of their settlements. Census data is used to analyse trends in occupational patterns, the age and sex composition of the population, and the port city's changing economic links with its hinterland.

298 **A fatal friendship: the Nawabs, the British and the city of Lucknow.**
Rosie Llewellyn-Jones.   New Delhi: Oxford University Press India, 1985. 285p. bibliog.

A fascinating account of the north Indian city of Lucknow from the time that Nawab Asaf ud-Daula, head of the post-Mughal Muslim successor state of Awadh (Oudh), established his capital there until the British annexation of the province in 1856. The author recreates the mode of life in the city, describes its architectural glories, and analyses its position at the meeting point during this period of Eastern and Western cultures.

299 **Studies in Indian urban development.**
Edwin Smith Mills, Charles M. Becker, with a contribution by Satyendra Verma.   New York: Oxford University Press, 1986. 214p.

A World Bank-sponsored study of urban development in India carried out by two American economists. The work identifies historical trends and regional differences in Indian urbanization and makes comparisons with the experience of other developing countries. It also reviews growth trends for different size categories of urban centres and the effects of government programmes to influence the pattern of urban development. In chapter five there is a case study of urbanization in Madhya Pradesh, measuring the effects of migration. A feature of the volume is the application of economic theory and the construction of mathematical models. Mills and Becker, along with Jeffrey Gale Williamson, have also produced a useful supplementary monograph, *Indian urbanization and economic growth since 1960* (Baltimore, Maryland: Johns Hopkins University Press, 1992. 328p.).

300 **Million cities of India.**
Edited by R. P. Misra. New Delhi: Vikas, 1978. 405p. bibliog.

A careful historical and geographic survey of the emergence of the nine cities in India which had a population in excess of one million at the time of the 1971 census: Ahmedabad, Bangalore, Bombay, Calcutta, Delhi, Hyderabad, Kanpur, Madras and Poona. A separate chapter is devoted to each city. In addition, two introductory and two concluding chapters synthesize the findings from individual studies and reflect on problems associated with the rise of the megalopolis in India.

301 **Calcutta.**
Geoffrey Moorhouse. Harmondsworth, England: Penguin, 1986. new ed. 400p. maps. bibliog.

A historical portrait of the second largest city in the British empire and the fourth largest city in the world, which served as the administrative capital of the Raj until 1911. Moorhouse uses Calcutta to portray how the British empire was created in India, and what happened to India when the empire ended. The picture painted is of a city both monstrous and marvellous, violent and yet cultured, a child of the industrial revolution yet the most representative of the third world. Moorhouse's popular, accessible work can be supplemented by *Calcutta – the living city* (Calcutta: Oxford University Press India, 1990. 2 vols.), edited by Sukanta Chaudhuri, a collection of illustrated, scholarly essays on the city's history, growth, culture and development, from its foundation in 1690 to the present day.

302 **Agricultural, industrial and urban dynamism under the Sultans of Delhi, 1206-1555.**
Hameeda Khatoon Naqvi. New Delhi: Munshiram Manoharlal, 1986. 205p. bibliog.

This volume provides an up-to-date, revisionist analysis of urban development and economic growth during the era of the Delhi Sultanate. The picture presented is one of 'urban upturn' related to innovations in craft production and increased cash-cropping and long-distance commercial exchanges. This provided the basis for the highpoint in premodern Indian urbanization which was reached during the Mughal era, when as many as a sixth of the population may have lived in urban centres. Naqvi is the author of a valuable earlier narrative history of Mughal urbanization: *Urbanisation and urban centres under the Great Mughals: an essay in interpretation* (Simla: Indian Institute of Advanced Study, 1971. 197p.).

303 **Cities, crafts and commerce under the Kusanas.**
Kameshwar Prasad. New Delhi: Agam Kala Prakashan, 1984. 202p. bibliog.

This interesting work details the growth in urban centres, craft industries and the arts during the early centuries of the Christian era as a Kusana empire, spanning between Bihar and Central Asia, became established. The author's analysis is based on careful use of archaeological and literary evidence and details the many functions, commercial, craft industrial, administrative, and religio-cultural, performed by cities during this period. The general overview of urban growth in ancient India provided in the introductory chapter can be supplemented by the detailed work of Vijay Kumar Thakur, *Urbanisation in ancient India* (New Delhi: Abhinav, 1981. 368p.).

304   **Urbanization and urban systems in India.**
        R. Ramachandran.   New Delhi: Oxford University Press India, 1991.
        364p. maps.

An original study of the process of urbanization in India from earliest times to the present day. Written from a geographical perspective, the author provides a brief history of Indian urbanization, but devotes the bulk of the text to an analysis of macro patterns of urbanization and to descriptions of settlement systems and rural-urban linkages. The problems of overcrowding and unplanned growth are recognized and the hope is expressed that the development of smaller cities and towns may provide some relief.

305   **Urbanization in India: spatial dimensions.**
        V. L. S. Prakasa Rao.   New Delhi: Concept, 1983. 327p. bibliog.

An excellent conceptual and empirical work by India's foremost urban geographer which looks at both the spatial pattern of India's process of urbanization and the internal structure of Indian cities. Section one examines macro aspects of recent urbanization. This reveals growth to have been very unbalanced both regionally and in terms of urban settlement size classes. Regional urban hierarchies are also plotted, drawing upon central-place system theories. Section two, on city spatial structures, draws heavily upon Prakasa Rao's detailed studies of the fast-growing south Indian metropolis of Bangalore.

306   **Urban decay in India (c. 300 – c. 1000).**
        Ram Sharan Sharma.   New Delhi: Munshiram Manoharlal, 1987.
        235p. maps. bibliog.

Stimulated by the author's earlier researches on Indian feudalism (see item no. 145), this volume analyses the process of urban degeneration which, according to Sharma, was experienced in north India from the 5th century AD – during the Gupta dynasty's supposed 'golden age'. Sharma draws upon recent archaeological data pertaining to more than 130 sites and also literary and epigraphic sources. The volume is arranged on regional lines, with separate chapters devoted to urban development in the north, the middle Gangetic plains and east India, central and western India, and the south. The author links urban decay to the emergence of a new pattern of production marked by agrarian expansion, the emergence of landed magnates, and the remuneration of service and artisan castes through land grants as the exchange economy atrophied.

307   **Mathura: the cultural heritage.**
        Edited by Doris Meth Srinivasan.   Columbia, Missouri: South Asia
        Books and the American Institute of Indian Studies, 1989. 405p.

A collection of conference papers presented in 1980 by Western and Indian specialists from a wide range of disciplines: history, sociology, economics, religious studies, numismatics, archaeology, linguistics and literature, epigraphy, art and iconography. The theme of the work is the important place of Mathura (Muttra), a city situated in north India on the Yamuna (Jumna) river, in India's 'second urbanism' between ca. 500 BC and 300 AD. (The 'first urbanism' occurred in the Harappan civilization of the second millennium BC). Mathura was a centre for Buddhism, Hinduism and Jainism and performed a variety of administrative, commercial and religio-cultural roles.

308 **City of gold: the biography of Bombay.**
Gillian Tindall.   Harmondsworth, England: Penguin, 1992. new ed.
210p. bibliog.

An evocative history of the growth of Bombay, India's most cosmopolitan city, in the 18th and 19th centuries. According to Tindall, Indians and Europeans alike flocked to Bombay to make their fortunes and to participate in the benefits of the industrial revolution and Western culture. The position of women, the growth of cultural institutions, the construction of palatial houses, and the emergence of the modern tradition in Indian journalism are described, with emphasis on the contributions of a host of prominent individuals. Originally published in 1982, the book is now available as a Penguin paperback. This includes a new introduction, reviewing changes in the city during the 1980s, but omits the photographs contained in the earlier hardback edition.

Minorities and Tribal Communities

General

309 **Ethnicity and nation-building in South Asia.**
Urmila Phadnis. New Delhi: Sage Publications, 1989. 328p. bibliog.
An appraisal of the dynamics of ethnic identity and an analysis of ethnic movements in the states of South Asia in a comparative framework. The text includes five case studies of autonomist-secessionist manifestations of ethno-nationalism.

310 **'Minorities' on themselves.**
Edited by Hugh Van Skyhawk. Stuttgart, Germany: Franz Steiner Verlag, 1985. 212p. (South Asian Digest of Regional Writing, no. 2).
A collection of eleven papers presented at a 1985 seminar at Heidelberg University which discussed the self-images found in the literatures of South Asian minority communities. The 'minorities' comprise religious groups (Virasaivas, Christians, Muslims, Sikhs, Buddhists, and Jains), Indian expatriates (Singapore Tamilians), and peoples of peripheral regions (Garhvalis).

The Anglo-Indian community

311 **Anglo-Indians: a historical survey of Anglo Indian community in 19th century India.**
Lal Bahadur Varma. New Delhi: Bhasha Prakashan, 1979. 228p. bibliog.
Focusing on the 19th century, this work surveys the origin and emergence of the Anglo-Indian community and its economic, social and political life. The connecting

theme running through the volume is the community's uncertainty of and search for a clear identity and status within colonial society.

312 Anglo-Indians: neglected children of the Raj.
Coralie Younger. New Delhi: BR Publishing, 1987. 196p. bibliog.

Based on interviews with Anglo-Indians living in Bangalore city and Australia, this work captures the attitudes and lifestyles of the community during the British Raj and after. Younger shows how prejudice imposed severe psychological pressures on this mixed race community who were placed in a buffer position between two dominant groups, the British ruling élite and the Indian masses. The text is divided chronologically between the periods 1919-47 and 1947-83 and includes chapters on Anglo-Indian employment, social relations, sexual mores, and politics.

Tribal peoples

313 The hour of the fox: tropical forests, the World Bank, and indigenous people in central India.
Robert S. Anderson, Walter Huber. Seattle, Washington: University of Washington Press, 1988. 158p. 2 maps. bibliog.

A compelling analysis of the plight of tribal peoples in the central Indian state of Madhya Pradesh as a consequence of deforestation and major World Bank-funded irrigation projects which have led to the displacement of the tribal population.

314 Tribalism in India.
Kamaladevi Chattopadhyay. New Delhi: Vikas, 1978. 302p.

A popular account of tribal life intended for the lay reader, based on the experiences of the author who lived with various tribes while helping them to develop their crafts. There are essays on nineteen different tribes from almost all parts of India. Chattopadhyay believes that, in spite of many surface differences, tribal life throughout different areas of India is the same – with a high degree of psycho-social integration, high standards of craftsmanship, the blending of the sacred and the profane, and complex kinship systems.

315 Tribal women in India.
Pratap C. Dutta (and others). Calcutta: Indian Anthropological Society, 1978. 199p. bibliog.

A collection of essays by Indian anthropologists, written in popular style, this book covers a wide range of variations in the life and activities of tribal women throughout India. Tribal women as coal miners, industrial workers, agricultural labourers, and food gatherers are discussed. Other chapters deal with tribal women's involvement in politics. In another chapter, 'Beautiful, hardy and wealthy yet weak and exploited', nomadic women are described. Included are several profiles of tribal women.

316 **Tribal guerrillas: the Santals of West Bengal and the Naxalite movement.**
Edward Duyker. New Delhi: Oxford University Press India, 1987. 201p. bibliog.

A lucid history of the Santals, tribals of south Bihar, the background to the communist-inspired Naxalite insurgency of 1967 to 1971, and Santal participation within the rebellion. The author provides a brief description of the evolution of the Santals from a slash-and-burn communal society to a landless group of sharecroppers who migrated to clear jungles in various parts of Bengal. He also notes the ability of the Naxalites to tie Santal tradition, notably the millenarianist rebellion of 1855, to their contemporary insurgency.

317 **The kingdom of the young: abridged from *The Muria and their ghotul*.**
Verrier Elwin. Bombay: Oxford University Press India, 1968. 261p. maps. bibliog.

This is the author's abridgement of his 1947 definitive study of the Muria Gond tribe of central India. In the *ghotul* or youth dormitory, all boys and girls live together and are socialized into adult psycho-sexual life. Elwin discusses the membership rites, discipline, recreation, sexual attitudes, moral standards, and marriage of this tribal community, especially its young. The life story of the Oxford-educated Elwin, who, influenced by Gandhi, devoted his life to studying, working among, and serving India's tribal communities, is reproduced in his *The tribal world of Verrier Elwin: an autobiography* (New York: Oxford University Press USA, 1964. 356p.). A new reprint of *The Muria and their ghotul* (New Delhi: Oxford University Press India, 1991. 730p.), along with, *Leaves from the jungle: life in a Gond village* (New Delhi: Oxford University Press India, 1993. new ed. 200p.), are now available.

318 **The aboriginal tribes of India.**
Stephen Fuchs. New York: St. Martin's Press, 1977. 308p.

An introductory survey and description of the tribal communities of India designed for the non-specialist. It comprises a chapter on prehistory and on the contemporary racial and ethnographic tribal situation, five chapters describing tribes in detail by region, and a concluding chapter on tribal work. The work is old-fashioned in its style and content, drawing heavily on colonial linguistic surveys, census reports and 'tribes and castes' volumes, and uses a somewhat crude and obsolete evolutionary framework to arrange tribes on a scale from less to more 'advanced'. Despite these defects, it usefully presents data on the geographic location and basic ethnography of various tribal peoples. It can be read alongside *The tribals of India* (New Delhi: Oxford University Press India, 1994. 144p.), by Sunil Janah, which documents tribal life across India as recorded during the author's thirty-year sojourn in various tribal villages.

319 **The Santals, a tribe in search of a great tradition.**
Martin Orans.   Detroit, Michigan: Wayne State University Press,
1965. 149p. bibliog.

An account of the shifting historical pressures for and against acculturation and
assimilation, and of the impact of a spreading market economy and industrialization
on the Santal tribe of eastern India. Based on fieldwork on Santal migrants to the
industrial town of Jamshedpur, the book examines the role of the 'great tradition'
(those elements of Indian civilization that have persisted almost all over the
subcontinent over an enormously long period of time) in modifying the 'little
tradition' (elements that are local, fleeting, and accepted only by particular groups),
but without totally destroying the distinctiveness of a tribal culture.

320 **Tribal movements in India.**
Edited by K. S. Singh.   New Delhi: Manohar, 1982-83. 2 vols. maps.
bibliog.

The author is a member of the Indian Administrative Service, who, having studied
backward communities in central India, became director of the Anthropological
Survey of India (ASI) and was placed in charge of the planning of all-India surveys
designed to profile tribal society. These volumes comprise papers presented at an ASI
workshop in 1976. Volume one focuses on tribal movements in northeast India,
including the Nagas, Khasis and campaigns in Assam and Manipur. Volume two
includes papers on movements elsewhere, including, most notably, the movement to
establish a state in Jharkhand.

321 **The tribal culture of India.**
Lalita Prasad Vidyarthi, B. K. Rai.   New Delhi: Concept, 1977. 487p.
maps. bibliog.

A well-written survey of Indian tribal life. Topics covered include tribal dimensions
of the civilization of India, tribal economic, political, religious, and kinship
structures, tribal art and folklore, settlement patterns of various Indian tribes, and
cultural changes induced in tribal areas by government-sponsored programmes. There
is also a fascinating chapter on the growth of Indian anthropological studies, first
under British influence, and lately (since 1950) under American influence.

322 **Tribal populations and cultures of the Indian subcontinent.**
Christoph Von Fürer-Haimendorf.   Leiden, the Netherlands:
E. J. Brill, 1985. 182p.

An excellent introductory overview of the cultural and ethnic homogeneity of India's
tribal peoples by an anthropologist whose observations began in 1936. The author
presents a cross section of tribal cultures, providing brief accounts of thirty-one
distinctive communities, eighteen of which are based on personal research. A
complementary volume by the author, with contributions from Michael Yorke and
Jayaprakash Rao, is *Tribes of India: the struggle for survival* (Berkeley, California:
University of California Press, 1989. new ed. 342p.). This touches on the issue of
government and tribal relations, including land issues and forest policy, and on
relations with non-tribals.

323 **The Todas of south India: a new look.**
Anthony R. Walker.   New Delhi: Hindustan Publishing Corp., 1986.
371p. maps. bibliog.

A study of the Todas of the Nilgiri Hills, which, based on the author's fieldwork between 1962 and 1981, updates the classic monograph on the community, William Halse R. Rivers' *The Todas* (London: Macmillan, 1906). Walker provides an account of the Todas' buffalo dairy cult and life cycle, a social history of the community from 1819 to 1981, focusing on changing marriage and kinship structures and employment patterns, and discusses the impact of British colonial land legislation and missionary activities.

Muslim communities.
See item nos. 420-33.

Indians Abroad

324 Hinduism in Great Britain: the perpetuation of religion in an alien cultural milieu.
Edited by Richard Burghart.   London: Tavistock, 1987. 290p. map. bibliog.

A collection of papers on the Indian community in contemporary Britain and its practice of Hinduism. These show the strength of the Hindu faith, there being more than a hundred Hindu temples in Britain today, but also the diversity of its traditions of thought and practice. An excellent bibliography is provided by Helen Kanitkar and there are specialist papers on Gujarati Hindu organizations in Bradford, the development of the Sathya Sai Baba movement, the fortunes of the Ramakrishna Mission, and the Indianization of IKSON (International Society for Krishna Consciousness). For Sikhism in Britain, see *Sikhs in England* (New Delhi: Oxford University Press India, 1987. 2nd ed. 282p.), by Arthur W. Helweg, which comprises a detailed study of the contemporary Sikh community of Gravesend.

325 South Asians overseas: migration and ethnicity.
Edited by Colin Clarke, Ceri Peach, Steven Vertovec.   Cambridge: Cambridge University Press, 1990. 395p. 7 maps.

A collection of conference papers on the Indian diaspora, presented at Oxford University in 1987. The work is divided into two main sections. The first, covering migration in colonial and post-colonial contexts, includes papers by H. Tinker (on Burma), S. Vertovec (Trinidad), M. Twaddle (East Africa), and J. Beall (Natal), and on Indians in Fiji, South Africa, and the French colonies. Part two covers contemporary migration streams to the West and to the Middle East. Six of the eight papers here deal with the UK experience. The volume, while setting out recent research findings, also includes concise and useful general and thematic introductions for the non-specialist. A recent work concerning one area not covered by this volume is *Turbans and traders: Hong Kong's Indian communities* (New Delhi: Oxford University Press India, 1994. 256p.), by Barbara-Sue White.

326   **Passage from India: Asian Indian immigrants in North America.**
Joan Jensen.   New Haven, Connecticut; London: Yale University
Press, 1988. 350p. bibliog.

This study examines the phenomenon of Indian migration into North America at the
turn of the century. Drawn predominantly from Punjab, and comprising mainly Sikhs,
the Indians settled in California and Canada's west coast, working initially, alongside
Japanese, Chinese and Koreans as *coolie* labourers on the expanding railroads. They
faced mounting white hostility and were often targets of mob violence and
exclusionist legislation. This drew the Indian community closer together and resulted
in the formation of sometimes militant and anti-imperialist Indian organizations. Only
after the Second World War were anti-Asian immigration codes gradually dismantled,
leading to the number of South Asians in the United States exploding from 76,000 in
1970 to nearly a million today. The contemporary Indian community in the US,
specifically Atlanta, and its family, economic, religious and cultural life, is reviewed
in John Y. Fenton's *Transplanting religious traditions: Asian Indians in America*
(New York: Praeger, 1988. 270p.).

327   **Migration, remittances and capital flow: the Indian experience.**
Deepak Nayyar.   New Delhi: Oxford University Press India, 1994.
148p. bibliog.

A sophisticated analysis of the profile of labour migration from India, its macro-
economic impact, and the significance of associated financial flows for the national
economy.

328   **Roma: the Panjabi emigrants in Europe, central and middle Asia,
the USSR and the Americas.**
Weer Rajendra Rishi.   Patiala, India: Punjabi University, 1976. 119p.
maps. bibliog.

Based on a close study of etymology, linguistics, material culture, religious beliefs
and practices, and historical evidence, the author validates the widely accepted belief
that the gypsies, or Roma, are of Punjabi origin, most of them descending from
Punjabis escaping the Muslim invaders of India.

329   **The banyan tree: overseas emigrants from India, Pakistan, and
Bangladesh.**
Hugh Tinker.   New York: Oxford University Press, 1977. 204p. bibliog.

A survey of South Asian expatriates in fifty-three countries of the world. Tinker, a
former director of the Institute of Race Relations in Britain, points out that South
Asians have a poor share in the political power of the countries of their adoption
irrespective of their number or economic power. He considers multiracialism as
possible in Malaysia, but impossible in East and South Africa. The study's conclusion
is pessimistic: Indians appear to be doomed to second-class status as citizens abroad
due both to their refusal to integrate and to the suspicion of the majority towards
Indians in the diaspora. This work builds upon Tinker's earlier volume, *A new system
of slavery: the export of Indian labour overseas, 1830-1920* (London: Hansib
Publishing, 1993. 2nd rev. ed. 434p.), first published in 1974, which surveys the
export of Indian indentured labour to the plantations of Mauritius, South and East
Africa, the Caribbean, Sri Lanka, Fiji, and Malaysia during the 19th century.

330 *Ayahs, lascars* **and princes: Indians in Britain 1700-1947.**
Rozina Visram.   London: Pluto Press, 1986. 304p. bibliog.

A fascinating account of the changing experiences of Indians working and living in Britain over the course of two and a half centuries. They came as students, professionals, sailors (the *lascars* who kept the British merchant fleet moving), servants to British families returning from India, and soldiers (during the two World Wars). Their contribution and experiences were varied. Duleep Singh became squire of Elvedon Hall in East Anglia and Dadabhai Naoroji the first Asian MP at Westminster in 1892. Others returned home as even more committed nationalists, having seen British society 'warts and all' and experienced its class, race and sex distinctions.

Languages

General

331 **The Indianization of English: the English language in India.**
Braj B. Kachru.   New Delhi: Oxford University Press India, 1983.
280p. maps. bibliog.
'Indian English', spoken by more than eighteen million people, including the economic, industrial, professional and political élite, is a vitally significant language. This volume brings together important papers written on the topic by Braj Kachru, an authority on Indian linguistics. The work examines the motives and processes which have resulted in Indianization, that is the acculturation, or 'nativization', of the English language in the subcontinent. Included are chapters on Indian English vocabulary and other non-native Englishes, revealing characteristics shared with West African and Caribbean English.

332 **South Asian languages: structure, convergence and diglossia.**
Edited by B. H. Krishnamurti, Colin P. Masica, Anjani K. Sinha.
New Delhi: Motilal Banarsidass, 1986. 390p.
A collection of thirty selected papers presented by Western and Asian scholars to a 1980 international conference on South Asian languages and linguistics. The volume is divided into three parts arranged around the themes of structure, convergence, and diglossia (the coexistence of high, or socially prestigious, and low varieties of a language).

333 **South Asian languages: a handbook.**
Edited by Christopher Shackle. London: School of Oriental and African Studies, External Services Division, 1985. 62p. 6 maps. bibliog.

A short, accessible guide to South Asian languages produced by staff at London University's School of Oriental and African Studies. A brief history and description of each language and its script is provided and there is also a review of literature and the language's current position. This work can be read in conjunction with *Languages of South Asia: a guide* (London: Routledge & Kegan Paul, 1982. 231p.), by G. A. Zograph (translated by G. L. Campbell), which describes the phonology and morphology of Indian languages.

334 **People of India: languages and scripts, Vol. IX.**
Edited by K. S. Singh, S. Manoharan. New Delhi: Oxford University Press India, 1994. 450p.

This work, part of the 'People of India' project (see item no. 42), sets out the distribution of India's different language families and analyses the spread of regional languages such as Hindi, Urdu, Telugu, and Marathi.

335 **English in Indian bilingualism.**
Kamal K. Sridhar. New Delhi: Manohar, 1989. 177p. bibliog.

This slim volume brings together ten recent studies of the role of English in India by an American-based Indian linguist. As Sridhar notes, India, with its ethnic and linguistic diversity, is a classic field for the study of bilingualism. Over the centuries, pan-Indian élites have used a series of 'link languages'. Since the early 19th century English has performed this role. Today a sixth of the Indian population is bilingual, though bilingualism in English is a predominantly urban, middle class phenomenon. This work blends together linguistic theory and empirical studies, in the state of Karnataka in southern India and among the Kannada-speaking community in New York.

336 **Sanskrit studies of M. B. Emeneau: selected papers.**
Edited by B. A. Van Nooten. Berkeley, California: University of California Press, 1988. 213p. (Occasional Paper, no. 13).

A selection of literary, philological, and linguistic Sanskrit studies written between 1939 and 1980 by the eminent Indologist, Murray B. Emeneau. Included are papers on Indian literature and textual interpretation and studies of Indo-Aryan linguistics, primarily etymologies (origins of words), as well as essays on dialectal variations and onomastics. In the foreword, Emeneau sketches the scholarly and autobiographical context in which the papers originated.

Grammars

337 Tamil.

R. E. Asher. London: Croom Helm, 1985. 265p. (Croom Helm Descriptive Grammars).

Part of a series of descriptive grammars, this work is more accessible, though less scholarly, than the classic traditional grammar of Albert H. Arden, *A progressive grammar of the Tamil language* (Madras: Christian Literature Society, 1976. 5th rev ed. 342p.), revised by A. C. Clayton. Other titles in the *Croom Helm* series include: *Punjabi* (London: Routledge, 1989. 300p.), by T. Bhatia; *Marathi* (London: Routledge, 1989. 300p.), by R. Pandharipande; and *Kannada* (London: Routledge, 1990. 349p.), by S. N. Sridhar.

338 A Marathi reference grammar.

Maxine Berntsen, Jai Nimbkar. Philadelphia: University of Pennsylvania, South Asia Regional Studies, 1975. 206p.

Prepared originally for American Peace Corps volunteers, this is a carefully designed volume setting forth the basic grammatical rules of Marathi. The introductory chapters deal with the Marathi sound system and the Devanagari script, and they are followed by a discussion of the parts of speech and an explanation of sentence structures. For closely related Konkani, a useful work is *A Konkani grammar* (New Delhi: Asian Educational Services, 1986. 439p.), by A. F. X. Maffei.

339 A history of the Hindi grammatical tradition: Hindi-Hindustani grammar, grammarians, history and problems.

Tej K. Bhatia. Leiden, the Netherlands: E. J. Brill, 1987. 229p.

This work is the first real attempt to trace the development of the Hindi grammatical tradition from 1698 to the present day. In what is a broadly chronological approach, Bhatia gives special attention to the linguistic, sociolinguistic (attitudes of grammarians) and pedagogical situation in India during the past three centuries. Over 400 grammars are analysed, including the key works of John Gilchrist (1796) and the Rev. S. H. Kellogg (1876/1893), as well as a number of unpublished and hitherto 'lost' grammars. A related work is *A house divided: the origin and development of Hindi-Urdu* (New Delhi: Oxford University Press India, 1991. new ed. 322p.), by Amrit Rai.

340 A progressive grammar of the Malayalam language.

Ludwig Johannes Fröhnmeyer. New Delhi: Asian Educational Services, 1979. 2nd rev. ed. 366p.

Originally published in 1913, this is a pedagogical (instructional) and reference grammar. There are twenty-one lessons dealing with the alphabet, parts of speech, and sentence structure, all accompanied by graded exercises. The appendices have examples of 'Malayalisms' and foreign words in the Malayalam language. An authoritative Malayalam dictionary is *English-Malayalam dictionary* (New Delhi: Asian Educational Services, 1984. new ed. 1,376p.), compiled by T. Zacharias.

341 A reference grammar of Punjabi.

Harjeet Singh Gill, Henry A. Gleason. Patiala, India: Department of
Linguistics, Punjabi University, 1969. rev. ed. 157p.

A standard grammar of modern spoken and written Punjabi. The introductory section
dicusses the history of the language and earlier grammars. In the phonology section,
the Punjabi language is compared to Hindi and other northern languages. A useful
pedagogical grammar, designed for Western readers, is *An intensive course in
Punjabi: dialogues, drills, exercises, vocabulary, notes on grammar, and word index*
(Mysore, India: Central Institute of Indian Languages, 1985. 430p.), by Motia Bhatia.

342 *Devavanipravesika*: an introduction to the Sanskrit language.

Robert P. Goldman, Sally J. Sutherland. Berkeley, California:
University of California Press, 1987. 2nd rev. ed. 460p. bibliog.

An accessible and innovative Sanskrit primer which, with its emphasis on
composition, memorization, and correct pronunuciation, presents Sanskrit to students
as a living language. The reading selections at the end of each lesson present a
sequential narration in gradually more advanced Sanskrit of the *Ramayana* epic. As
far as possible, this popular textbook is Indological (Indian-orientated) as opposed to
classical or comparative in its approach. Designed for the general Western reader,
Teach yourself Sanskrit (London: Hodder & Stoughton, 1985. new ed. 528p.), by M.
Coulson, is a useful paperback.

343 A reference grammar of Kashmiri.

Braj. B. Kachru. Urbana, Illinois: Department of Linguistics,
University of Illinois, 1969. 416p. bibliog.

A pedagogically orientated introductory reference manual of Kashmiri. The
introductory section deals with the origin of the Kashmiri writing system and the
emergence of the Kashmiri literary tradition. Other chapters deal with phonology;
word formation; word classes; noun, verb, and adverbial phrases; and sentence types.

344 A grammar of modern Telugu.

B. H. Krishnamurti. J. P. L. Gwynn. New Delhi: Oxford University
Press India, 1986. 473p.

Telugu is the most extensively spoken language in southern India, with more than
seventy million speakers. This work is a clearly written pedagogical and reference
grammar.

345 Outline of Hindi grammar with exercises.

Ronald Stuart McGregor. New Delhi: Oxford University Press India,
1988. 3rd ed. 261p. bibliog.

A popular, traditional pedagogical and reference grammar for post-beginners used
extensively for university teaching and *Linguaphone* courses. Chapters deals with
nominal forms, verbs, post positions, adverbs, conjunctions, rules of *sandhi*
(coalescence of final and initial letters of words), and formation of words. There are
twenty-six lessons with associated vocabulary and translation exercises. A companion
work, *Urdu study materials for use with Outline of Hindi Grammar* (New Delhi:
Oxford University Press India, 1992. 175p), is a useful conversion text, containing

Urdu text, vocabularies, and grammatical notes. Two other useful recent textbooks are: *An introduction to Hindi and Urdu* (New Delhi: Munshiram Manoharlal, 1993. 330p.), by Richard Barz and Yogendra Yadav; and *Teach yourself Hindi* (London: Hodder & Stoughton, 1989. 192p.), by Rupert Snell and S. C. R. Weightman, which provides a basic introduction to Hindi for the Western visitor to India.

346 Comparative grammar of the Prakrit languages.
Richard Pischel, translated from the German by Subhadra Jha. New Delhi: Motilal Banarsidass, 1981. 653p. bibliog.

First published in German in 1900, this reference grammar remains the most elaborate on Prakrit, the vernacular of the common people of classical northern India. There is a long introduction on the history of these languages and early Prakrit grammarians. This is followed by grammatical rules. An invaluable companion volume is *Comprehensive Prakrit-Hindi dictionary* (New Delhi: Motilal Banarsidass, 1986. new ed. 580p.), compiled by P. H. D. T. Sheth.

347 A reference grammar of Bengali.
Punya Sloka Ray. Chicago: University of Chicago Press, 1966. 2 vols.

A descriptive, but authoritative, grammar. Introductory chapters deal with general and historical backgrounds and an outline of the history of the Bengali language. Later chapters deal with phonology, morphology, literary and colloquial language, Bengali metre, and a sketch of the Assamese language.

348 Hindi and Urdu since 1800: a common reader.
Christopher Shackle, Rupert Snell. London: School of Oriental and African Studies, 1990. 224p. 2 maps. bibliog.

The first volume in a projected series of SOAS South Asian Texts, this book is targeted at intermediate students possessing an elementary knowledge of modern South Asian languages. The core of the work is devoted to a selection of twenty-four Hindi and Urdu passages, dating from 1801 to 1972, each prefaced by a contextualizing introduction and followed by detailed notes. In part one there is an excellent introduction which explains the evolution of Hindi and Urdu. The book's central theme is that both languages share a common heritage and close relationship, yet historical and cultural factors led to their bifurcation. Sanskrit, the progenitor of both languages, is the source of script and higher vocabulary for Hindi, while Arabic, the language of Islam, and Persian, the court language of the Mughals, perform the same functions for Urdu.

Dictionaries

349 **_Bhargava's_ standard illustrated dictionary of the Hindi language: Hindi-English edition.**
Varanasi, India: Bhargava Book Depot, 1980. rev. enlarged. ed. 1,280p.

Lists over 100,000 Hindi words. Though usage is not indicated for the words included, this is the best dictionary available for the purpose. Parts of speech and guides to pronunciation and grammar are included. The work includes numerous topical appendixes.

350 **Universal English-Gujarati dictionary.**
Pandurang Ganesh Deshpande. New Delhi: Oxford University Press India, 1989. 968p.

A comprehensive dictionary. Deshpande has also compiled an intermediate dictionary, which was first published in 1969 under the auspices of the Gujarati University, Ahmedabad: _Concise English-Gujarati dictionary_ (New Delhi: Oxford University Press India, 1987. new ed. 468p.). One of the best Gujarati grammars is _A Gujarati reference grammar_ (Philadelphia: University of Philadelphia Press, 1965. 188p.), by George Cardona.

351 **Hanklyn-Janklin: a treasury of Indian and Indo-British words.**
Nigel B. Hanklin. New Delhi: Banyan Books, 1993. 261p.

This book, written by a retired British embassy attaché based in India for more than four decades, is designed to help foreign travellers unravel the mysteries of subcontinental English. It includes definitions of commonly used Indian words, particularly those which appear in India's English-language newspapers, for example _gherao_, the art of surrounding offices during labour disputes, and _darshan_, used to describe fleeting sightings of deities and politicians. The title of the glossary, which includes 1,200 entries, is both an allusion to the Indian penchant for echo words and a tribute to the classic 19th-century lexicon _Hobson-Jobson: a glossary of colloquial Anglo-Indian words and phrases_ (London: Linguasia, 1994. 3rd ed. 1,022p.), compiled by Col. Henry Yule and A. C. Burnell and edited by William Crooke.

352 **Kittel's Kannada-English dictionary.**
Ferdinand Kittel, revised and enlarged by M. Mariappa Bhat.
Madras, India: University of Madras, 1968-69. 4 vols.

One of the most exhaustive and useful dictionaries of ancient and modern Kannada words. The introduction traces the history of Kannada lexicography. Originally published in 1894, it contains grammatical information and literary references. The single volume, _The English-Kannada pocket dictionary_ (New Delhi: Asian Educational Services, 1985. 684p.), compiled by P. M. Rau, is a more succinct alternative.

353   **People's own dictionary: English to Bengali and Bengali to English.**
Edited by A. S. Mahmud, compiled by M. Quamruzzaman.   Dacca: Academic Publishers, 1971. 1,665p.

A comprehensive dictionary. Numerous appendixes include proverbs, biographies, and trade and financial information. Grammatical information and levels of usage are indicated.

354   **English and Marathi dictionary.**
J. T. Molesworth, T. Candy.   New Delhi: Asian Educational Services, 1984. new ed. 974p.

Originally published in 1831, this standard dictionary contains etymological information.

355   **Student's diamond dictionary of words, phrases and idioms: Anglo-Oriya.**
Compiled by Jagan Mohan Patnaik, edited by Girija Sankar Ray.
Cuttack, India: Cuttack Publishing House, 1962-64. 2 vols.

A comprehensive dictionary. Entries include parts of speech, levels of usage, and illustrative phrases. A useful grammar for beginners is *A grammar of the Oriya language* (Copenhagen: Danish Missionary Society, 1959. 134p.), by A. Andersen.

356   **A dictionary of Urdu, classical Hindi, and English.**
John Thompson Platts.   New Delhi: Oriental Books Reprint Corp., 1977. reprint. 1,259p.

Originally published in 1884 and frequently reprinted, Platts' dictionary continues to be the best available for working with classical, and especially courtly, Urdu. Entry words are preceded by a code letter which indicates the language to which the word belongs (ie. S = Sanskrit, P = Persian). Entries include etymological information. Platts also produced an Urdu grammar which remains invaluable, *A grammar of the Hindustani or Urdu language* (New Delhi: Munshiram Manoharlal, 1969. reprint of 1884 ed. 399p.). *A Sanskrit grammar for beginners in Devanagri and Roman letters throughout* (New Delhi: Asian Publication Service, 1975. 2nd ed. 230p.), by F. Max Muller, first published in 1866, is an excellent reference work.

357   **Pali-English dictionary.**
Edited by T. W. Rhys Davids.   New Delhi: Motilal Banarsidass, 1994. new ed. 501p.

Originally published in 1921 and reprinted many times, this is the standard dictionary of Pali words, their etymology, uses, and English equivalents, containing over 160,000 entries. A useful reference Pali grammar is *Introduction to Pali* (London: Routledge, 1986. new ed. 480p.), by A. K. Warder.

358   **Telugu-English dictionary.**
Paluri Sankaranarayana.   New Delhi: Asian Educational Services,
1986. new ed. 1,307p.

Originally published in 1900, this dictionary has been revised and enlarged frequently. Copious English synonyms and definitions of technical terms are included.

359   **The Punjabi dictionary.**
Compiled and edited by Maya Singh.   Patiala, India: Language
Department, Punjabi University, 1972. 1,221p.

Originally published in 1895 and thoroughly revised in 1961, this is the standard Punjabi (Gurumukhi) to English dictionary. Words are given in Romanized form as well as in the Gurumukhi script. Both the etymology of the word and its various usages are clearly explained.

360   **Sanskrit-English dictionary.**
Monier Monier Williams.   New Delhi: Marwah, 1986. new ed.
1,333p.

The best one-volume dictionary of the Sanskrit language, with over 180,000 words. It is based on the definitive seven-volume *Sanskrit-Wörterbuch*, compiled and published by Otto Von Böhtlingk between 1858 and 1877, and revised by Ernst Leumann and Carl Cappeller.

361   **A comprehensive Tamil-English dictionary.**
M. Winslow.   New Delhi: Asian Educational Services, 1984. new ed.
990p.

A comprehensive, authoritative work. Grammatical information is provided.

Religion

General

362 **Religion in modern India.**
Edited by Robert D. Baird. New Delhi: Manohar, 1989. 2nd rev. ed. 501p.

An encyclopedic collection of nineteen essays by leading Western scholars on Indian religious movements and religious thinkers since the early 19th century, arranged in two parts. In part one, the movements covered include the Brahmo Samaj, the Arya Samaj, the Ramakrishna Movement, the Singh Sabhas, the Parsi community, and Christianity. In part two, there are chapters on, among others, Ram Mohan Roy, Swami Dayananda Sarasvati, Swami Vivekananda, Mohammad Iqbal, Mahatma Gandhi, Sri Aurobindo, and Sarvepalli Radhakrishnan. Another useful recent collection of essays on religious ideas and practices in India is *The religious culture of India: power, love and wisdom* (Cambridge: Cambridge University Press, 1993. 500p.), edited by Friedhelm Hardy.

363 **Indian religion.**
Edited by Richard Burghart, Audrey Cantlie. London: Curzon Press, 1985. 258p. (Collected Papers on South Asia, no. 7).

A collection of nine papers, by Indologists and social anthropologists, which look at a wide range of Indian religious practices and beliefs. Particularly outstanding are the essays by Jonathan Parry on the Aghori ascetics of Banaras and by Christopher J. Fuller on priestly rituals in a south Indian temple.

364 **Utopias in conflict: religion and nationalism in modern India.**
Ainslie T. Embree. Berkeley, California: University of California
Press, 1990. 144p.

In this collection of six essays, the author, an eminent American scholar, tackles such
crucial topics as religion and nationalism, the question of Hindu tolerance, the
contemporary politics of religion, and the position and dilemmas of Muslims and
Sikhs in India in the late 20th century. Aware of the huge complexity of Indian
society, the author disaggregates carefully, making it clear that there have been and
still are many different Muslim groups in India, with distinctive experiences and
concerns, as well as many Hindu visions of truth. Published at a time of resurgent
communalism, Embree argues that, while Christianity and Islam have proved
historically and culturally adaptable, Hinduism, contrary to popular perceptions, has
eschewed genuine tolerance or dialogue and has sought instead to encapsulate other
religious systems.

365 **Socio-religious movements in British India (The New Cambridge
History of India III:1).**
Kenneth W. Jones. Cambridge: Cambridge University Press, 1990.
243p. bibliog.

An impressive compendium of recent scholarship on socio-religious reform
movements in 19th- and early 20th-century India by a scholar who has written an
excellent, specialist monograph on the Arya Samaj: *Arya Dharm: Hindu
consciousness in 19th century Punjab* (New Delhi: Manohar, 1989. 343p.). The
volume is arranged along chronological and regional lines, with the sections on
northern and western India being particularly strong. A wide range of individual
movements, Hindu and non-Hindu, are covered. The earlier classic text by John Nicol
Farquhar, *Modern religious movements in India* (New York: Garland, 1980. 471p.),
written in 1914 from a liberal missionary perspective, has been substantially
superseded by Jones' work.

366 **Religion in India.**
Edited by Triloki Nath Madan. New Delhi: Oxford University Press
India, 1991. 448p. bibliog. (Oxford in India Readings in Sociology and
Social and Cultural Anthropology).

A collection of important readings on Indian religion which are intended to introduce
students and general readers to the strands of theoretical debate on the topic and
exhibit the diversities of approach in the existing literature. The editor has written a
general, theoretical introduction. The remaining twenty-six papers are arranged in five
analytical sections: sacred knowledge; sacred space; sacred time; sacred persona; and
reorientations to the sacred. There are pieces by Louis Dumont, David Pocock, Ann
Grodzins Gold, Diana Eck, Mysore N. Srinivas, Verrier Elwin, Lawrence Babb,
Christopher Fuller, R. S. Khare, Lionel Caplan, and Mark Juergensmeyer.

367   **Religion in South Asia: religious conversion and revival movements in South Asia in medieval and modern times.**
Edited by G. A. Oddie.   New Delhi: Manohar, 1991. 2nd rev. ed. 272p.

A collection of excellent essays on the themes of religious conversion and revival movements. The particular concern of the contributors is with the economic and social motives and effects of the various conversion movements.

Buddhism

368   **The social dimensions of early Buddhism.**
Uma Chakravarti.   New Delhi: Oxford University Press India, 1987. 238p. bibliog.

A balanced and perceptive investigation of the relationship between early Buddhism and the society in which it developed. The author analyses aspects of the social, political, religious, and economic environment of the Buddha's era. She describes the existence of two distinct types of political formations: centralized monarchies, in which private land control prevailed, and republics (*gana-samghas*), where there was collective control by the ruling clans. The period covered is ca. 600-500 BC.

369   **Buddhism: its essence and development.**
Edward Conze.   New York: Harper, 1975. reprint of 1951 ed. 212p. bibliog.

A popular and reliable introduction by one of the most respected scholars in the field. The author traces the major doctrinal developments in Buddhism from its origins to the Tantric period. The opening forty pages are especially helpful for the general reader because in them the author places Buddhism within the context of world religions, and he specifically addresses such usually disregarded questions as 'Is Buddhism atheistic?'. The work concludes with a handy seventeen page chronological chart of major dates and events in Buddhist history.

370   **Buddhist monks and monasteries of India.**
Sukumar Dutt.   New Delhi: Motilal Banarsidass, 1988. new ed. 395p. bibliog.

A thorough and definitive study of the Buddhist monastic community (*sangha*) in ancient India. Dutt traces the growth of the *sangha* from its earliest days and establishes its connection with the tradition of *sanyasins* (wandering ascetics). Included is a history of the rise and fall of the great Buddhist monastic universities of India and their curricula. This book can be read usefully in conjunction with *Buddhist saints in India: a study in Buddhist values and orientation* (New York; Oxford: Oxford University Press, 1994. 448p.), by Reginald A. Ray.

371 **Theravada Buddhism: a social history from ancient Benares to modern Colombo.**
Richard F. Gombrich. London: Routledge & Kegan Paul, 1988. 237p. bibliog.

An excellent overview of the Theravada branch of Buddhist thought which developed after Buddha's death and is established today in Sri Lanka and Southeast Asia. This 'School of the Elders', also known as *Hinayana* (Lesser Vehicle), emphasizes the mendicant, meditative life as the way to break the cycle of *samsara* (death and rebirth). Its scriptures are written in Pali.

372 **An introduction to Buddhism: teachings, history and practices.**
Peter Harvey. Cambridge: Cambridge University Press, 1990. 374p. map. bibliog.

A wide-ranging, clearly written and well illustrated introductory text. The opening chapter portrays the Buddha in his specific Indian and historical context. In the core of the text, Harvey describes and explains Buddhist beliefs and practices. The rest of the work is given to a review of the historical development of Buddhism within India and its spread to Sri Lanka, Southeast Asia, China, Japan and the world beyond. The concluding chapters examine Buddhism's modern history.

373 **Divine revelation in Pali Buddhism.**
Peter Masefield. London: George Allen & Unwin, 1986. 187p. bibliog.

A controversial revisionist work which argues that conventional ideas about the way to enlightenment as embodied in the main texts of Pali Buddhism are wrong. Masefield argues that the *Nikayas* (Pali Buddhist texts) reveal an original Buddhist teaching that has been obscured by the misunderstandings of monks and modern scholars over thousands of years. They show that the way to salvation is via the Buddha's divine grace rather than through individual striving and merit, and that Buddhist social attitudes were by no means egalitarian, but were concerned, like Brahminical Hinduism, with protecting the purity of the Aryan *varnas* (classical social divisions).

374 **Indian Buddhism: a survey with bibliographical notes.**
Hajime Nakamura. New Delhi: Motilal Banarsidass, 1987. 423p. bibliog. (Buddhist Traditions, vol. 1).

This work is unusual in that the bibliographic notes actually take precedence over the survey text. This makes the work an excellent guide to scholarship, including Japanese. It can be read usefully in conjunction with Warder (see item no. 377). Another excellent annotated bibliography on Buddhism, containing several thousand entries, is *Guide to Buddhist religion* (Boston, Massachusetts: G. K. Hall, 1981. 415p.), edited by Frank E. Reynolds and John Holt.

375 **What the Buddha taught.**
Walpole Rahula. London: Fraser, 1978. rev. ed. 151p. bibliog.

This is the best available treatment of the basic teachings of early Buddhism. It is less complex and philosophical than Conze (see item no. 369). Nowhere else are such difficult-to-understand doctrines as *annata* (no-self) expounded so clearly. Explanations are illustrated with appropriate quotations from Buddhist scriptures. A useful short biography of the life of Buddha, Prince Gautama Siddhartha (ca. 563-ca. 483 BC), is *The awakened one: a life of the Buddha* (London: Phoenix, 1994. 153p.), by Sherab Chodzin Kohn.

376   The Buddhist religion: a historical introduction.
Richard H. Robinson, Willard L. Johnson.   Belmont, California: Dickenson, 1982. 3rd ed. 290p. bibliog. (Religious Life of Man Series).

This short book, of great beauty, is one of eight in a series on world religions intended for the general reader. First published in 1970, the book includes personal interpretations of various aspects of Buddhism by Robinson, one of America's foremost Buddhist scholars. Following an initial chapter that describes the present religious scene in various Buddhist countries, there is a traditional presentation of Buddhism and the life and teachings of Gautama, a chapter on the development of Indian Buddhism, and a chapter on developments outside India. This book is more readable but less sophisticated than Conze (see item no. 369).

377   Indian Buddhism.
Anthony Kennedy Warder.   New Delhi: Motilal Banarsidass, 1980. 2nd rev. ed. 627p. maps. bibliog.

A definitive study of Buddhism in India by a leading Pali scholar. Following an introductory section in which Warder examines Indian civilization before and during the Buddha's lifetime, the author attempts to separate the probable facts about the Buddha's life from the legends that have grown up over the years. Two lengthy chapters discuss Buddhist teachings and Buddhist schisms.

Christianity and Judaism

378   Saints, goddesses and kings: Muslims and Christians in south Indian society, 1700-1900.
Susan Bayly.   Cambridge: Cambridge University Press, 1989. 520p. bibliog. (Cambridge South Asian Studies, no. 43).

A careful study of the spread and development of the Islamic and Christian faiths in south India during the pre- and early-colonial periods through conversions. The author shows that both faiths evolved in this region traditions of worship which were marked by accommodation to indigenous Hindu patterns of practice. Part one is devoted to an analysis of Islamic worship and part two to a study of four groups of Christians. Two recent specialist studies of Christianity within a sub-region of south India are: Susan Viswanathan, *The Christians of Kerala: history, belief, and ritual among the Yakoba* (New Delhi: Oxford University Press India, 1994. 298p.); and Kenneth Ballhatchet, *Priests, peasants and fishermen: caste, class and Catholicism in India 1789-1914* (London: C. Hurst, 1992. 224p.).

379 **Class and culture in urban India: fundamentalism in a Christian community.**
Lionel Caplan. Oxford: Clarendon Press, 1987. 320p. bibliog.

A wide-ranging study of the Protestant community of Madras city, where Christians constitute, with seven per cent of the population, the largest minority. Drawing upon fieldwork carried out during 1974-75 and 1981-82, the author discerns two distinctive strands of urban Protestantism: an ecumenical, middle class, liberal-social gospel, derived from early 20th-century liberal Western Christianity; and a more direct, lower class, evangelical pietism introduced by 19th-century missionaries. Each has its own distinctive style of consumption and worship. The latter is particularly uncompromising to Hinduism and its adherents have been attracted during recent years to Pentecostalism and Christian fundamentalism promoted by American organizations.

380 **Mother Teresa.**
Navin Chawla. New Delhi: Gulmohar Press; London: Sinclair-Stevenson, 1992. 231p.

A solid account of the life and work of Mother Theresa of Calcutta, the Roman Catholic nun and missionary who was awarded the Nobel prize for peace in 1979. Born in Yugoslavia in 1910, Theresa first went to India in 1928, leaving her convent to work alone in the slums in 1948 and to help lepers from 1957. Her own sisterhood, the Orders of the Missionaries of Charity, was founded in 1950. Today, it has a congregation of 4,000 sisters and novices in 468 branch houses around the globe.

381 **Caste and Christianity: attitudes and policies of Anglo-Saxon Protestant missions in India.**
Duncan B. Forrester. London: Curzon Press, 1980. 227p. bibliog.

The central narrative thread in this fine monograph concerns how ideas about caste first came into the thinking of Protestant Christian missionaries from Europe and America and how these ideas changed and developed in reponse to alternating social climates before and after the 1857 Rebellion. Attention is focused on the policies of different missionary organizations and on the attitudes of both European Christians and Indian Christians, the latter as converts seeking to accommodate their new faith to old conventions. Forrester interestingly shows that Christian missions, far from being the 'handmaiden of imperialism', far predated it and were treated warily by a British Raj which was conscious of its inherited role as a sponsor and protector of Hindu institutions.

382 **A history of Christianity in India.**
Stephen Neill. Cambridge: Cambridge University Press, 1984-85.
2 vols. maps. bibliogs.

Conceived of as a trilogy, tracing the history of Christianity in India from 1498 to the present day, the author, Bishop Neill, died before the third volume could be completed. Volume one, *The beginnings to 1707,* focuses on the Mughal era, a period characterised by limited Indian contacts with Christianity, concentrated in coastal regions. Volume two, *1707-1858,* examines the confrontation between Christianity, Hinduism and Islam which occurred as British authority was extended across the subcontinent. Bishop Neill, himself a prominent member of the Church of South India, undogmatically accords fair and sympathetic treatment to all the various forms of the Christian faith – Roman Catholic, Anglican, Protestant, the Thomas Syrian Christians – as their ministers and missionaries made contact with India.

383 The children of Israel: the Bene Israel of Bombay.
Schifra Strizower. New Delhi: Oxford University Press India, 1971. 176p. bibliog.

A classic socio-religious analysis of the Bene Israel Jews who constitute over eighty per cent of Indian Jewry and live predominantly in Greater Bombay. Strizower discusses both the religious and social differences between and among the Bene Israelites, the Baghdadi Jews, and the Cochin Jews. Their claim to be descended from the Ten Tribes of Israel is examined, as is their lack of knowledge of the Pentateuch, the Talmud, Hebrew, and traditional synagogue rituals. A more recent work is S. B. Isenberg, *India's Bene Israel: a comprehensive inquiry and sourcebook* (London; New Delhi: Sangam Books, 1989. 443p.).

384 Jews in India.
Edited by Thomas A. Timberg. New Delhi: Vikas; New York: Advent Books, 1986. 347p.

A collection of fifteen essays, eight original and the remainder reprinted or appearing in English for the first time, which shed scholarly light on various facets of the life, history and practices of the Jewish community in India. The essays are arranged in five thematic sections: review articles; classical studies; the Cochin and Malabar Jews; Baghdadi Jews in India's port cities; and the Bene Israel. Particularly useful are the bibliographic introduction by the editor and his paper on the economic history of the Calcutta Jews. Two seminal essays by David G. Mandelbaum and S. S. Koder on social stratification among Cochin Jews are included.

Communalist tensions

385 Riot after riot: reports on caste and communal violence in India.
M. J. Akbar. New Delhi: Penguin India, 1988. 177p.

In this collection of fifteen essays and feature articles, written by the accomplished journalist M. J. Akbar for his newspaper, *The Telegraph*, and the magazine *Sunday* during the 1980s, the mounting cycle of caste and communal violence in India is chronicled and analysed. The Moradabad massacre in 1980, the slaughter of Uttar Pradesh *harijans* in 1981, and the Ayodhya Babri Masjid controversy are all covered by an author who makes clear his commitment to secularism, humanity and truth and his rejection of religion as symbol of hate. Though pessimistic in its conclusions, this book makes compelling reading. A related work is Zebab Banu's *Politics of communalism: a politico-historical analysis of communal riots in post-independence India with special reference to the Gujarat and Rajasthan riots* (London: Sangam Books, 1989. 226p.).

386   **The brotherhood in saffron: the Rashtriya Swayamsevak Sangh and Hindu revivalism.**
Walter K. Anderson, Shridhar D. Damle.   Boulder, Colorado:
Westview Press; New Delhi: Sage Publications, 1987. 317p. bibliog.

An authoritative, detailed examination of the Rashtriya Swayamsevak Sangh (RSS), its early growth in the pre-independence period, its organization, the function of its various officers, and the evolution of its ideology. The RSS's goal has been to create a stable, proper Hindu society and culture, protected from the 'corruption' of Christian and Islamic values. It has sought to inculcate its ideas and values throughout Indian society via its newspapers, the *Organiser*, *Shakti*, and *Panchjanya*, student societies, labour unions and its religious forum, the Vishwa Hindu Parishad. The RSS has also trained political workers who have campaigned as allies of the Jana Sangh Party and, most recently, the Bharatiya Jana Sangh. Anti-secularist, it has done much to fan the flames of communal tensions.

387   **Fundamentalism, revivalists and violence in South Asia.**
Edited by James Warner Bjorkman.   Riverdale, Maryland: The
Riverdale Company, 1988. 220p.

A collection of summary essays and case-studies presented to a 1984 workshop at the University of Wisconsin held on the themes of Sikh and Islamic fundamentalism and Hindu revivalism in contemporary South Asia. Particular attention is paid to the Damdani Taksal Sikh movement of Sant Jarnail Singh Bhindranwale (1947-84) in Punjab and the Hindu Sabha and Rashtriya Swayamsevak Sangh (RSS) in the Hindi heartland. Contributors include Robert Frykenberg, Lloyd and Susanne Rudolph, Surjit Mansingh, Kenneth Jones, and Paul Wallace.

388   **Communalism in modern India.**
Bipan Chandra.   New Delhi: Vikas, 1987. 2nd rev. ed. 391p.

In this analysis, the author, a nationalist historian, argues that communalism was not based on real conflict between India's Hindu and Muslim communities, but on a distorted reflection of real conflict, a 'false consciousness'. The literature on communalism in colonial and independent India has been voluminous during recent years. Among the best works are: Gyanendra Pandey's *The construction of communalism in colonial north India* (New Delhi: Oxford University Press India, 1992. new ed. 297p.); K. N. Panikkar's (editor) *Communalism in India: history, politics and culture* (New Delhi: Manohar, 1991. 228p.); Suranjan Das's *Communal riots in Bengal 1905-1947* (New Delhi: Oxford University Press India, 1991. 311p.); and Sarvepalli Gopal's (editor) *Anatomy of a confrontation: Ayodhya and the rise of communal politics in India* (London: Zed Books, 1993. 240p.).

389   **Collective action and community: public arenas and the emergence of communalism in north India.**
Sandria B. Freitag.   Berkeley, California: University of California
Press, 1989. 328p. bibliog.

A wide-ranging and innovative study which analyses community consciousness and communalism through focusing on the competitive world of festivals, processions and other cultural spectacles in the towns of Uttar Pradesh during the 19th and early 20th centuries. There are case studies of religious processions and their impact in Banaras,

Bareilly, Agra, Kanpur, and Lucknow, and of the aggressive Cow Protection Leagues of the early 1890s. The author argues that the 'symbolic rhetoric' and 'codes of behavior' of these public activities, when combined with late 19th-century developments in communication, notably 'print capitalism', provided the basis for the transition from face-to-face relational communities to exclusivist, pan-Indian Hindu and Muslim sectarian identities.

390   **Religious nationalism: Hindus and Muslims in India.**
Peter Van der Veer.   Berkeley, California: University of California Press, 1994. 234p. bibliog.

A study in the relationship between religion and politics in India. Using an interdisciplinary approach, the author draws on history, anthropology and social theory to show how religious identities in India have been shaped by migration, pilgrimage, language, and the media.

Hinduism

391   **Redemptive encounters: three modern styles in the Hindu tradition.**
Lawrence A. Babb.   Berkeley, California: University of California Press, 1986. 257p. bibliog. (Comparative Studies in Religion and Society, no. 1).

The subjects of this fascinating monograph are the 'Hindu religious imagination', or Hindu modes of perceiving religious meanings in a variety of historical, visionary and interpersonal experiences, and the 'dynamics of contemporary Hindu religious movements'. Three distinctive modern movements are examined: the north Indian centred Radhasoamis, which traces its roots to a 19th-century guru from Agra; the millenarianist Brahma Kumaris, who emerged in Sind in the 1930s; and devotees of the contemporary miracle-worker Sai Baba, a living guru. Each movement presents a marked contrast to traditional forms of Hinduism.

392   **The sacred cow: the evolution of classical Hinduism.**
Arthur Llewellyn Basham, edited by Kenneth G. Zysk.   London: Rider, 1990. 160p. map. bibliog.

A short, vivid survey of India's early religious history by the author of the monumental, *The wonder that was India* (see item no. 143). Published posthumously, this work, which originated as a series of public lectures, contains several interesting new theories, including an attempt to assign portions of the *Bhagavad-gita*, the Hindu equivalent of the Christian New Testament, to three distinct authors over a period of about two hundred years. The opening chapter examines the prehistorical religion of South Asia, dating from ca. 2700-1700 BC. The volume's English title is misleading, since it contains only a passing reference to the sanctity of cattle in the Hindu tradition. In the US it carries the more representative title, *The origins and development of classical Hinduism* (Boston, Massachusetts: Beacon Press, 1989. 159p.).

393 **The Hindu religious tradition: a philosophical approach.**
Pratima Bowes. London; Boston: Routledge & Kegan Paul, 1977.
322p.

An exploratory and critical study of the philosophical ideas and social practices in the
Hindu religious tradition. The author believes that the most unique features of the
Hindu faith are the acceptance of polytheism, monism, yogic perfectionism, and
various forms of monotheism as valid forms of religious expression, and the Hindu
attempt at self-integration with the religious reality at various levels – cosmic, social,
and individual. The work includes insightful analyses of the Hindu notions of *karma*
and free will, reincarnation, and *lila* (play).

394 **The sacred thread: Hinduism in its continuity and diversity.**
John L. Brockington. Edinburgh: Edinburgh University Press, 1981.
222p. bibliog.

An excellent survey of ancient Indian religious traditions, tracing the history of the
ideas associated with the wearers of the sacred thread since Vedic times. The work
concentrates on the Vedic and classic periods and is based on the Brahminical
tradition. The closing chapter is devoted to consideration of modern interpretations of
the tradition.

395 **Hinduism: a religion to live by.**
Nirad C. Chaudhuri. Oxford: Oxford University Press; New Delhi:
BI Publications, 1979. 340p. bibliog.

A provocative, idiosyncratic analysis of the development of Hinduism by a renowned
Indian writer (see items no. 3, 853). The author takes issue with those who stress the
'life renunciation' element within Hinduism and, instead, argues that, in practice,
Hindus are concerned not with escape from the world, but with obtaining worldly
power. A contrasting interpretation is provided in *Hinduism: anthropology of a
civilization* (New Delhi: Oxford University Press India, 1994. new ed. 200p.), by
Madeleine Biardeau (translated from the French by Richard Nice).

396 **Ganesa: lord of obstacles, lord of beginnings.**
Paul B. Courtright. New York: Oxford University Press USA, 1985.
274p. bibliog.

Blending textual analysis with anthropological field research in Maharashtra, the
author presents an illuminating analysis of the mythology and worship of the
elephant-god Ganesa, a central deity within Siva's cluster. Courtright applies
Freudian analysis to Ganesa's family relationships as recounted in the *Puranas* and
concludes that he emerged as eternally submissive to his mother with an ambiguous
and immature male sexuality. Complementary works on Indian deities include: John
Stratton Hawley, D. M. Wulff's (editors) *The divine consort: Radha and the
goddesses of India* (Berkeley, California: University of California Press, 1982.
432p.); and D. Kinsley's *Hindu goddesses: visions of the divine feminine in the Hindu
religious tradition* (Berkeley, California: University of California Press, 1988. 289p.).

397 **Guide to Hindu religion.**
David J. Dell (and others).   Boston, Massachusetts: G. K. Hall, 1981.
461p. bibliog.

A comprehensive, annotated bibliography on Hinduism that contains several thousand entries grouped under twelve headings: history of Hinduism; Hindu religious thought; authoritative and sacred texts; popular practices; the arts; Hinduism in social life and politics; rituals; ideal beings; mythology; sacred locations; soteriology; and research aids. There are author, title and subject indexes.

398 **An outline of the religious literature of India.**
John Nicol Farquhar.   New Delhi: Asia Book Corp., 1984. new ed.
451p.

An indispensable guide to the basic contents of principal Hindu, Buddhist, and Jain writings, from the *Vedas* to about 1800 AD. Chapters are arranged by schools of thought within historical periods.

399 **The camphor flame: popular Hinduism and society in India.**
Christopher J. Fuller.   Princeton, New Jersey: Princeton University Press, 1992. 306p. bibliog.

An excellent, wide-ranging text on Hinduism which rejects the traditional Orientalist approach of textual analysis and seeks instead, through a 'synchronic, ethnographically-based analysis', to interpret Hinduism's characteristics in terms of social phenomena and portray it as a vibrant, living religion. The author analyses the interrelationship between Hindu gods, great and little; royal and village rituals; Hindu attitudes towards misfortunes; devotional movements; and popular Hinduism during pilgrimages. Two key themes in the work are that Hinduism sees no sharp divide between humanity and divinity and that hierarchical inequality is deeply rooted in the religion.

400 **Encyclopaedia of the Hindu world.**
Edited by Ganga Ram Garg.   New Delhi: Concept, 1992- . 3 vols.

An ambitious publishing project, which will continue into the next century. Forty volumes are planned, covering in detail all aspects of the Hindu religion: sects, deities, cults, *rishis* (seers), mystics, saints, customs, festivals, temples, pilgrim centres etc. The encyclopaedia is being produced in an alphabetical A-Z format, each volume containing between 1,000-2,000 entries. Indian and foreign scholars have been commissioned to write entries on specialist topics. The first three volumes covering the letter 'A' were published in 1992. Volume one contains a ninety page introductory essay on Indian geography, culture, religion, arts, literature and history written by G. R. Garg, a leading Indologist and Arya Samajist, who is also editor of the *International Encyclopaedia of Indian Literature.*

401 **The lord as guru: Hindu *sants* in the northern Indian tradition.**
Daniel Gold.   New York: Oxford University Press USA, 1987. 256p. bibliog.

In this scholarly work, the author examines the *nirguna bhakti* devotional tradition, which involves the worship of a living guru as a manifestation of transcendent reality. In part one, Gold analyses the *nirguna sant* tradition in north India, describing its socio-historical and religious context and chronicling the rise of lineages of holy men, particularly the Radhasoamis. Part two compares two formative *sants*, Namdev and Kabir, with two 18th-century *sants*, Paltu Sahib and Charandas. Part three discusses the roots of *sant* tradition in Hinduism, Buddhism, and *sufism*. This is a book which succeeds in showing the continuity of the *sant* tradition to the present day.

402 **The Hindu religious tradition.**
Thomas J. Hopkins. Encino, California: Dickenson, 1971. 156p. bibliog.

A widely used college text. The volume has two major parts: the first deals with developments up to 900 AD, when, according, to Hopkins, the Hindu tradition reached its classical zenith, and from then to the present, a period during which only minor changes in that tradition have taken place.

403 **J. Krishnamurti: a biography.**
P. Jayakar. New Delhi: Penguin India; New York: Harper & Row, 1987-89. 528p.

An excellent biography of Jiddu Krishnamurti (1895-1986), the Madras-born Indian theosophist who, in 1925, was proclaimed the Messiah by Annie Besant (1847-1933). Theosophy, a religio-philosophical system based on intuitive insight into the nature of the divine, was based on the Hindu ideas of *karma* and reincarnation.

404 **Dayananda Saraswati: his life and ideas.**
J. T. F. Jordens. New York: Oxford University Press, 1979. 368p. bibliog.

An accurate, comprehensive account of the founder of the Arya Samaj, a Hindu reform organization, and his influence on Hinduism in 19th-century northern and western India and on 20th-century Hindu nationalism. Jordens examines Swami Dayananda's (1824-83) novel interpretations of the Hindu scriptures and argues that these have to be taken seriously. There is an excellent and thorough bibliography.

405 **A survey of Hinduism.**
Klaus K. Klostermaier. Albany, New York: State University of New York Press (SUNY), 1989. 649p. bibliog.

An accessible and comprehensive textbook covering a great many aspects of Hinduism: its history, sacred writings, central ideas, branches (Vaisnavism, Saivism, Saktism etc), pantheon of gods and goddesses, and new developments in the 19th and 20th centuries. The work is divided into three parts. Part one analyses Hinduism's historical development and defining features and also reviews the basic writings that possess canonical value, including, for example, a useful four-page summary of the narrative of the great *Ramayana*. Part two describes the salient features of Hinduism's 'three ways': the paths of work, knowledge, and loving devotion. Part three identifies the structural supports of Hinduism: the social order, the physical reality of India, and sacred time and space. There is a detailed chronology and sixty-five page bibliography. An excellent introductory work.

406   **The Brahmo Samaj and the shaping of the modern Indian mind.**
David Kopf.   New Delhi: Archives, 1988. reprint. 399p. bibliog.
Originally published in 1979, this classic account of the genesis and ideas of the early
19th-century Hindu reformist Brahmo Samaj (estd. 1828) places the movement in its
historical context of early colonial Bengali society. Kopf sees the members of the
Brahmo Samaj as religious and social reformers, and as pioneers of liberal political
consciousness and Indian nationalism. An excellent biography of the Brahmo Samaj's
founder, Ram Mohan Roy (1774-1833), is now available: *Ram Mohan Roy: social,
political and religious reform in nineteenth century India* (New York: Paragon
House, 1987.), by S. Cromwell Crawford.

407   **The presence of Siva.**
Stella Kramrisch, photographs by Praful Patel.   Princeton, New
Jersey: Princeton University Press, 1981. 514p. bibliog.
A unique critical study of the myth, metaphysics, and artistic expressions of Lord
Siva, perhaps the most elusive member of the Hindu pantheon, by a leading art
historian. Kramrisch handles a huge variety of literary and archaeological materials
with imagination and delicacy. She narrates and interprets Saivite myths on both
ontological and metaphysical levels. A work of wisdom.

408   **Divine passions: the social construction of emotion in India.**
Edited by Owen M. Lynch.   Berkeley, California: University of
California Press, 1990. 312p.
A collection of essays which provide vivid observational data on the current practice
of devotional *bhakti* worship in north India, particularly in the pilgrimage centres
devoted to the Hindu god Krishna. These accounts show how the concept *rasa*
(transcendental emotion), drawn from Sanskritic aesthetic theory, constitutes the
emotional experience of Krishna's devotees. The most significant essays are by Owen
Lynch, Paul Toomey, Peter Bennett, Frederique Apffel Marglin, and Charles Brooks.
Arranged in five sections, there are also essays on emotion in Indian family life.

409   **Non-renunciation: themes and interpretations of Hindu culture.**
Triloki Nath Madan.   New Delhi: Oxford University Press India,
1987. 184p. bibliog.
This book is an important corrective to the stereotypical notion in the West that
renunciation, the rejection of worldly pursuits and pleasures to pursue the ideal of the
sadhu and the *fakir*, is central to the Hindu faith. The author, a distinguished
anthropologist, explores the tensions and moral dilemmas that arise from the dialogue
between the renouncer and the man-in-the-world in chapters with such titles as
'Asceticism and eroticism', 'The desired and the good', and 'Living and dying'. He
concludes that, under the influence of Western liberal values of material prosperity,
political democracy, and secularism, the ideal balance between renouncer and man-
in-the-world is being tilted irretrievably in favour of the latter.

410   **Social roots of religion in ancient India.**
Ramendra Nath Nandi.   Calcutta: Bagchi, 1986. 218p. bibliog.
This work relates changes in religious ideology and practices to changes in the
productive forces and material culture of India between the 3rd and 12th centuries

AD. There are fifteen chapters, arranged in three chronological sections: Brahmanism (3rd-6th centuries); Vaisnavism, Saivism, and Jainism (7th-12th centuries), the early feudal age; and Virasaivism.

411 **Siva: the erotic ascetic.**
Wendy Doniger O'Flaherty. New York; Oxford: Oxford University Press, 1981. 386p.

An important, original, stimulating, and convincing interpretation of sexual excitement and repression both by gods and ascetics in the Indian tradition. Based on a wide array of *Puranic* and epic texts and myths, the book explores stories associated with Siva and Kama, using psycho-sexual interpretations. O'Flaherty is also editor of a useful companion volume, *Textual sources for the study of Hinduism* (Manchester, England: Manchester University Press, 1988. 211p.).

412 **Many *Ramayanas*: the diversity of a narrative tradition in South Asia.**
Edited by Paula Richman. New Delhi: Oxford University Press India, 1993. 273p.

The *Ramayana*, detailing the story of Rama, the virtuous Prince of Ayodhya, is the most popular of Hinduism's epic poems, and for modern Hindu revivalist parties Rama has become a war cry for what they depict to be a monolithic, homogenous Hinduism. This scholarly work is an important critique of the revivalist interpretation. It shows that different traditions, at different times, in different places, and with differing needs have moulded the Rama to suit their own aesthetic. Furthermore, there is no definitive *Ramayana* text: the widely used version by Valmiki is the most popular, but not the only rendition.

413 **Vaisnavism: contemporary scholars discuss the Gaudiya tradition.**
Edited by Steven J. Rosen. New York: Folk Books, 1992. 162p.

The editor is a disciple of A. C. Bhaktivedanta Swami, the founder of IKSON, or the Hare Krishna movement. In this work, Rosen provides extracts from interviews held with twenty-five Western and Indian writers and academics interested in different aspects of Gaudiya Vaisnavism. This introduction to modern scholarship can be read usefully alongside *A source-book of modern Hinduism* (London: Curzon Press, 1994. 228p.), by Glyn Richard, a balanced selection of texts with commentaries.

414 ***Bhakti* and the *bhakti* movement: a new perspective.**
Krishna Sharma. New Delhi: Munshiram Manoharlal, 1987. 342p. bibliog.

An original work which seeks to deconstruct the concept of *bhakti*, presented by European Indologists, as a devotional, monotheistic Hinduism largely in Christianity's image. Instead, the author, an adherent to the devotionally and nationalistically tinged version of *Advaita Vedanta* associated with the intellectuals Swami Vivekananda and Sarvepalli Radhakrishnan, proposes that *bhakti* be understood as a broad generic term. It encompasses both *nirguna-bhakti* (the worship of the living guru as a manifestation of transcendent reality) monist and *saguna-bhakti* (the worship of immanent gods through divine images) monotheistic forms of devotion. A complementary work is: *Lord divine: studies in bhakti and devotional mysticism* (London: Curzon Press, 1994. 244p.), a collection of essays edited by Karel Werner.

415 The universal Gita: Western images of the *Bhagavad-Gita,* a bicentenary survey.

Eric J. Sharpe.   London: Duckworth, 1985. 188p. bibliog.

This volume was written to commemorate the 200th anniversary of the publication, in 1785, of the first English translation of the *Bhagavad-Gita* ('song of the blessed'), Hinduism's supreme religious work, by Charles Wilkins. It examines changing Western interpretations, beginning with a discussion of the views of late 18th-century Orientalists and 19th-century missionaries and closing with those of writers such as T. S. Eliot. The author notes that the closing quarter of the 19th century marked a turning point for the text as, with the printing and communications revolution within India, direct access to it was widened beyond the ranks of the religious élite and the *Gita* found itself at the centre of a renaissance of Hindu thought. The work is complemented by Arvind Sharma's *The Hindu Gita: ancient and classical interpretations of the Bhagavadgita* (London: Duckworth, 1986. 269p.), which looks at a much earlier period of *Gita* interpretations.

416 Hinduism: new essays in the history of religions.

Edited by Bardwell L. Smith.   Leiden, the Netherlands: Brill, 1976. 231p. bibliog.

A careful examination of selected aspects of Vaisnava *bhakti* ('devotion') and mythology, principally in Bengal. Included are two essays on Caitanya, another two on Ramakrishna, one on the pilgrimage to Ramadevra in Rajasthan, and another on the bibliography of the medieval *bhakti* movement.

417 A dictionary of Hinduism, its mythology, folklore, and development, 1500 BC-AD 1500.

Margaret Stutley, James Stutley.   Bombay: Allied, 1977. 372p.

This is perhaps the most comprehensive and yet concise encyclopaedia on Hinduism. Its approximately 2,500 subject headings include rites, practices, concepts, functionaries, myths, places, literary texts, religiously significant fauna and flora, gods and goddesses, legends, symbols, music, and philosophical and religious terms. The book provides comparative references from other ancient religions, such as those in the Near East. It is published in the United States as *Harper's dictionary of Hinduism: its mythology, folklore, philosophy, literature, and history* (New York: Harper & Row, 1977. 372p.).

418 A new face of Hinduism: the Swaminarayan religion.

Raymond B. Williams.   Cambridge: Cambridge University Press, 1984. 217p.

The Swaminarayan movement, though less than two centuries old, today has more than five million followers in India and among emigrants abroad. It is a regional religion, tracing its origins to the teachings of a Gujarati, Sahajanand Swami, also known as Swaminarayan (1781-1830), who was influenced by a Vallabhaite form of Vaisnavism and to some degree by Jainism. The author traces the movement's history, the community's organization, its distinctive Hindu theology, and its religious practices. Williams shows that the movement owes much to aspects of the Brahminical Hindu tradition that came before it, but it is unusual in its emphasis on the divine presence of the guru, its congregational form of religious fellowship, and the extreme form of non-violence it advocates.

419 **The experience of Hinduism: essays on religion in Maharashtra.**
Edited by E. Zelliot, M. Berntsen. Albany, New York: SUNY, 1988. 387p. bibliog.

A collection of short articles, poems, stories, interviews and reminiscences on Hinduism in the western Indian state of Maharashtra which have been produced over the last thirty years by mainly American scholars. Notable papers are those by Gunther Sontheimer on the religion of the Dhangar nomads, by Anne Feldhaus on contemporary Mahanubhav practice, and by Iravati Karve on a pilgrimage to Pandharpur. A valuable source-book for Western students of Hinduism.

Islam

420 *Sufis* **of Bijapur, 1300-1700: social roles of** *sufis* **in medieval India.**
Richard Maxwell Eaton. Princeton, New Jersey: Princeton University Press, 1978. 358p. bibliog.

A superb book dealing with the role that the mystical *sufi* orders played in spreading Islamic popular culture to south India – a topic that is generally neglected in other historical surveys. Eaton examines the life and times of the various Bijapur *sufis* and their relationship with the *ulama* (Islamic doctors of law), the Bijapur court, and the Hindu population. His chapter on saint-worship and the tomb-cult of the Indian *sufis* is perhaps the most literate account on the subject. Eaton has produced an excellent supplementary volume, *The rise of Islam and the Bengal frontier, 1204-1760* (Berkeley, California: University of California Press, 1994. 359p.), which analyses the spread of Islam to Bengal – now home to the world's second largest Muslim ethnic population – from early medieval times.

421 *Shari'at* **and ambiguity in South Asian Islam.**
Edited by Katherine P. Ewing. Berkeley, California; London: University of California Press, 1988. 321p. maps. bibliog.

The essays in this volume examine the codes of behaviour by which South Asian Muslims live their lives and their interrelationship, often ambiguous, with the Islamic *sharia* (body of regulations). Contributors include historians and anthropologists. A complementary work is the collection of essays on the ideal of *adab* (proper behaviour) which is edited by Barbara D. Metcalf, *Moral conduct and authority: the place of adab in South Asian Islam* (Berkeley, California: University of California Press, 1984. 389p.).

422 **The Muslims of British India.**
Peter Hardy. Cambridge: Cambridge University Press, 1972. 306p.
5 maps. bibliog. (Cambridge South Asian Studies, no. 13).

An excellent survey of the historical experience of South Asia's Muslim community
from the late Mughal era to what Hardy terms the 'dual partition' of both India and
Pakistan and of the Muslim population between them. The author carefully surveys
the impact of British rule, contrasting the intellectual trends between those exposed to
colonial educational institutions and those trained at traditional religious seminaries,
and analyses the motives and successes of Muslim political participants and
movements.

423 **The Shia of India.**
John Norman Hollister. New Delhi: Oriental Books Reprint Corp.,
1979. 2nd ed. 440p. bibliog.

A religious and historical account of the growth of the Shia sect of Islam and its
major denominations, especially the *mustalians* and the *nizarians*, in India. Hollister
discusses the theological roots of Ithna Ashariya (those Shias who recognize only
twelve imams), the expansion of the Shia community in the south under Bahmani and
succeeding kingdoms and in the north under the Mughals, the emergence of the
Ismailiyas, and the adjustments made by the Shia with the Hindu faith and traditions.

424 **Islamic Culture.**
Hyderabad, India: Islamic Culture Board, 1927- . quarterly.

A longstanding journal devoted to Islamic history and culture in South Asia. It is
published in Hyderabad, a centre of Islamic culture in India.

425 **Muslim endowments and society in British India.**
Gregory C. Kozlowski. Cambridge: Cambridge University Press,
1985. 211p. bibliog. (Cambridge South Asian Studies, no. 35).

An interesting examination of the impact of British colonial rule on Islam via the
policy adopted towards the legal treatment of *waqfs* (religious endowments of land or
revenue rights). In the late 19th century, British courts came to insist that *waqfs*
should be applied only to charitable purposes and not for private purposes, as had
been the case in the pre-colonial period. Although the *Waqf* Validating Act in 1913
restored the status quo, the author argues that the preceding protracted debate
between British administrators and Muslim leaders had the effect of emphasizing a
narrow view of the Islamic community which obscured its diversity.

426 **Muslim women in India: political and private realities, 1890s-1980s.**
Shahida Lateef. London: Zed Books, 1990. 238p.

In this work, Lateef draws attention to the distinction that exists between the public,
conservative face of political Islam and the private, much more adaptable, face of
Islam in personal lives. She draws on survey data of more than 1,300 women in nine
major Indian cities undertaken for the National Committee on the Status of Women in
India in 1974, as well as interviews with fifty (male and female) community leaders.
She argues that excessive emphasis has been placed on religious differences, and that
the difficulties faced by Muslim women owe more to regional culture and social and
economic pressures.

427 **The rose and the rock: mystical and rational elements in the intellectual history of South Asian Islam.**
Edited by Bruce B. Lawrence. Durham, North Carolina: Duke University Press, 1979. 200p. bibliog. (Comparative Studies on Southern Asia, no. 15).

This volume contains six essays. Sheila McDonough's essay shows that India's great Muslim philosopher, Iqbal, was both traditional and progressive, Islamic and Western, and opposed to both secularism and rationalism. Bruce Lawrence's essay points out that Sayyid Ahmad Khan (see item no. 263), who is often viewed as the supreme rationalist of modern Indian Islam, was at heart influenced by Delhi mysticism. Annemarie Schimmel's articles analyse the role of Amir Ali in introducing the rational element into the understanding of the Prophet Muhammad. Two other essays examine the mystical element in the poetry of Bedil and Ghalib.

428 **Islamic revival in British India: Deoband, 1860-1900.**
Barbara D. Metcalf. Princeton, New Jersey: Princeton University Press, 1982. 386p. 7 maps. bibliog.

An absorbing specialist study of Islamic revival in colonial north India. The focus is the *madrasa* (seminary) established at the provincial town of Deoband which subsequently provided religious leadership for South Asia's Muslims. The author provides an integrated account of the institution – its origins, organization, ideas of its founders, eminent scholars, and their social mileu – and sets developments within the wider context of Islamic reform movements in late 19th-century India. Deoband's *ulama* (Islamic doctors of law) are depicted by Metcalf as renewers, working within the established Islamic tradition, rather than modernists who reached out to new sources of inspiration. The work complements the earlier study by David Lelyveld, *Aligarh's first generation: Muslim solidarity in British India* (Princeton, New Jersey: Princeton University Press, 1978. 380p.), which examines the early years of the Muslim Anglo-Oriental college founded in 1875 at Aligarh by Sir Sayyid Ahmad Khan (see item no. 263), and which, through imparting a cohesiveness to its scholars drawn from divergent backgrounds, equipped them to provide future political leadership to the community.

429 **The Indian Muslims.**
Mohammed Mujeeb. New Delhi: Munshiram Manoharlal, 1985. 1st Indian ed. 590p. bibliog.

The author, an Indian Muslim, has portrayed the life and thought of the Muslims in India. The approach is chronological, but each period (early, middle, modern) is examined from various perspectives. The treatment of politics and politicians, poets and writers, the arts and architecture, and social life is particularly illuminating. The writer argues that the Muslims' desire to maintain the identity of their faith has come often into conflict with the desire to be fully integrated in India, leading the 'separatist' elements to emphasize the former and the 'secular' forces to seek the latter. This authoritative account from the 'nationalist Muslim' perspective, first published in 1967, can be contrasted usefully to the work *The Muslim community of the Indo-Pakistan subcontinent (610-1947): a brief historical analysis* (Karachi: Ma'aref, 1977. 2nd ed. 385p.), written by Ishtiaq Husain Qureshi, a Pakistani Muslim.

430   **A history of** *sufism* **in India.**
Saiyid Athar Abbas Rizvi.   New Delhi: Munshiram Manoharlal,
1978-83. 2 vols. bibliogs.

A detailed scholarly account, using Persian sources, of the saints who belonged to the
silsilas ('orders of *sufis*'). The author describes each major figure and details their
thinking. There are also chapters on *sufis'* relationship to Hindu traditions of
mysticism, on *sufi* poetry, and on *sufi* conceptions of politics. Volume one is titled,
Early sufism and its history in India to 1600 AD, and volume two, *From sixteenth
century to modern century.*

431   **Islam in the Indian subcontinent.**
Annemarie Schimmel.   Leiden, the Netherlands: E. J. Brill, 1980.
303p. bibliog.

A careful, balanced survey of the history and situation of Islam in India, Pakistan, and
Bangladesh. Schimmel describes and evaluates the cultural activities of devoted
mystical leaders who won over many Hindus to the Islamic faith and generated a
Hindu-Muslim religio-cultural synthesis against the background of an Islamic
political tradition which was intolerant of Hinduism and which kept Hindu-Muslim
tensions alive.

432   **Modern Islam in India: a social analysis.**
Wilfred Cantwell Smith.   New Delhi: Manohar, 1985. reprint of
1946 ed. 396p. bibliog.

A vigorous Marxist class analysis of Islamic religious movements and trends in the
Indian subcontinent from the last third of the 19th century until the 1940s. The author
deals first with individual writers and their followers, for example Sayyid Ahmad
Khan (see item no. 263), Amir Ali and Iqbal. He then examines political groups and
movements, including the radical Ahrars and Khaksars. Smith characterizes the
Muslim League as initially a reactionary movement which later became bourgeois
nationalist in character.

433   **Islam in India: studies and commentaries.**
Edited by Christian Wilhelm Troll.   Various publishers. 4 vols.
1982-89.

Designed as a scholarly annual of Islamic studies in India, four volumes were
published between 1982 and 1989, each comprising essays on a different theme and
edited by the India-based German Christian, C. W. Troll. The titles of the four
volumes are: *Vol. 1: The Akbar mission and miscellaneous studies* (New Delhi:
Vikas, 1982. 231p.); *Vol. 2: Religion and religious education* (New Delhi: Vikas,
1985. 315p.); *Vol. 3: Islamic experience in contemporary thought* (New Delhi:
Chanakya, 1986. 293p.); and *Vol. 4: Muslim shrines in India: their character, history
and significance* (New Delhi: Oxford University Press India, 1989. 327p.).

Jainism

434 The assembly of listeners: Jains in society.
Edited by Michael B. Carrithers, Caroline Humphrey. Cambridge: Cambridge University Press, 1991. 328p.

This volume comprises a collection of papers written by anthropologists, sociologists and Indologists, presented originally at a colloquium on the Jain community. The book is well structured into four sections: Jain ideals and Jain identity; local Jain communities; Jains in the Indian world; and new Jain institutions in India and beyond. Useful summaries of ensuing arguments have been contributed by the editors. Primarily documentary and ethnographic, this wide-ranging empirical work goes beyond the paradoxical stereotypes of Jain society – extreme asceticism and ostentatious displays of wealth – seeking to relate these to each other and to the wider world.

435 A comprehensive history of Jainism up to 1000 AD.
Asim Kumar Chatterjee. Calcutta: Firma KLM, 1980. 400p. bibliog.

A history of the birth and growth of Jainism in India during the formative period from 800 BC to early medieval times. Based on Vedic and Anga texts, this book provides a historical narrative on the origins, development, and contributions of the Digambara and Svetambara sects of Jainism.

436 The Jaina path of purification.
Padmanabh S. Jaini. Berkeley, California: University of California Press, 1979. 374p. bibliog.

A capable, scholarly, general introduction to the Jains and their religion, written in a lucid, expository style. Jaini draws on both Digambara and Svetambara historical traditions in order to depict the beginnings of Jainism, the life and career of the founder, Mahavira, and the early development of the Jaina tradition. The concluding chapter discusses Jainism's historical development.

437 The central philosophy of Jainism (*anekanta-vada*).
Bimal Krishna Matilal. Ahmedabad, India: L. D. Institute of Indology, 1981. 72p.

This work, which reconstructs the history of *anekanta-vada*, Jainism's central philosophy of non-radicalism, originated as a series of lectures. Matilal shows *anekanta-vada* to have arisen through a synthesis of different metaphysical and ontological theories of ancient India. It is a theory of non one-sidedness which emphasizes the many-sided nature of reality.

Pilgrimage and pilgrim centres

438 **Hindu places of pilgrimage in India: a study in cultural geography.**
Surinder Mohan Bhardwaj.   Berkeley, California: University of California Press, 1983. 2nd ed. 258p. maps. bibliog.

A detailed study of India's Hindu pilgrimage system written from the perspective of cultural geography. The author examines pertinent historical and religious literature, including the *Mahabharata* and the *Puranas*, to provide an analysis of the distribution of *tirthas* (holy places), pilgrimage routes and perceptions of *tirtha* rankings. Then, drawing upon the findings of fieldwork conducted during 1967-68, which involved the interview of more than 5,000 pilgrims, Bhardwaj provides details of the caste composition of pilgrims and the frequency and purpose of visits.

439 **Banaras: city of light.**
Diana L. Eck.   London: Routledge & Kegan Paul, 1983. 427p. maps. bibliog.

An elegantly produced and illustrated historical and descriptive account of the Hindu holy city, Banaras (Varanasi). Eck, a professor of Hindu religion at Harvard University, is also author of *Darshan: seeing the divine image in India* (Chambersburg, Pennsylvania: Anima Books, 1985. 2nd ed. 97p.), an evocative study of images and their functions. In this work she analyses Banaras' elaborate and thriving rituals, myths and literature. Available in paperback format, it forms both a scholarly reference work and also an informative guidebook for visitors to the holy city. Raghubir Singh's *Banaras: the sacred city of India* (London: Thames & Hudson, 1988. 120p.) forms a sumptuous photographic companion volume.

440 **Servants of the goddess: the priests of a south Indian temple.**
Christopher J. Fuller.   Cambridge: Cambridge University Press, 1984. 232p.

An anthropological study of the priests of the Minakshi Temple of Madurai, in Tamil Nadu, south India. The author describes and analyses the myths of the temple, the social structure of the priesthood, and the relationships of the priests to the state and to other Brahmin caste groups. He explains their current feelings of demoralization. This specialised monograph work can be read usefully in conjunction with Burton Stein's edited volume, *South Indian temples: an analytical reconsideration* (New Delhi: Vikas, 1978. 155p.).

441 **Journey through the twelve forests: an encounter with Krishna.**
David L. Haberman.   New York; Oxford: Oxford University Press, 1994. 272p. 2 maps. bibliog.

An account of a Krishna pilgrimage in the Indian region of Braj, situated south of Delhi. Drawing upon his own experience of the event, the author places the pilgrimage in its historical and cultural context, and recounts the tales of Krishna around which the pilgrimage revolves. This work can be read usefully in conjunction with *Braj: centre of Krishna pilgrimage* (New Delhi: Bagchi, 1987. 554p.), by A. D. Entwistle.

442 **Pilgrimage in the Hindu tradition: a case study of West Bengal.**
E. A. Morinis. New Delhi: Oxford University Press India, 1984.
350p. bibliog.

An excellent study of the practice and significance of pilgrimages for rural society in West Bengal. Other similar works on pilgrimages in other parts of India include: Ann Grodzins Gold's *Fruitful journeys: the ways of Rajasthan pilgrims* (Berkeley, California: University of California Press, 1988. 333p.); and Dighambar Balkrishna Mokashi's *Palkhi: an Indian pilgrimage* (Albany, New York: State University of New York Press (SUNY), 1987. 291p.), translated from the Marathi by Philip C. Engblom, which is an account of the popular large-scale pilgrimage to Pandharpur in southern Maharashtra.

443 **Death in Banaras.**
Jonathan P. Parry. Cambridge: Cambridge University Press, 1994.
380p. bibliog.

A fascinating study of the 'sacred specialists' who serve the millions of pilgrims and mourners attracted to the holy city of Banaras (Varanasi) each year. Parry explores the way the priests organize their business and their understanding of the rituals over which they preside. An excellent complementary volume is *Culture and power in Banaras: community, performance and environment, 1800-1980* (Berkeley, California: University of California Press, 1989. 290p.), edited by Sandria B. Freitag, which comprises an important collection of scholarly essays on various aspects of north Indian culture as found in Banaras. There are contributions on the connections between pilgrimage and disease (D. Arnold), railroad construction and environmental degradation (R. G. Varady), and on folk music and Hindi drama.

444 **Religion under bureaucracy: policy and administration for Hindu temples in south India.**
Franklin A. Presler. Cambridge: Cambridge University Press, 1987.
179p. bibliog.

A richly documented and lucid study of the introduction of contested and sometimes contradictory state policies regarding the administration of Hindu temples in 19th- and 20th-century south India. Presler shows how, through religion, the modern Indian state has shaped relations between centre and locality, and between public and private domains.

445 **Gods on earth: the management of religious experience and identity in a north Indian pilgrimage centre.**
Peter Van der Veer. London; Atlantic Highlands, New Jersey: The Athlone Press, 1988. 310p. bibliog. (Monographs on Social Anthropology, vol. 59).

A study of the north Indian Hindu *tirtha* (holy city) of Ayodhya by an anthropologist. The author provides illuminating descriptions of the Ramanandi *sadhus,* the dominant renunciant order which controls many of its temples and monasteries, and Brahmin *pandits* (priests) who serve as pilgrim guides and carry out a lucrative trade in bathing and life-cycle rituals on the banks of the sacred river Sarayu. There is also a valuable historical narrative which traces the changing fortunes of Ayodhya, the city of Rama, since the 18th century. This history supplements that provided by the Sanskritist Hans

Bakker in his excellent monograph, *Ayodhya* (Groningen, the Netherlands: Egbert Forsten, 1986. 3 vols in one), which covers the city's development from pre-Buddhist times to the late Mughal era.

Sikhism

446 **Who is a Sikh?: the problem of Sikh identity.**
William Hewat McLeod.   Oxford: Clarendon Press, 1989. 140p.
bibliog.

A stimulating, but in the current political climate in Punjab, controversial work by the leading scholar of Sikh studies in the West. Designed as a series of lectures, which were not presented due to the author's ill-health, the essays in this slim volume examine the historical process by which the Sikh tradition emerged and grew. From an early loose body venerating the Gurus, there emerged during the 18th century a distinct, militant-fundamentalist grouping, the *Khalsa*, which lay emphasis on the code of behaviour called the *rahit*. This group grasped power and entered a claim to orthodoxy and between 1873-1920, via the Singh Sabha and Gurdwara Reform movements, Sikhism established a powerful, highly visible identity, clearly separate from Hinduism. Amplified discussions of the themes raised are to be found in McLeod's *The Sikhs: history, religion, and society* (New York: Columbia University Press, 1989. 161p.).

447 **The construction of religious boundaries: culture, identity and diversity in the Sikh tradition.**
Harjot Oberoi.   New Delhi: Oxford University Press India, 1994.
300p. bibliog.

Drawing on post-structuralist theory, the author reinterprets religion and society in India and suggests an alternative to earlier scholarly narratives that saw Sikhism, Hinduism and Islam as historical categories encompassing self-conscious units of religious identity.

448 **A history of the Sikhs. Volume 1: 1469-1839. Volume 2: 1839-1964.**
Khushwant Singh.   New Delhi: Oxford University Press, 1991.
2nd ed. 2 vols. maps. bibliog.

A definitive history of the Sikhs, their religion, and their political fortunes, written by one of India's foremost journalists. Singh considers Sikhism to be a *melange* of the Hindu *bhakti* and Muslim *sufi* traditions of medieval India. His contention that the rise of Sikhism and the resurgence of Punjabi nationalism are synonymous is not generally accepted by Sikh theologians. Appendixes contain translations of hymns from the *Adi Granth/Guru Granth Sahib* (holy book of Sikhism) and *Dasam Granth* (collection of the tenth Sikh guru, Gobind Singh).

449 **The divine master: life and teachings of Guru Nanak.**
Sewa Ram Singh, edited by Prithipal Singh Kapur.   Jalandhar, India:
ABS Publications, 1988. 222p. bibliog.

A study of the life and teachings of Guru Nanak (1469-1539), founder of the Sikh
religion. The Guru's doctrines are set out in the *Adi-Granth*, which fused elements of
Brahmanism and Islam, but also added distinctive new ideas. A classic earlier account
of Guru Nanak's life and teachings is: *Guru Nanak in history* (Chandigarh, India:
Panjab University, 1969. 348p.), by J. S. Grewal.

450 **Selections from the sacred writings of the Sikhs.**
Translated by Trilochan Singh (and others), revised by George S.
Fraser.   New York: S. Wiser, 1973. 1st American ed. 288p.

Prepared by a panel of Sikh scholars and sponsored by UNESCO, this is a
comprehensive anthology of Sikh writings. The translations were polished by the
Irish poet George S. Fraser. An introduction by Sarvepalli Radhakrishnan, the
philosopher and second president of India, explains the fundamental tenets of the
Sikh religion.

Zoroastrianism

451 **Zoroastrians: their religious beliefs and practices.**
Mary Boyce.   Boston, Massachusetts: Routledge & Kegan Paul,
1979. 252p. maps. bibliog.

An introduction to the Zoroastrian religion as it is practised by the Parsee community
of India, written by its foremost contemporary expert. The book provides a history of
the religion and its practitioners from Indo-Iranian times to the present. It examines
the influence of Zoroastrianism not only on three great Iranian empires but also on
Buddhism, Judaism, Christianity, and Islam.

452 **The Parsis.**
Piloo Nanavutty.   New Delhi: National Book Trust, 1980. 2nd ed.
184p.

A straightforward survey of the history of India's Parsee community from its Iranian
origins to the present day. The volume includes a brief account of Parsee religious
beliefs and customs. However, its chief focus is on the community's contribution to
the evolution of modern India, including reviews of Parsee achievements in politics,
commerce and industry, science and medicine, and art and literature. It can be read
usefully alongside *Parsees in India: a minority as an agent of social change* (New
Delhi: Vikas, 1994. 300p.), by Eckehard Kulke.

Philosophy

453 Thinkers of the Indian renaissance.
Edited by Donald H. Bishop.   New Delhi: Wiley Eastern, 1982. 408p.
An analysis of the life, ideas and impact of nineteen Indian philosophers and political thinkers of the 19th and 20th centuries. Standard figures, such as Mahatma Gandhi, Rabindranath Tagore, Ram Mohan Roy, Sri Aurobindo, and Sarvepalli Radhakrishnan are considered. There are also essays on less mainstream thinkers, for example Ananda Kentish Coomaraswamy, K. C. Bhattacharya, Ramana Maharshi, Iswar Chandra Vidyasagar, and M. N. Roy. An invaluable work.

454 A history of Indian philosophy.
Surendra Nath Dasgupta.   Cambridge: Cambridge University Press, 1965-69. reprint of 1922-25 ed. 5 vols. bibliog.
A monumental work by one of the greatest specialists in the field. The author has undertaken not only a survey of the better-known Indian philosophical systems, but also an in-depth analysis of many obscure philosophical schools. The fifth volume, completed posthumously by the author's widow, examines Saivite thought. There is an abridgement of these volumes by R. Agarwal and S. K. Jain (Allahabad, India: Kitab Mahal, 1969. 230p.), with the same title. A more recent study of Indian philosophy since Vedic times is *Studies in the history of Indian philosophy* (Calcutta: Bagchi, 1990. new ed. 3 vols.), edited by Debiprasad Chattopadhyaya.

455 The philosophy of the *Upanishads*.
Paul Deussen.   New York: Dover, 1966. reprint of 1905 ed. 417p. bibliog.
Written by a German Kantian scholar, this definitive study of the *Upanishads* emphasizes the idealistic element in Vedantic philosophy without ignoring the variety of thought present in the texts. Part one discusses the key concept of Brahman; part two Vedantic cosmology; part three the psychology of the *atman* ('self'); and part four the concept of transmigration and salvation.

456 **The *Bhagavad Gita*.**
Edited by Eliot Deutsch. Washington, DC: University Press of
America, 1982. 192p. bibliog.

A scholarly, readable translation of India's most important religious text. Deutsch has
written a marvellous introductory essay about the importance of the book and its
central characters, Krishna and Arjuna. A concluding chapter, in four parts, examines
the principal message of the *Gita*. The total effect, therefore, is to present the message
of the *Gita* clearly and accurately. Another useful critical translation of the *Gita* is
Bhagavad Gita: translation and commentary (New Delhi: Motilal Banarsidass, 1985.
245p.), by Richard Gotshalk.

457 **Perception, knowledge, and disbelief: a study of Jayarasi's
scepticism.**
Eli Franco. Stuttgart, Germany: Franz Steiner Verlag, 1987. 584p.
bibliog. (Alt- und Neu-Indische Studien 35).

This work comprises a copiously annotated and authoritative translation of the first
half of the *Tattvopaplavasimha* ('The critique of philosophical principles'), an
important treatise by the 8th-century philosopher Jayarasi. The Sanskrit text is printed
en face. Jayarasi's work is the only full-fledged text on materialist scepticism in the
Indian tradition. With great subtlety, it refutes the theories of perception developed by
Nyaya, Mimamsa, Buddhism, and Samkhya.

458 **Outlines of Indian philosophy.**
Mysore Hiriyanna. London: Allen & Unwin, 1975. new ed. 419p.

A college-level text for students of religion and philosophy, which was originally
published in 1932. Though the scope of the volume is limited to Vedic, early post-
Vedic, and other early systems, culminating in the philosophy of Ramanuja (d. 1137),
all the principal Indian philosophical doctrines are clearly delineated. Unfortunately
the author, an eminent Indian philosopher, has omitted any discussion of the Tantric
tradition.

459 **Sri Aurobindo: a biography and a history.**
K. R. Srinivasa Iyenagar. Pondicherry, India: Sri Aurobindo
International Centre of Education, 1972. 3rd rev. enlarged ed. 2 vols.
bibliog.

A comprehensive biography of Aurobindo Ghose (1872-1950), college professor,
political revolutionary, and philosopher. The book describes Aurobindo's lonely years
in England, his efforts to obtain an appointment to the Indian Civil Service, his
employment in the princely state of Baroda, his relationship with Tilak and other
political revolutionaries during 1902-10, and his activities as a poet-philosopher in
Pondicherry between 1910 and 1950 after renouncing politics for yogic philosophy
and establishing the Auroville *ashram*. A more concise biography is *Sri Aurobindo: a
biography* (New Delhi: Oxford University Press India, 1989. 172p.), by Peter Heeks.

460 **The moral and political writings of Mahatma Gandhi.**
Edited by Raghavan Iyer. Oxford: Clarendon Press, 1986-87. 3 vols.
bibliog.

This selection of the moral, political and philosophical writings of Mahatma Gandhi is designed to complement the editor's own analysis of Gandhi's thought, *The moral and political thought of Mahatma Gandhi* (Oxford; New York: Oxford University Press, 1973. 385p.). The most important items from the ninety volumes of Gandhi's *Collected Works* are reproduced in these three volumes, with the titles: *I: Civilization, politics, and religion; II: Truth and non-violence;* and *III: Non-violent resistance and social transformation.* The single volume, *The essential writings of Mahatma Gandhi* (New Delhi: Oxford University Press India, 1991. 441p.), edited by Iyer, collects together Gandhi's seminal writings.

461 **Journal of Indian Philosophy.**
Dordrecht, the Netherlands: D. Reidel, 1970- . quarterly.

Published in the Netherlands under the editorship of an Indian philosophy professor, this journal is the only Western publication exclusively devoted to Indian philosophy. It contains few book reviews.

462 **The perennial Vivekananda: a selection.**
Compiled by Swami Lokeswarananda. New Delhi: Sahitya Akademi, 1988. 300p.

Swami Vivekananda (1863-1902), organizer of the now world-wide Ramakrishna Mission, once described himself as 'condensed India', by which he meant he represented every individual, every sect and community of India. This selection is taken from his lectures, letters, inspired talks, and poems.

463 **Logic, language and reality: an introduction to Indian philosophical studies.**
Bimal Krishna Matilal. New Delhi: Motilal Banarsidass, 1985. 448p.
bibliog.

The author, a Sanskrit scholar familiar with contemporary Western analytic philosophy, seeks to demonstrate in this work the continuing relevance of classical Indian philosophy. Particularly interesting is the section on the history of Indian logic and Jaina attempts to steer a middle path between the metaphysical extremes of being and becoming and Buddhist idealism. The volume is complex in places and assumes readers have some prior background familiarity with Indian philosophy.

464 **Perception: an essay on classical Indian theories of knowledge.**
Bimal Krishna Matilal. Oxford: Clarendon Press, 1986. 438p.
bibliog.

This volume shows the relevance of classical Indian epistemology to modern philosophical debates. Arranged in four parts, it comprises twelve chapters dealing with such topics as Indian philosophical method/argument, nature, knowledge and illusion, perception, and world views. The author is particularly vigorous in his defence of Nyaya realism against Buddhist phenomenalism.

465 **Six pillars: introduction to the major works of Sri Aurobindo.**
Edited by Robert A. McDermott. Chambersburg, Pennsylvania:
Wilson Books, 1974. 198p. bibliog.

Aurobindo Ghose (see item no. 459), a Cambridge-educated classicist and author of thirty volumes of religio-philosophical interpretations of Vedanta and his own teachings, had a profound influence on modern Indian philosophy. In this slim volume, six experts examine his ideas on the spiritual transformation of the modern world; his interpretation of the *Gita*; his philosophical theories about existence, knowledge and spiritual evolution; and his long epic poem *Savitri*. This is the best introduction to Aurobindo.

466 **Essays on Indian philosophy, traditional and modern.**
J. N. Mohanty, edited by Purushottama Bilimoria. New Delhi:
Oxford University Press India, 1994. 386p. bibliog.

A selection of essays by the author written over a forty year period. Topics covered include metaphysics, epistemology, social ethics, religion and the differences between Eastern and Western philosophy.

467 **Radhakrishnan: his life and ideas.**
K. Satchidananda Murty, Ashok Vohra. Albany, New York: State
University of New York (SUNY) Press, 1990. 239p. bibliog.

A solid, balanced account of the career and ideas of the Madras-born Dr. Sarvepalli Radhakrishnan (1888-1975), one of the great Indian intellectuals of the 20th century. Educated in Protestant mission schools, well read in both Eastern and Western philosophical and religious literature, a prolific writer and translator of the Indian classics, an international academic, and a diplomat and India's president between 1962-67, Radhakrishnan was a universalist figure and a non-sectarian Hindu who stressed the importance of spirituality. These intellectual concerns are brought out in two complementary works: Ishwar C. Harris's *Radhakrishnan: the profile of a universalist* (Columbia, Missouri: South Asia Books; Calcutta: Minerva, 1982. 306p.); and Sarvepalli Gopal's *Radhakrishnan: a biography* (London: Unwin Hyman, 1989. 408p.).

468 **Encyclopaedia of Indian philosophies.**
Edited by Karl H. Potter, Sibajiban Bhattacharyya, Gerald James
Larson, Ram Shankar Bhattacharya, Harold G. Coward, K. Kunjunni
Raja. Princeton, New Jersey: Princeton University Press; New Delhi:
Motilal Banarsidass, 1970-93. 6 vols. bibliog.

As of 1994 only six of the projected twenty-eight volumes had been published. The first volume, a bibliography of over 9,000 entries, contains complete information on Sanskrit philosophical texts and their authors, chosen for their enduring theoretical and philosophical value. Volumes two and six deal exclusively with the the Nyaya and Vaishesika philosophical systems, and commentaries on those systems up to 1350 and 1510 respectively. The third volume deals with Advaita-Vedanta, and commentaries on it. Volume four, which is edited by G. L. Larson and R. S. Bhattacharya, covers the Samkhya dualist tradition from ancient to modern times. Volume five, edited, by H. G. Coward and K. Kunjunni Raja, deals with the philosophy of the Grammarians. A work for research scholars which can be read with

Guide to Indian philosophy (Boston, Massachusetts: G. K. Hall, 1988. 159p.), edited by Karl H. Potter, Austin B. Creel and Edwin Gerow, a bibliographic guide which includes 884 annotated entries and has name and subject indexes.

469 The principal *Upanishads*.
Translated by Sarvepalli Radhakrishnan. New York: Humanities, 1978. 958p. bibliog.

A careful and extremely readable translation of the fifteen major *Upanishads* (sacred scriptures) and five short ones. Radhakrishnan has been criticized for sacrificing literalness for readability. The translator's introductions to the texts reflect the position of the school of commentators led by Sankaracarya (788-820 AD), one of India's greatest philosophers, but they also include interesting comparisons with Western religious ideas wherever appropriate.

470 A sourcebook in Indian philosophy.
Edited by Sarvepalli Radhakrishnan, Charles A. Moore. Princeton, New Jersey: Princeton University Press, 1967. 683p. bibliog.

This anthology successfully accomplishes its two stated objectives: to supply Western readers with basic source material on Indian philosophy in convenient and usable form, and to present material on all the major philosophical systems and perspectives of India. Selections from the Vedas, *Upanishads*, *Gita*, *Mahabharata*, *Manusmriti*, *Arthasastra*, *Carvakas*, Jainism, Buddhism, the six principal schools of philosophy, Sankara, Ramanuja, Aurobindo, and Radhakrishnan have been included. Not all the translations are original. The translation of the *Gita* is exceptionally good.

471 Structural depths of Indian thought.
P. T. Raju. Albany, New York: State University of New York (SUNY) Press, 1985. 599p. bibliog. (SUNY Series in Philosophy).

An authoritative and accessible overview of the entire range of Indian philosophy, written by a leading expert in the fields of Indian and comparative philosophy. This work is designed to serve as a companion to the more comprehensive volumes of Dasgupta (see item no. 454). The author stresses the intellectual, as opposed to the religious or cultural, aspects of Indian thought, revealing it to be rich in rational discussion of many of the same epistemological, metaphysical, and logical issues as have been considered in the West. The closing chapter on contemporary Indian philosophy includes discussions of Radhakrishnan, Aurobindo, Tagore, Gandhi, and Krishnamurti. This is the best introductory textbook to Indian philosophy.

472 Universals: studies in Indian logic and linguistics.
J. Frits Staal. Chicago: University of Chicago Press, 1988. 267p. bibliog.

A collection of twelve reprinted papers, seven on Indian logic and five on Indian linguistics, and seven reviews, which seek to demonstrate that Indian contributions to the general area of philosophical thought are 'similar and not dissimilar to Western contributions'. Staal shows that Indian *pandits* (learned men) discovered the same universals that were discovered in the West. In a useful introductory essay, the author discusses his ideas concerning such universals.

473   **The yogi and the mystic: studies in Indian and comparative mysticism.**
Karel Werner.   London: Curzon Press, 1994. 208p. bibliog.

A study which covers a wide range of aspects of Indian and comparative mysticism. The author examines the structural patterns in mystical experiences and the mystical paths of different traditions and schools.

Society

General

474 Contributions to Indian Sociology.
New Delhi: Sage Publications, 1957- . biannual.

Edited by Triloki Nath Madan, author of *Pathways: approaches to the study of society in India* (New Delhi: Oxford University Press India, 1994. 289p.), a critical analysis of studies of Indian society over the past fifty years, this is the leading international journal for research on Indian and South Asian societies. Two other important journals are: *Social Scientist*, a well-established journal produced by the Indian School of Social Sciences, at Trivandrum, India; and *Indian Journal of Social Science*, a new quarterly produced since 1988 by Sage Publications.

475 Fluid signs: being a person the Tamil way.
E. Valentine Daniel. Berkeley, California: University of California Press, 1984. 320p. bibliog.

An imaginative, original work which provides a new interpretation of south Indian village culture. The author, a native Tamil speaker, carried out fieldwork in a village near Trichinopoly, in Tamil Nadu, during 1975-76 and participated in the famous Ayyappan pilgrimage. Villagers' dreams are interpreted with cultural insight and there are chapters on such topics as the household and sexuality. The work exemplifies the Chicago University '*jati* theory', which emphasises the centrality of *jati* (genus or ranked substance) rather than caste, and focuses on flows of 'substance' between persons and places.

476 The hollow crown: ethnohistory of an Indian kingdom.
Nicholas B. Dirks. Cambridge: Cambridge University Press, 1987. 458p. bibliog. (Cambridge South Asian Studies, no. 39).

A study of the 'ethnohistory' of local chiefly families and kingdoms in south India based on late medieval, early modern and imperial inscriptional and textual sources and ethnographic fieldwork. The author seeks to redress the previous emphasis on the religiosity of Indian society and neglect of the underlying political reality and 'poetics of power'. Dirks concludes that crowns in India were never so hollow, nor kings so inferior, as Orientalism made them out to be.

477 *Homo hierarchicus*: **the caste system and its implications.**
Louis Dumont, translated from the French by Mark Sainsbury.
Chicago: University of Chicago Press, 1980. rev. English ed. 386p.
maps.

An important intellectual and comparative analysis of the Indian caste system and Western egalitarianism. Dumont, a French structuralist, argues that purity and pollution concepts underlie the caste system. The book assumes considerable knowledge of Indian sociological literature and contemporary anthropological theory, and it has been criticized for ignoring the occupational dimension of the caste system. A milestone in the continuing debate on the nature of caste. A related recent work, *Status and sacredness: a general theory of status relations and an analysis of Indian culture* (New York: Oxford University Press USA, 1994. 384p.), by Murray Milner, challenges the view that India's caste system is a unique phenomenon and contends that caste distinctions are similar to status differentiation found elsewhere.

478 **The inner conflict of tradition: essays in Indian ritual, kingship and society.**
Jan C. Heesterman.   Chicago: University of Chicago Press, 1985.
255p. bibliog.

A collection of essays, some previously published, which make the forbidding technicality of Vedic ritual accessible and provide a cohesive interpretation of Indian civilization. The author's central idea of 'inner conflict' refers to a perceived disjuncture in Indian civilization between the transcendent realm of *dharma* (natural law) and its associated ritual order, which reigns but does not rule, and the world of power and interest. This 'inner conflict' is most clearly manifested in the relationship between brahmin and king, who are respectively dependent upon each other for material support and legitimation, yet remain irreconcilable. The work also includes essays on Vedic myth and ritual, the *Arthasastra* (see item no. 132) and the state, caste and *karma,* the Mughal Empire and the British Raj, and Max Weber.

479 **Caste, cult and hierarchy: essays on the culture of India.**
Pauline Kolenda.   Meerut, India: Folklore Institute, 1981. 350p.

This volume collects together essays written by the author between 1957 and 1978. Three main topics are addressed: indigenous views of caste, pollution and patron-client *jajmani* relationships, based on fieldwork in the north Indian village of Khalapur; village shamanism (popular, low-caste Hindu religious beliefs); and analyses of the views of Louis Dumont (see item no. 477). The review of literature on changes taking place in the *jajmani* (quasi-ritual patron-client service relationship) and *hali* (bonded labour) systems is particularly useful, comparing the models posited by Wiser, Leach, Gould, and Beidelman.

480 **Friends, brothers and informants: fieldwork memories of Banaras.**
Nita Kumar. Berkeley, California: University of California Press,
1992. 271p.

An honest, self-critical account of fieldwork carried out by a distinguished Indian anthropologist among the artisans of Banaras. The author draws attention to the problems faced in communication and understanding by Western-schooled, urban middle class Indian scholars – Kumar was born and raised in the Lucknow cantonments – and poor, illiterate working class artisans. The volume gives an insight into the approaches and philosophies of anthropologists, with Kumar advocating the use of indigenous literature to supplement oral testimonies and ethnographic observation.

481 **Society in India.**
David Goodman Mandelbaum. Berkeley, California: University of
California Press, 1970-72. 2 vols. bibliog.

A readable, reliable, and comprehensive survey of Indian society and its principal components – the individual, the family, the caste system, and village life. The author has also identified the patterns and extent of social mobility and institutional change in India. Though somewhat dated, Mandelbaum's conclusions have stood the test of time.

482 **An anthropological bibliography of South Asia together with a
directory of recent anthropological field work.**
Compiled by Elizabeth Von Fürer-Haimendorf, Helen Kanitkar.
Paris: Mouton, 1958-76. 4 vols.

Almost 13,000 Western-language items on South Asia, the bulk of them on India, are listed, though not annotated. With the exception of Indian census publications, government publications have been excluded. The volumes have one general and nineteen regional sections, each covering the following categories: cultural and social anthropology, material culture and applied art, folklore and folk art, prehistoric archaeology, physical anthropology, and miscellanea.

Family and marriage

483 **Society from the inside out: anthropological perspectives on the
South Asian household.**
Edited by John N. Gray, David J. Mearns. New Delhi; Newbury
Park, California: Sage Publications, 1989. 263p.

A collection of scholarly papers concerned with an 'inside out' approach to the study of the South Asian household, that is with analysing links between the household and wider society. The contributions on India include a paper by Pauline Kolenda which discusses factors, such as the need for cooperative work teams and the low age of marriage, that promote the joint family in Rajasthan, and by Sylvia Vatuk on the diversity of household composition in southern India.

484 **Kinship organization in India.**
Irawati Karmarkar Karve. New York: Asia, 1968. 3rd. ed. 431p.
maps. bibliog.

First published in 1953, this is a classic comprehensive survey of national patterns and regional differences in Indian kinship organization. The book begins with a discussion of caste and family and examines kinship usages as detailed in ancient and historical literature. Subsequent chapters discuss regional and intra-regional variations in kinship organization and the Hindu law of property, inheritance and succession in various areas of India.

485 **Regional differences in family structure.**
Pauline Kolenda. Jaipur, India: Rawar Publications, 1987. 390p.
bibliog.

A useful collection of largely previously published essays by an expert on Indian domestic structures. Kolenda uses the detailed information collected by the 1961 census for exploring regional differences in household organization. This work can be complemented by *Family, kinship and marriage in India* (New Delhi: Oxford University Press India, 1993. 502p.), a collection of scholarly essays edited by Patricia Uberoi.

486 **Concepts of person: kinship, caste and marriage in India.**
Edited by Akos Ostor, Lina Fruzzetti, Steve Barnett. Cambridge, Massachusetts: Harvard University Press, 1982. 276p.

A collection of American conference papers, dating from 1976, concerned with new approaches to South Asian caste, kinship, and marriage, stimulated by the work of Louis Dumont (see item no. 477) and David Schneider, for whom descent is not simply a concrete biological fact from which social rights flow, but is pre-eminently symbolic and conceptual. There are interesting comparisons by Fruzzetti and Ostor of kinship ideas in Bengal and south India, a paper on Kashmiri *pandits* by T. N. Madan, and kinship concepts in central and western Uttar Pradesh are analysed by R. S. Khare and Pauline Kolenda.

487 **Punjabi century, 1857-1947.**
Prakash Tandon. Berkeley, California: University of California Press, 1968. 274p. map.

488 **Beyond Punjab, 1937-1960.**
Prakash Tandon. Berkeley, California: University of California Press, 1971. 222p.

489 **Return to Punjab, 1961-1975.**
Prakash Tandon. Berkeley, California: University of California Press, 1981. 211p.

The above three entries constitute the autobiography and family history of the Tandons, a family of western Punjab, written by a leading business executive. The first volume deals with the changing urban lifestyle in north India under British rule, the second with the author's spectacular rise in the Indian corporate universe, and the third with his tenure in state-controlled banking and trade enterprises. While substantial portions of these volumes deal with corporate organization and behaviour, there is a wealth of information on family life in India during the last 150 years.

Social structure and social change

490 Modernization and social change among Muslims in India.
Edited by Imtiaz Ahmad. New Delhi: Manohar, 1983. 281p.

A collection of well-written essays which reveal new approaches to the study of social change among the contemporary Muslim community in India. In the introduction, the editor reviews writings on this theme by past generations of anthropologists and sociologists. The remainder of the work is devoted to more specialist papers. Aspects of Muslim women's status are addressed in contributions by Shahida Lateef and Neisha Haniff, while Peter Mayer, John Eale, and Mattison Mines analyse the position of the Muslims of Bengal and south India, who are somewhat detached from the community's north India-based Urdu speaking élite.

491 The Hindu caste system.
Harold A. Gould. New Delhi: Chanakya, 1987-90. 3 vols.

These three volumes collect together essays written by the author during three decades of the study of Indian social structure. *Vol. 1: The sacralization of a social order* (1987) focuses on the traditional system of social stratification. It sees the origin of the caste system as lying in the success which Brahmin priests had in making a religion out of the social order, especially the occupational system, hence the volume's title. *Vol. 2: Caste adaptation in modernizing Indian society* (1988) looks at adaptive transformations of the caste system under the impact of modernity and includes essays on Sanskritization and case studies in the north Indian cities of Lucknow and Kanpur. *Vol. 3: Politics and caste* (1990) emphasises the relationship between caste and politics in modern India and contains recent essays on the Congress Party in Faizabad district, east Uttar Pradesh.

492 Social stratification.
Edited by Dipankar Gupta. New Delhi: Oxford University Press India, 1992. 518p. bibliog. (Oxford in India Readings in Sociology and Social Anthropology).

An excellent introductory text which has collected together more than thirty key readings by anthropologists and sociologists on Indian social structure. The work, which includes an introductory chapter by the editor, is divided into four parts: caste; caste profiles; class; and caste, class and conflict. There is also an appendix which includes extracts from the thoeretical work of, among others, Max Weber and Louis Dumont. There are readings from such key writers as M. N. Srinivas, G. S. Ghurye, McKim Marriott, Pauline Kolenda, T. N. Madan, André Beteille, Gerald Berreman, R. S. Khare, Morris D. Morris, Daniel Thorner, Kathleen Gough, F. G. Bailey, Jan Breman, and Romila Thapar.

493 **The coming of the *Devi*: *Adivasi* assertion in western India.**
David Hardiman.   New Delhi: Oxford University Press India, 1987.
248p. bibliog.

A fascinating study, drawing on oral testimonies, of a struggle for assertion by the tribal *Adivasi* community in western India against local landlords and Pasi liquor dealers. This occurred after, in 1922, a goddess (*Devi*), known as Salabhai who expressed her teachings through spirit mediums, commanded the *Adivasis* to change their established way of life, give up alcoholic drink, meat consumption, and engage in a non-violent movement. The author argues that such struggles highlight the power of religion in peasant society and the impact of the rise of capitalism and nationalism.

494 **Untouchable! Voices of the *Dalit* Liberation Movement.**
Edited by Barbara R. Joshi.   London: Zed Books, 1986. 166p.
bibliog.

A fascinating collection of writings, published in English for the first time, by the traditionally disadvantaged low-caste Indian minorities, or *dalits* (poor and downtrodden). The book is divided into six sections dealing with: the historical background; current social and economic conditions; the evolution of a new culture; problems confronting *dalit* grassroots organizational efforts; untouchability and Indian public institutions; and strategies for successful change. Each section is preceded by a useful contextual introduction by the editor. It is argued that, despite four decades of legislation to abolish untouchability, there has been little improvement in the lot of *dalits* and violence continues to be directed against untouchables. However, *dalits* are responding to discrimination through organizing a coherent movement of opposition to the Indian social system. This work provides a platform for the *Dalit* Liberation Movement's most active and articulate leaders.

495 **Religion as a social vision: the movement against untouchability in twentieth-century Punjab.**
Mark Juergensmeyer.   Berkeley, California: University of California Press, 1982. 357p. map. bibliog.

This monograph traces the rise and fall of the Ad Dharm (estd. 1925), a movement concerned with low-caste social and religious advancement, and its leader Mangoo Ram (1886-1980). It looks at the social context in which the movement emerged, its impact on rural and urban areas, attempts to resuscitate Ad Dharm during the 1970s, and at such related movements as the Ravidas, Arya Samaj, Ambedkar movements, Valmikhi Sabha, Christianity, and the Radhasoamis.

496 **The untouchable as himself: ideology, identity, and pragmatism among the Lucknow Chamars.**
Ravindra S. Khare.   Cambridge: Cambridge University Press, 1984.
208p. bibliog. (Cambridge Studies in Cultural Systems, no. 8).

A sensitive study of what it means to be an untouchable (*harijan*) in contemporary India, based on fieldwork among the Chamar community in the north Indian city of Lucknow. The author describes the Chamar's cultural ideology and allows urban Chamar reformers, leaders and ordinary persons to speak for themselves. Although untouchability has been legally abolished, *Harijans* continue to experience social resistance and deprivation, while changing socio-economic circumstances have generated new expectations. This book can be read usefully alongside *The backward classes in contemporary India* (New Delhi: Oxford University Press India, 1992. 117p.), by André Beteille.

497   Caste: the emergence of the South Asian social system.
Morton Klass.   Philadelphia: Institute for the Study of Human Issues, 1980. 212p. bibliog.

An historic overview of the development of India's caste system in which the author rejects the two competing established views of the origins of caste – the racial hypothesis (that it arose out of the racial antipathies of the Aryan conquerors for the indigenous Dravidians) and the occupational hypothesis (which sees castes as guilds with a special concern for rank or purity) – and presents his own interpretation. For Klass, the caste system is essentially a socio-economic system concerned with gaining and maintaining differential access to agricultural surplus and is based around 'marriage-circles' which have originated from equalitarian, common-descent clans. He dates its emergence to ca. 2000 BC, when rice and hard grain cultivation spread throughout the subcontinent. A useful related work, focusing on the *varna* classificatory scheme is *Classifying the universe: the ancient Indian varna system and the origins of caste* (New York: Oxford University Press USA, 1994. 448p.), by Brian K. Smith.

498   An untouchable community in south India: structure and consensus.
Michael Moffatt.   Princeton, New Jersey: Princeton University Press, 1979. 323p. bibliog.

This superb study of five untouchable castes in a Tamilian village argues that untouchables are among the most fervent believers in the system that oppresses them. In social terms, the untouchables have adopted a system of caste-specific roles among themselves that replicates the larger caste system. Also, culturally, untouchables believe in the same hierarchically graded pantheon as do upper castes.

499   Caste, conflict and ideology: Mahatma Jotirao Phule and low-caste protest in nineteenth-century western India.
Rosalind O'Hanlon.   Cambridge: Cambridge University Press, 1985. 326p. map. bibliog. (Cambridge South Asian Studies, no. 30).

A scholarly analysis of the career of Jotirao Govind Phule (1827-90). A gardener by caste, he became the chief leader and ideologue of a powerful low and untouchable caste protest movement in late 19th-century Maharashtra which criticized the Indian National Congress for being too Brahminist and urban-centred in outlook. Phule founded the Truth-seeking Society in 1873, as a liberating vehicle for rural-based social and religious protest, and developed a powerful critique of Brahmin power. The author exhibits great skill in handling Marathi materials and empathy for her subject and accords ideology a central position in her analysis. There are also excellent descriptions of Maharashtra's social structure – the 'Maratha-*kunbi* caste complex' – and of the activities of other early Hindu reformers and Christian missionaries.

500 **Caste and kinship in Kangra.**
Jonathan P. Parry.   London: Routledge & Kegan Paul, 1979. 353p.
bibliog.

A case-study of how the Indian principle of hierarchy based on religious concepts of purity and pollution affects thoughts and action in India's western Himalayan (Kangra) region. The author, strongly influenced by Dumont (see item no. 477), argues that hierarchy underlies divisions within and between castes and families, as well as between men and gods. The special strength of this book is its examples of how people's ideas and behaviour are moulded by caste.

501 **When a great tradition modernizes: an anthropological approach to Indian civilization.**
Milton Singer.   New York: Praeger, 1972. 430p. bibliog.

A careful and empirical rejection of the view that traditional Indian society is resistant to change. Using Madras as a case study, and utilizing information on the industrial leadership of the city and on the Vaisnavite tradition, Singer concludes that the Indian tradition has utilized adaptive strategies for several centuries. He points out that, given the long history of the Hindu civilization of India, the process of modernization is likely to be complicated and not easily discernible.

502 **Caste in modern India and other essays.**
Mysore N. Srinivas.   London: J. K. Publishers, 1978. reprint of 1962
ed. 171p. bibliog.

According to Srinivas, three processes of social change are active in modern India: Sanskritization (the gradual availability of higher caste rituals to the untouchables), Westernization, and secularization. The author argues that Westernization and secularization, with the help of urbanization, have reduced the differences between subcastes, but the progress in Sanskritization continues to be painfully slow in modern India. This is an influential work.

503 **Dimensions of social change in India.**
Edited by Mysore N. Srinivas, S. Seshaiah, V. S. Parthasarathy.
Bombay: Allied, 1977. 518p. map. bibliog. (National Seminar on
Social Change, Bangalore, India, 1972).

A collection of thirty, consistently excellent, papers dealing primarily with social change among rural caste, tribal, and religious groups. After establishing the constituents of socio-economic development, the contributors examine changes in rural power structure, social stratification, the concept of dominant caste, the status of women, and the place of Muslims in Indian society.

Social problems, health and welfare

504 Colonizing the body: state medicine and epidemic disease in nineteenth-century India.
David Arnold. Berkeley, California; London: University of California Press, 1993. 354p. bibliog.

An innovative analysis of medicine and disease in colonial India, combining detailed empirical research with acute political economic analysis. The author analyses the role of the colonial state in medical and public health activities and argues that Western medicine became a critical battleground between the colonized and the colonisers. A recent collection of essays on a related theme is *Public health and preventive medicine in British India, 1859-1914* (Cambridge: Cambridge University Press, 1994. 344p.), edited by Mark Harrison.

505 South Asian systems of healing.
Edited by E. Valentine Daniel, Judy F. Pugh. Leiden, the Netherlands: E. J. Brill, 1984. 126p. (Contributions to Asian Studies, Vol. 18).

A collection of eight specialist essays by Western and Indian scholars, five of which were presented to a 1980 University of Wisconsin conference on Asian medical systems and which are concerned with analysing the epistemological basis of Indian medicine. Judy Pugh's paper focuses on astrological counselling in Banaras; Margaret Egnor analyses the cultural context of smallpox and turberculosis and the changing character of Mariamman, a mother deity; Katherine Ewing relates how Muslim *pirs* (wandering Muslim religious teachers) sometimes function as *hakims* (Muslim physicians), dispensing medicines; Debora Bhattacharyya reviews folk concepts of mental disorder in West Bengal; and Daniel describes the practice of pulse feeling in Siddha medicine.

506 Pills against poverty: a study of the introduction of Western medicine in a Tamil village.
Goran Djurfeldt, Staffan Lindberg. New Delhi: Macmillan, 1980. 232p. bibliog.

A study based on fieldwork in a coastal village twenty miles south of Madras, inhabited mostly by untouchables. The book describes the incidence of disease and mortality, the use of indigenous and Western-allopathic systems of medical practices, and the minimal success of the family planning programme in the village. Especially valuable is the examination of the relationships between the indigenous medical system and local religious values, and between the values of the dominant urban policy-makers and the Western medical system.

507 Mad tales from the Raj: the European insane in British India, 1800-1858.
Waltraud Ernst. London, New York: Routledge & Kegan Paul, 1991. 195p. bibliog.

An unusual study of the treatment of the European insane in India during the first half of the 19th century. The author, a practising psychologist, examines how colonial conditions gave lunatic policy a distinctive character in India. There were three significant deviations in practices from domestic models: inmates were segregated within asylums on a race basis; the European insane were not given manual labour since it was viewed as beneath their status; and European lunatics were institutionalized much earlier in India than would have been the case in Britain since they were seen as a special threat to the prestige of the colonial ruling class.

508 The social and cultural context of medicine in India.
Edited by Giri Raj Gupta. New Delhi: Vikas, 1981. 356p. bibliog.

This interesting work brings together fourteen papers by Indian and Western anthropologists and sociologists on a wide range of aspects of Indian medicine in its social and cultural context. Particularly interesting are the papers on north Indian folk medicine (R. S. Khare) and healers (E. O. Henry), homeopathy (S. M. Bharadwaj), and 'Who chooses modern medicine and why?' (T. N. Madan). There is also a paper by D. Banerji which, ranging from ancient times to the present day, charts the development of the Indian health service. Banerji concludes that, contrary to colonial myths, villagers have long shown an interest in acquiring curative and preventive services of a Western type and that it has been inadequate service provision which has let them down rather than their own resistance.

509 Indian Journal of Social Work.
Bombay: Tata Institute of Social Sciences, 1940- . quarterly.

One of the oldest Indian quarterlies, devoted to the 'promotion of professional social work'. It contains articles on various social issues including child welfare, juvenile delinquency, labour welfare, physically and mentally handicapped, criminology. Some book reviews are included.

510 The politics of health in India.
Roger Jeffrey. Berkeley, California: University of California Press, 1988. 348p. bibliog.

An objective analysis of the politics of health policy in India during the colonial and post-independence periods. During the colonial era, the author notes that, while changes in food distribution and famine policy helped to reduce mortality, sanitary reform and preventive medical services were underfunded. The crude death rate continued to fall after independence and clearer emphasis began to be given to rural and primary health care. Jeffrey interprets the 1970s community health workers' initiative as a response to popular pressures generated by both Gandhian and socialistic rhetoric.

511 Primary health care and traditional practitioners.
D. N. Kakar. New Delhi: Sterling, 1988. 195p. bibliog.

A survey and analysis of the therapeutic role of traditional medical practitioners based on Kakar's studies of the work of sixty-four full-time, local registered practitioners in Haryana. Seventy per cent of the practitioners interviewed had no formal qualification or training in an Indian system of medicine, yet they supplied three-quarters of all primary health care in rural areas. The author notes that most of these 'doctors' prescribe, sell, and inject Western (allopathic) medicines as well as *Ayurvedic* prescriptions, yet base their knowledge of treatments on the advice of salesmen from pharmaceutical companies. Kakar recommends improvements in their training, monitoring, and equipping.

512 **Shamans, mystics, and doctors.**
Sudhir Kakar. New York: Knopf, 1982. 306p. bibliog.

A fascinating, descriptive analysis of mystical cults, shamans, indigenous doctors, and the 'sacred' component of Indian culture, concerned with 'healing' mental disorders in India. Kakar explores in depth the healing practices of a *sufi* saint, a Tantric mystic, and an *Ayurvedic* doctor in the context of modern psychotherapy. Written by a Western-trained Hindu psychotherapist, the book finds that modern psychoanalysis and other psychiatric therapies are of only marginal relevance to the mental health situation in India.

513 **Studies on Indian medical history.**
Edited by G. Jan Meulenbeld, Dominik Wujastyk. Groningen, the Netherlands: Egbert Forsten, 1987. 247p.

A collection of fourteen papers presented by medical historians to an international workshop sponsored by the European *Ayurvedic* society. The two main sections are titled 'The Classical Tradition' and 'Colonial Interactions'. They contain essays on such themes as *Ayurvedic* pharmacology, the philosophical background of the *Carakasamhita* (medical encyclopaedia composed by Caraka during the reign of the Kusana king, Kanishka), relations between Indian and European medical practitioners, and Indian claims to have discovered smallpox vaccination before Jenner.

514 **Health status of Kerala: paradox of economic backwardness and health development.**
P. G. K. Panikar, C. R. Soman. Trivandrum, India: Centre for Development Studies, 1984. 159p. bibliog.

A pioneering analysis of the operation of the successful health care programme which has been implemented during recent decades in the economically backward south Indian state of Kerala. The authors examine various components of health status – income distribution, working and living conditions, water supply and sanitation, education, and health care facilities – and note that government and private sector expenditure on health is high in the state. Specific recommendations are made to increase community participation in decision-making and cost sharing and for ways of improving nutritional levels.

515 **Asceticism and healing in ancient India.**
Kenneth G. Zysk. Oxford: Oxford University Press, 1991. 200p. bibliog.

An impressively researched history of the evolution of Indian medicine between 800-100 BC, which employs the multiple tools of historical and socio-religious approaches rather than the purely philological method. The work is concerned with a 'paradigm shift' from preceding early Vedic medicine (1700-800 BC), based on magical rituals and exorcism, to the scientific, empirico-rational *Ayurvedic* medicine of the period 200 BC – 400 AD, as set out in the classical manuals of Caraka, Bhela and Susruta. The key players in this shift were, according to the author, wandering physicians, excluded from the inner circles of Brahminic religion and society, who made common cause with ascetic intellectuals, mainly Buddhist, to give rise to new, empirically grounded medical knowledge.

Village life

516 Hindus of the Himalayas: ethnography and change.
Gerald Duane Berreman. Berkeley, California: University of California Press, 1972. rev. ed. 440p. bibliog.

A detailed anthropological examination of the role and significance of kinship, caste, and community in a village of the Garhwal region in the Himalayan foothills. The culture of the villagers is examined within the broad context of north Indian traditions. The revised edition includes observations on the author's return to the village ten years after the initial field survey and the lack of social progress in the intervening period.

517 Caste, class and power: changing patterns of stratification in a Tanjore village.
André Beteille. Berkeley, California: University of California Press, 1971. 238p. map. bibliog.

A pioneering and detailed study of a south Indian village in the Tanjore district, written from a Marxian and Weberian point of view by an Indian sociologist. The author postulates that power, prestige, and wealth have become detached from caste status in recent years, and concludes that, as a result of rapid economic change, caste stratification will be seriously damaged, leading to a new and mobile balance among castes.

518 Palanpur: the economy of an Indian village.
Christopher John Bliss, N. H. Stern. Oxford: Clarendon Press, 1982. 340p. bibliog.

A clearly-presented study of chiefly economic aspects of a small north Indian village (population 762) situated in the wheat and sugar-cane growing Muzzafarnagar district, northeast of Delhi. The fieldwork was carried out during 1974-75. The opening chapters describe the social and landholding structure of the Thakur and Murao dominated village and chapter three reviews relevant development theories. The remainder of the work analyses the village economy: markets (labour, credit, agricultural produce), share tenancy arrangements, and wheat cultivation. A basic knowledge of economic theory by the reader is assumed, with regression analysis being used to examine leasing, output and income. The authors conclude that peasant behaviour in the village is complex and differential, but find that agricultural productivity is invariant to farm size, rather than negatively correlated, as commonly believed.

519 Beyond patronage and exploitation: changing agrarian relations in south Gujarat.
Jan Breman. Berkeley, California: University of California Press, 1994. 304p. bibliog.

This work is a revised edition of *Patronage and exploitation: changing agricultural relations in south Gujarat*, published in 1974. Case studies of two villages show how the traditional system of labour exchange (*jajmani*) has broken down and has been replaced by the employer-employee relationship, with its inherent conflict. According to Breman, the social and economic position of the service castes has deteriorated, and government intervention in village social and political life has not mitigated the position of the village landless poor. A new section analyses the dynamics of poverty.

520 Indian village.
Shyama Charan Dube.   London: Routledge, 1965. 248p. bibliog.

A classic account by an eminent sociologist of social structure, ritual activities, and extra-village activities in the late 1940s. The beginnings of change, as it affects family, caste, and village justice, are documented. According to Dube, growing individualism leads to frequent migration, the diminished authority of tradition, occupational diversification, weakened hereditary principles and paternalistic justice. A synoptic account of Dube's analysis of Dewara, a Deccani village, appears in *India's villages* (London: J. K. Publishers. 1960. 2nd. rev. ed. 218p.). This volume, edited by Mysore N. Srinivas, also includes classic essays on various villages in south India by Kathleen Gough, David Mandelbaum and Eric Miller, in north and central India by G. Morris Carstairs, McKim Marriott, and Marian Smith, and in Orissa by F. G. Bailey.

521 Karchana: lifeworld-ethnography of an Indian village.
Oyvind Jaer.   Oslo: Scandinavian University Press, 1994. 400p. bibliog.

This work, originally a 1990 doctorate thesis by a Norwegian anthropologist, is an impressive account of the economic, social and cultural life and institutions of a Hindu village community of thirty-five castes and 3,900 members, situated near Allahabad in the Ganges plain of northern India. 'Lifeworld' refers to the horizons of experience of villagers, and in this account the author supplements conventional chapters on social structure and land-usage patterns with interesting chapters on the 1989 *Kumbh Mela* religious festival, death rituals, and local commercial interchanges. The volume interweaves observations gleaned from fourteen months fieldwork between 1985 and 1989 with meticulous archival research.

522 Vilyatpur 1848-1968: social and economic change in a north Indian village.
Tom G. Kessinger.   Berkeley, California: University of California Press, 1974. 227p. 2 maps.

A path-breaking study of changing economic and social patterns in a Punjabi village in Jullundur district between the mid-19th century and the early years of the green revolution. Previous village studies carried out by anthropologists had been synchronic, describing the village structure at one specific point of time. Kessinger, both an historian and anthropologist, is concerned with patterns of change. Combining contemporary observation and oral testimonies with the scrutiny of official and unofficial village records, including family histories and pilgrimage records, he describes how the village coped with more than a doubling of its population between 1848 and 1968, while improving its living standards. Cultivation became more intensive, occupational patterns more diversified, family organization and patron-client *jajmani* relationships evolved, and significant outmigration occurred, bringing access to new remittance wealth.

143

523 **Village studies: data analysis and bibliography. Volume 1: India 1950-1975.**
Edited by Claire M. Lambert. Epping, England: Bowker, for the Institute of Development Studies at the University of Sussex, Brighton. 1976. 329p. bibliog.

A bibliography of individual research studies undertaken in rural areas of India. The focus is on the information obtained and the analyses completed of individual villages between 1950 and 1975: a highpoint period for ethnographic village studies. In addition to the annotations, the compilers have given computer-coded, numerical classification to the various categories of village life explored in these studies.

524 **Changing village, changing life.**
Prafulla Mohanti. London: Viking, 1990. 288p.

The author, an Indian domiciled in England, has constantly been pulled back to his village, Nanpur, situated in Orissa, throughout his life. In *My village, my life: portrait of an Indian village* (New York: Praeger, 1974. 230p.), Mohanti evocatively described various aspects of village life, including the joint family, festivals, caste, food, religion, and the position of women, through letting villagers speak for themselves. In this volume, the author records new impressions gained from his visits during the later 1980s. There are chapters on such topics as farming, *harijans* (untouchables), medicines and drugs, crime, and elections and politics.

525 **The poison in the gift: ritual, prestation and the dominant caste in a north Indian village.**
Gloria Goodwin Raheja. Chicago: University of Chicago Press, 1988. 286p. bibliog.

A study of the patterns and significance of gifting in Pahansu, a relatively prosperous village situated north-east of Delhi in which Gujars are the dominant caste. According to the author, the major concern of the dominant castes in giving *dan* ('gifts') is the transfer of inauspiciousness from the donor to the recipient rather than hierarchical considerations, as posited in the theory of Dumont (see item no. 477). The author reveals new ways of looking at ritual (birth, marriage, death, and the annual cycle), kinship, and caste.

526 **The politics of inequality: competition and control in an Indian village.**
Miriam Sharma. Honolulu, Hawaii: University of Hawaii Press, 1978. 262p. maps. bibliog.

An intimate view of the many subtle ways through which the dominant caste in an eastern Uttar Pradesh village exercises its authority. Sharma finds evidence that class interests have very slowly begun to replace caste as an organizing principle in the countryside. She examines the role of developing capitalist relations in agriculture and of the green revolution in the process. A complementary work, examining the changing patterns of caste and class stratification in a manner influenced by Beteille (see item no. 517), is D. B. Miller's *From hierarchy to stratification: changing patterns of social inequality in a north Indian village* (New Delhi: Oxford University Press India, 1975. 229p.).

527 **Remembered village.**
Mysore N. Srinivas. Berkeley, California: University of California Press, 1976. 356p.

When the field notes of the author, a leading Indian sociologist, about Rampura village in Karnataka were burned in a fire, he decided to abandon the traditional, problem-oriented monograph and revert to ethnography. The result is a masterful account of a Mysore village in the late 1940s. Ecology, caste, marriage and family functions, religion and agriculture are some of the topics addressed in this sensitive work. A number of other essays by Srinivas on Rampura are collected together and reproduced in *The dominant caste and other essays* (New Delhi: Oxford University Press India, 1987. 208p.).

528 **Struggling with destiny in Karimpur, 1925-1984.**
Susan S. Wadley. Berkeley, California: University of California Press, 1994. 319p. 2 maps.

Anxious to overcome the inherent limitations of traditional static, synchronic village studies, this innovative diachronic analysis presents a portrait of an Indian village as it has changed over a sixty-year period. The author examines alterations in agriculture, labour relations, education and family ties, as related by villagers of different castes, economic status and gender. The village, Karimpur, had earlier been studied by W. H. and C. M. Wiser (see item no. 529).

529 **Behind mud walls, 1930-1960: with a sequel: the village in 1970.**
William H. Wiser, Charlotte M. Wiser. Berkeley, California: University of California Press, 1971. rev. ed. 287p.

A little classic, this book describes the life of a north Indian village, Karimpur, near Agra, in which the Wisers lived for several years. The authors write movingly of the quality of Indian village life, as well as of the capacity of the villagers to accept some modern advances. William Wiser shows himself to be a particularly acute observer of the changing *jajmani* (quasi-ritual patron-client service relationship) system, on which he had written expertly before. The concluding sequel was written by Mrs. Wiser who visited the village alone after her husband's death. A warm human document.

530 **Third class ticket.**
Heather Wood. Harmondsworth, England: Penguin, 1984. 331p. maps.

A land-owner of Bengal, in a gesture uncharacteristic of her class, bequeathed her wealth to finance an all-India railroad tour for her fellow villagers. The author, a foreign research scholar, met these villagers by chance and accompanied them on part of their journey. The result is a sensitive recording of the villagers' thoughts and feelings, at once simple and profound, and of village life, with its superstitions, phobias and traditions. A wonderful introduction to India's village ethos.

Women

531 The Indian women's search for identity.
Shoma A. Chatterji. New Delhi: Vikas, 1988. 256p. bibliog.

A forceful and impassioned analysis of the situation of women as the underprivileged in Indian society which focuses on the impact of state and judicial policies. There are four sections: women at home; women in society; women at work; and women and health. Chatterji's coverage of the wide range of problems faced by women is comprehensive. Issues covered include: rape; death because of the non-payment of dowry; sexist rules preventing women from working night shifts; and the detrimental effect of current contraceptive practices on the health of lower-class women.

532 Women and society in India.
Neera Desai, Maithreyi Krishnaraj. New Delhi: Ajanta, 1987. 404p. bibliog.

This volume, written from an interdisciplinary feminist perspective, is designed as a textbook for undergraduate studies in India. The book opens with a short overview of the status of women from Vedic times to the present. This is followed by six analytical chapters on education, the family, violence, health, 'action for change' (political issues and movements), and women's economic issues.

533 Women in Indian society: a reader.
Edited by Rehana Ghadially. New Delhi: Sage Publications, 1988. 380p. bibliog.

A collection of key readings on a wide range of issues affecting women in India. The work is designed for gender studies courses. A biannual journal, *Indian Journal of Gender Studies* (New Delhi, London: Sage Publications, 1994-), is now available as an academic forum.

534 Women's quest for power: five Indian case studies.
Devaki Jain, assisted by Nalini Singh, Malini Chand. New Delhi: Vikas, 1980. 272p. bibliog.

Four of these case-studies deal with the efforts of low-income women to undertake cooperative income generation, and the fifth with efforts for social reform. Each case-study includes a discussion of the origins of the organization, its goals and activities, the characteristics of its organizers and members, its operational techniques, and, most importantly, an assessment of the organization's impact on the quality of women's lives. Devaki Jain's introductory essay is at once romantic and highly analytical.

535 The perfect wife: the orthodox Hindu woman according to the *Stridharmapaddhati* of Tryambakayajvan.
I. Julia Leslie. New Delhi: Oxford University Press India, 1989. 375p. bibliog. (Oxford University South Asian Studies Series).

The main part of this book comprises a translation of the *Stridharmapaddhati* ('Manual on the duty of women'), a Sanskrit text from an outpost of Brahminical culture, 18th-century Tanjore. It deals with ideals rather than actualities, enjoining in great detail women's daily duties and required obedience as wives, and includes a discussion of the nature of women. Dr Leslie intersperses the text with informed explanations of its arguments and excursuses on the history of the ideas it contains. An interesting collection of scholarly essays on the position and role of women during an earlier period is, *Position and status of women in ancient India* (Varanasi, India: Banaras Hindu University, 1988. 352p.), edited by L. K. Tripathi.

536 **Daughters of independence: gender, caste and class in India.**
Joanna Liddle, Rama Joshi.   London: Zed Books; New Brunswick, New Jersey: Rutgers University Press, 1986-89. 262p. bibliog.

An accessible, multi-disciplinary account of educated, urban women's issues in the late 1970s. The authors, drawing on fieldwork in Delhi, consider three issues in particular: the concept of patriarchy; the influence of the West on women's liberation in India; and the social processes which link the gender system with caste and class structures. The authors suggest controversially that the notion of female inferiority was introduced into India during the imperial period. They argue that earlier female segregation in the upper castes into the domestic sphere was related to the maintenance of caste purity rather than any inferior evaluation.

537 **Women's seclusion and men's honor: sex roles in north India, Bangladesh and Pakistan.**
David Goodman Mandelbaum.   Tucson, Arizona: University of Arizona Press, 1988. 153p. bibliog.

In this, the last book he wrote before his death in 1987, the American anthropologist examines the position of women in South Asia and the significance of *purdah* ('seclusion'). The book, not based on original fieldwork, is a work of synthesis. Mandelbaum argues that gender relations are related to men's honour and prestige and notes significant differences between *purdah* in north and south India and between Hindu and Muslim cultures. Three important related books on the same issue are: Prem Chowdhry, *The veiled woman: shifting gender equations in rural Haryana 1880-1990* (New Delhi: Oxford University Press India, 1994. 368p.); Patricia Jeffrey, *Frogs in a well: Indian women in purdah* (London: Zed Books, 1979. 187p.); and Hanna Papanek and Gail Minault (editors), *Separate worlds: studies of purdah in South Asia* (Columbia, Missouri: South Asia Books; New Delhi: Chanakya, 1982. 317p.).

538 **Indian women and patriarchy: conflicts and dilemmas of students and working women.**
Maria Mies, translated from the German by Saral K. Sarkar.   New Delhi: Concept, 1980. 311p. bibliog.

This study, by a Western scholar with long experience in India, deals with the conflicts and dilemmas of Indian women students and working women within a family system characterized as patriarchal. Biographical case-studies complement texts to reveal the role conflicts in India's changing society. Mies concludes by saying that, no matter how educated they are, urban women are still tied down by established patriarchal norms, and that a broad-based women's movement has not developed because urban and educated women remain unaware of the problems of rural women. A thought-provoking book.

539 **The extended family: women and political participation in India and Pakistan.**
Edited by Gail Minault. New Delhi: Chanakya, 1981. 312p.
This collection of essays is concerned particularly with political participation rather than the extended family in the sociological sense. The pre- and post-independence periods are covered. The essays focus on Indian women. For European *memsahibs* during the British Raj, the outstanding work is, *The memsahibs: the women of Victorian India* (London: Century, 1989. new ed. 210p.), by Pat Barr. For women's contemporary political involvement, *Towards empowerment: women and movement politics in India* (Boulder, Colorado: Westview Press, 1992. 230p.), by Leslie J. Calman, should be consulted.

540 **Women, work and marriage in urban India: a study of dual- and single-earner couples.**
G. N. Ramu. New Delhi, London: Sage Publications, 1989. 206p. bibliog.
A comparative study of middle class dual- and single-earner urban families in the fast-growing south Indian city of Bangalore. Based on interviews undertaken in 1979 and 1984, the author examines how gender roles have been affected by the employment of wives and mothers outside the home. He concludes that employment of middle-class women has resulted in little change in gender-role ideology and behaviour since they continued to remain responsible for housework and childcare. However, Ramu also provides evidence that employed wives have increased freedom with regard to dress and choice of friends, greater marital happiness, and enhanced participation in family decision-making. A complementary Bangalore study is, *Status of single women in India: a study of spinsters, widows and divorcees* (New Delhi: Uppal, 1987. 191p.) by N. S. Krishnakumari, which focuses on the social, psychological and economic condition of single urban women.

541 **Narrowing the gender gap.**
Geeta Somjee. New York: St. Martin's Press, 1989. 155p. bibliog.
An absorbing account of urban and rural Gujarati women's political and economic participation since the late 1960s and specific organized efforts to overcome the 'gender gap'. The work is arranged in four parts: a summary of relevant literature; a generational analysis of urban women; a study of successful 'regenerative' projects by élite female leaders; and economic and political involvement in rural communities. There is a sophisticated analysis of women's relationships with employers and economic organizations, including an account of Ela Bhatt's founding in Ahmedabad of the Self-Employed Women's Association.

542 **Women, poverty and resources.**
Ponna Wignaraja. New Delhi, London: Sage Publications, 1990. 241p. bibliog.
This volume, commissioned by UNICEF and written by a development expert associated with innovative experiments in poverty alleviation in the Third World, reviews post-1970 alternative development efforts in South Asia addressing issues of gender and poverty. Examples described relating to India are the Working Women's Forum and the Credit Society. The author contends that the involvement of women is essential for the success of any development effort and donors should identify homogenous groups of women who can be organized for long-term action.

Politics and Government

General

543 Government and politics in South Asia.
Craig Baxter, Yogendra K. Malik, Charles H. Kennedy, Robert C.
Oberst.   Boulder, Colorado: Westview Press, 1987. 415p. 8 maps.
A textbook designed for area courses which covers government and politics in all the states of South Asia. Part one, written by Yogendra Malik, contains eight analytical chapters on India, examining its political culture, social structure, party system, bureaucracy, interest groups, and leadership and succession.

544 India Briefing.
Edited by Marshall M. Bouton, Philip K. Oldenburg.   Boulder,
Colorado: Westview Press, 1987- . annual.
An annual collection of essays published in cooperation with the Asia Society. Each volume begins with an analysis of Indian politics during the previous year.

545 Political system in India.
Edited by Verinder Grover.   New Delhi: Deep & Deep, 1989. 10 vols.
A wide-ranging anthology of 411 articles on various facets of India's political system. The volumes average more than 700 pages in length.

546 India: government and politics in a developing nation.
Robert L. Hardgrave, Stanley A. Kochanek.   San Diego, California:
Harcourt Brace Jovanovich, 1993. 5th ed. 466p. map. bibliog.
This edition updates, to 1993, a useful introductory text, designed for university students, first published in 1970. Hardgrave and Kochanek use development theory to highlight key issues in Indian politics. The book has succinct chapters on India's

historical background, its constitution, institutional structures, interest groups, political parties, electoral behaviour, and foreign policy. This edition was written in the aftermath of the assassination in May 1991 of Rajiv Gandhi, marking the end of a dynasty that had dominated the politics of 'the world's largest democracy' for nearly half a century, and at the height of the Hindu-Muslim dispute over Ayodhya.

547 **India under pressure: the prospects for political stability.**
Robert L. Hardgrave. Boulder, Colorado: Westview Press, 1984.
214p. bibliog.

A very readable, balanced and concise study of the sources of, threats to, and prospects for India's political stability, based on research commissioned by the US State Department. The author analyses the linkages between social change, unrest and instability, producing projections for the period between 1984-89, including (with remarkable prescience) assassination scenarios. There is also a review of institutions responsible for maintaining stability – political parties, the bureaucracy, and the military – and a succinct description of India's foreign policy making process. Hardgrave concludes that future social unrest will remain 'manageable'. On a similar theme, but written ten years on at a time of reduced optimism, *India's violent democracy* (London: Frances Pinter Publishers, 1994. 128p.), by Dennis Austin, is penetrating in its analysis.

548 **Indian Journal of Political Science.**
New Delhi: Indian Political Science Association, 1939- . quarterly.

This quarterly carries scholarly articles on all aspects of politics, with primary emphasis on India. Contributions are mainly from Indian, American, and British political scientists. Some book reviews are included. A quarterly *Indian Political Science Review* is also published by Delhi University.

549 **India's democracy: an analysis of changing state-society relations.**
Edited by Atul Kohli, Pranab Bardhan (and others). Princeton, New Jersey: Princeton University Press, 1990. new ed. 350p. map.

An excellent collection of essays on the theme of democracy in India and the functioning of related institutions which were written during the optimistic early months of Rajiv Gandhi's premiership. The contributions are grouped around three themes: the changing character of political institutions (parties, political leadership, and the military); economic and ethnic pressures; and the efforts of socio-economic interest groups to influence the political process. Contributors include Henry Hart, James Manor, Stephen Cohen, Paul Brass, Pranab Bardhan, Ghanshyam Shah, and Francine Frankel.

550 **Contemporary Indian politics.**
Madhu Limaye. London: Sangam Books, 1987. 467p.

An analysis of the current dilemmas affecting Indian politics written by a distinguished socialist politician, who served as a general secretary of the Janata Party. A variety of themes are discussed: the centralization of authority; increasing authoritarianism and corruption; the decline of institutions and the retreat from 'rational politics' to traditional regional, caste and religious identities; and the 'decrepitude' of the welfare apparatus and the planned economy. Written at the height of the Punjab crisis, Limaye's analysis of India's problems is careful, but gloomy.

551 **Foundations of Indian political thought: an interpretation (from Manu to the present day).**
V. R. Mehta.   New Delhi: Manohar, 1993. 303p.

A lucid, interpretive analysis of various streams of political thought in India since ancient times. The thirteen chapters are arranged in three chronological parts: the ancient period (chapters two to six); medieval India (chapter seven); and the modern age (chapters eight to twelve). The thinkers examined include Manu, Valmiki, Vyasa, Kautilya, Barani, Abu'l Fazl, M. N. Roy, Nehru, Mahatma Gandhi, and Rammanohar Lohia. A useful complementary collection on political ideas in contemporary India is, *Political thought in modern India* (New Delhi: Sage Publications, 1986. 362p.), edited by T. Pentham and K. L. Deutsch.

552 **Government and bureaucracy in India, 1947-1976.**
Bankey Bihari Misra.   New Delhi: Oxford University Press India, 1986. 416p. bibliog.

A solid, largely descriptive analysis of India's post-independence government system. The author notes continuities from the pre-independence period: the federal constitution descends from the Government of India Act, 1935, while the non-executive president has authorities akin to those of a Dominion-style constitutional monarch. The Indian Administrative Service (IAS), successor to the Indian Civil Service (ICS) of the colonial era, has continued to act as the 'steel frame' of the Indian Union.

553 **The government and politics of India.**
Wyndraeth Humphrey Morris-Jones.   Huntingdon, England: Eothen Press, 1987. 4th rev. ed. 291p. 3 maps. bibliog.

An established study of Indian politics, first published in 1964, by the former director of the Institute of Commonwealth Studies at London University. A strength of this work is the linkages which the author reveals between contemporary Indian governmental and administrative arrangements and those of both pre-British and the colonial eras. However, the author questions whether a Westminster parliamentary model has been suitable for a country riven with so many centrifugal forces, and linguistic and regional separatism.

Post-independence political history

554 **India: the siege within.**
M. J. Akbar.   Harmondsworth, England: Penguin, 1985. 325p. map.

An examination of the origins and nature of the contemporary strains on Indian unity which have deep historical roots. The author, a renowned journalist, provides a synopsis of India's political and social history since 1947 and devotes two parts of the work to the genesis of the crises in Punjab and Kashmir. There are accounts of a meeting with the Sikh fundamentalist leader Sant Jarnail Singh Bhindranwale, and the 1984 army operation in Amritsar and subsequent assassination of Indira Gandhi. A complementary work, which includes excellent studies of the Shramik Sanghatana and Bhoomi Sena movements in Maharashtra and the Srikakulam Naxalite movement in Andhra Pradesh, is *Protest in democratic India: authority's response to challenge* (Boulder, Colorado: Westview Press, 1985. 160p.), by Leslie J. Calman.

555   India's simmering revolution: the Naxalite revolution.
Sumanta Banerjee.   London: Zed Books, 1984. 2nd ed. 327p. maps.

A detailed study of revolutionary communism in India between 1967 and 1972, written by a journalist for *The Statesman* who was arrested in 1975 during the Emergency. The author describes the efforts of Charu Mazumdar (d. 1972), the Maoist leader and theorist of the Communist Party of India (Marxist-Leninist), who rejected attempts to work through the parliamentary framework and launched, in Bihar and West Bengal, a violent campaign of land confiscation and the 'annihilation' of landlords, moneylenders, and other 'enemies' of the people. The hoped-for nationwide communist uprising failed to occur, but the Naxalites shocked the Indian government profoundly.

556   The politics of India since independence (Vol. IV:1 in The New Cambridge History of India).
Paul Richard Brass.   Cambridge: Cambridge University Press, 1992. new ed. 360p. maps. bibliog.

Building upon nearly three decades of research on Indian politics, ethnicity, nationalism and political economy – viz. *Language, religion, and politics in north India* (New York: Cambridge University Press, 1974. 467p.) – Brass provides here a general, analytically arranged, overview of political developments in India since independence. The central theme is that national leaders, particularly in the post-Nehru era, have sought increasingly to centralize power, decision-making and control of economic resources, disregarding India's cultural diversity and social fragmentation. The consequences have been a weakening of the effectiveness of political organizations and an intensification of ethnic, religious, caste and regional conflicts. The result has been a systemic crisis of the Indian polity.

557   Agrarian struggles in India after independence.
Edited by Akshayakumar Ramanlal Desai.   New Delhi: Oxford University Press India, 1986. 666p.

This massive volume contains papers on virtually all the important politically-based agrarian movements and conflicts in post-independence India. The essays are arranged in two broad sections. The first, containing two hundred pages, focuses on the 'all-India situation' and includes documents, such as the Home Ministry's famous 1969 report on the causes and nature of current agrarian tensions, and theoretical papers, notably by Gail Omvedt on caste, agrarian relations, and agrarian conflict, and K. S. Singh on the agrarian dimension of tribal movements. The second section offers a 'panorama' of regional struggles selected from all regions of India. The editor provides an overview pulling together the key elements.

558 Dominance and state power in modern India: decline of a social order.
Edited by Francine R. Frankel, M. S. A. Rao.   New Delhi: Oxford University Press India, 1989-90. 2 vols.

These studies in state-society relations from colonial times through to 1985 give special attention to class structure, caste stratification, ethnicity and dominance. Using an historical and comparativist perspective, the contributors consider most of the major areas of India, including Tamil Nadu, Bihar, and Kerala, to develop an empirical theory of Indian political and economic change. A paperback edition was produced in 1994.

559 Social ferment in India.
Alexandra George.   London: Athlone Press, 1986. 320p. bibliog.

Drawing on fieldwork conducted in Uttar Pradesh, Madhya Pradesh, West Bengal, and Rajasthan, and interviews with leading academics, politicians and officials, this book is a journalistic account of social, economic and political pressures and turmoil in contemporary India. A particular focus is the impact of economic development and India's hierarchical social structure on groups at the bottom of society. There are cases studies of tribals in backward districts in south Rajasthan and in industrializing areas of the Chotanagpur plateau near Ranchi. Growing caste and ethno-religious conflicts are analysed and there is a postscript on unrest in Punjab and Gujarat in 1985.

560 Indira Gandhi's India: a political system reappraised.
Edited by Henry C. Hart.   Boulder, Colorado: Westview Press, 1976. 313p. bibliog.

Nine chapters by Hart and his colleagues examine the origins, course, and likely consequences of the Emergency proclaimed by Indira Gandhi in 1975. The book's insights into the workings of India's political institutions continue to be valid. It can be usefully complemented by two contrasting works: Dilip Hiro, *Inside India today* (New York: Monthly Review Press, 1979. rev. ed. 338p.), a neo-leftist, partisan indictment of Mrs. Gandhi's 'constitutional coup' of June 1975; and Pramila Lewis, *Reason wounded: an experience of India's Emergency* (New Delhi: Vikas, 1978. 207p.), a first-hand account of the 1975-77 Emergency written by a social worker who was arrested during her attempts to organize labourers in the Delhi area.

561 The state, political processes and identity: reflections on modern India.
Edited by Zoya Hasan, S. N. Jha, Rasheeduddin Khan.   New Delhi, London: Sage Publications, 1989. 324p.

A useful collection of essays by Indian political scientists on various aspects of the political situation during the late 1980s. Hasan is a specialist on north Indian politics and author of *Dominance and mobilisation: rural politics in western Uttar Pradesh, 1930-1980* (New Delhi: Sage Publications, 1989. 195p.).

562 **Democracy and discontent: India's growing crisis of governability.**
Atul Kohli.   Cambridge: Cambridge University Press, 1990. 420p.
bibliog.

An acute analysis of political changes in India from the late 1960s to the late 1980s focusing on the increasing role of violence in Indian politics and what Kohli sees as the consequent 'crisis of governability'. The book is based on fieldwork during 1985-86 and was written before the 1989 general election. Kohli, the author of *The state and poverty in India: the politics of reform* (Cambridge: Cambridge University Press, 1987. 262p.), concludes that the roots of the governability crisis are political rather than socio-economic. It is linked to a process of 'overpoliticization', as an interventionist, but ineffectual, national government dealing with a poor economy has become the object of increasingly intense competition by political activists, and political parties have become fragmented.

563 **India: the years of Indira Gandhi.**
Edited by Yogendra K. Malik, D. K. Vajpeyi.   Leiden, the
Netherlands: E. J. Brill, 1988. 148p.

An assessment of the legacy of Indira Gandhi, the dominant figure in Indian politics between 1964 and 1984, in nine brief essays written by area specialists. Topics covered comprise Indira Gandhi's personality, India's constitutional structure, India's economy, security and defence, family planning, science and technology, and foreign policy. The authors are impressed by Indira Gandhi's successes in defence, security, and foreign policy, but are disturbed by her mixed performance on the domestic scene and, in particular, the legacy left of social polarization, unresolved ethnic and communal conflict, and an increasingly repressive state.

564 **India: creating a modern nation.**
Edited by Jim Masselos.   New Delhi: Sterling, 1990. 435p.

A collection of papers presented at an international conference held in 1988 at the University of Sydney, Australia. The essays are arranged in three chronological sections, organized around the bench-mark years of 1947, 1967 and 1987. The aim is to encapsulate the changing character of the new nation over its first forty years. The two contrasting themes which are stressed are those of success and relative achievement in the economic and technological spheres, where a bourgeois revolution (see item no. 21) has been accomplished, but of enduring social discrimination and underdevelopment. In addition to political and social themes, the papers focus on such topics as cultural and linguistic changes, food crisis management, debt bondage, and dowry practices.

565 **A family affair: India under three prime ministers.**
Ved Mehta.   New York: Oxford University Press USA, 1982. 166p.

Another of the author's volumes of lucid reportage on contemporary India, this one begins with Indira Gandhi's massive 1977 electoral defeat. It chronicles the unravelling of the Janata Party coalition that succeeded her and her triumphant return to power in 1980. The book is especially noteworthy for a revealing interview with Janata prime minister Morarji Desai. For Mehta's pre-1977 reportage see, *Mahatma Gandhi and his apostles* (New York: Viking, 1977. 260p.) and *The new India* (New York: Viking, 1977. 174p.), both equally readable. Covering the 1980s, *Rajiv Gandhi and Rama's Kingdom* (New Haven, Connecticut: Yale University Press, 1995), examines the closing years of Indira Gandhi and the subsequent rise and death of her son, Rajiv Gandhi.

566   **The story of the integration of the Indian states.**
Vapal Pangunni Menon.   New York: Arno, 1972. 511p. maps. bibliog.
Before independence the Indian subcontinent contained over 550 princely states (see item no. 167), many feeble in power and extremely limited in territory, but practically all ruled far more autocratically than British India. After independence all of these states were integrated into India and their rulers pensioned off. Mr. Menon was one of the four architects of this integration – the other three were Mountbatten, the last viceroy; Nehru; and Vallabhbhai Patel, the home minister. This lucid book presents a detailed account of the process of integration.

567   **Domestic conflicts in South Asia.**
Edited by Urmila Phadnis, S. D. Muni, Kalim Bahadur.   New Delhi: South Asian Publishers, 1986. 2 vols.
Two collections of scholarly papers presented at a conference on domestic crises in the South Asia region held at Jawaharlal Nehru University, New Delhi. There are essays on all of the states of South Asia. Volume one, *Political dimensions*, includes a paper by Mahendra Prasad Singh on the crisis in Indian pluralism and the party system. Volume two, *Economic and ethnic dimensions*, contains contributions by Phadnis on ethnic conflicts in South Asia and by Kamta Prasad on poverty trends in India.

568   **India 2000: the next fifteen years.**
Edited by James R. Roach.   Riverdale, Maryland: The Riverdale Company, 1986. 228p.
A broad-ranging collection of papers which were presented to a symposium at the Centre for Asian Studies at the University of Texas, Austin, during the 1985-86 Festival of India. They examine India in change and include predictions of future developments.

569   **From Raj to Rajiv: 40 years of Indian independence.**
Mark Tully, Zareer Masani.   London: BBC Books, 1988. 174p. map. bibliog.
Written by Tully, chief of the BBC's Delhi Bureau, and Masani, a television producer and author of *Indira Gandhi: a biography* (New York: Thomas Crowell, 1976. 341p.), this book explores a wide range of themes in India's political, social, economic and cultural post-independence history. The authors draw on interviews with a broad cross-section of the population, searching for the authentic voices of the 'real India'. Contrasting the achievements of India's technological revolution with the economic deprivation of urban slum-dwellers and village labourers, and the traditional ritual of temples and mosques with the new found radicalism of women and untouchables, they highlight the contradictions of a complex nation with insight and empathy. Tully has also co-authored, with Satish Jacob, a journalistic account of the Operation Blue Star storming of the Golden Temple in Amritsar, which provoked the retributive assassination of Indira Gandhi in October 1984: *Amritsar: Mrs Gandhi's last battle* (London: Jonathan Cape, 1985. 238p.).

570 **The painful transition: bourgeois democracy in India.**
Achin Vanaik. London, New York: Verso, 1990. 302p. bibliog.
Written from a 'New Left' perspective, this work analyses the political economy of contemporary India. Topics addressed include: the decline of one-party dominance; Hindu nationalism; centre-state relations; the segmented character of Indian society; and the position of the Left and its way forward. The body of the text was written before Congress (I)'s defeat in the November 1989 general election, but the author has included a postscript interpreting the election result.

Political parties and elections

571 **The Annual Register of Indian Political Parties.**
New Delhi: S. Chand, Indian Institute of Applied Political Research, 1972/73- . annual.
This useful reference annual is a comprehensive record of organizational information and documents of all the major national political parties, and several regional and communal parties. The strengths of these parties in the parliament and state assemblies are provided in a tabular form. An invaluable publication. In recent years the editor has been A. M. Zaidi.

572 **Khaki shorts, saffron flags: a critique of the Hindu right.**
Edited by Tapan Basu, Sumit Sarkar, Sambuddha Sen. Bombay: Orient Longman; London: Sangam Books, 1993. 116p. (Tracts for the Times).
A title in the series, *Tracts for the Times*, which examines key issues of contemporary concern, this slim volume analyses the growth of the Hindutva brigade and its role in the communalization of Indian society. The authors are academics from Delhi University. The focus of the work is the growth of the Hindu chauvinist Rashtriya Swayamsevak Sangh (RSS), founded as a paramilitary organization in 1925 by Dr. Keshav Hedgewar, and which was banned in 1948 and 1976, and of the Vishwa Hindu Parishad (VHP), which has helped to disseminate the doctrine of Hindu nationalism. The authors highlight the rigidly disciplined structure of the RSS, the sinister, phantom nature of its funding, and discuss its role in communal riots.

573 **Radical politics in South Asia.**
Edited by Paul Richard Brass, Marcus F. Franda. Cambridge, Massachusetts: MIT Press, 1973. 449p. bibliog.
A comparative study of socialist and communist parties in six regions of India, Bangladesh, and Sri Lanka that lays to rest the bogey of Moscow's meddling in the affairs of Indian communist parties. The thesis of the book is that the tactics of radical parties in South Asia change as a result of factional, ideological, and personal disputes, and that external pressures, whether from Russia or elsewhere, have very little to do with the development of radical politics in contemporary India.

574 A compendium of Indian elections.

David Butler, Ashok Lahari, Prannoy Roy.   New Delhi: Arnold-Heinemann India, 1984. 281p. bibliog.

A compendium of data on the seven general elections held in India between 1951 and 1980. The electoral histories of *Lok Sabha* (federal parliament) constituencies are tabulated, party vote shares shown and swings tabulated. The appendixes include details of by-election results and the numbers of candidates and lost deposits in each election. Three brief introductory chapters analyse vote-seat relationships, the sizes of electoral swings, and party splits.

575 The Indian left: critical appraisals.

Edited by Bipan Chandra.   New Delhi: Vikas, 1983. 452p.

This collection of essays, written by Marxist political scientists, explores the reasons for the failure of communists in India, unlike those in China and Indo-China, to establish themselves as a dominant force in the nationalist movement or to maintain a strong presence in independent India. The chief answer presented is that before 1947 India's communists remained inflexibly wedded to ideological orthodoxy – the 'Moscow line' of centralized control by a vanguard of the proletariat. This prevented them from taking advantage, in a 'united-front' manner, of the upsurge of peasant discontent at the end of the 1920s. After independence, the Indian Communist Party fractured as three different ideological wings battled for hegemony.

576 Hindu nationalism and Indian politics: the origins and development of the Bharatiya Jana Sangh.

Bruce Desmond Graham.   Cambridge: Cambridge University Press, 1990. 283p. bibliog. (Cambridge South Asian Studies, no. 47).

This work analyses the Bharatiya Jana Sangh (BJS), the most robust of the first generation of Hindu nationalist parties, during the first two decades of its history from 1951. The BJS failed to establish itself as the dominant party among the Hindu community. Graham attributes its restricted appeal to the limiting scope of its founding doctrines, organizational and leadership weaknesses, and its inability to establish a firm socio-economic support base. This book should be read in conjunction with M. A. Jhangiani, *Jan Sangh and Swatantra: a profile of the rightist parties in India* (Bombay: Manaktalas, 1967. 223p.).

577 Political parties in India.

Horst Hartmann.   Meerut, India: Meenakshi, 1982. 4th ed. 355p. bibliog.

First published in 1971, *Political parties in India* is widely used as a textbook in India and abroad. The author systematically analyses the political parties in terms of their organizational structures, party-building techniques, and the roles they play in Indian politics and elections. He emphasizes the positive aspects of the constitution in strengthening the political consensus and national integration. He believes that democracy is suited to Indian pluralism and can provide stable government. An excellent bibliography and summaries of various election statistics and party manifestos are included.

578 **Socialism in India.**

Sohail Jawaid. London: Sangam Books, 1987. 320p. bibliog.

A careful survey of the progress of socialism in India across forty years of independence. The work covers the breakaway from Congress in 1948 of the Congress Socialist Party (CSP), which had been founded in 1934 by Jayaprakash Narayan, Rammanohar Lohia and Acharya Narendra Deva as a 'ginger group', and which renamed itself the Socialist Party and, later, the Praja Socialist Party (PSP). It also chronicles factional splits which led to Lohia leaving to form the Samyukta Socialist Party (SSP), and socialist involvement in the Janata government which came to power in 1977. It can be usefully complemented by Surendranath Dwivedy's *Quest for socialism: fifty years of struggle in India* (London: Sangam Books, 1987. 373p.), an insider's account written by a former parliamentary leader of the PSP.

579 **Congress in Indian politics: a centenary perspective.**

Edited by Ram Joshi, R. K. Hebsur. Riverdale, Maryland: The Riverdale Company; New Delhi, London: Sangam Books, 1988. 299p.

This work comprises an introduction, by the editors, and fourteen studies of various aspects of the Congress Party (Indian National Congress) during its century-long history between 1885 and 1985. Contributors focus on institutional dimensions of Congress politics and policies, Congress relations with specific social groups and minorities, and the general nature of Indian politics. There are papers by W. H. Morris-Jones, Ghanshyam Shah, Richard Sisson, and Baldev Raj Nayar. The volume can be read profitably in conjunction with another excellent centenary collection of essays, more historical in approach, *Indian National Congress and Indian society, 1885-1985: ideology, social structure, and political dominance* (New Delhi: Chanakya, 1987. 480p.), edited by Paul R. Brass and Francis Robinson.

580 **Ethnicity and equality: the Shiv Sena party and preferential politics in Bombay.**

Mary Fainsod Katzenstein. Ithaca, New York: Cornell University Press, 1979. 237p. bibliog.

A book about the political movement in Bombay city to obtain preferential treatment in employment opportunities for Maharashtrians. This study explores the conflict between meritocratic recruitment, irrespective of ethnic and caste affiliation, and preferential employment based on ethnic and regional representation. Katzenstein makes no normative assessment of the policy of preferential treatment, but argues that such treatment is here to stay and need not be considered contrary to democratic principles.

581 **Elections in India: its [sic] social basis.**

Susheela Kaushik. Calcutta: Bagchi, 1982. 238p. bibliog.

Taking the view that most Indian election studies are 'too microscopic, time bound, and territorially delimited', this neo-Marxist scholar tries to incorporate the dynamics of political economy in her analysis. Kaushik presents a lucid picture of rural and urban Indian society. Her interpretation of such stand-bys in Indian electoral analysis as the 'wave' phenomenon, vote banks, and primordial voter identification are refreshing.

582   **The Congress Party of India: the dynamics of one-party democracy.**
Stanley A. Kochanek.   Princeton, New Jersey: Princeton University Press, 1968. 516p. bibliog.

Examines the relationship between and among the president and the working (executive) committee of the Congress Party, the prime minister, and the cabinet. The author's view is that since independence India has been a one-party democracy. He regards the loss of hegemony by the Congress Party in 1967 as a minor episode. The analysis of the party's success in remaining a viable force under changing political conditions is penetrating. Neat periodization is the book's main asset.

583   **Hindu nationalism in India: rise of the Bharatiya Janata Party.**
Yogendra K. Malik, Vijay Bahadur Singh.   Boulder, Colorado: Westview Press, 1994. 225p. bibliog.

Effectively a reincarnation of the old Jana Sangh, which was incorporated into the Janata Party in 1977, the Bharatiya Janata Party (BJP), founded in 1980, was initially a moderate, Gandhian-oriented centrist force. After its crushing defeat in the 1984 general election, it returned to its roots as a staunchly Hindu nationalist, right-of-centre party, allied with the militant Rashtriya Swayamsevak Sangh (RSS). The author charts the party's ideological shifts and the increasing electoral success it has enjoyed. This culminated in its capturing a fifth of the national vote in the 1991 general election after mobilizing the Hindu community of northern India over the Babri Masjid Ramjanmabhumi issue at Ayodhya.

584   **Indian communism: opposition, collaboration and institutionalization.**
Ross Mallick.   New Delhi; Oxford; New York: Oxford University Press, 1994. 277p. bibliog.

A clear analysis of the strategy and achievements of communists in India since the early 1960s. The volume was written in the wake of the global collapse of communism after 1989. The author is critical of Indian Communists' achievements in office at the state level and pessimistic about their chances of achieving a political breakthrough. This is because of their anxiety to mobilize landed rural interests and unionized workers, classes who are opposed to a fundamental socialist transformation, instead of seeking to radicalize less privileged classes.

585   **1984 *Lok Sabha* elections: massive mandate for Rajiv Gandhi (UNI-DCM computer-based study).**
G. G. Mirchandani, K. S. R. Murthi.   New Delhi: Sterling, 1985. 244p.

A record of the political background to and the campaign events of the December 1984 general election. Held just two months after the assassination of prime minister Indira Gandhi by her Sikh bodyguards, her son Rajiv secured a record national mandate for the Congress (I) party. The authors draw upon a computerized database maintained by the *United News of India* to provide statistical analysis of an election in which there were a record 5,000 candidates. The 1980 election, which resulted in the return to power of Indira Gandhi, is chronicled in *India at the polls, 1980: a study of the parliamentary elections* (Washington, DC: American Enterprise Institute, 1987. 198p.), by Myron Weiner.

586 **The Indian political parties: a historical analysis of political behaviour up to 1947.**
Bankey Bihari Misra.   New Delhi: Oxford University Press India, 1976. 665p. bibliog.

An analysis of the framework within which political parties evolved and operated in India between 1905 and 1947. Several chapters are devoted to the behaviour of these parties in provincial and federal legislative bodies, and others to the development of party ideologies. Misra argues that the primary goal of these parties was to obtain power and that ideologies were always subservient to that goal.

587 **Communism in India.**
Gene D. Overstreet, Marshall Windmiller.   Berkeley, California: University of California Press, 1959. 603p. bibliog.

A thorough study of the growth of communism in India, its history, organization and leadership. The discussion of the failure of the communist movement to come to terms with Gandhian nationalism is treated most refreshingly. Equally impressive is the discussion of communist drives in the first decade of India's independence, a period which saw the movement divide into two – those who worked through 'constitutional' means, and those who, as in Telengana, took extralegal, often violent, measures to seize land from the landholders, establish a parallel government, and develop a communist sanctuary on the 'soviet' model. There is also an excellent discussion of the Communist Party's relationship with the Comintern and Stalin.

588 **Elections and political development: the South Asian experience.**
Norman D. Palmer.   London: C. Hurst; Durham, North Carolina: Duke University Press, 1975. 340p. bibliog.

An important study, for the specialist, of South Asian electoral and voting behaviour, based on analysis and personal observation of elections since 1951 and the sampling of voters' opinions. The author believes that, despite their shortcomings, elections have given political stability to India, but, writing in 1974, he expresses caution concerning the future.

589 **The Naxalites and their ideology.**
Rabindra Ray.   Oxford: Oxford University Press, 1989. 251p. bibliog.

An excellent analysis of the political philosophy of the Naxalites of West Bengal and their strategy of agrarian mass revolution allied with urban terror, which shook the Indian political system between 1967 and 1972. The author carefully sets the Naxalite movement in the context of Bengali agrarian and urban society and the development of communism in the state.

590 **Party and democracy in India.**
S. N. Sadasivan.   New Delhi: Tata-McGraw-Hill, 1977. 537p. bibliog.

An encyclopaedic examination and classification of more than 200 parties. Sadasivan sketches the history, socio-economic bases, internal structure and functioning of local, regional, and national parties.

591　Communism in Indian politics.

Bhabani Sen Gupta.　New York: Columbia University Press; New Delhi: Young Asia, 1978. 471p. bibliog.

This highly informative book provides an excellent review of the role of communism in Indian politics since 1964. The development of three rival communist parties is fully explored and their attitude towards participation in India's parliamentary system, as in labour and peasant movements, is carefully examined. In a useful follow-up volume, *CPI-M: promises, prospects, problems* (New Delhi: Young Asia, 1979. 296p.), Sen Gupta reviews the strides made by the Communist Party of India-Marxist. The author analyses the party's success in mobilizing peasants, as well as workers and lower-middle class civil servants, in West Bengal, Tripura, and Assam, and its lack of success in Kerala.

592　Elections in India: data handbook on *Lok Sabha* elections, 1952-85.

Compiled by Vijay Bahadur Singh, Shankar Bose.　New Delhi, London: Sage Publications, 1986. 2nd ed. 682p.

An invaluable collection of data setting out detailed *Lok Sabha* results by parties and regions for the eight general elections held between 1952 and 1984. In all these contests, except for 1977, the Congress Party won a plurality of the national vote. By-election results are also presented. An analytical companion volume is *India decides: elections 1952-1991* (New Delhi: Living Media, 1991. 380p.), by David Butler, Ashok Lahari, and Prannoy Roy, which provides methodical commentary.

593　Elections in India: data handbook on *Lok Sabha* elections, 1986-91.

Compiled by Vijay Bahadur Singh, Shankar Bose.　New Delhi, London: Sage Publications, 1994. 320p.

Provides detailed data on the 1989 and 1991 general elections. In the November 1989 contest Congress (I) was faced, unusually, in 400 constituencies by a straight fight with a single candidate from the National Front-Bharatiya Janata Party-Left electoral coalition. Congress (I) won a plurality of the national vote, but the opposition mustered enough seats to form a coalition government The May 1991 election witnessed contests between 9,000 candidates for 537 seats in the *Lok Sabha* before an electorate of 514 million. Two companion volumes are: *1989-1991 general elections in India, including November 1991 by-elections* (New Delhi: Associated Publishing House, 1992. 212p.), by M. L. Ahuja and Sharda Paul; and *India votes: alliance politics and minority governments in the ninth and tenth general elections* (Boulder, Colorado: Westview Press, 1992. 454p.), edited by Harold Alton Gould and Sumit Ganguly.

594　Party building in a new nation: the Indian National Congress.

Myron Weiner.　Chicago: Chicago University Press, 1967. 509p. maps. bibliog.

A classic empirical work based on five distinct Congress Party branches in five different states. The thesis of the book is that the party has been eminently successful in mediating conflicting demands of modernization and of traditional society. The book, unfortunately, lacks any case study from the 'Hindi heartland' of India.

595 **The encyclopaedia of the Indian National Congress.**
Edited by A. Moin Zaidi, Shaheda Zaidi. New Delhi: S. Chand &
Co. [Vols. 1-26] and Indian Institute of Applied Political Research
[Vol. 27], 1976-94. 27 vols.

A comprehensive sourcebook for students of the Indian National Congress. Each
volume covers a chronological period of roughly four years, commencing with the
movement's founding in 1885 and reaching, in volume twenty-seven, 1990. Materials
reproduced are texts of the plenary session of Congress and its Working Committee,
presidential addresses, resolutions, and summaries of important speeches. Lists of
conference delegates are included in the appendix.

State and local politics

596 **Indian federalism: problems and issues.**
Edited by Tarun Chandra Bose. Calcutta: Bagchi, 1987. 239p.

A collection of papers by Indian political scientists which explore a range of issues in
centre-state relations. It can be supplemented by: *State governments in India* (New
Delhi: Macmillan, 1979. 328p.), by Shriram Maheshwari, a clear survey of state
administration, the constitutional framework, the role of the governor, and centre-
state relations; and *Centre-state budgetary transfers* (New Delhi: Oxford University
Press India, 1988. 324p.), edited by I. S. Gulati, a collection of papers which examine
the federal financial relationship in India.

597 **Dynamics of state politics, Kerala.**
Edited by N. Jose Chander. New Delhi: Sterling, 1986. 224p.

A collection of nine studies of political trends and developments in the south Indian
state of Kerala in which the Communist Party is the dominant political force. The
papers include overviews of the state's political history, party system, political
culture, the 'uprisings' of 1959 and 1970, and electoral trends. The leading themes are
the persistence of middle class-led caste and communal groups as a counterpoint to
lower-class communist mobilization, and the fragmentation of the party system.

598 **State politics in India.**
Babulal Fadia. New Delhi: Radiant, 1984. 2 vols. bibliog.

The first volume of this work comprises a synthesis of literature on Indian federalism
and state politics. It includes historical surveys of Indian states from late Mughal
times through to reorganization in 1956. The second volume focuses on political
developments in ten states. The author asks why has the Communist Party been
successful in Kerala and West Bengal and why has factionalism predominated in
some states but not in others.

599   **What's happening to India?: Punjab, ethnic conflict, Mrs.**
Gandhi's death and the test for federalism.
Robin Jeffrey.   Basingstoke, England: Macmillan, 1986. 249p.
7 maps. bibliog.

Intended for the general reader, this book explains the background to the communal
explosions in Punjab during the early 1980s and the challenge they posed to Indian
federalism. The author stresses the unique aspects of Punjab, with its frontier
location, violent history, and place at the centre of Sikh religion. He also shows how
modernization in this leading green revolution state reacted with Punjabi culture, and
how short-term political machinations ignited the volatile mixture.

600   **Sikh separatism: the politics of faith.**
Rajiv Alochan Kapur.   London: Allen & Unwin, 1986. 272p.

An excellent account of the stages by which fundamentalist Sikhs in the Punjab came
to launch a violent demand for a separate Sikh state, Khalistan, and the Sikh political
party, Akali Dal, became increasingly radicalized. The work includes coverage of the
traumatic events of 1984 when the Golden Temple at Amritsar was stormed by
government troops, claiming the lives of more than 500 Sikhs, and prime minister
Indira Gandhi was assassinated by her Sikh bodyguards.

601   **Marxist state governments in India: politics, economics and**
society.
T. J. Nossiter.   London, New York: Frances Pinter Publishers, 1988.
212p. map. bibliog. (Marxist Regimes Series).

A detailed, clearly-written overview of the development of communism in India,and
the performances of Marxist state governments in Kerala and West Bengal and the
Communist Party in Tripura. Nossiter notes the constraints imposed upon India's
communists by the requirements of a competitive multi-party political system and
also by the federal power structure. The resulting 'Indian form of communism' has
been non-revolutionary, adjusting Marxist-Leninist teachings to Indian circumstances.
An excellent case-study of a communist government in practice is *Development
policy of a communist government: West Bengal since 1977* (Cambridge: Cambridge
University Press, 1993. 240p.), by Ross Mallick.

602   **Patterns of *Panchayati Raj* in India.**
Edited by G. Ram Reddy.   New Delhi: Macmillan, 1977. 213p. maps.
bibliog.

Panchayati Raj - the administration of rural units by elected local leaders – has long
been considered an ageless institution of participatory democracy in the Indian
countryside. Reddy's introductory chapter discusses the modernization of this
institution and its relationship to the state bureaucracy. Fifteen other essays analyse
Panchayati Raj in the states. This useful survey can be complemented by: *Local
politics: the law of the fishes* (New Delhi: Oxford University Press India, 1988.
368p.), by M. S. Robinson, a study of the impact of local politics on the poor; and
State and district administration in India (New Delhi: National, 1976. 387p.), by J. D.
Shukla, which describes the structure of local-level administration.

603 **The expansive élite: district politics and state policy making in India.**
Donald B. Rosenthal.   Berkeley, California: University of California Press, 1977. 337p. maps. bibliog.

A case-study of how rural local élites in two districts in Maharashtra influence the course of state and national politics and policy-making. The book is based on extensive interviews. An epilogue, written during the 1975-77 Emergency, shows how most of the features delineated earlier are of continuing significance.

604 **State elections in India: data handbook on *Vidhan Sabha* elections, 1952-1985.**
Compiled by Vijay Bahadur Singh, Shankar Bose.   New Delhi, London: Sage Publications, 1987-88. 5 vols.

A comprehensive collection of data on the results of state elections in independent India. The volumes range in length from 500 to 760 pages. The regions covered are: *I: The North Pt. 1 (Haryana, Himachal Pradesh, Jammu & Kashmir, Punjab, Rajasthan, and Delhi); II: The West (Maharashtra, Gujarat, Madhya Pradesh, and Goa); III: The East and Northeast (Assam, West Bengal, Orissa, Manipur, Meghalaya, Nagaland, Sikkim, Tripura, Arunachal Pradesh, and Mizoram); IV: The North Pt. 2 (Bihar and Uttar Pradesh);* and *V: The South (Andhra Pradesh, Karnataka, Tamil Nadu, Kerala, and Pondicherry).*

605 **State politics in contemporary India: crisis or continuity?**
Edited by John R. Wood.   Boulder, Colorado: Westview Press, 1985. 257p.

A collection of essays on political developments in seven different Indian states – Uttar Pradesh, Maharashtra, West Bengal, Karnataka, Kerala, Gujarat, and Bihar – by eminent Western and Indian political scientists. Particularly interesting are the essays by James Manor on the imposition of Gundu Rao as chief minister of Karnataka, Atul Kohli on the factors behind the rise of the Communist Party in West Bengal, and Wood on the Congress Party's caste-based strategy in Gujarat. Unfortunately, there are no papers on Punjab or Assam.

Structure of government

606 **India's parliament.**
Edited by Phul Chand.   New Delhi: The Institute of Constitutional and Parliamentary Studies, 1984. 315p. bibliog.

A very useful analytical exposition of the working of the parliamentary institution in India. The fourteen chapters, contributed by academics and politicians, cover a variety of topics. These include: the evolution of the Indian parliament; the legislative process and parliamentary procedures; the role of the Speaker; the parliamentary secretariat; the constitutional position and membership of the *Rajya Sabha* (upper house); and parliament's relationships with the president, the judiciary, and the media.

607 **The president of India.**
Bhaskar Chandra Das. New Delhi: S. Chand, 1977. 499p. bibliog.
A detailed examination of the powers of the president of India as prescribed by the constitution and the role this office has assumed in actual practice. Das believes that in times of political crisis the president can be of pivotal importance and can act independently of the advice offered by the prime minister. The author indicates that India's federal parliamentary system has the possibility of evolving into a French-style executive presidential system.

608 **The office of the governor: its constitutional image and reality.**
N. S. Gehlot. Allahabad, India: Chugh, 1977. 320p. bibliog.
The governor's powers, such as dissolution of the state legislature and naming chief ministers, are limited as long as one party has a clear majority and provides checks to his powers. However, since 1967, the governor's role has assumed special importance due to the emergence of shaky coalition regimes or one-party cabinets based on razor-thin majorities. This well-organized book examines the governor's role in India's changing political environment. A series of case studies and appendixes add to the book's value.

609 **Nehru to Narasimha Rao: the changing office of prime minister in India.**
Edited by James Manor. London: C. Hurst, 1994. 276p.
An up-to-date examination of the evolution of the office of prime minister which takes into account recent changes as India has had to readjust to the ending of the 'Gandhi dynasty'. The focus is on the prime minister's role and authority in relation to parliament, the bureaucracy, the judiciary, the foreign and defence establishment, and other social and political forces.

610 **The bureaucracy in India: an historical analysis of development up to 1947.**
Bankey Bihari Misra. New Delhi: Oxford University Press India, 1977. 421p. bibliog.
A clear exposition of the development of India's bureaucracy. The work is arranged in a chronological format, divided into three periods: to 1858; 1858 to 1919; and 1919 to 1947. There are separate analytical chapters on developments in bureaucratic concepts in the West, the training and education of India's civil servants, Indianization, and the relationship between bureaucracy and democracy in India.

611 **The office of the prime minister of India.**
R. N. Pal. New Delhi: Ghanshyam, 1983. 279p. bibliog.
A detailed study of the role and evolution of the office of Indian prime minister. The author shows how, through the rising power of the prime minister's secretariat at the expense of the cabinet secretariat, the prime minister has come to assume a role more akin to a US president than a parliamentary leader. The office has benefitted from the 'nationalization' of politics and the 'personalization' effect of the mass media. However, as the Janata coalition period revealed, much of the premier's strength also depends on the relative balance of party power within parliament.

612   **India's political administrators, 1919-83.**
       David C. Potter.   Oxford: Clarendon Press, 1986. 289p.

This book describes the work of the Indian Civil Service (ICS) and its lineal descendant, the Indian Administrative Service (IAS), and explains how and why the colonial administrative tradition persisted without change after independence. Drawing upon both historical records and interviews with former ICS and IAS officers, Potter stresses the 'political' nature of both services, deeply involved in all phases of the policy-making process, and demonstrates how, through recruitment and training, a 'gentleman-administrator' ethos has been inculcated. Recognizing it as the crucial 'steel frame', which had helped to maintain centralized political control, efficiency and order, the political leaders of independent India, most fervently Vallabhbhai Patel, opted to maintain the ICS/IAS tradition.

613   **History of Indian administration.**
       Baij Nath Puri.   Bombay: Bharatiya Vidya Bhavan [Vols. 1-2];
       New Delhi: Munshiram Manoharlal [Vol. 3], 1968-82. 3 vols.

A detailed, factual account of the changing character of Indian central administration since early times. Volume 1, *Ancient period*, includes descriptions of Mauryan and Gupta administrative systems. Volume 2, *Medieval period*, published in 1975, covers the Delhi Sultanate and Mughals, as well as chronicling Rajput, Maratha and Sikh administrative practices. The final volume, *Modern period*, focuses on the British Raj (to 1947), describing the home government, the role of the viceroy, provincial, district and revenue administration, the police and judiciary, and the development of the administrative services.

Constitution and Legal System

614 **Police power and colonial rule: Madras 1859-1947.**
David Arnold. New Delhi: Oxford University Press India, 1986.
277p. bibliog.
This work is concerned with the increase in state power that transformed the state's relation to society through the colonial period. The author, a prominent member of the *Subaltern* (see item no. 179) school of radical social historians, shows how an increasingly militarized and repressive police force, developed on the model of the Irish Constabulary, represented the essence of mature colonialism and a central feature of India's colonial legacy. The first half of the book analyses the development of police organization in south India, demonstrating how Indians who predominated in the force became alienated from society and socialized into the colonial ethos through recruitment, training, and discipline. The second half describes police deployment against rural unrest, proletarian upheaval, and nationalist agitation, particularly from the 1930s. A more conventional police history is *The police and political development in India* (Princeton, New Jersey: Princeton University Press, 1969.), by David H. Bayley.

615 **The Indian constitution: cornerstone of a nation.**
Granville Austin. Bombay: Oxford University Press India, 1972.
Indian ed. 390p. bibliog.
A political history describing how the constitution of India was shaped between 1946 and 1949. The author investigates the interplay of ideals and personalities, past constitutional practices in British India and future aspirations, and the economic and social assumptions implicit in the document. The discussion of the constitution's Directive Principles is extremely lucid.

616 **The Indian Supreme Court and politics.**
Upendra Baxi. Lucknow, India: Eastern Book, 1980. 272p. bibliog.
In India, as in the United States, the resolution of key political questions has often been left to the Supreme Court, which has issued conflicting opinions based on

constitutional provisions. This lively, opinionated, but informed, book explains why the court is using a loose 'constructionist' approach and is gradually moving to a populist direction. It can be supplemented with *Judicial review in India* (New Delhi: Sangam Books, 1988. 162p), by Vijay Lakshmi Dudeja.

617   **Valiant victims and lethal litigation: the Bhopal case.**
       Compiled by Upendra Baxi, Amita Dhanda.   Bombay: N. M. Tripathi
       1990. 608p. bibliog.
Produced under the auspices of the Indian Law Institute, this work comprises a compilation and review of the litigation records of the Bhopal Union Carbide chemical plant disaster case. A compelling account of the December 1984 disaster, the worst industrial accident ever, which claimed 8,000 lives and injured an estimated 300,000, is provided in *A killing wind: inside Union Carbide and the Bhopal catastrophe* (New York: McGraw-Hill, 1987. 297), by Dan Kurzman.

618   **Readings in the constitutional history of India, 1757-1947.**
       Edited by Desika Char.   New Delhi: Oxford University Press India,
       1983. 789p. bibliog.
A compilation of official and non-official source materials chronicling India's constitutional development. The work is arranged chronologically in seven parts and includes more than 400 extracts from original records.

619   **Religion, law and the state in India.**
       John Duncan Martin Derrett.   London: Faber & Faber, 1968. 615p.
       bibliog.
A classic collection of essays on ancient Hindu law and religion, Islamic law, and the role of religion in modern Indian law. Derrett, both a barrister and academic, is also author of *The death of a marriage law: epitaph for the rishis* (New Delhi: Vikas, 1978. 228p.), an account of the Indian parliament's 1976 liberalization of Hindu law to permit the dissolution of marriage by mutual consent and the consequences of the decision.

620   **Judges and the judicial power: essays in honour of Justice V. R.**
       Krishna Iyer.
       Edited by Rajeev Dhavan, R. Sudarshan, Salman Khurshid.   London:
       Sweet & Maxwell, 1985. 340p.
An excellent collection of essays by Indian and Western scholars and legal practitioners in honour of the radical, pioneering Kerala Justice Krishna Iyer. Contributors include: J. D. M. Derrett, who compares the current powers of judges to invalidate unconstitutional executive actions with those enjoyed in ancient times; J. Narain, reviewing redistributive justice; Marc Galanter and Robert Hardgrave, analysing affirmative action policies; and Upendra Baxi, examining 'social action litigation'.

621 Competing equalities: law and the backward classes in India.
Marc Galanter. Berkeley, California: University of California Press, 1984. 625p. bibliog.

The definitive legal work on law and the Indian backward classes. The author describes the government programmes of protective advancement for backward classes that have been implemented during recent decades and traces the development of case law surrounding such 'compensatory discrimination'. Galanter is less clear in his assessment of the effectiveness of the programmes, and notes that the Indian government has failed to carry out systematic evaluations. Galanter (1898-1988) is also the author of an excellent general textbook, *Law and society in modern India* (New Delhi: Oxford University Press India, 1989. 329p.), which was edited posthumously by Rajeev Dhavan.

622 Police brutality: an analysis of police behaviour.
Sailendra Misra. New Delhi: Vikas, 1986. 139p.

Written by a serving deputy inspector-general of police and director of the National Police Commission, 1977-80, this frank 'insider's account' summarizes what is known about police brutality in modern India, analyses its causes, and recommends solutions. Misra confirms that police brutality is extensive and deep-rooted and attributes it to tradition, expectations of colleagues and the public for vengeance against suspected criminals, lust for money, and overwork. He expects the situation to become worse as crime and group violence increase, along with physical attacks on police officers.

623 India's constitution.
Moolamattom Varkey Pylee. New Delhi: S. Chand & Co., 1992. 5th rev. ed. 471p. maps. bibliog.

An up-to-date and comprehensive examination of the principles and provisions of the Indian constitution which has long served as a popular undergraduate text. Following a brief introduction, the book is divided into six sections that mirror the constitution itself: preamble; territory and citizenship; fundamental rights and directive principles; machinery of the Union and state governments; the federal system; and miscellaneous provisions. Two readable and succinct alternative works are: *The Indian constitution and its working* (New Delhi: Sangam Books, 1986. new ed. 236p.), by R. Joshi; and *Shorter constitution of India* (New Delhi: Prentice-Hall of India, 1988. 10th ed. 423p.), by Durga Das Basu, which includes all major amendments to the constitution and leading court decisions.

624 Crime and criminality in British India.
Edited by Anand A. Yang. Tucson, Arizona: University of Arizona Press, 1985. 192p.

A collection of essays by Western social historians on various themes in the history of Indian crime during the colonial period. The work shows how the colonial state defined crime and criminality and how marginal groups, such as *dacoits* (bandits), pastoralists and tribals, were gradually pacified through integration into the mainstream of Indian society, culminating in the passing of the Criminal Tribes Act in 1871, which specified where defined 'criminal tribes' could live and work. The volume places the analysis of South Asian crime in the larger context of social history and fresh theoretical approaches, such as the concept of informal 'social control'.

Defence and Military Affairs

625 **India's nuclear bomb.**
Shyam Bhatia. Sahibabad, India: Vikas, 1979. 169p. bibliog.

India's nuclear policy from independence through to India's 1974 nuclear explosion is sketched in broad outline by a prominent journalist. It is argued that, although the nuclear weapons option was not ignored in earlier years, the 1964 Chinese nuclear explosion resulted in rising pressures within India for nuclear weapon development. Bhatia suggests that the Shastri-Gandhi decision for a test explosion was a way to accommodate demands for weapons without actually producing them. This book should be read alongside the later, *Nuclear proliferation: the US-Indian conflict* (New Delhi, London: Sangam Books, 1993. 474p.), by Brahma Chellaney.

626 **The Indian army: its contribution to the development of a nation.**
Stephen Philip Cohen. New Delhi: Oxford University Press India, 1990. new ed. 254p. bibliog.

A social and political history of the Indian army. Well documented and clearly-written, with extensive quotes from records and interviews, the book describes how the British created in India one of the largest, best disciplined volunteer armies in modern times. Cohen carefully examines the disputes between Whitehall and Delhi, and between British rulers and Indian politicians on the role and character of the Indian armed forces. Unfortunately, the discussion of the period 1947-71 is extremely brief.

627 **Armies of the Raj: from the Mutiny to independence, 1858-1947.**
Byron Farwell. London: Viking Penguin, 1989. 399p. bibliog.

This work, accompanied with many illustrations, gives a flavour of what life was like in the Indian army during the British Raj. It describes the system of organization and recruitment, arms and equipment, and recounts the army's role in such events as the Amritsar Massacre (1919) and its campaigns during the First and Second World Wars. This readable work can be complemented by Charles Chenevix-Trench, *The Indian army and the King's enemies, 1900-1947* (London: Thames & Hudson, 1988.

312p), which vividly recounts Indian army military campaigns; and *The sepoy and the Raj: the politics of the Indian army, 1860-1940* (London: Macmillan, 1994. 313p.), by David Omissi, which focuses on the several million Indian peasant-soldiers who served the colonial power.

628 *Naukar*, **Rajput and** *sepoy*: **the ethnohistory of the military labour market in Hindustan, 1450-1850.**
Dirk H. A. Kolff.   Cambridge: Cambridge University Press, 1990. 217p. bibliog.

This interesting revisionist work, focusing on north Indian military recruitment and service during the 16th and 17th centuries, shatters the monolithic stereotype of the Rajput as a saffron-robed warrior-prince on horseback. The author introduces the concept of the 'military labour market' and shows how military service had a distinct life cycle and exchange value which was integral to early modern South Asian society.

629 **A matter of honour: an account of the Indian army, its officers and its men.**
Philip Mason.   New York: Holt; London: Jonathan Cape, 1974. 580p. bibliog.

A critical study of the growth and development of the Indian army from its 18th-century beginnings to India's independence in 1947. Mason argues that there was a bond of honour between the Europeans and the Indians, and among the Indians of various castes and linguistic groups who served in the armed forces. The characters of such diverse military leaders as Field Marshals Lord Roberts of Kandahar (1832-1914), Sir Claude Auchinleck (1884-1918), and Sir William Slim (1891-1970), who saw service in both India and elsewhere, are drawn with compassion and understanding.

630 **Armies of the Great Mughals (1526-1707).**
Raj Kumar Phul.   New Delhi: Oriental Publishers, 1978. 372p. bibliog.

Intended to supersede *Army of the Great Mughals*, a classic work written by William Irvine in 1902, this volume provides a detailed, connected account of the development of the Mughal army since the time of Changiz. Part one, which contains twelve chapters, describes the administrative structure of the Mughal army: the *mansabdari* system, recruitment, salaries, titles, strength, equipment, weapons, its artillery wing, cavalry, infantry, and navy. Part two, with eight chapters, analyses the army in the field: its military camps, strategy, tactics, and siege techniques.

631 **Military history of India.**
Jadunath Sarkar.   Bombay: Orient Longman, 1970. 179p. maps. bibliog.

A study of the development of military science, originally published posthumously in 1960. Sarkar discusses great battles and campaigns from Alexander the Great's invasion of the Punjab in the 4th century BC through to the 18th-century Maratha campaigns against the tottering Mughal authority. The author argues that superior technology, organization, strategy and tactics, and an adequate economic base eventually proved more important than the number of soldiers employed.

632 **Indian security policy.**
Raju G. C. Thomas.   Princeton, New Jersey: Princeton University
Press, 1986. 312p. map.
An excellent analysis of Indian defence policy since 1947 within the context of the
regional strategic triangle of India, Pakistan and China, and of economics,
technology, and budgetary considerations. The author notes that while India
maintains the fourth largest army in the world and faces the danger of a nuclear arms
race in South Asia, as a result of Pakistan's nuclear programme, it remains 'one of the
few bastions of stability in the Third World'.

Foreign Relations

633 India's foreign policy and relations.
Angadipuram Appadorai, M. S. Rajan.   New Delhi: South Asia
Publishers, 1988. new ed. 709p. bibliog.
An authoritative and comprehensive textbook overview of India's foreign policy
since independence. Most of the book is devoted to analysis of the period between
1947 and 1972. There are separate chapters on India's relations with its neighbours
and the various regions of the world. Developments since 1982 are reviewed in a
separate chapter.

634 India's strategic future: regional state or global power?
Edited by Ross Babbage, Sandy Gordon.   New York: St. Martin's;
Basingstoke, England: Macmillan, 1992. 184p. map.
A collection of eight papers presented to a 1990 conference held at the Australian
National University. The contributors argue that India is faced today with two new
threats to its national security: Pakistan's secret development of nuclear weapons,
challenging India's military superiority; and the distraction of mounting levels of
domestic violence. However, India's strategic position has been improved by three
developments: the formation of new bodies for regional cooperation, notably the
South Asian Association for Regional Cooperation (SAARC), established in 1983;
the cultivation of a more balanced relationship with other global powers, notably the
USA; and the improvement in the nation's naval defences.

635 The making of India's foreign policy: determinants, institutions, processes, and personalities.
Jayantanuja Bandhyopadhyaya.   New Delhi: Allied, 1980. 2nd ed.
286p. bibliog.
An excellent brief analysis of India's foreign policy-making process, focusing on the
Ministry of External Affairs and the personal role of the foreign minister. The book's
thesis is that India's foreign policy is determined not only by its national interests and

the state of the world, but also by the personal style of political leaders in power. The more recent *Politics and economics of India's foreign policy* (London: C. Hurst, 1994. 306p.), by Ramesh Thakur, looks at economic factors as well.

636 **India, Pakistan, and the great powers.**
William J. Barnds. New York: Praeger; London: Pall Mall Press, 1972. 388p. 3 maps. bibliog.

An exhaustive survey of the role of the major world powers – the US, USSR, and China – on the Indian subcontinent. While critical of excessive United States involvement, the book nevertheless makes a strong case for continued American participation in the subcontinent's long-term economic development and defence. Written by a former US government intelligence analyst, the book is balanced, well documented, and sensitive to Indian national aspirations. Unfortunately, the Indo-Pakistan conflict receives inadequate attention.

637 **India's foreign policy since 1971.**
Robert W. Bradnock. London: Frances Pinter Publishers, Royal Institute of International Affairs, 1990. 128p. bibliog.

An exceptionally succinct analysis of the dynamics of Indian foreign policy since 1971, when India's regional dominance was confirmed by the break up of Pakistan. The author describes the foreign policy institutional structure, economic aspects (aid and investment), and the primacy placed on political and economic independence. This work is available in paperback.

638 **India, Pakistan, Bangladesh, and the major powers: politics of a divided subcontinent.**
G. W. Choudhury. New York: Free Press; London: Collier Macmillan, 1975. 276p. bibliog.

An analysis of the relations between the countries of the Indian subcontinent and the USSR, USA, and China, especially in the context of the Bangladesh crisis of 1971. The author considers that the great powers, particularly the Soviet Union, have complicated the way to peace on the subcontinent.

639 **The security of South Asia: American and Asian perspectives.**
Edited by Stephen Philip Cohen. Urbana, Illinois: University of Illinois Press, 1987. 290p. maps.

An interesting and unusual collection of essays addressing the topics of the relationship between India and Pakistan and the involvement of the United States in South Asia. The Indian, Pakistan and American contributors, strategic experts, were asked to place themselves in the position of counterparts from another state and propose policy approaches from this different perspective. The papers in part one are arranged around perceptional themes, while part two is concerned with speculations on the future. In the first appendix, the military power balance, circa 1985, on the subcontinent is tabulated. In the second, a prediction is made concerning the likely consequences of an India-Pakistan nuclear war. In one scenario, entailing 'counter-city strikes', the computed immediate death toll exceeds fifty millions.

640 **Soviet policy toward India: ideology and strategy.**
Robert H. Donaldson. Cambridge, Massachusetts: Harvard
University Press, 1974. 338p. bibliog.

Based mainly on Russian sources, this is the best study of Indo-Soviet relations up to
1972. Donaldson carefully analyses Soviet attempts to modify Marxist-Leninist
policy doctrines to suit changing patterns of Soviet interest in India. A useful, more
recent work is *Soviet relations with India and Vietnam* (Basingstoke, England:
Macmillan, 1992. 315p.), by Ramesh Thakur.

641 **India's foreign policy.**
V. P. Dutt. New Delhi: Vikas, 1984. 447p.

Written by a former member of the Indian Parliamentary Consultative Committee on
Foreign Affairs, this opinionated book focuses on Indian foreign policy during the
period between 1966 and 1976 when Indira Gandhi was prime minister. It records
India's economic and political relations with the United States, the USSR, China,
Pakistan, and other immediate neighbours. The final chapter deals briefly with
developments between 1977 and 1984.

642 **The origins of war in South Asia: Indo-Pakistani conflicts since
1947.**
Sumit Ganguly. Boulder, Colorado: Westview Press, 1994. 2nd ed.
145p. bibliog.

A study of three Indo-Pakistani conflicts: 1947-48, 1965, and 1971. Ganguly's
analysis of the last conflict should be read alongside *War and secession: Pakistan,
India, and the creation of Bangladesh* (Berkeley, California: University of California
Press, 1990. 338p.), by Richard Sisson and Leo E. Rose, which is a masterly
reconstruction of the decisions which led to the 1971 Bangladesh war. The authors
draw on many previously unpublished sources and interviews conducted with key
participants and political leaders.

643 **Cooperation and conflict in South Asia.**
Partha S. Ghosh. New Delhi: Manohar, 1989. 265p. bibliog.

An examination of five areas of discord in South Asia: the relations between India,
the region's predominant power, and its smaller neighbours – Pakistan, Bangladesh,
Nepal, Bhutan, and Sri Lanka. The author notes that the difficulties that India has
experienced with at least three of its neighbours are tied directly to ethnic and
ideological bases of nation- and state-building. A straightforward textbook covering
political processes in South Asia is *The International Politics of South Asia*
(Manchester University Press 1992, 243p.) by V. M. Hewitt. It analyses bilateral
relations between states in the region, relationships with neighbouring states and the
superpowers, and South Asia's position within the world economy.

644 **Kashmir: a study in India-Pakistan relations.**
Sisir Gupta. Bombay; London: Asia Publishing House, 1966. 511p.
maps. bibliog.

A carefully documented, definitive analysis of Indo-Pakistani relations *vis-à-vis*
Kashmir from 1946 to 1965. With minute details, Gupta examines the background to
the 1947-48 hotilities in Kashmir, the main UN resolutions on Kashmir, and Indian

legal claims to the territory. The volume, completed before the 1965 Indo-Pakistan war, ends with a plea for the restoration of amicable relations between the two neighbouring states on the basis of legitimization of the present cease-fire line into a permanent boundary. This book can be supplemented with *Kashmir: the troubled frontiers* (New Delhi: Lancer, 1994. 396p.), by Afsir Karim.

645 A diplomatic history of modern India.
Charles H. Heimsath, Surjit Mansingh. Bombay: Allied Publishers, 1971. 559p. maps. bibliog.

A straightforward historical narrative of Indian diplomacy, with emphasis on the Nehru era. The book is rich in detail and is amply documented from government sources. It should be read together with the more analytical work of Bandhyopadhyaya (see item no. 635) in order to provide a balanced basis for the study of India's foreign policy.

646 International Studies.
New Delhi: Vikas, 1959- . quarterly.

Quarterly publication of the Indian School of International Studies, Jawaharlal Nehru University, Delhi. Contains scholarly articles on international law, international organization, and international relations, with emphasis on India's policies and its role in international affairs. There is a good book review section, and it carries an annual bibliography of Indian publications on India in world affairs.

647 India and the non-aligned world: search for a new order.
Hari Jaisingh. New Delhi: Vikas, 1983. 155p. bibliog.

Written at the time of the 1983 New Delhi Non-Aligned Summit, held during a period of intensified 'cold war' rhetoric, this book outlines the genesis, development, achievements, and tasks ahead of the non-aligned movement. The author is a journalist passionately committed to the movement's ideals. The appendix list of summit attendances shows the growing strength of the movement: twenty-five full members attended the 1961 Belgrade summit and ninety-seven members the 1983 New Delhi summit.

648 India's foreign policy, 1947-92: shadows and substance.
Harish Kapur. New Delhi, London: Sage Publications, 1994. 231p. bibliog.

A succinct analysis of how and why India's foreign policy has evolved during the post-independence decades and its international image changed. The first part of the book reviews India's four key foreign policy goals: the quest for security; the diplomacy of development; the desire for regional hegemony; and the search for an international role. Part two examines the foreign-policy decision-making process, specifically the institutional framework and the personality factor.

649 Yearbook on India's Foreign Policy.
Edited by Satish Kumar. New Delhi: Sage Publications, 1985- . annual.

A useful annual reference work which analyses significant features of Indian foreign policy during each year. The first issue, published in 1985, covered 1982-83. Each issue contains specially commissioned essays by academics, diplomats and journalists on issues of current concern. There are also country profiles, and key documents and statistics are collected together in an appendix.

650   Problems of India's foreign policy.
Madhu Limaye.   New Delhi: Atma Ram, 1984. 320p. bibliog.

This book collects together the author's writings on foreign affairs during the period between 1947 and 1984 and also includes several previously unpublished essays. Limaye, a committed socialist, explores ways of reconciling the claims of idealism and morality with the need for national security, and explores the meeting ground of universalism and nationalism in a country which for many centuries has been subject to foreign rule. The book's format is chronological, with chapters on Nehru's early foreign policy, the Sino-Indian conflict, non-alignment, Janata international policy, and the new international economic order.

651   India's search for power: Indira Gandhi's foreign policy 1966-1982.
Surjit Mansingh.   New Delhi, London: Sage Publications, 1984. 405p.

A comprehensive and sympathetic study of Indira Gandhi's response to the changing international environment that India faced during the post-Nehru decades. The author, a former Indian Foreign Service officer, notes that Indira Gandhi's foreign policy, unlike Nehru's, which was underpinned by an ambitious world vision, was characterized by pragmatism, flexibility and a new emphasis on security, territory, and prestige. Included are solid surveys of India's bilateral relationships with the United States, the Soviet Union, Pakistan, and China. A useful collection of related essays is *Indian foreign policy: the Indira Gandhi years* (New Delhi, London: Sangam Books, 1990. 244p), edited by A. K. Damodaran and Uma Shankar Bajpai.

652   The cold war on the periphery: the United States, India and Pakistan.
Robert J. McMahon.   New York: Columbia University Press, 1994. 420p. bibliog.

An examination of American policy towards the Indian subcontinent, focusing on the period between independence in 1947 and the Indo-Pakistani War of 1965. It analyses the motivations behind America's pursuit of Pakistan and India as strategic cold war prizes. It should be read alongside: *Superpower rivalry in the Indian Ocean: Indian and American perspectives* (New York; Oxford: Oxford University Press, 1989. 309p.), edited by Selig S. Harrison and K. Subrahmanyam; and *The hope and the reality: US-India relations from Roosevelt to Reagan* (Boulder, Colorado: Westview Press, 1992. 231p.), edited by Harold Alton Gould and Sumit Ganguly, which covers the period up to the late 1980s.

653   Indian foreign policy: the Nehru years.
Edited by Bal Ram Nanda.   New Delhi, London: Sangam Books, 1989. new ed. 279p. bibliog.

The foreign policy performance of India's first prime minister is evaluated by prominent Indian academics, journalists, and diplomats in this collection of lectures delivered at the Nehru Memorial Museum and Library, New Delhi. The volume, originally published in 1976, is organized thematically and regionally. India's policies of disarmament and non-alignment, and her relations with Pakistan, the Muslim world, the superpowers, China, and Southeast Asia are discussed. An introduction by the museum's director ably synthesizes all the contributions. Well worth reading.

654 Strategies of British India: Britain, Iran and Afghanistan, 1798-1850.

Malcom E. Yapp. Oxford: Clarendon Press, 1980. 682p. 8 maps. bibliog.

A meticulously-researched monograph on the foreign policy of the British Raj during the early 19th century. The volume deals with the Russian frontier and imperial policies before a Northwest Frontier was definitively established.

Economy

General

655 **The economy of India.**
V. N. Balasubramanyam.   London: George Weidenfeld & Nicolson, 1984. 241p. bibliog.

A clearly-written, analytical survey of the performance of the Indian economy between 1950 and 1980 and the policy strategies which were pursued, designed for the general reader and students of development economics. Individual chapters deal with the following topics: population structure; overall growth performance; savings and investment; the agricultural sector; manufacturing; private foreign investment; foreign aid; and overseas trade. In his conclusion, Balasubramanyam recommends the adoption of more outward-looking economic policies, greater reliance on market forces and the price mechanism, and reduced bureaucratic controls. Such a shift in development strategy has occurred, gradually, since 1984.

656 **India in transition: freeing the economy.**
Jagdish Natwarlal Bhagwati.   Oxford: Clarendon Press, 1993. 108p.

Originally presented as a series of Oxford University lectures in 1992, this work was conceived soon after the new minority Congress (I) administration, headed by P. V. Narasimha Rao, had embarked on an apparently determined programme of liberal economic reforms. Bhagwati, an academic who had worked briefly in the Planning Commission during the 1960s and had become critical of the inhibiting effects of bureaucratic controls and overly rigid planning, reveals here his optimism in this new policy course. This slim volume is arranged around the themes of 'what went wrong' during the planning era, the steps taken by the Rao government, and future prospects.

657 **The Indian economy: poverty and development.**
Pramit Chaudhuri. London: Crosby Lockwood Staples; New Delhi:
Vikas, 1978-79. 279p. bibliog.

A well-written introductory text for anyone with a basic knowledge of economics.
Focusing on internal problems and relationships, this book does full justice to the
complexity of India's problems. Like many others, Chaudhuri observes that the
Indian economy developed steadily until 1967 after which structural constraints led to
stagnation. The author soundly criticizes the vagueness of planning goals in Indian
politics. A short and readable book.

658 **The Indian economy and its performance since independence.**
Edited by R. A. Choudhury, Shama Gamkhar, Aurobindo Ghose.
New Delhi: Oxford University Press India, 1990. 315p.

A collection of twenty-one papers which were presented by Indian scholars at a 1985
University of Delhi seminar held to take stock of the achievements and failures of the
Indian economy after four decades of independence. Included are also three
previously published seminal essays by the distinguished economists Amartya Sen,
Sukhamoy Chakravarty and Raj Krishna. The contributors approach their analyses of
post-independence economic performance from diverse perspectives: statistical-
empirical, political-economic, and liberal neo-classical. There is general agreement
that although there has been economic growth since independence, the rate has been
low in comparative Third World terms, while severe inequalities and deprivation
persist. A new developmental strategy of structural change is advocated. There are
interesting analyses of state capitalism in India, the role of the bureaucracy, inter-state
disparities in development, Rajiv Gandhi's New Economic Policy, the 'trickle-down'
theory of rural growth, and state industrial policy. *Growth and income distribution in
India: policy and performance since independence* (New Delhi: Sage Publications,
1987. 356p.), by R. M. Sundrum, and *India's national income, 1950-1980: an
analysis of economic growth and change* (New Delhi: Sage Publications, 1983.), by a
former cabinet member V. K. R. V. Rao, provide additional information on the socio-
economic and macro impact of postwar economic changes.

659 **The Indian economy: recent development and future prospects.**
Edited by Robert E. Lucas, Gustaf F. Papanek. Boulder, Colorado:
Westview Press, 1988. 350p.

An excellent collection of papers on recent trends in the Indian economy and likely
developments. It should be read alongside *The Indian economy: problems and
prospects* (New Delhi: Viking Penguin, 1992.), edited by Bimal Jalan, a symposium
which examines the early economic reforms of the Narasimha Rao Congress (I)
government, which came to power in 1991.

660 **South Asia: the narrowing option.**
Brian Slocock. London: Economist Intelligence Unit (EIU), 1988.
119p. map. (EIU Special Report No. 110).

A lucid, opinionated analysis by the *Economist Intelligence Unit* of recent economic
development in the countries of South Asia and prospects for the future. The report
notes common problems faced by the South Asian states: balance of payments
deficits, being propped up by immigrant remittances, foreign aid, and increased debt;

a too narrow and dated range of exports; excessive protection of domestic industries; a restricted tax base due to poverty, evasion, and special privileges for agriculture; and increasing political corruption.

661 **India's economic problems: an analytical approach.**
Edited by J. S. Uppal. New York: St. Martin's Press, 1979. 2nd ed. 409p. bibliog.

Intended for a general audience, this collection of articles deals with the national economy, human resources, agriculture, industry, Gandhian economics, labour, economic policy, black money, and a variety of other topics. Most of the essays are excellent and do not require in-depth knowledge of India's economy.

Economic history

662 **An Indian rural economy, 1880-1955: the Tamilnad countryside.**
Christopher John Baker. Oxford: Clarendon Press; New Delhi: Oxford University Press India, 1984. 616p. maps. bibliog.

A hugely impressive economic history focusing on the rural economy of the southern state of Tamil Nadu, but which ranges widely. The opening chapter provides a *longue durée* overview of the historical evolution of Tamilnad since ancient times and introduces the three subregional economies – the valleys, the plains, and Kongunad – whose contrasting fortunes are at the heart of the study. There are also separate chapters on colonial trade, rural markets, and the urban economy. The picture drawn is one of agricultural commercialization between the late 19th century and the 1920s in response to European and Southeast Asian demands. During the 1930s rural capital was redirected into urban pursuits as agricultural prices slumped and food availability declined. The work should be read in conjunction with *The south Indian economy: agrarian change, industrial structure and state policy, c. 1914-1947* (New Delhi: Oxford University Press India, 1991. 292p.), edited by Sabyasachi Bhattacharya, Sumit Guha, Raman Mahadevan, Sakti Padhi, D. Rajasekhar, and G. N. Rao.

663 **Cambridge economic history of India.**
Cambridge: Cambridge University Press, 1982. 2 vols. bibliog.

The first volume, edited by Tapan Raychaudhuri and Irfan Habib, Professor of History at Aligarh Muslim University, covers chiefly the period between 1200 and 1750, when Islamic dynasties dominated. It is subdivided into two parts – the pre-Mughal and the Mughal eras – and comprises analytical chapters dealing with economic sectors and specific macro-regions. The authors are established Indian and Western scholars. The second volume, edited by Dharma Kumar and Meghnad Desai, covers the period between 1757 and 1970. Considerably longer, it analyses the changes introduced into Indian economic life as a result of British colonial rule, closer integration within the international economy, and demographic expansion. Two concluding chapters review post-independence economic policies and trends. These are clearly written expositions of the state of existing knowledge. Both volumes are essential reading.

664 **British rule and the Indian economy, 1800-1914.**
Neil Charlesworth.   London: Macmillan, 1982. 73p. bibliog. (Studies in Economic and Social History).

Part of a popular series sponsored by the Economic History Society (U. K.), this slim volume provides a succinct overview of traditional historiography and recent specialist research on the performance of the Indian economy during the colonial period. There are thematic sections dealing with the rural sector, industry, trade and foreign investment, and government policy. There is also an invaluable bibliography. The author challenges the nationalist interpretation of India's economic development which holds that growth was hindered by British rule, and argues that the imperial impact was much weaker and more differential than once believed. A classic exposition of the older nationalist interpretation is *India in the Victorian age: an economic history of the people* (New Delhi: Low Price, 1993. new ed. 628p.), by Romesh C. Dutt, which was originally published in 1904.

665 **A history of Indian economic thought.**
Ajit Kumar Dasgupta.   London: Routledge, 1993. 206p. bibliog.

This chronologically arranged work begins with chapters covering Buddhist economic thought, the economic values set out in Kautilya's *Arthasastra*, and the economic ideas of the Muslim period of predominance. The remaining six chapters cover the 19th and 20th centuries. Four are devoted to various strands of nationalist economic thought: Dadabhai Naoroji's 'drain theory'; M. G. Ranade's critique of overdependence on agriculture; late nationalist ideas of 'discriminating protection'; and 'Gandhian economics'. The closing chapter reviews post-independence Indian economic thinking, including the Mahalanobis planning model. This volume can be complemented by William J. Barber's *British economic thought and India, 1600-1858: a study in the history of development economics* (Oxford: Clarendon Press, 1975. 243p.), which surveys changes in British economic thinking in relation to India.

666 **Arrested development in India: the historical dimension.**
Edited by Clive J. Dewey.   New Delhi: Manohar, 1988. 377p.

A collection of fourteen scholarly papers by, predominantly Western, economic and social historians re-examining India's economic development during the immediate pre-colonial and colonial periods. The concept of 'arrested development' is dissected, and commonly-held beliefs about India's economic retardation are challenged. Particularly notable are the papers on the supposed 'anarchy' of the 18th century (Burton Stein and Christopher and Susan Bayly), the impact of the inter-war depression on agriculture in western India (Neil Charlesworth), cropping trends in Punjab (M. Islam), and de-industrialization in the 19th-century south Indian textile industry (Konrad Specker). An earlier volume, *Economy and society: studies in Indian economic and social history* (New Delhi: Oxford University Press India, 1979. 358p.), edited by Kirty N. Chaudhuri and Clive J. Dewey, also contains significant papers highlighting new directions in Indian economic history research.

667 **The agrarian economy of the Bombay Deccan, 1818-1941.**
Sumit Guha.   New Delhi: Oxford University Press India, 1985. 215p. bibliog.

A modern analysis of trends in the agrarian economy of the Deccan in western India during the period of British rule. Individual chapters are devoted to the revenue system, agricultural technologies, agrarian social structure, and population movements. The author concludes that the periods between 1820-50 and 1920-40 were ones of stagnant or declining per capita output, between 1850-75 there was expansion (during the cotton boom), while the years 1875-1920 saw more complex differential trends punctuated by several severe famines.

668 Indian Economic and Social History Review.
New Delhi: Vikas, 1963- . quarterly.

A scholarly journal devoted to social and economic history, edited at Delhi School of Economics by an international board of Indian and foreign scholars. The principal focus is on the modern period. The *Journal of the Economic and Social History of the Orient* (Leiden, the Netherlands: E. J. Brill, 1958-), with three issues a year, provides good coverage of ancient Indian economic and social history.

669 The Hindu equilbrium.
Deepak Lal. Oxford: Clarendon Press; New Delhi, Oxford University Press India, 1989. 2 vols. maps. bibliogs.

An ambitious work which looks at the broad sweep of Indian economic history from ancient to modern times. The second volume – *Aspects of Indian labour* – focuses on labour markets. In volume one, *Cultural stability and economic stagnation: India c.1500 BC – 1980 AD*, Lal seeks to explain the evolution and survival of the caste system and related local socio-political structures. He argues that a social and economic equilibrium was fashioned by the ancient Hindus to suit a situation in which labour was a scarce resource and where climatic and political factors created great uncertainties. This equilibrium survived throughout the subsequent centuries of Muslim and British rule since it provided, by pre-modern standards, a not unimpressive average standard of living and reliable local structures for appropriation of the rural surplus.

670 Class structure and economic growth: India and Pakistan since the Moghuls.
Angus Maddison. London: George Allen & Unwin, 1971. 181p. bibliog.

A popular broad historical analysis which discusses the links between the social structure of the Indian subcontinent and economic growth. Though dated in places, the work has two particular strengths: its focus on government attempts to change the underlying social structure and its presentation of detailed national income data.

671 The economy of the Mughal empire c. 1595: a statistical study.
Shireen Moosvi. New Delhi: Oxford University Press India, 1987. 442p. 11 maps. bibliog.

A pioneering attempt to apply statistical analysis to the economy of Mughal India around the year 1600. Using data from the *A'in-i Akbari* (see item no. 121), the great official compilation of the time, Moosvi provides estimates of the extent of cultivation, crop yields, the distribution of the rural surplus among the ruling class, price movements, the urbanization level, and the size of the population of the Mughal empire. Moosvi refrains from computing a Mughal GNP in this volume, but has subsequently provided an estimate which suggests that, in per capita terms, it exceeded that of early 20th-century India. A bold, but controversial work, which has been criticized for containing too many 'guesstimates' and macro extrapolations.

672   **India at the death of Akbar: an economic study.**
William Harrison Moreland.   New Delhi: Sunita, 1989. reprint. 306p.
2 maps.

A classic work, originally published in 1920, which foreshadowed later research (see item no. 671) by attempting to quantify wherever possible. The author, W. H. Moreland (1868-1938), a former district officer in the Indian Civil Service, drew upon Persian documents, notably the *A' in-i Akbari* (see item no. 121), to establish trends in commerce, population movements and agrarian production. Though outmoded in places, the work remains a coherent account of economic and social conditions during the age of the Great Mughals. Moreland was also the author of *From Akbar to Aurangzeb: a study in Indian economic history* (New Delhi: Vinod, 1988. reprint. 364p.), and *The agrarian system of Moslem India* (New Delhi: Kanti, 1988. reprint. 296p.).

673   **An economic history of India (from pre-colonial times to 1986).**
Dietmar Rothermund.   London: Croom Helm, 1988. 214p. bibliog.

A solid, conventional analysis of India's economic evolution over the very long term – since ancient times. The work is organized chronologically, but greatest emphasis is given to the 20th century, with two-thirds of the book being devoted to the period since 1914. In the opening section, there is a description of the structure of the traditional, pre-colonial economy. Under colonial rule, Rothermund sees the 'evolution of a parasitical symbiosis' between an agrarian state and a Western capitalist corporation, the East India Company. This part of the book summarizes conclusions already presented in the author's *The Indian economy under British rule and other essays* (New Delhi: Manohar, 1983. 223p.). The remainder of the book is devoted to a description and analysis of the causes of India's aborted growth and restricted development.

674   **Perspectives in social and economic history of early India.**
Ram Sharan Sharma.   New Delhi: Munshiram Manoharlal, 1983.
262p. bibliog.

An outstanding work of synthesis by India's foremost social and economic historian of the ancient and early medieval eras (see items no. 145, 306). The work is divided into two parts, social history and economic history, and contains sixteen analytical chapters. The author provides an overview of the successive stages through which the economy and social structure passed. There are also chapters on the position of women, the role of astrology and divination, irrigation, usury and numismatics, land grants and historiography.

675   **Survey of research in economic and social history of India.**
Edited by Ram Sharan Sharma.   New Delhi: Ajanta, 1986. 283p.

Sponsored by the Indian Council of Social Science Research (ICSSR), this useful volume contains six papers which review the existing literature on the economic and social history of India during the ancient, medieval and modern periods. The contributors are S. Bhattacharya, Satish Chandra, Irfan Habib, S. Jaiswal, D. N. Jha, and Dharma Kumar. The bibliographical notes are extensive.

676   **The shaping of modern India.**
Daniel Thorner. New Delhi: Allied, 1980. 404p. bibliog.
This book contains an extract from Thorner's unpublished 1948 interpretive essay on
the British period in Indian history. In addition, the book includes a selection of
articles and other writings that span the subsequent quarter century of the author's
career The twenty essays presented in the volume include Thorner's critique of the
theories of Marx and Chayanov, of the studies of H. H. Mann, S. L. F. D. Nyle, and
Henry Maine, and his own bold thesis on the emergence of capitalist agriculture in
India. Thorner's work is of supreme value because it combines a depth of first-hand
knowledge of India with a first-rate grasp of the relevant social science theory.

677   **The economy of modern India, 1860-1970 (Vol. III:3 in The New
Cambridge History of India).**
Brian Roger Tomlinson.   Cambridge: Cambridge University Press,
1993. 234p. maps. bibliog.
An excellent analysis of the process of economic change in India from colonial times
which synthesizes the findings of recent specialist monographs and articles and the
author's own research on the inter-war Indian economy. The opening chapter
addresses the debates over imperialism, development and underdevelopment. There
are then separate chapters on the agricultural sector, trade and manufacture during the
colonial period and a chapter on the state and the economy between 1939 and 1970.
The picture presented is one of some output growth and technical change, but in
which overall development was constrained by weak market structures,
underdeveloped institutions, and inappropriate and debilitating government policies.
The thirteen page annotated bibliography is particularly useful.

Economic and social journals, abstracts and indicators

678   **Commerce.**
Bombay: Commerce Ltd, 1910- . weekly.
India's oldest journal dealing with economic and financial affairs. Usual features
include a special article on some aspect of the economy, analysis and interpretation of
government statistical data, an in-depth survey of a particular industry, and company
news. The fortnightly *Business India* (Bombay: Advani, 1978-), produced in the
style of the popular US weekly *Business Week*, also provides excellent coverage of
Indian business developments. It is written from a corporate, free-enterprise
perspective.

679   **Economic and Political Weekly.**
Bombay: Sameeksha Trust, 1966- . weekly.
This influential weekly reviews, from a radical perspective, economic and political
affairs with emphasis on India. Both Indian and foreign scholars and journalists

contribute. Occasional special issues are devoted to themes such as a 'Review of Agriculture'. Articles are scholarly in tone. Two other important economic journals are the *Indian Economic Journal* (University of Bombay) and the *Indian Journal of Economics* (Allahabad).

680 **Economic Survey.**
Department of Economic Affairs, Ministry of Finance. New Delhi, 1963- . annual.
This succinct annual review is the most comprehensive description of the functioning of the Indian economy. A brief topical review of the economy as a whole pinpoints major achievements and shortfalls. Chapters on agriculture, infrastructure, industry, prices, price policy, budgets and fiscal policy, banking, and foreign trade are followed by a brief chapter outlining the tasks for the year ahead. The second part of the survey has cumulative statistical tables on production, money supply, finance, employment, balance of payments, foreign trade, and other relevant topics. A useful *India, Economic Information Yearbook* (New Delhi: National, annual), is also available, edited by A. N. Agrawal, H. O. Varma, and R. C. Gupta.

681 **Far Eastern Economic Review.**
Hong Kong: Far Eastern Economic Review, 1946- . weekly.
The liveliest and most extensive weekly coverage of Asian economic and political affairs. The review's editorial outlook is liberal. International trade and aid, foreign investment, and the activities of transnational corporations receive special attention. Indispensable for keeping abreast of Asian affairs and India's role in them. The publishers also produce an annual *Asia Yearbook* which summarizes each year's events.

682 **ICSSR Journal of Abstracts and Reviews: Economics.**
New Delhi: Indian Council of Social Science Research, 1972- . quarterly.
The Indian Council of Social Science Research started this quarterly abstracting service in 1972. Items are classified according to the American Economic Association's nomenclature. Abstracts of selected articles from over forty Indian economic journals are given. Each issue includes a few book reviews. Similar abstracts are produced by the ICSSR for anthropology and sociology, and political science. Since 1987 a specialist annotated and selected bibliography of English language publications on Indian social and economic conditions has been produced annually by Sage Publications, *Indian Social and Economic Development: an index to the literature*. It includes research reports, seminar papers, articles, annual reports, official documents, and some books, but excludes books published by well known publishers and articles from popular journals. The number of entries has averaged around 500 in each issue.

683 **Statistical Abstract, India.**
New Delhi: Central Statistical Organisation, 1949- . annual.
This annual abstract contains the latest available data on economic and social development. The data covers periods of five to ten years, with brief explanatory notes preceding each section and primary sources cited under each table. The *Statistical Pocket Book – India* (1956-) and *National Account Statistics* (1956-) are also produced annually by the Central Statistical Organisation.

Planning and development

684 **The state and development planning in India.**
Edited by Terence James Byres. New Delhi: Oxford University Press India, 1994. 567p. (SOAS Studies on South Asia).

This collection of essays provides a comprehensive analysis of the nature, achievements and limitations of Indian development planning from the 1950s to the late 1980s. The papers are arranged in three sections: state development planning and structural change; critical domestic issues; and planning and the foreign dimension (aid, trade and investment). A wide range of topics is addressed, including agricultural development, regional disparities in growth, problems of plan implementation, and the rise and decline of development planning.

685 **Development planning: the Indian experience.**
Sukhamoy Chakravarty. Oxford: Clarendon Press, 1987. 128p. bibliog.

A lucid, intelligent analysis of India's planning experience by an economist and former member of the Planning Commission. Chakravarty, while admitting that errors were made and that not enough emphasis was placed either on exports or on seeking efficiency in the state industries, defends vigorously the basic thrust of Indian planning with its emphasis on redistribution and the state sector.

686 **Indian planning at the crossroads.**
Bhabatosh Datta. New Delhi: Oxford University Press India, 1992. 251p.

This collection of essays, written by the author between 1985 and 1991, provides a running commentary on the problems of the Indian economy during the Seventh Plan (1986-90) period and at the start of the 1990s. The author reviews the contemporary debates over the respective merits of a choice between growth-oriented and employment-oriented development strategies, between encouraging large-scale modern industries or labour-intensive smaller scale enterprises, and between different sources of finance. There are separate chapters on the New Economic Policy of 1985-86, export performance, exchange rate policy, government debt, and central budgets.

687 **Direct attacks on rural poverty: policy, programmes, and implementation.**
Prabhu Ghate. New Delhi: Concept, 1984. 597p. bibliog.

A detailed analysis of the conceptualization, working and impact of non-land-based government programmes designed to benefit the landless and near landless rural poor in Ghazipur district, situated in eastern Uttar Pradesh, in north India. A wide range of programmes, from blanket weaving to 'food for work', are examined and the author concludes that they serve as palliatives, rather than a direct attack on rural poverty. What is really required is more fundamental state intervention to bring about changes in the region's inegalitarian social structure.

688 **The process of planning: a study of India's five year plans, 1950-1964.**
A. H. Hanson. Oxford: Oxford University Press, for the Royal Institute of International Affairs, 1966. 560p.

A standard account of the planning process during the 1950s and 1960s. Two complementary works are: *Planning for industrialization: India's industrialization and trade policies since 1951* (Oxford: Oxford University Press, for the OECD, 1970. 537p.), by Jagdish N. Bhagwati and Padma Desai, which examines the machinery of planning and the first three five-year-plans; and *The crisis of Indian planning: economic planning in the 1960s* (Bombay: Oxford University Press India, 1968. 416p.), edited by Paul Streeten and Michael Lipton. All three works were written at a time when the Indian economy was subject to temporary food shortages and a foreign exchange crisis.

689 **Development in South Asia.**
Basil Leonard Clyde Johnson. Harmondsworth, England: Penguin, 1983. 250p. bibliog.

A succinct, yet comprehensive, review of the rural and industrial development of the Indian subcontinent during the first three and a half decades after independence. Johnson, an Australian geographer, assesses agricultural development from the perspective of the technological changes brought about by irrigation and the green revolution, and assesses the effect of land reform and opportunities offered by colonization. The author examines industrial development in relation to the resource bases of the states of South Asia (India, Pakistan, Bangladesh, Sri Lanka, and Nepal) and in the context of national planning ideologies. There are also chapters on trade and living standards.

690 **Growth and justice: aspects of India's development experience.**
Christopher Thomas Kurien. New Delhi: Oxford University Press India, 1992. 295p. bibliog.

A collection of essays written during the 1980s by Kurien, an economist from the Madras Institute of Development Studies. The author is critical of a simplistic emphasis on growth simply in quantitative terms, stressing the need for it to be broadly based in social terms to constitute real development. The volume includes both theoretical and empirical chapters. The latter focus on analyses of the New Economic Policy of the administration of Rajiv Gandhi (1984-89) which sought to use the resources generated by quantitative growth to alleviate poverty via targetted programmes. However, Kurien notes that the record of employment generation during the 1980s was particularly disappointing. Kurien is also editor, with E. R. Prabhakar and S. Gopal, of *Economy, society and development: essays and reflections in honour of Malcolm S. Adiseshiah* (New Delhi: Sage Publications, 1991. 331p.), which includes sixteen essays covering various aspects of the Indian economy, development and planning, and education.

691   **Does aid work in India? : a country study of the impact of official development assistance.**
Michael Lipton, John Toye.   London, New York: Routledge, 1990. 276p. bibliog.

This volume is a revised and updated version of a case study report carried out for the World Bank in 1984. Individual chapters set aid inflows in their macro- and micro-economic contexts, showing their relative importance over time, in terms of overall public investment, and the impact of aid on Indian poverty. Some sixty evaluations of project aid to India are examined.

692   **Western economists and Eastern societies: agents of change in South Asia, 1950-70.**
George Rosen.   London; Baltimore, Maryland: Johns Hopkins University Press, 1985. 270p.

A review of the role of Western economists in the post-independence development process in India and Pakistan. The author focuses on programmes funded by the American Ford Foundation, a private philanthropic organization with political underpinnings, and interviewed many officials and development economists. The work is divided chronologically into four parts. Part two analyses agricultural programmes, economic institution building in India, and the Calcutta urban development plan. Rosen concludes that, unlike Pakistan, India sought just economic and technical aid, not advice on political and economic ideology, and ended the period with a more mature economics profession and stronger related institutions.

693   **Economic development and environment: a case study of India.**
Edited by Kartik C. Roy, Clement Allan Tisdell, Raj Kumar Sen.
Calcutta: Oxford University Press India, 1992. 164p.

A collection of essays by five contributors which examine the environmental issues related to India's planned development. In the opening chapter, a comparison is drawn between Nehru's centralized planning programme and Mahatma Gandhi's concept of 'sustainable development'. In the following chapters there are empirical reviews of the environmental impact of India's post-independence development, focusing on such topics as deforestation, industrial pollution and the effects of irrigation projects. There is also an analysis of the controversial Narmada Valley Project and National Missile Testing Range at Baliapal in Orissa, both of which provoked popular agitations.

694   **The great ascent: the rural poor in South Asia.**
Inderjit Singh.   Baltimore, Maryland: Johns Hopkins University Press, for the World Bank, 1990. 444p. bibliog.

This work is a challenge to interpretations of the green revolution as being of benefit only to the rural élite. Singh, who defines the rural poor as underemployed small farmers (cultivating less than five acres) and agricultural labourers, sees this group as also benefitting from the introduction of high-yielding grain varieties. This was because productivity increased and so did labour demand in rural areas, both in agricultural and service activities, as purchasing power grew. However, Singh is critical of the failure to precede or accompany the green revolution with land reform so as to redistribute rural assets and enable the poor to benefit even more. He also notes that agricultural mechanization, specifically tractorization encouraged by cheap credit, and the influx of migrant labourers have ensured that rural wages have remained depressed.

695 **Reaching out to the poor: the unfinished rural revolution.**
Geeta Somjee, A. H. Somjee.   Basingstoke, England: Macmillan, 1989. 152p. bibliog.

The theme of this work is the constraints of economic and social relationships within which India's rural poor are trapped and their inability to escape from poverty by themselves. The authors argue that the poor require socially concerned individuals to mobilize them and economic organizations to target them for development. This theme is explored by a detailed analysis of the work of four major milk cooperatives in western India. The performances of the cooperatives in areas such as health provision are impressive, yet still the authors find that a 'social queue' exists, with better off groups benefiting first, followed by agriculturist castes, with the landless and *Adivasis* (tribals) the last to be reached.

696 **Public expenditure and Indian development policy 1960-1970.**
John Toye.   Cambridge: Cambridge University Press, 1981. 270p.
bibliog. (Cambridge South Asian Studies, no. 25).

A careful, empirical analysis of the relationship between public expenditure and Indian economic performance during the 1960s. In part one, the author critically assesses Indian statistics on public expenditure and theories on public expenditure and state accumulation. In part two, Toye considers how far the public authorities were responsible for causing the industrial recession of the late 1960s, measures inter-state differences in public expenditure growth, and discovers a growing disjunction between expenditure control and planning. In part three, the broad historical trajectory of Indian planning is sketched. Toye describes it as characterized by 'mimetic nationalism' - the defensive copying of developed countries. This was seen most clearly in a pro-heavy-industry bias in the allocation of investment and indiscriminate import substitution, which resulted in unbalanced growth.

Political economy

697 **The political economy of development in India.**
Pranab Bardhan.   Oxford: Basil Blackwell, 1984. 118p.

A short, very readable, though polemical, analysis of India's post-independence economic development and related class structure. The author, an economist noted for detailed micro-level surveys of Indian poverty and rural social structures, presents a general hypothesis that India has remained trapped in a low-level equilibrium trap for decades – experiencing annualized per capita GDP growth of barely 1.5 per cent – as a result of constraints imposed by its class structure. A plurality of classes has dominated the political economy, generating pressures for patronage and subsidies which have stifled the potential for more rapid and egalitarian state-primed economic growth. A contrasting analysis is *India: a political economy of stagnation* (Oxford:

Oxford University Press, 1980. 300p.), by Prem Shankar Jha. This lays the blame for the Indian economy's halting performance on the shoulders of the 'intermediate' class of the commercial and industrial sector self-employed who have profited from a regime of shortages.

698 India's political economy, 1947-1977: the gradual revolution.
Francine R. Frankel. Princeton, New Jersey: Princeton University Press, 1978. 600p. maps. bibliog.

This book grapples with the dilemmas and contradictions inherent in India's development goal of rapid improvement in the living conditions of the poorest without the chaos of revolution. Frankel argues that India's strategy of 'accommodative politics and radical social change' has resulted in growing socio-political conflict and sluggish economic growth. The evidence presented suggests that without a direct attack on the propertied castes and classes, economic development and social change will continue at their current unsatisfactory rate. This is an authoritative analysis of India's political economy. A contrasting, neo-liberal, Friedmanite critique of post-independence Indian economic management is presented in *Foundations of India's political economy: towards an agenda for the 1990s* (New Delhi: Sage Publications, 1992. 304p.), by Subroto Roy and William E. James.

699 India in transition: issues of political economy in a plural society.
F. Tomasson Jannuzi. Boulder, Colorado: Westview Press, 1989. 164p. bibliog.

An inquiry into the economic components of the contemporary Indian political situation by a scholar with special expertise on eastern India. Jannuzi describes how intricate and self-reinforcing social-structural impediments impede rural development and have resulted in a propensity to violent confrontation and social breakdown. The author believes that the increasing build-up and use of military and paramilitary units to suppress civil disorder threatens the constitutional stability of India and may presage growing military intervention in government.

700 In pursuit of Lakshmi: a political economy of the Indian state.
Lloyd Irving Rudolph, Susanne Hoeber Rudolph. Chicago: University of Chicago Press, 1987. 529p. bibliog.

An important analysis of the dynamics of the contemporary Indian state which gives primacy to the influence of material forces and economic conditions. Political party support bases are described and it is noted that the influence exercised by prosperous, especially urban, groups over the Congress Party served to delimit Nehru's reformist aspirations. The authors conclude that social classes have played a relatively minor role in India's post-independence political process. However, caste groups (*jatis*) and other interest, or 'demand', groups narrower than classes have been influential. This has given rise to centrist politics and 'involuted pluralism' within the context of a 'strong-weak state'.

Finance and Banking

701   **Political economy and monetary management: India 1766-1914.**
Srinavasan Ambirajan.   Madras, India: Associated East-West Press,
1984. 203p. bibliog.

A succinct exposition of Indian financial policy over a 150-year period which argues
that economists contributed significantly to monetary policy making. Three distinct
periods are covered: the late-18th-century integration of the gold-based systems of
south India with the silver-based systems of north India; the early to mid-19th-century
regulation of the Agency Houses and establishment of a modern banking system; and
the late-19th-century silver debate and resulting Indo-British financial arrangements.

702   **The evolution of the State Bank of India.**
Amiya Kumar Bagchi.   Bombay: Oxford University Press India, 1987
and 1990. 2 vols.

The official history of the State Bank of India (founded 1955) and its predecessors,
the Imperial Bank of India (1921) and the Presidency Banks of Bengal, Bombay and
Madras. The first two volumes respectively cover the periods 1806-76 and 1876-
1914. Bagchi, a distinguished economic historian, sets developments in the context of
broader changes in the colonial economy. A narrower, complementary study is
Towards a new frontier: history of the Bank of Baroda, 1908-1983 (New Delhi:
Manohar, 1985. 309p.), by Dwijendra Tripathi and Priti Misra.

703   **Pricing and inflation in India.**
Pulapre Balakrishnan.   New Delhi: Oxford University Press India,
1991. 271p. bibliog.

An econometric analysis of Indian inflation between 1950 and 1980 which includes
separate chapters on the relationship between foodgrain and manufacturing output
and price movements and changes in the money supply. Balakrishnan ascribes India's
inflation during the period before 1965 to the rapid pace of industrialization within an
underdeveloped economy. Since 1965 he suggests that government intervention in the

foodgrain economy has created a measure of 'structural inflation'. This book can be read in conjunction with *War against inflation: the story of the falling rupee: 1943-77* (New Delhi: Macmillan, 1979. 338p.), by Chandulal Nagindas Vakil; and *Pricing policies and price controls in developing countries: the case of India* (London: Frances Pinter Publishers, 1987. 220p.), by K. D. Saksena.

704 Credit, markets, and the agrarian economy of colonial India.
Edited by Sugata Bose.   New Delhi: Oxford University Press India, 1994. 333p. bibliog.

Peasant indebtedness, as described in the accounts of S. S. Thorburn (see item no. 711) and Malcolm Lyall Darling (see item no. 748), was a cause of colonial concern. It was viewed as a sign of poverty and as a reason for the lack of dynamism in agriculture. These scholarly essays demonstrate how the study of rural credit has moved beyond the simple issues of poverty and prosperity. A useful supplement is *National savings movement in India* (New Delhi: Atma Ram, 1978. 444p.), by Gokaran Nath Mehrotra, which describes government efforts to stimulate 'small' savings and use them in the development effort.

705 Indian banking: towards the 21st century.
Edited by A. S. Chawla.   New Delhi: Bagchi, 1988. 185p.

A collection of essays by Indian economists and financial writers assessing the current state of Indian banking and prospective trends. A related work, analysing the operations of the commercial banking and the cooperative credit structure is *Indian banking since independence* (New Delhi: Ashish, 1988. 360p.), by K. Deb.

706 The financial development of India, 1860-1977.
Raymond William Goldsmith.   London; New Haven, Connecticut: Yale University Press, 1983. 240p. bibliog.

Using a wide range of secondary statistical sources, Goldsmith, an American economist, provides statistical indicators of the financial structure of South Asia and the Indian Union from colonial times. The work is arranged in chronological chapters and includes many tables. A notable feature is the annual series of data on national income per capita, price levels, money supply, bank assets and sectoral investment. An impressive work which ranges more widely than its title might suggest.

707 Reserve Bank of India Bulletin.
Bombay: Reserve Bank of India, 1947- . monthly.

The most authoritative source on Indian banking and finance. In general, each issue contains a monthly review of finance and the economy, seasonal trends in prices, national debt, current statistics, and one or two articles. Some issues are accompanied with supplements. This publication provides a cumulative index decennially.

708 The imperial monetary system of Mughal India.
Edited by John F. Richards.   New Delhi: Oxford University Press India, 1987. 382p. maps.

A collection of conference papers on the theme of monetary integration in Mughal and immediate post-Mughal India. The seven contributors include: Irfan Habib, writing about the effects of the silver influx into early modern India; Stephen Blake, on monetary exchange in the Mughal empire; Frank Perlin, on money use in late pre-colonial India; and Om Prakash. The editor provides a useful introduction.

709 **Money and the market in India, 1100-1700.**
Edited by Sanjay Subrahmanyam. New Delhi: Oxford University Press India, 1994. 300p. bibliog.

In this volume the growing use of money is seen as indicative of an increasing orientation towards the market of producers (agriculturalists and manufacturers). India's experience of increasing monetization and commercialization is traced in this collection of specialist essays which range from medieval Tamil Nadu to colonial times. Covering the preceding period, *Living without silver: the monetary history of early medieval India* (New Delhi: Oxford University Press India, 1990. 369p.), by John S. Deyell, is an authoritative monograph.

710 **The Indian financial system.**
V. K. Subramanian. New Delhi: Abhinav, 1979. 233p. bibliog.

A descriptive account of the Indian financial system. The book covers such key issues as the fiscal provisions of the constitution, state and federal financial administration, legislative control over finances, the role of planning and finance commissions, the taxation system, public debt, the Reserve Bank of India and the banking system, foreign borrowing, and rural credit. There are numerous statistical tables and lists of financial and industrial institutions.

711 **Mussalmans and money-lenders in the Punjab.**
S. S. Thorburn. New Delhi: Mittal, 1983. 198p.

Originally published in 1886, this classic work is a passionate plea by a colonial government official for the introduction of measures to protect the Muslim agriculturalists of the Punjab from becoming hopelessly indebted to and, as a consequence, the effective serfs of Hindu moneylenders. The book initiated a debate which resulted in the passing of the 1900 Punjab Alienation of Land Act, prohibiting all transfer of land to non-agriculturalists in Punjab – a strategic province for the Raj.

Trade, Traders and Commerce

Trade and commerce

712 **Foreign trade regimes and economic development: India.**
Jagdish N. Bhagwati, T. N. Srinivasan.   New York: Columbia
University Press, 1975. 261p. map. bibliog.

This study examines the interaction between India's foreign trade and domestic
policies and objectives. The pre-1966 import substitution policies are compared
unfavourably with liberalized trade policies following the 1966 currency devaluation.
The authors argue that the earlier restrictive foreign exchange allocation and
industrial licensing policies, together with import controls and restricted exports,
encouraged wasteful resource allocation and blunted inter-firm competition.

713 **The trading world of Asia and the English East India Company,
1660-1760.**
Kirty N. Chaudhuri.   Cambridge: Cambridge University Press, 1978.
629p. 8 maps. bibliog.

A sophisticated analysis of the activities and role played by the English East India
Company in the economy of South Asia during the late-17th and first half of the 18th
century. The work includes general chapters on trade and monetary fluctuations and
the politics of early modern commerce, and more specialized chapters devoted to
individual commodities, such as pepper, silk, coffee, and textiles. Five long statistical
appendixes provide annual series of imports and exports for these items between 1664
and 1759. A complementary work, which examines the activities of an important
commercial rival, is *The Dutch East India Company and the economy of Bengal,
1630-1720* (Princeton, New Jersey: Princeton University Press, 1985. 292p.), by Om
Prakash.

714 **India and the Indian Ocean: 1500-1800.**
Edited by Ashin Dasgupta, Michael Naylor Pearson. Oxford: Oxford
University Press, 1987. 363p. map.
A collection of specially commissioned essays on different aspects of early modern
Indian Ocean trade. The editors have contributed two useful introductory chapters.
Other notable papers are by Om Prakash, on the Dutch East India Company, and by
Ahsan Jan Qaisar, on life on Indian ships during the 16th and 17th centuries. The
volume can be complemented by: Kirty N. Chaudhuri, *Asia before Europe: economy
and civilisation of the Indian Ocean from the rise of Islam to 1750* (Cambridge:
Cambridge University Press, 1990. new ed. 477p.), a work of impressive scope; and
Satish Chandra (editor), *The Indian Ocean: explorations in history, commerce and
politics* (New Delhi: Sage Publications, 1987. 334p.), which, ranging from antiquity
to the present day, includes chapters on 19th-century harbour development and
India's incorporation into the modern capitalist world system after 1750.

715 **Ancient India and ancient China: trade and religious exchanges,
AD 1-600.**
Xinru Liu.   New Delhi: Oxford University Press India, 1988. 231p.
bibliog.
Combining literary sources with archaeological and numismatic data, the author has
reconstructed ancient trade routes between India and China during the Kusana, Shaka,
and Gupta eras. The factors behind this long-distance commerce are clearly
explained. They were threefold: the marketless exchange of gifts among Indian and
Chinese rulers; a taste for costly exotica among ruling élites in both states; and the
donation of treasures to Buddhist monasteries, a practice which was believed to
transfer merit to the donor. A fascinating work.

716 **India's exports and export policies in the 1960s.**
Deepak Nayyar.   New York: Cambridge University Press, 1976.
392p. bibliog.
A valuable analysis of India's export performance and policies in the 1960s. The
author empirically examines eleven traditional as well as non-traditional items that
together constitute sixty per cent of India's total export earnings. The author believes
that India's relatively poor export performance is primarily due to internal factors:
rising domestic demand, inappropriate export promotion policies, and substantial
inflow of foreign remittances from Indians overseas. Two useful books on the same
theme, but covering later periods, are: *India's export performance: some policy
implications* (New Delhi: Intellectual Publishing, 1981. 243p.), by K. S. Dhindsa; and
India's trade policy and the export performance of industry (New Delhi, London:
Sage Publications, 1994. 225p.), by Pitou Van Dijck and K. S. Chalapati Rao.

717 **Encounters: the westerly trade of the Harappa civilization.**
Shereen Ratnagar.   New Delhi: Oxford University Press India, 1981.
292p. maps. bibliog.
In six chapters the author examines the geographical scope, articles of trade,
technologies of overland and sea transport, the significance of clay seals, and the
institutional organization of the urban Harappan civilization which flourished in the
Indus basin between 2500 and 1500 BC. Recent archaeological discoveries, indicating

a much larger territory within the confines of the Indus Valley Civilization than previously assumed, have been fully exploited by the author in documenting her views.

718 **The political economy of commerce: southern India, 1500-1650.**
Sanjay Subrahmanyam. New York; Cambridge: Cambridge University Press, 1990. 401p. maps. bibliog. (Cambridge South Asian Studies, no. 45).

An astute and original analysis of south Indian commerce during the 16th and 17th centuries, based upon Portuguese and Dutch archival sources. The author explores the relationship between long-distance trade and economic and political structures. He demonstrates how local developments in early modern south India interacted with larger international processes and how an influential group of what he terms 'portfolio capitalists', with interests in commerce, land control and revenue farming, gradually emerged as advisers to regional rulers. Covering the 9th to the mid-14th centuries, *Two medieval merchant guilds of south India* (New Delhi: Manohar, 1988. 273p.), by Meera Abraham, describes the activities of merchant guilds, and their links with rulers, temples and overseas traders, in early medieval south India.

719 **Periodic markets and rural development in India.**
Sudhir Wanmali. New Delhi: B. R. Publishing, 1981. 236p. maps. bibliog.

This is an analysis of local rural marketing systems in contemporary India based on fieldwork carried out in Singhbhum district in southeast Bihar. The author, a geographer, draws upon central-place theory in his descriptions of the market hierarchy and periodicity. He describes how traders service the market system and how they are also used by government to foster rural development.

The trading community

720 **Partner in empire: Dwarkanath Tagore and the age of enterprise in eastern India.**
Blair B. Kling. Berkeley, California: University of California Press, 1976. 276p. bibliog.

Dwarkanath Tagore (1794-1846), grandfather of the Nobel Prize-winning poet Rabindranath Tagore (see item no. 856), was a key figure in the 'Bengal renaissance' of the early 19th century and dominated Calcutta commercial and civic endeavour from the collapse of the old Agency Houses between 1830 and 1833 until the fall of his own Union Bank in 1846-47. This excellent biography describes Dwarkanath's rise as a businessman, prospering by serving the British, and his promotion of cultural and civic enterprises, including the Brahmo Samaj (see item no. 406) social and religious reform movement.

721 **Indian business and nationalist politics 1931-39: the indigenous capitalist class and the rise of the Congress Party.**
Claude Markovits. Cambridge: Cambridge University Press, 1985. 230p bibliog. (Cambridge South Asian Studies, no. 33).

A systematic study of the political attitudes of Indian big business during the final, crucial phase of the nationalist struggle. The author draws on both private papers of prominent businessmen and official sources to depict an Indian capitalist class diverse in its interests and lacking political unity. Early support for nationalism came from only a section of the business community, many of whom, notably Hindu *banias* (traders), were traditional in outlook and were attracted by the Gandhian religious component. However, from the late 1930s a decisive realignment occurred, and from 1944 onwards Indian big business as a whole shifted clearly into the Congress camp. This work should be read in conjunction with *Businessmen and politics: rising nationalism and a modernising economy in Bombay, 1918-1933* (New Delhi: Manohar, 1978. 323p.), by A. D. Gordon, which covers the preceding period, and *Business and politics in India: a historical perspective* (New Delhi: Manohar, 1991. 375p.), edited by Dwijendra Tripathi.

722 **The warrior merchants.**
Mattison Mines. Cambridge: Cambridge University Press, 1985. 192p. maps. bibliog.

A study by an American anthropologist of an important artisan-merchant community, the weavers, who form the second largest sector of the south Indian economy. The author traces the role of weaver-merchants in the organization of south Indian states and society from the medieval period to the present. He shows that for centuries they have maintained supralocal organizations to represent their interests and administer their affairs and that, at times in their history, they have rivalled the status and power of agriculturalists.

723 **Indian capitalist class: a historical study.**
V. I. Pavlov. New Delhi: People's Publishing House, 1964. 408p. bibliog.

The textbook of Indian Marxists, this classic Marxist-Leninist analysis examines two key issues: the role of trading and moneylending regimes during the Mughal and British periods; and the origin and development of the Indian bourgeoisie, especially as a result of British capitalism. Separate chapters are devoted to the development of the Gujarati, Marwari, Marathi, and Bengali bourgeoisies. The author challenges the conventional wisdom that the Indian middle class developed largely as a service élite to meet British imperial needs rather than as an autonomous economic class.

724 **Caste and capitalism in colonial India: the Nattukottai Chettiars.**
David Rudner. Berkeley, California: University of California Press, 1994. 320p. bibliog.

An ethnographic and historical analysis of the Nattukottai Chettiars, a successful southern Indian merchant banking subcaste. Rudner explores the impact of colonial rule on the Chettiars' commercial systems, analysing their response to the opportunities created in financing commodity production in neighbouring Empire dependencies, notably Myanmar (Burma), Sri Lanka and Malaysia. The author also challenges the conventional assumption that caste structures are incompatible with the conduct of business.

725 The Marwaris: from traders to industrialists.

Thomas A. Timberg. New Delhi: Vikas, 1978. 268p. maps. bibliog.
An outstanding study of the emigrant business community from the semi-arid regions of Marwar in modern Rajasthan, who now control between one-half and two-thirds of all industrial assets and production in the private sector of India. The Marwari diaspora began in the 18th century and gained momentum in the late-19th and early-20th centuries when many of them came to control business houses in Calcutta and Bombay. Timberg provides regional details of their migration, their business methods, and information on changes in their attitudes, values, and social and kinship structure.

726 Business communities in India: a historical perspective.

Edited by Dwijendra Tripathi. New Delhi: Manohar, 1984. 288p.
A collection of fourteen papers which examine the socio-economic characteristics, religious and cultural values, and historical developments of some of the most important commercial communities in India. Nearly all areas of India are covered and a number of the papers go back as far as the 16th and 17th centuries. The contributors include Rajat Kanta Ray, J. S. Grewal, Amalendu Guha, V. D. Divekar, S. Nurul Hasan, and G. D. Sharma. Focusing on western India, *Business houses in western India: a study in entrepreneurial response, 1850-1956* (London: Jaya, 1990. 223p.), edited by Dwijendra Tripathi and Makrand Mehta, is another excellent volume of essays.

Industry

General

727 Productivity and growth in Indian manufacturing.
Isher Judge Ahluwalia. New Delhi: Oxford University Press India,
1991. 242p. bibliog.

Utilizing econometric techniques, Ahluwalia computes and compares trends in
industrial productivity during different periods of India's recent economic history. Up
to 1965, during the 'Mahalanobis period', growth was significant, being explained by
investment in new manufacturing capacity. The period between 1965 and 1975 was
characterized by stagnation, dealt more fully in Ahluwalia's *Industrial growth in
India: stagnation since the mid-sixties* (New Delhi: Oxford University Press India,
1985. 235p.). This is ascribed to overly rigid government planning policies. Since the
late 1970s the trend in manufacturing productivity has been reversed, growth being
faster than could be explained by the inputs used. This Ahluwalia links to an easing of
government controls and the pursuit of more liberal economic policies.

728 Indian industrialization: structure and policy issues.
Edited by Arun Ghosh, K. K. Subrahmanian, Mridul Eapen, Haseeb A.
Drabu. New Delhi: Oxford University Press India, 1992. 364p.

A collection of essays reviewing Indian industrial trends in the light of the 1980s
retreat from state planning and shift to a policy of economic liberalization. The chief
editor, Arun Ghosh, a former member of the Indian Planning Commission, ascribes
the current problems of low industrial productivity and slackening growth to this
policy change. He advocates greater government intervention to promote research and
development, upgrade technologies, and enhance competition. A completely different
analysis is provided in *Industrial development policy of India* (Tokyo: Institute of
Developing Economies, 1992. 163p. Occasional Paper Series No. 27), by Kyoko
Inoue, who sees the solution to India's industrial ills as enhanced liberalization.

729   **Kothari's Economic and Industrial Guide to India.**
Madras: Kothari, 1936- . biennial.
This biennial guide continues Kothari's *Economic Guide and Investor's Handbook of India*. It gives detailed information about major companies, which are classified according to their broad industrial categories. It provides information on taxation, import-export regulations, foreign aid, national economic plans, national and per capita income, agriculture, and other economic and social indicators. A useful guide for foreign investors.

730   **Industrial growth and stagnation: the debate in India.**
Edited by Deepak Nayyar.   New Delhi: Oxford University Press India, 1994. 350p.
This volume brings together a selection of essays, published in the *Economic and Political Weekly* (see item no. 679), on the problems of industrializing India. The papers have made a significant contribution to recent policy decisions. A related collection of essays is *Economic liberalisation, industrial structure and growth in India* (New Delhi: Oxford University Press India, 1990. 254p.), edited by Ashok S. Guha.

731   **Industrialization in India: growth and conflict in the private corporate sector, 1914-47.**
Rajat Kanta Ray.   New Delhi: Oxford University Press India, 1979. 384p. bibliog.
This volume gives the story of the growth of corporate enterprise and its failure to transform India's agricultural economy into a predominantly industrial one. The author points out that during 1913-38 Indian industrial growth was much above the world average, while that of the 'small' sector was pitiable. According to Ray, it was the failure of the 'small' sector to achieve high growth rates before independence in 1947 that caused Indian industrialization on the whole to lag behind. The volume includes brief descriptions of development experience in fifteen industries and also describes the 'radicalization' of the Indian business community and emergence of a consensus on economic policy. Ray has also edited a collection of essays on the emergence of entrepreneurs and industries in India over the colonial period, *Entrepreneurship and industry in India 1800-1947* (New Delhi: Oxford University Press India, 1992. 276p.). Another outstanding work on early industrialization in India is *Private investment in India, 1900-1939* (Cambridge: Cambridge University Press, 1972. 482p.), by Amiya Kumar Bagchi, which mixes applied economic theory with case studies of seven major industries.

732   **Industrial policy and planning, 1947 to 1991: tendencies, interpretations and issues.**
Jasvantlal Chimanlal Sandesara.   New Delhi: Sage Publications, 1992. 211p. bibliog.
An excellent analysis of changes in India's industrial policy during the post-independence period. The work describes the early emphasis on state intervention through Five-Year-Plans, the encouragement given to heavy industries, the later wave of rationalization in older industries, and the adoption, from the mid-1980s, by the Congress (I) governments of Rajiv Gandhi and P. V. Narasimha Rao, of a strategy of greater economic liberalization.

Large-scale sector

733 **India's textile sector: a policy analysis.**
Sanjiv Misra.   New Delhi: Sage Publications, 1993. 278p. bibliog.
The textile industry is a key sector of the Indian economy, accounting for the largest share of employment, value-added in manufacturing, and exports. One of the earliest of industries to be established in India, during recent decades it has been characterized by sluggish growth. In export markets, India has lost out to other Asian producers. As a result, there have been enforced closures in the organized mill sector and increasing general indications of a sickness. Sanjiv Misra explains these developments and concludes that growth in the textile industry in India has been stifled by a restrictive policy framework. He advocates greater deregulation and the scrapping of a number of controls put in place originally to protect labour interests. A complementary work, analysing growth and productivity trends in the sector between 1950 and 1980, is *The cotton mill industry in India* (New Delhi: Oxford University Press India, 1984. 134p.), by Davangere Umpathi Sastry.

734 **Japan enters Indian industry: the Maruti-Suzuki joint venture.**
Raja Venkataramani.   London: Sangam Books, 1990. 248p. bibliog.
A study of inward foreign investment by the Japanese conglomerate Suzuki and the anticipated transformation of the Indian automobile industry through its joint venture with Maruti. This work shows the 'New Economic Policy' of liberalization in action.

Small-scale sector

735 **The artisans of Banaras: popular culture and identity, 1880-1986.**
Nita Kumar.   Princeton, New Jersey: Princeton University Press, 1988. 279p. bibliog.
An excellent, wide-ranging historical-anthropological study of the artisan community of the north Indian holy city of Varanasi (Banaras). The author provides a fascinating insight into the working life of craft workers and their sense of occupational solidarity. Of particular importance is Kumar's depiction of popular culture, describing the ties of neighbourhood and such leisure foci as wrestling *akharas*, musical performances, and festivals. Covering an earlier period, *The Company weavers of Bengal: the East India Company and the organization of textile production in Bengal, 1750-1813* (Oxford: Oxford University Press, 1988. 211p.), by Hameeda Hossain, is a fine work on the handloom industry.

736 **Small scale enterprises in industrial development: the Indian experience.**
Edited by K. B. Suri.   New Delhi: Sage Publications, 1988. bibliog. 348p.
In India small-scale industries have been accorded an important place in the planning framework for both ideological and employment-generating reasons. However, in

recent years the rationale behind and the effectiveness of this development strategy have been called into question. This volume brings together fifteen papers presented by Indian and Western economists to a conference held in New Delhi in 1985 and sponsored jointly by the World Bank and the Institute of Economic Growth, Delhi. The papers are arranged in five sections under the headings, 'Data base', 'Relative efficiency', 'Industry studies', 'Factor and product markets and linkages', and 'Government policy'. An excellent comparative work is *Small manufacturing enterprises: a comparative analysis of India and other economies* (New York: Oxford University Press USA, for the World Bank, 1987. 362p.), edited by Ian Malcom David Little, Dipak Mazumdar and John M. Page.

737 **The small industries policy in India.**
Nasir Tyabji. Calcutta, India: Oxford University Press India, 1989. 223p. bibliog.

An analysis of the set of policy measures for small producers which have evolved gradually through the course of India's political-economic development during the past half century. The author acknowledges the influence of Gandhian ideals on post-independence policies to safeguard the small-scale sector, notably the Khadi and Village Industries Commission, and during the Janata administration of the late 1970s led by Charan Singh, but argues that the spirit of Gandhism has been largely ignored as a result of the compulsions of capitalistic development. On future prospects for the sector, *Modern small industry in India: problems and prospects* (New Delhi: Sage Publications, 1988. 193p.), by Ram Krishna Vepa, is a useful work.

Industrialists

738 **India's industrialists.**
Margaret Herdeck, Gita Piramal. Washington, DC: Three Continents Press, 1985. 467p. maps. bibliog.

The first of a projected three-volume survey of India's leading industrial families. Thirteen families are covered in this first volume: Ambani, Bajaj, Birla, Goenka, Kirloskar, Mafatlal, Mahindra, Modi, Oberoi, Tata, Thapar, TTK, and Walchand. A profile is provided of each, based on interviews. Included are basic details of each family's history, the scope of its present activities, photographs and charts.

739 **Lala Shri Ram: a study in entrepreneurship and industrial management.**
Arun Joshi. New Delhi: Orient Longman, 1975. 708p.

A meticulously researched biography of a pioneering north Indian industrialist. Lala Shri Ram (1884-1962) was born into a Punjabi *Agarwal* banking family which rendered services to the British during the 1857 Indian Rebellion and set up the Delhi Cloth Mills in 1888. He joined the family company in 1909 and oversaw a dramatic expansion in the scale and range of its industrial and commercial interests into sugar, fertilisers, heavy chemicals, PVC resins, engineering, sewing machines and ceramics. Though, in comparison to the Tatas and Birlas, the Shri Ram group remained a minnow, the work is a fascinating and richly detailed study of Indian entrepreneurship in the *mofussil* (interior).

740 **Beyond the last blue mountain: a life of J. R. D Tata (1904-1993).**
Russi M. Lala. New Delhi: Penguin (India), 1993. new ed. 400p.

An excellent biography of the industrial magnate Jehangir Ratanji Dadabhoy Tata which is divided into four parts. Parts one, three and four examine Tata's background, personality, and his friendship with such figures as the Congress politicians, Mahatma Gandhi, Jawaharlal Nehru, and Indira Gandhi. They reveal that he was born in France, where his father, Ratanji Dadabhoi Tata, was living with his French wife. Part two describes J. R. D's forty-six years as chairman of Tata Industries and the leading role he took in developing India's aviation industry.

741 **Enterprise and economic change: 50 years of FICCI.**
H. Venkatasubbiah. New Delhi: Vikas, 1977. 176p. bibliog.

A study of the role of Indian industrialists, organized as the Federation of Indian Chambers of Commerce and Industry (FICCI), in critical economic and political issues between 1927 and 1976. The author points out that FICCI responses were often developed not by Indian capitalists but rather by their 'managers' such as T. T. Krishnamachari and G. L. Mehta, who later played a significant role in India's planning as Union ministers. Venkatasubbiah's painstaking study clearly shows that the Indian government has had a positive bias towards free enterprise and 'bigness' but has steadfastly opposed monopolies.

Agriculture and Food

Agricultural production and rural social structure

742 **Sugarcane and sugar in Gorakhpur: an inquiry into peasant production for capitalist enterprise in colonial India.**
Shahid Amin. New Delhi: Oxford University Press India, 1984. 336p. maps. bibliog.

A fascinating historical reconstruction of the cultivation and processing of sugarcane in Gorakhpur district, Uttar Pradesh, and the crop's impact on peasant lives. Drawing upon a wide range of official and unofficial records and oral testimonies, Amin provides a 'bottom up' *Subaltern* (see item no. 179) insight into the activity. Focusing on the period between 1890 and 1940, there are detailed descriptions of 'sugarcane culture' (tillage techniques and harvest cycles) processing, transport and marketing, and a penetrating analysis of small peasant dependence on capitalist merchants and feudal-capitalist landlord financiers. For the contemporary situation, *The political economy of Indian sugar: state intervention and structural change* (New Delhi: Oxford University Press India, 1990. 225p.), by Sanjaya Baru, and *Raising cane: the political economy of sugar in western India* (Boulder, Colorado: Westview Press, 1992. 366p.), by Donald W. Attwood, are useful works.

743 **Agricultural trends in India, 1891-1947: output, availability and productivity.**
George Blyn. Philadelphia: University of Pennsylvania Press, 1966. 370p. maps. bibliog.

A classic study of the production of food and cash crops in the provinces of British India from 1891. Blyn shows that over the period as a whole non-foodgrain output grew at a rate ahead of population growth, but foodgrain output rose more slowly. All-India crop output increased to ca. 1911, but during the inter-war years began to be outstripped by the fast-growing population. The statistics reproduced by Blyn, which include a hundred page appendix showing all-India and provincial acreage and output trends by crops, reveal significant regional differences in performance, with Bengal and Bihar standing out as the worst performing provinces. This volume should be read alongside *Growth, stagnation or decline?: agricultural productivity in British India* (New Delhi: Oxford University Press India, 1992. 288p.), edited by Sumit Guha, which includes a critique of the reliability of the data on which Blyn based his analysis.

744   **Peasant labour and colonial capital: rural Bengal since 1770 (Vol. III:2 in The New Cambridge History of India).**
Sugata Bose.   Cambridge: Cambridge University Press, 1993. 203p. maps. bibliog.

A fine work of synthesis and interpretation on the theme of agrarian change under British colonial rule. Developing findings from his earlier monograph, *Agrarian Bengal: economy, social structure and politics, 1919-1947* (Cambridge: Cambridge University Press, 1986. 306p.), Bose emphasizes the crucial connections between rural credit networks and the global system of commodity exchange which increasingly subordinated peripheral rural Bengal to the core capitalist economies. The author also analyses the relationships between demography, commercialization, class structure, and peasant resistance and makes comparisons with regional agrarian histories of other parts of South Asia.

745   **Agrarian impasse in Bengal: institutional constraints to technological change.**
James K. Boyce.   Oxford, New York: Oxford University Press, 1987. 308p. maps. bibliog.

This clearly-written work analyses the agricultural performance of West Bengal and Bangladesh between 1949 and 1980, with a specific focus on demographic, technological and institutional determinants. Controversially, Boyce rejects the neo-Malthusian notion that rural impoverishment has resulted from overpopulation. Instead, he views water control – irrigation, drainage and flood control – as the key to agricultural development in this region. Furthermore, Boyce believes that the agrarian social and political structure has acted as a barrier to the development of necessary cooperative institutions above the level of the individual farm.

746   **The state and rural economic transformation: the case of Punjab, 1950-85.**
G. K. Chadha.   New Delhi: Sage Publications, 1986. 369p. bibliog.

A careful analysis of the dynamics of rural transformation in Punjab since independence, with particular focus on the impact of the green revolution (new seed fertilizer technology). The author examines changes in land-use patterns, cropping intensity and input structure; agriculture's relative terms-of-trade *vis-à-vis* industry; and rural social structure in terms of employment patterns, asset distributions, marketable surpluses, and income distribution. Chadha concludes that rapid agricultural growth in Punjab did result in a discernible decline in the incidence of rural poverty and did not just benefit the upper strata of cultivators. This volume can be complemented by Holly Sims' *Political regimes, public policy and economic development: agricultural performance and rural change in the two Punjabs* (New

Delhi: Sage Publications, 1988. 206p.), which analyses the political economy of the Punjab.

747 **A glossary of north Indian peasant life.**
William Crooke, edited by Shahid Amin. New Delhi: Oxford University Press India, 1989. 290p.
An important late-19th-century compendium on the north Indian countryside, originally published in 1879. It is reissued with an excellent introduction by the editor and is accompanied by monochrome and colour illustrations of rural implements and activities. Arranged thematically, the work covers the economic, agricultural, material, domestic and ritual life of north India's peasants as observed by Crooke, a district officer. There are seven appendixes, providing information on the harvest calendar, indigenous cloth and clothes, and agricultural sayings.

748 **The Punjab peasant in prosperity and debt.**
Malcolm Lyall Darling, edited by Clive J. Dewey. New Delhi: Manohar, 1977. reprint of 1925 ed. 291p.
A classic study of the peasant economy of early-20th-century Punjab by a British district officer. The focus of the work is on the financing of agricultural operations and peasant indebtedness. The editor, an economic historian, provides an excellent scene-setting introduction. The work can usefully be read in conjunction with Darling's later book, *Rusticus loquitur, or the old light and the new in the Punjab village* (London: Oxford University Press, 1930. 400p.).

749 **Agrarian power and agricultural productivity in South Asia.**
Edited by Meghnad Desai, Susanne Hoeber Rudolph, Ashok Rudra. Berkeley, California: University of California Press, 1984. 384p.
A mixed collection of theoretical and empirical essays by Indian and Western economists and social historians on various aspects of agricultural production and rural power structures in India. Particularly good are the papers by Ronald Herring on the 'Economic consequences of local power configurations' and Lloyd and Susanne Rudolph on the 'Determinants and varieties of agrarian mobilization'. There is also an excellent chapter on the economic history of sugar production by Donald Attwood and a review of relevant literature by David Ludden.

750 **India's changing rural scene 1963-1979.**
Gilbert Etienne. New Delhi: Oxford University Press India, 1982. 231p. map. bibliog.
A first hand account of how rural India changed during the 1960s and 1970s green revolution period. The author conducted surveys between 1963-64 and 1978-79 in a variety of districts across India. They included districts which experienced relatively rapid growth and diversification, such as Bulandshahr in western Uttar Pradesh, Guntur in Andhra Pradesh, and Thanjavur in Tamil Nadu, and ones, such as Varanasi in eastern Uttar Pradesh and Muzzafarpur in Bihar, which have been characterized by very slow development. Part two of the work deals with planning problems. In his conclusion, Etienne stresses the importance of increasing the supply of agricultural inputs and improving soils and water management, rather than focusing on credit and other programmes. An analysis of the rural scene a decade on is provided in Etienne's

Agriculture and Food. Agricultural production and rural social structure

Food and poverty: India's half won battle (New Delhi: Sage Publications, 1988. 272p.).

751 Land to the tiller: the political economy of agrarian reform in South Asia.
Ronald J. Herring. New Haven, Connecticut: Yale University Press, 1983. 314p. maps. bibliog.

An excellent review of the aims and concrete results of the land reform policies which have been adopted since independence in India, Pakistan, and Sri Lanka. The author distinguishes between land reform, representing only one factor of production, and agrarian reform, which involves the structural transformation of the total rural political economy. He analyses the working of three models of land reform: tenure reform, raising issues of just rents and security of tenure; land-ceiling legislation, based on the concept of a just holding and an efficient holding size; and 'land to the tiller', which, as pursued in Kerala, raises issues of social development and justice. Herring favours the last type of reform, but stresses that all land reform programmes face the obstacles of local power and political structures. Useful companion volumes are: *A study of land reforms in Uttar Pradesh* (Honolulu, Hawaii: Hawaii University Press, 1986. 287p.), by B. Singh and S. Misra; and *India's persistent dilemma: the political economy of agrarian reform* (Boulder, Colorado: Westview Press, 1994. 250p.), by F. Tomasson Jannuzi.

752 Agriculture and social structure in Tamil Nadu: past origins, present transformations, and future prospects.
Joan P. Mencher. Durham, North Carolina: Academic Press, 1978. 314p. bibliog.

Based on detailed village studies over an eight-year period in a growing district, this book synthesizes statistics, archival materials, interviews, and secondary sources to create a broad-based analysis of India's rural problems. The volume constitutes a pathbreaking social anthropology of paddy cultivation, including excellent accounts of land tenures, absenteeism and the role of caste in agriculture. The author argues that rural inequalities have been reinforced by present developmental strategies and are the basic impediment to increasing agricultural productivity. A complementary work on agrarian change in post-independence south India is *Dynamics of rural transformation: a case study of Tamil Nadu, 1950-75* (New Delhi: Orient Longman, 1981. 151p.), by Christopher Thomas Kurien.

753 In defence of the irrational peasant.
Kusum Nair. Chicago: University of Chicago Press, 1979. 154p. bibliog.

A thought-provoking and stimulating challenge to neo-classical agricultural economics. Nair compares Punjab's progress with Bihar's stagnant agriculture and argues that socio-cultural patterns rather than purely economic factors are the main determinant of difference.

754   **The political economy of agrarian change: Nanchilnadu 1880-1939.**
M. S. S. Pandian.   New Delhi: Sage Publications, 1990. 192p. bibliog.

A case study of agrarian change during the colonial period in India, focusing on the rice-growing region of Nanchilnadu, situated at the southernmost tip of India. Today, Nanchilnadu is part of the state of Tamil Nadu, but during the colonial period it was situated within the princely state of Travancore. Pandian describes the ancient system of agriculture, based on an elaborate irrigation system, and argues that it was undermined by hamfisted 'development' projects undertaken by the Travancore State during the late-19th and early-20th centuries.

755   **Peasant class differentiation: a study in method with reference to Haryana.**
Utsa Patnaik.   New Delhi: Oxford University Press India, 1987. 229p.

Critical of existing methods of analysing agrarian structure and changes in it, Patnaik formulates an empirical criterion based on labour use for capturing class status. This is then applied to farm households in Haryana. The results suggest the need to critically re-examine preconceptions of 'peasant' and 'capitalist' farming in India. In particular, Patnaik reveals the adoption of green revolution technology to have been far more concentrated with the labour-hiring classes than suggested by conventional analysis and, as a result, income gains have been skewed.

756   **Organizational issues in Indian agriculture.**
Kakkadan Nandanath Raj.   New Delhi: Oxford University Press, 1990. 227p. bibliog.

A collection of twelve papers and lectures written and presented over a period of three decades (1956-86) by one of India's foremost agricultural economists. The volume includes comparative papers, which contrast India's experience of agrarian development with that of Mexico, China, Taiwan, and South Korea. There are also analyses of rural credit, taxation, underemployment labour, 'sacred cows' and 'surplus cattle', village economics, and the ownership and distribution of land in India, based on data from 1954-55.

757   **Essays on the commercialization of Indian agriculture.**
Edited by Kakkadan Nandanath Raj, Neeladri Bhattacharya, Sumit Guha, Sakti Padhi.   Oxford; New York: Oxford University Press, 1985. 354p.

This volume contains twelve papers on the theme of the commercialization of the Indian countryside since the mid-19th century. The contributors comprise three distinguished economists – K. N. Raj, Krishna Bharadwaj, and Amit Bhaduri – and nine social and economic historians. The essays written by the economists are typically theoretical. In contrast, the historians provide detailed studies focusing on facets of economic and social change in specific Indian micro-regions. Topics include the tobacco industry in Guntur district, emigration from Orissa between 1901 and 1921, and post-independence class relations and commercialization in Punjab and Uttar Pradesh.

758 **A history of agriculture in India.**
Mohinder Singh Randhawa.   New Delhi: Indian Council of
Agricultural Research, 1980-86. 4 vols.
A comprehensive history of Indian agriculture from earliest times to the present day,
relating Indian developments to international changes. The volumes range in length
from between 500 and 700 pages and include information on tillage practices and
crops grown. The titles and publication dates of the volumes are: *I: Beginning to 12th
century* (1980); *II: Eighth to eighteenth century* (1982); *III: 1757-1947* (1983); and
IV: 1947-1981 (1986).

759 **Rural India: land, power and society under British rule.**
Edited by Peter Robb.   London: Curzon Press for the School of
Oriental and African Studies, London University, 1983. 314p.
A collection of essays by Western and Indian social historians on aspects of the rural
economy and society of 19th- and 20th-century British India. The editor provides an
introductory overview of the debate concerning the extent of change engendered by
British rule and a paper on peasant indebtedness in late 19th-century Bihar. Other
significant papers, include Ian Catanach on plague and the Indian village, Neil
Charlesworth on the fragmentation of landholdings, Dharma Kumar on the term 'land
control', and Anand Yang on the development of local control institutions in Bihar.

760 **Studies in the development of capitalism in India.**
Ashok Rudra (and others).   Lahore, Pakistan: Vanguard, 1978. 459p.
bibliog.
A collection of essays examining the debate among neo-Marxist scholars on whether
the predominant mode of production in Indian agriculture is semi-feudal or capitalist.
Among the more important essays are those by Ashok Rudra, Daniel Thorner, Utsa
Patnaik, Paresh Chattopadhyay and Dalip Swamy. The book is useful for its detailed
and empirical consideration of class relations in the Indian countryside. Recent
advances in the theory of agrarian relations are expounded in *Agrarian economic
relations and Indian agriculture* (New Delhi: Oxford University Press India, 1994.
256p.), edited by Kaushik Basu, and *Agrarian relations and accumulation: the 'mode
of production' debate in India* (Bombay: Oxford University Press India, 1990. 272p.),
edited by Utsa Patnaik.

761 **Agricultural development and rural poverty.**
Ajit Kumar Singh.   New Delhi: Ashish, 1987. 372p. maps. bibliog.
A comprehensive study of post-independence agrarian change in the large north
Indian state of Uttar Pradesh (UP). The author subdivides the state into five regions
for his analysis of land utilization, cropping patterns, social structure, and
technological and institutional change. It is shown that, while agricultural output and
productivity have expanded significantly in all regions since 1950, the growth rate
has been below the all-India average. Within the province, the well-irrigated, wheat-
growing west UP has far outperformed the east, leading to widening inter-regional
income disparities.

762 **Understanding green revolutions: agrarian change and development planning in South Asia (essays in honour of B. H. Farmer).**
Edited by Sudhir Wanmali, Tim R. Bayliss-Smith. Cambridge: Cambridge University Press, 1984. 384p.

A collection of essays by Indian and Western scholars on the progress of the green revolution in the states of South Asia, presented in honour of the Cambridge University geographer, Bertram Hughes Farmer (see item no. 6). Another useful book which analyses the impact of the green revolution within India specifically is *Technical change and income distribution in Indian agriculture* (Boulder, Colorado: Westview Press, 1994. 160p.), by David G. Abler, George S. Tolley, and G. K. Kripalani.

Irrigation

763 **Managing canal irrigation: practical analysis from South Asia.**
Robert Chambers. Cambridge: Cambridge University Press, 1988. 279p. bibliog.

An excellent, practical analysis of irrigation management in contemporary India. The author, a former Ford Foundation staff member in New Delhi, draws upon his first-hand experience to advance proposals to improve the management of irrigation systems for the benefit of producers and consumers. Chambers describes the operation of canal irrigation, noting that, if effective, it can increase agricultural output threefold over rainfed conditions. He emphasizes the importance of 'main system management' in contrast to the professional fixation on water management 'below the outlet'. He also discusses the effects of corruption by irrigation officers and advocates promoting farmer participation in canal irrigation management.

764 **India's water wealth: its assessment, uses, and projections.**
K. L. Rao. New Delhi: Orient Longman, 1979. rev. ed. 267p. maps. bibliog.

This book, by a former minister in the Indian government, is divided into three parts. The first deals with water resources of India, the second with water uses, and the third with growing water demand. In his coverage of irrigation, hydro-electric power, flood control, and navigational projects, Rao admits that India has not yet made rapid strides in the harnessing of river waters for economic development. Two complementary volumes, focusing on agricultural uses and the social impact of large-scale irrigation projects, are: *Irrigation in India's agricultural development: productivity, stability, equity* (New Delhi: Sage Publications, 1987. 280p.), by B. D. Dhawan; and *Big dams, displaced people: rivers of sorrow, rivers of change* (New Delhi: Sage Publications, 1992. 199p.), edited by Enakshi Ganguly Thukral.

765 **Canal irrigation in British India: perspectives on technological change in a peasant economy.**
Ian Stone. Cambridge: Cambridge University Press, 1984. 374p. maps. bibliog. (Cambridge South Asian Studies, no. 29).
A detailed study of the qualitative and quantitative effects on the sub-regional economy of western Uttar Pradesh of the irrigation canals constructed by British engineers during the 19th century. The author examines the impact on cropping patterns, production techniques and organization, protection from famine, and social and economic relations between 1860 and 1920. An analysis of the larger-scale Punjab canal-colonies project, entailing massive agricultural colonization of the formerly arid *doabs* between the rivers Jhelum, Chenab, and Sutlej from the 1880s, is contained in Imran Ali's *The Punjab under imperialism, 1895-1947* (Princeton, New Jersey: Princeton University Press, 1988. 264p.).

766 **Village republics: economic conditions for collective action in south India.**
Robert Wade. Cambridge: Cambridge University Press, 1988. 213p. bibliog. (Cambridge South Asian Studies, no. 40).
A fascinating analysis of village cooperation in the sphere of water management in contemporary south India. The author studied intensively one village, Kottapalle, and collected data on forty other socio-economically similar neighbouring villages in Kurnool district in Andhra Pradesh with the aim of seeking explanations for variations in levels of collective action. Wade concluded that villages were most active in water control efforts where the benefits to be obtained from cooperation were the greatest. The size of benefits was determined by geophysical factors, viz. placement on the canal system (whether at the risky tail-end or higher up) and soil fertility.

Food and famine

767 **Famine in South Asia: political economy of mass starvation.**
Mohiuddin Alamgir. Cambridge, Massachusetts: Oelgeschlager, Gunn & Hain Publishers, 1980. 421p. bibliog.
A sophisticated analysis of past and contemporary famines in the Indian subcontinent, blending theory and empirical findings. In the opening chapters, the author presents a definition and theory of famine and reviews the historical records on past Indian famines. The remainder of the work comprises analytical chapters on such topics as famine victims and societal response, foodgrain stocks and availability, price movements, and trends in employment, wages and real incomes. Some of the more recent empirical data is drawn from Bangladesh.

768 **Famines in India: a study in some aspects of the economic history of India with special reference to food problems, 1860-1990.**
Bal Mokand Bhatia. New Delhi: Konark, 1991. 3rd. rev. ed. 383p. bibliog.

This popular textbook narrates the famines and scarcities that have occurred in India since 1860 and examines their causes. The author believes that the economic distortions of colonialism were the main cause of these calamities, which increased in frequency during the 19th century. Economic dislocations expanded the underclass and government efforts to remedy the situation were too little and invariably too late. The book, written from a nationalist perspective, includes a chapter on the 1943 famine in Bengal, but fails to satisfactorily explain the absence of famines between 1908 and 1943. Bhatia is also author of the useful, *Indian agriculture: a policy perspective* (New Delhi: Sage Publications, 1988. 191p.).

769 **Unstable agriculture and droughts: implications for policy.**
Edited by C. H. Hanumantha Rao, S. K. Ray, K. Subbarao. New Delhi: Vikas, 1988. 192p.

A collection of scholarly essays which examine climatic and agricultural conditions in India, noting the proneness of certain regions to drought and the implications this has for government policy. A fine complementary work is *Food policy in India: a survey* (New Delhi: Bagchi, 1988. 414p.), by R. N. Chopra.

770 **Food, society and culture: aspects in South Asian food systems.**
Edited by Ravindra S. Khare, M. S. A. Rao. Durham, North Carolina: Carolina Academic Press, 1986. 336p.

A varied collection of essays on cultural and dietetic aspects of food in the Indian subcontinent. Part one examines the preparation and distribution of food offerings to deities at south Indian pilgrimage sites between 1359 and 1640 AD, Muslim secular and religious feasts in Delhi, and the gastrodynamics (changing food habits) of migration. The contributors are Carol Breckenridge, Christopher Murphy, and M. S. A. Rao. Part two addresses food classifications as they relate to health, and food distributions through charity, hospitality, rationing, and the global network.

771   **Subject to famine: food crises and economic change in western India, 1860-1920.**
Michelle Burge McAlpin.   Princeton, New Jersey: Princeton University Press, 1983. 288p. 6 maps. bibliog.

A revisionist study of rural economic change in colonial western India. The author uses an econometric approach to attack the traditional nationalist analysis – propounded most clearly by R. C. Dutt (see item no. 664) – which blamed over-taxation and forced commercialization for the apparently increasing severity of famines during the late 19th century. McAlpin contends that a communications revolution, in the form of railroads and improved bullock carts, and more settled political conditions resulted in internal commercial and market development and a transition from real 'food scarcity famines' to famines caused by a lack of purchasing power arising from unequal distribution in a situation of plenty. Included are analyses of climatic uncertainty in peasant agriculture, the development of 'insurance systems', the demographic impact of famines, colonial land revenue systems, price movements, changing cropping patterns, and the evolution of colonial famine relief policies.

Transport and Communications

772 **Steamboats on the Ganges: an exploration in India's modernization through science and technology.**
Henry T. Bernstein.   London: Sangam Books, 1988. new ed. 230p. bibliog.

Originally published in 1960, this is a classic study of the introduction of steam navigation on the Ganges river system by the British colonial regime from the 1830s. Bernstein describes the early problems encountered by the new technology in Indian conditions and the gradual adaptations which were made. These enabled steamboats to enjoy a decade of success before the onset of competition from the new railroads from the 1860s.

773 **Transport and communications in India prior to steam locomotion: Vol. 1. Land transport.**
Jean Deloche, translated from the French by James Walker.   New Delhi: Oxford University Press India, 1993. 327p. map. bibliog. (French Studies in South Asian Culture and Society, no. VII).

An excellent, well-illustrated, descriptive account of forms of land transportation in India before the railway era commenced in the mid-19th century. The author describes the road network, road engineering, human and pack transport, bullock carts, the *banjaras*, who carried grain, sugar and salt across the subcontinent in huge pack-animal convoys, and Mughal *sarais* (rest-houses). The French edition first appeared in 1980.

774 **Distance and development: transport and communications in India.**
Wilfred Owens.   Washington, DC: Brookings Institution, 1968. 170p. bibliog. (Transport Research Program).

A classic study of the role of transport and communications in the social and economic development of India. Owen argues that a well-organized system of transport and communications is necessary to build the nation, to exploit natural resources, and to develop agriculture and industries. He examines the problems of inter-city and rural transportation networks, as well as the role of telecommunications in the India of the 1960s.

775 **Transport geography of India: commodity flows and the regional structure of the Indian economy.**
Moonis Raza, Yash Aggarwal. New Delhi: Concept, 1986. 299p. maps. bibliog.

A sophisticated, geographical analysis of commercial flows in contemporary India, noting the focus on the metropolises of Bombay, New Delhi, Calcutta, and Madras.

776 **Railways of the Raj.**
Michael Satow, Ray Desmond. London: Scolar Press, 1980. 118p. bibliog.

An album of prints, paintings, and photographs assembled and interpreted by two railroad enthusiasts. Both the text and the illustrations vividly recreate the era when major urban centres built lavish railroad stations with their pavilions, waiting and dining rooms, and noteworthy architecture. The descriptions of Bombay's Victoria Terminus, the model railroad of the Maharaja of Gwalior, and the night-soil trolleys of Jodhpur are fascinating.

777 **Railways of India.**
John N. Westwood. Newton Abbot, England: David & Charles, 1974. 192p. maps. bibliog.

Intended for the general reader, this book provides a brief survey of the development and operations of railroads in India from their mid-19th-century beginnings to the early 1970s. Three long descriptive chapters, dealing with the periods 1850-70, 1870-1947, and 1947-72, are followed by a survey of infrastructure and rolling stock. Brief appendixes include information on major types of locomotives, nine zonal railway maps, and many photographs. A more discursive work is O. S. Nock's *Railways of Asia and the Far East* (London: A & C Black, 1978. 226p.), the first part of which is devoted to the Indian subcontinent.

Energy

778 **India: the energy sector.**
Patrick David Henderson. London: Oxford University Press, for the
World Bank, 1975. 191p. maps. bibliog.
Henderson, a World Bank specialist, presents a careful and balanced study of India's
energy sources and their utilization. He provides a thorough review of India's coal,
petroleum, hydro-electric, thermal, nuclear, and biomass resources. Some chapters
deal with the development of fuel and power industries, energy shortages, and
policies for the future.

779 **Energy and economic development in India.**
Rajendra Kumar Pachauri. New York: Praeger, 1977. 187p. bibliog.
This book attempts to present a total picture of the role of India's energy sector in the
nation's economic development. Demand, resources, and alternative technologies, as
well as the power sector, are discussed. The author argues that greater conservation
efforts need to be made and believes that coal, solar and other alternatives to
petroleum need to be vigorously pursued.

780 *Zamindars*, **mines and peasants: studies in the history of an Indian
coalfield and its rural hinterland.**
Edited by Dietmar Rothermund, D. C. Wadhwa. New Delhi:
Manohar, 1978. 236p. (University of Heidelberg South Asia
Interdisciplinary Regional Research Programme, no. 9).
This volume, part of the Dhanbad Research Project, analyses the impact of coalfield
development in Bihar on the rural hinterland during the 19th and 20th centuries and
the sources of labour supply for the industry. It should be read in conjunction with:
*Urban growth and rural stagnation: studies in the economy of an Indian coalfield and
its rural hinterland* (New Delhi: Manohar, 1980. 493p.), edited by D. Rothermund, E.
Kropp, G. Dienemann; and A. B. Ghosh's *Coal industry in India* (New Delhi:
Manohar, 1977).

781 **Energy resources and economic development in India.**
Wallace Edward Tyner.   Leiden, the Netherlands; Boston,
Massachusetts: Martinus Nijhoff, 1978. 139p. bibliog.
An exploration of the relationship between energy resource development and economic growth in India. The author believes that inadequate attention has been paid to developing the power and petroleum sectors, consequently economic development has been constrained by energy shortages. There are chapters on energy resource endowments, trends in energy consumption, oil and natural gas, electric power, and biogas and other alternative energy sources.

782 **Rural energy: consumption, problems and prospects.**
D. R. Veena.   New Delhi: Ashish, 1988. 336p. bibliog.
An analysis of the nature, causes and magnitude of energy consumption in India's rural areas. The author puts forward an action-plan to deal with mounting problems in this area.

Labour and
Employment

783 **Rethinking working-class history: Bengal, 1900-1940.**
Dipesh Chakrabarty. Princeton, New Jersey: Princeton University
Press, 1989. 245p. bibliog.

A fascinating study of the Calcutta-Howrah proletariat and jute industry which relates
the Indian experience to thematic treatments of working-class history developed in
the West. The author presents a paradoxical picture of a militant working-class that
failed to develop trade unions. This is explained by the vitality of traditional pre-
capitalist cultural practices of status and power hierarchies. Chakrabarty, adopting a
neo-Marxist *Subaltern* (see item no. 179) perspective, provides insights into the
mentalities of jute mill workers, who drew on ties of kinship, language, religion, and
race during their informally structured protests, and the Scottish factory owners and
their managers.

784 **The origins of industrial capitalism in India: business strategies
and the working classes in Bombay, 1900-1940.**
Rajnarayan Chandavarkar. Cambridge: Cambridge University Press,
1994. 468p. bibliog. (Cambridge South Asian Studies, no. 51).

An impressive study of the relationship between labour and capital in India's early-
20th-century economic development, focusing on the cotton textile metropolis of
Bombay. The author describes the development of the cotton mill industry, its
particular problems in the 1920s and 1930s, and the millowners' and state's response.
The greatest strength of the work lies in its analysis of the mill workforce: its rural
roots, urban networks, class fragmentation, and agitational strategies during the eight
general strikes which occurred in Bombay between 1919 and 1940. The work can be
complemented by two very different studies of Bombay's millworkers: Richard
Newman, *Workers and unions in Bombay 1918-1929: a study of organization in the
cotton mills* (Canberra: Australian National University, 1981. 320p.), and Morris D.
Morris's classic study, *The emergence of an industrial labour force in India: a study
of the Bombay cotton mills, 1854-1947* (Berkeley, California: University of California
Press, 1965. 263p.).

219

785   **Capital accumulation and workers' struggle in Indian industrialization: a case study of Tata Iron and Steel Company, 1910-1970.**
Satya Brata Datta.   Stockholm: Almqvist & Wicksell International, 1986. 295p. bibliog. (Stockholm Studies in Economic History, no. 9).
An analysis of labour relations at Tata Iron and Steel Company (TISCO), collective organizations, and workers' resistance. Datta believes that management control over the labour process has been fundamental to TISCO's attempts to attain its profitability objectives since its inception in 1907.

786   **Industry and inequality: the social anthropology of Indian labour.**
Mark Holmström.   Cambridge: Cambridge University Press, 1984. 342p. bibliog.
A comprehensive summary and analysis of ecological, sociological, and anthropological data on Indian factory labour. The author discusses differences in the characteristics of industrial labour in different major urban centres and between the small-scale unorganized and large-scale organized sectors. Particularly impressive is the chapter on labour markets which provides fascinating information on how an Indian worker gets a job, retains it, and advances to a better position. Holmström draws on findings from his monograph *South Indian factory workers: their life and their world* (Cambridge: Cambridge University Press; New Delhi: Allied, 1976/1979. 158p.).

787   **Indian Labour Yearbook.**
New Delhi: Labour Bureau, Ministry of Labour, 1946- . annual.
This official annual presents a comprehensive picture of the latest developments in the field of labour. Included are data on employment, wages, prices, living standards, labour administration, industrial disputes, agricultural labourers, and Indian workers overseas. A bibliography of official publications dealing with labour and several topical appendixes provide additional useful information.

788   **Indian trade unions: a survey.**
V. B. Karnik.   New Delhi: Sangam Books, 1983. new ed. 431p. bibliog.
A broad survey of the trade union movement in India since the end of the First World War. Historical in scope, it describes and analyses the role of the Marxian, Gandhian, and other assorted socialists in the development, unity and diversity, and politicization of the Indian trade unions. There are several statistical tables and short biographical sketches of labour leaders.

789   **Chains of servitude: bondage and slavery in India.**
Edited by Utsa Patnaik, Manjari Dingwaney.   Madras: Sangam Books, 1985. 380p.
A collection of historically orientated and contemporary essays on forms of bonded labour and agrestic and domestic slavery in the Indian subcontinent from early times to the present day. Three historical chapters review the history of slavery and coerced and debt-bonded labour in ancient India, medieval India, and 19th-century colonial

India. There are also five contemporary regional studies. These show that bondage, defined by extra-economic coercion, continues unabated in Bihar and other areas.

790 Indian labour movement.
G. Ramanujam. New Delhi: Sterling, 1986. 423p.

A chronologically-arranged history of the century-old Indian trade union movement, written by the founder and leader of the non-Marxian Indian National Trade Union Congress (INTUC). Ramanujam focuses on the methods and operations of the different trade unions and their relationships to both employers and government through various codes, acts, and commissions. The book demonstrates that the Indian trade union movement, associated during its early years with the Indian freedom struggle, has remained largely political and has met with little success in economic matters.

791 Rural labourers in Bengal 1880-1980.
Willem Van Schendel, Aminul Haque Faraizi. Rotterdam, the Netherlands: Erasmus University, Comparative Asian Studies Programme, 1984. 146p.

An empirical survey of the characteristics of rural labourers in Bengal over the course of the last century. The authors find that the proportion of rural labourers remained stable during the late colonial period, but increased significantly after independence in 1947. Trends in real wages are computed and there is an interesting section on the survival strategies of impoverished rural labourers, including deciding to opt for unrestrained fertility, a choice which has short-term economic advantages but long-term costs. Over the period, labour relations became increasingly contractualized and depersonalized. A complementary volume of essays, focusing exclusively on the colonial period is *The world of the rural labourer in colonial India* (New Delhi: Oxford University Press India, 1992. 310p.), edited by Gyan Prakash.

792 Trade unions in India: concepts, cases and case law.
Pramod Verma, Surya Mookherjee. New Delhi: Oxford University Press India, 1982. 408p. bibliog.

A dynamic overview of contemporary Indian trade unionism. Eight case-studies are presented to evaluate major issues in Indian industrial and labour relations. A separate section examines ten leading court cases dealing with labour law and the impact of judicial rulings on Indian labour legislation.

Science and Technology

General

793 **Science and technology in India.**
Edited by Vadilal Dagli. New Delhi: Chand, 1982. 338p. bibliog.
Twenty-seven essays on the role of science and technology in India's development.
Several deal with Indian research and development efforts in such key sectors as
electronics, fuel and power, metallurgy, information systems, and the chemical
industry. Others deal with the development of technologies that are appropriate for
Indian agriculture and small rural industries. A group of essays examine such national
and broad issues as the relationship of science to economic development, manpower
for research, institutional management, and Indian science policy.

794 **Triveni: science, democracy and socialism.**
A. Rahman. Simla, India: Indian Institute for Advanced Study, 1977.
111p. bibliog.
A definitive statement of his views by the founder of science policy studies in India.
Rahman, a biochemist influenced by J. D. Bernal, argues that Indian scientists must
on the one hand develop alternative technologies which are appropriate to Indian
conditions, and on the other participate in building a nation committed to socialism
and secularism.

795 **Science and Culture.**
Calcutta: Indian Science News Association, 1935- . monthly.
Though this journal is increasingly publishing articles in the sciences, it carries a
large number of articles on the impact of science on society, research planning in
India, and analyses of investments in science for social welfare.

796   **India and the computer: a study of planned development.**
C. R. Subramanian.   Oxford: Oxford University Press, 1992. 383p.
bibliog.

An analysis of India's struggle in policy development and implementation in the field
of computers between 1968 and 1990. The first digital computer arrived in India in
1955 and the first commercial computer was installed in 1961. Thirty years later
India's information technology business was worth Rs. 22,140 million. The book
includes chapters on mainframe and software development and notes how,
encouraged by the more liberal economic strategy pursued by the government of
Rajiv Gandhi (1984-89), the private sector, in the form of such companies as HCL
and Wipro, began to take the lead from the 1980s.

797   **Organizing for science: the making of an industrial research
laboratory.**
Shiv Visvanathan.   New Delhi: Oxford University Press India, 1985.
279p. bibliog.

A study of Indian society's response to the phenomenon of industrial research, based
on a case study of a research laboratory in Delhi. The first three chapters chronicle the
rise of industrial research in India, commencing in the early 19th century, with the
Asiatic Society's promotion of scientific enquiry, and culminating in the creation after
independence of the Council of Scientific and Industrial Research (CSIR) and
establishment of five national laboratories and research stations.

History of science and technology

798   **A concise history of science in India.**
Edited by D. M. Bose, S. N. Sen, B. V. Subbarayappa.   New Delhi:
Indian National Science Academy, 1989. reprint. 689p. maps. bibliog.

A collection of articles, including a survey of sources and an overview by the editors,
dealing with Indian contributions to various branches of mathematics and the physical
and biological sciences. There are chapters on astronomy, mathematics, medicine,
chemistry, agriculture, botany, zoology, and the physical world, as well as a brief
discussion of Western science in India during the 19th century. This valuable survey
is enhanced by a chronological table, a detailed bibliography, and excellent drawings,
charts, and photographs.

799   **History of science and technology in ancient India – the
beginnings.**
Debiprasad Chattopadhyaya.   Calcutta: Firma K. L. Mukhopadhyaya,
1986. 556p. bibliog.

This work focuses on the Harappan age of urbanization and technological
development, ending ca. 1750 BC. Drawing upon materials from the succeeding 'dark
age', which continued until the 'second urbanization' occurred in the Ganges valley
from the 6th century BC, Chattopadhyaya posits the presence of mathematics and

astronomy in the Indus Valley Civilization, although it remains formally undocumented. This work can be complemented by H. C. Bhardwaj, *Aspects of ancient Indian technology* (New Delhi: Motilal Banarsidass, 1979. 212p.), a straightforward survey of technology in ancient India which includes chapters on glassmaking, pottery, and copper, iron, silver and gold metallurgy.

800   **The tentacles of progress: technology transfer in the age of imperialism, 1850-1940.**
       Daniel R. Headrick.   New York; Oxford: Oxford University Press, 1988. 405p. bibliog.

A wide-ranging overview of the transfer of technology, including equipment, techniques, and experts, from the West to colonies in Asia and Africa during the age of 'high imperialism'. The author argues that this transfer led to underdevelopment rather than industrialization since colonial rulers stifled cultural diffusion through restricting access to technical education and discouraging entrepreneurship among non-European subjects. This volume includes a chapter on the railways of India and sections on irrigation, the telegraph, urban sanitation improvements, the iron and steel industry, shipbuilding, and technical education in India. Headrick's earlier work, *The tools of empire: technology and European imperialism in the nineteenth century* (New York; Oxford: Oxford University Press, 1981. 221p.), also includes chapters on Indian railways and steam-shipping.

801   **History of science, technology and medicine in India.**
       Om Prakash Jaggi.   New Delhi: Atma Ram, 1977-86. 15 vols.

A comprehensive, fact-filled survey of the evolution of science, technology and medicine in India from earliest times to the present. Volumes range in length from 170 to 350 pages and bear the following titles: *I: Technology in ancient India*; *II: Science in ancient India*; *III: Folk medicine*; *IV: Ayurveda: Indian system of medicine*; *V: Yogic and Tantric medicine*; *VI: Indian astronomy and mathematics*; *VII: Science and technology in medieval India*; *VIII: Medicine in medieval India*; *IX: Science in modern India*; *X: Technology in modern India*; *XI: Impact of science and technology in modern India*; *XII: Western medicine in India: epidemics and other tropical diseases*; *XIII: Medical education and research*; *XIV: Public health and its administration*; and *XV: Western medicine in India: social impact*.

802   **The Indian response to European technology and culture, AD 1498-1707.**
       Ahsan Jan Qaisar.   New Delhi: Oxford University Press India, 1982. 225p. bibliog.

Building on Irfan Habib's articles on the social history of Indian technology, this book examines the Indian response to a wide variety of European technological devices in shipbuilding, navigation, land transport, printing, chronometry (precision measurement), and glass-making. Qaisar also discusses the Indian response to European innovations in painting. architecture, music, food, costume, and marriage customs. There are twenty-four pages of carefully selected plates of drawings and miniatures. A useful related work is *Homo faber: technology and culture in India, China and the West from 1500 to the present day* (The Hague, the Netherlands: Martinus Nijhoff; Bombay: Allied, 1979. 275p.), by Claude Alphonso Alvares.

803 **History of chemistry in ancient and medieval India incorporating the *History of Hindu chemistry* by Acharya Prafula Chandra Ray.** Edited by P. Ray. Calcutta: Indian Chemical Society, 1956. 494p. bibliog.

A chronological history of the development of chemistry in India from its alchemic roots, based on an earlier two-volume work by Prafula Chandra Ray which is copiously extracted. Indian skills in the art of making glazed pottery, the extraction and working of metals, and the preparation of caustic alkalies, oxides, sulphides of metals, and dyes are outlined. The author attributes the decline of the scientific spirit in India to the development of the caste system which separated theoretical speculation from practical experimentation.

Education

804 **Education in South Asia: a bibliography.**
Philip Geoffrey Altbach, Denzil Saldanha, Jeanne Weiler. New
York, London: Garland Publishing, 1987. 360p.
This reference works contains 1,419 bibliographic entries on education in South Asia.
They are arranged in thematic chapters covering sociological, organizational, and
pedagogical aspects of the subject.

805 **Higher education reform in India: experience and perspectives.**
Edited by Philip Geoffrey Altbach, Suma Chitnis. New Delhi: Sage
Publications, 1993. 438p.
A collection of twelve excellent essays on Indian educational policy, based on World
Bank funded research. Changes in higher education over the past four decades are
reviewed and there are case studies of four innovative programmes: adult education,
scientific research, Institutes of Technology, and distance teaching. The papers reveal
that the sector has undergone substantial unplanned expansion, but there has been
little real reform. Two useful complementary works are: *Crisis and collapse of higher
education in India* (New Delhi: Vikas, 1987. 255p.), by J. D. Sethi; and *From
isolation to mainstream: higher education in India* (London: Sangam Books, 1987.
314p.), by M. R. Bhiday.

806 **Life at school: an ethnographic study.**
Meenakshi Thapan. New Delhi: Oxford University Press India,
1991. 271p. bibliog.
An ethnographic study of the character and functioning of the Rishi Valley School, a
coeducational, residential public school in southern India run by the Krishnamurti
Foundation, based on fieldwork conducted in 1981. The author analyses the internal
organization and authority structure of the school, its ethos or ideology and culture,
and interpersonal relations between teachers and pupils. A complementary work,
which focuses on the content of school curricula and textbooks, is: *Image, ideology*

and inequality: cultural domination, hegemony and schooling in India (London, New Delhi: Sage Publications, 1993. 178p.), by Timothy J. Scrase.

807 **Universities Handbook: India.**
New Delhi: Association of Indian Universities, 1927- . biennial.
This handbook provides information about more than a hundred Indian universities and higher education institutions. Founding dates, names of officers, deans of faculties, courses of studies, degree requirements, and degrees awarded are given, as well as lists of constituent and affiliated colleges. The index contains references to subjects and courses at degree level. Doctoral degree programmes are also listed.

808 **The child and the state in India: child labor and education policy in comparative perspective.**
Myron Weiner. Princeton, New Jersey: Princeton University Press, 1991. 213p.
In India primary education is not compulsory, nor is child labour illegal. As a consequence, barely a half of children between the ages six and fourteen attend school, choosing employment instead in cottage industries, tea stalls, restaurants, as household workers and as agricultural labourers. This book explains why Indian policies towards children in education and employment differ from those of most other developing countries. Weiner shows that India's low per capita income and economic situation is less relevant as an explanation than the belief systems of the state bureaucracy and middle class. At the core of these beliefs are the Indian view of the social order, notions of the respective roles of upper and lower social strata, with education being assigned an important role in helping to maintain differentiations among social classes.

Literature

Classical literature in English translation

809 **The lord of the meeting rivers: devotional poems of Basavanna.**
Basavanna, edited and translated by K. V. Zvelebil. New Delhi:
Motilal Banarsidass; Paris: UNESCO, 1984. 176p.

This important work comprises a translated selection of 126 of the more than 1,400
devotional poems which were written by Basavanna (known also as Basava) a
charismatic 12th-century saint-poet and social reformer who was a leading figure in
the Virasaiva or Lingayat movement that revolutionized Karnatak society and culture.
The poems, written in Kannada, aim at social transformation based on the principles
of equality, dignity of labour, monotheism, and non-violence. The compiler and
translator has also provided a biographical sketch of the life of Basavanna, a lucid
outline of the Virasaiva philosophy and doctrine, and notes on the poems. A
masterpiece of Indian social and mystical literature.

810 **Bhartrihari: poems.**
Bhartrihari, translated by Barbara Stöler Miller. New York:
Columbia University Press, 1967. 156p. bibliog.

Bhartrihari composed three volumes of single-stanza lyrical poetry in the 5th century:
one devoted to love, another to indifference to sensual pleasures, and the third to wise
conduct. Every stanza stands as a poem in itself and expresses one idea completely.

811 **The ten princes: Dandin's *Dash-kumara-charitra*.**
Dandin, translated by Arthur W. Ryder. Chicago: University of
Chicago Press, 1980. reprint of 1927 ed. 240p.

A delightfully picaresque novel of the Gupta period, ably translated and originally
published in 1927. It depicts the low-life of courtesans, unfaithful wives, hypocritical
priests, unscrupulous ascetics, rakes, fervent lovers, and sinful gods. Dandin's moral
point is that none of us can reach perfection: duty, profit, and love are always in
conflict, and one of the three must be sacrificed to attain the other two.

812 **Songs of the saints of India.**
Compiled and translated by John Stratton Hawley, Mark
Juergensmeyer. New York; Oxford: Oxford University Press, 1988.
244p. bibliog.

An anthology of Hindu *bhakti* poems, which have been translated in fluent and vivid
verse. Helpful introductions have been provided by the compilers. Hawley is also
author of *Sur Das: poet, singer, saint* (Seattle, Washington: University of Washington
Press, 1984. 233p.), a biography of Sur Das (1478-1560), the blind poet of Agra
whose famous poetry in praise of Krishna was recited at the court of emperor Akbar.
This book includes beautifully translated texts.

813 ***Shilappadikaram*: the ankle bracelet.**
Illango-Adigal, translated by Alain Danielou. London: Allen &
Unwin, 1967. 211p.

An ancient Tamil tragic verse-epic of the 3rd century. The story has two contrasting
characters: a devoted wife with natural beauty and a woman of pleasure with
contrived virtues. Kovalan, a young, wealthy merchant, falls in love with the royal
courtesan. The poem ends tragically with the death of all three, but husband and wife
are reunited in heaven.

814 **Love song of the dark lord: Jayadeva's *Gitagovinda*.**
Jayadeva, edited and translated by Barbara Stöler Miller. New York:
Columbia University Press, 1977. 225p. (UNESCO Collection of
Representative Works, Indian Series).

Perhaps the most lyrical and sensuous poem in the entire Sanskrit literature, the *Gita
Govinda* (Song of Krishna) describes the estrangement of Radha from her divine
lover, Lord Krishna, the incarnation of Vishnu. Written by a Bengali court poet of the
12th century, the poem is an allegory of the human soul oscillating between erotic
and divine love and finally transcending them both. The editor's introduction explains
the poem's structure and its symbolism in excellent fashion.

815 **The origin of the young god: Kalidasa's *Kumarasambhava*.**
Kalidasa, translated by Hank Heifetz. Berkeley, California:
University of California Press, 1985. 180p.

The acknowledged master-poet and dramatist of Sanskrit, Kalidasa's literary
reputation rests on six surviving works from the 5th century, the two most important
of which are the romantic verse drama *Shakuntala* (see items no. 816, 817) and the
lyric narrative *Kumarasambhava*. This *mahakavya* (great poem) comprises more than

600 verses divided into eight cantos. A celebration of Siva, this epic poem presents complex images and descriptions of the sacred landscape of the Himalaya, the seasons, female beauty, and heroic battles, which all contribute to a unique aesthetic experience. This work can be supplemented by *The cloud messenger: Meghaduta* (Ann Arbor, Michigan: University of Michigan Press, 1964. 96p.), translated by Franklin and Eleanor Edgerton, a long lyrical poem by Kalidasa which was immensely popular at the time.

816 **Theater of memory: the plays of Kalidasa.**
Kalidasa, edited by Barbara Stöler Miller, translated by Edwin Gerow, David Gitomer, and Barbara Stöler Miller. New York: Columbia University Press, 1984. 387p. bibliog.

Comprehensive analyses and new translations of the three extant plays of Kalidasa, the master poet of the era of Candragupta II (ca. 375-415 A.D.). The first, *Shakuntala*, is a heroic romance with rich mythological layers. It later came to be known in Europe through the impact it made on Goethe. The second, *Vikramorvasiya*, is a fantastical tale whose main protagonists are a celestial nymph and a mortal king. The third, *Malavikagnimitra*, is a secular romance set in the king's palace and pleasure garden. All three plays are characterized by elaborately stylized plots, characters, poetry, dialogue, and dance gestures.

817 **Great Sanskrit plays in new English transcreations.**
Edited and translated by P. Lal. New York: New Directions, 1964. 396p. bibliog.

Six classical plays – Sudraka's *Toy cart*, Vishakadatta's *Mudrarakshasa (Signet ring)*, Bhasa's *Dream*, Bhavabhuti's *Latter story of Rama*, Harsha's *Ratnavali*, and Kalidasa's *Shakuntala* – have been 'transcreated' in modern idiom. An introductory essay and a concluding bibliography provide excellent information on Indian drama as a literary form.

818 **Poems of love and war: from the eight anthologies and the ten long poems of classical Tamil.**
Translated by Attipat Krishnaswami Ramanujan. New York: Columbia University Press, 1985. 337p.

A selection of translated poems from the Cankam Age (300 B.C. – A.D. 300) of classical Tamil Nadu, south India. The exquisite, evocative poems celebrate love and war and represent generalized human types set in idealized landscapes. A concluding essay by the translator summarizes Tamil poetics, describing the strict literary distinction that was made between an inner (*aham*) world haunted by concerns of family and love and an exterior (*puram*) world of kings and battles, elegies to the glory and sorrow of war. An earlier volume of classical Tamil translations by Ramanujan, *The interior landscape: love poems from a classical Tamil anthology* (Bloomington, Indiana: Indiana University Press, 1967. 128p.), was instrumental in initiating a critical re-evaluation of Indian studies in the United States.

819   **The *Panchatantra.*** Translated by Arthur W. Ryder.   Chicago: University of Chicago Press, 1964. 470p.

This is India's great treasury of animal fables dating back to the 2nd century BC, with over 200 different versions in at least fifty languages outside India. The translation is exquisite.

820   **The *Ramayana.*** Valmiki, translated by Hari Prasad Shastri.   London: Shanti Sadan, 1952-59. 3 vols.

The standard complete prose translation of India's second-longest and most popular epic, with detailed glossaries of Sanskrit proper names and epithets. A major retranslation has been undertaken by Princeton University Press, directed by Robert P. Goldman, with four volumes being produced between 1985 and 1994. For an abridged version of the epic, see *The Ramayana of Valmiki: condensed from Sanskrit and transcreated into English* by P. Lal (New Delhi: Vikas, 1981. 341p.), and *The Ramayana of R. K. Narayan: a shortened modern prose version of the Indian epic suggested by the Tamil version of Kamban* (New York: Penguin, 1977. 177p.), both of which cover the central life story of the exemplary Rama, his marriage, exile, the abdication of his wife, her later recovery, and the triumphant return to his kingdom.

821   **Two plays of ancient India: *The little clay cart, The minister's seal.*** Translated by Johannes Adrianus Bernardus Van Buitenen.   New York: Columbia University Press, 1968. 278p.

Two plays of the Gupta period: *The little clay cart,* by Sudraka, is a 'rambunctious comedy of manners'; and *The minister's seal,* by Vishakadatta, is a 'taut political drama'. In both plays urban characters such as gamblers, spies, courtesans, ministers, learned thieves, hypocritical monks, and rebel princes are carefully delineated. An introductory essay discusses several aspects of the Indian world-view and the role of drama in explaining it.

822   **The *Mahabharata* of Krishna Dwaipayana Vyasa.** Vyasa, translated by Kisari Mohan Ganguli.   Calcutta: Oriental, 1962. 12 vols.

A complete and faithful translation of India's longest epic. Originally published between 1884 and 1896 by Pratap Chandra Roy, these volumes have been listed inaccurately in earlier bibliographies as having been translated by Roy. A new complete translation was undertaken by Johannes A. B. Van Buitenen (*The Mahabharata,* University of Chicago Press, 1973-), but only three volumes were completed before the translator's death. For abridged versions, see *The Mahabharata of Vyasa: condensed from Sanskrit and transcreated into English* by P. Lal (New Delhi: Vikas, 1980. 3rd ed. 400p.), and *Mahabharata* retold by William Buck (Berkeley, California: University of California Press, 1981. 417p.).

Regional literature in English translation

823 Boatman of the Padma.

Manik Bandyopadhyay, translated from the Bengali by Hirendranath Mukherji. New Delhi: National Book Trust, 1977. 2nd ed. 144p.

Originally published in 1936, *Boatman* remains one of the truly great novels of Bengal. Written by a Marxist with keen Freudian insights, the story deals with the oppressed life of a boatman whose fortunes depend on the flow of the river and the water level in it, phenomena often in conflict with the desires of other villagers.

824 *Pather Panchali*: song of the road.

Bibhutibhushan Banerji, translated by T. W. Clark, Tarpada Mukherji. Bloomington, Indiana: Indiana University Press, 1975. 316p.

The odyssey of a Bengali Brahmin boy through childhood, youth, marriage, and despair, and the encounter of tradition with modernity are superbly told. The novel has achieved additional acclaim via Satyajit Ray's rendering in film: *The Apu trilogy*.

825 Another India: an anthology of contemporary Indian fiction and poetry.

Selected and edited by Nissim Ezekiel, Meenakshi Mukherjee. New Delhi: Penguin (India), 1990. 296p.

A selection and English translation of forty-four pieces of the best new Indian fiction and poetry which appeared in the celebrated literary journal *Vagaratha*. Writers featured include, B. S. Mardhekar, Gopinath Mohanty, Krishna Baldev Vaid, Nirendranath Chakrabarti, B. N. Saikia, U. R. Anantha Murthy, and, writing in English, Nissim Ezekiel, Arun Joshi, and Jayanta Mahapatra. Two excellent collections of contemporary Indian poetry are: *Ten twentieth-century Indian poets* (New Delhi: Oxford University Press India, 1989. new ed. 114p.), selected and edited by Rajagopal Parthasarathy; and *Two decades of Indian poetry, 1960-1980* (Sahibabad, India: Vikas, 1980. 176p.), edited by Keki N. Daruwalla.

826 The village had no walls.

Vyankatesh Digambar Madgulkar, translated from the Marathi by Ram Deshmukh. New York: Asia, 1967. 172p.

A distinguished short novel, originally entitled *Bangarwadi*, of a Marathi shepherd's village and the way it functions, as seen through the eyes of a school teacher.

827 The *Vikas* book of modern Indian love stories.

Edited by Pritish Nandi. New Delhi: Vikas, 1979. 212p.

Twenty-five stories from as many writers, with nineteen translated from various Indian languages, and devoted to intriguing facets of relationships between the opposite sexes. The translations are uniformly good. Included in the anthology are several distinguished writers such as Mulk Raj Anand, Amrita Pritam, Krishna Chander, Khushwant Singh, Vijay Tendulkar, Sasthi Brata, Manik Bandyopadhyay and Kamala Das.

828 *Chemmeen.*
Thakazhi Sivasankara Pillai, translated by Narayan Menon.
Westwood, Connecticut: Greenwood, 1979. 228p.
One of the finest contemporary Indian novels. set in Kerala, the theme is forbidden intercommunal love in a fishing village. The novel received the Sahitya Akademi's Award, and has been published in more than twenty Indian languages and at least twelve Western languages.

829 **The Third World and other stories.**
Phanishwar Nath Renu, translated by Kathryn G. Hansen.   New Delhi: Chanakya, 1986. 185p.
A collection of well-translated short stories set in rural Bihar, in north India, by Renu, who was the first Indian novelist after Premchand (D. R. Srivastava: see item no. 831) to return to the rural milieu. Included are 'The third vow' (*Tisri Kasam*), a tale about a rough cart driver who is hired to carry a beautiful *nautanki* starlet to a fair which was made into a successful film in 1966 by Basu Bhattacharya, and 'Queen of red betal' (*Lal Pan ki Begam*), which portrays the social life of a Bihari village in all its complexity.

830 **Modern Hindi short stories.**
Translated and edited by Gordon C. Roadarmel.   Berkeley, California: University of California Press, 1974. 211p.
Fifteen stories from as many writers, ably translated. Many depict middle-class city dwellers bound by tradition yet caught in a changing world. The prevalent theme is alienation. The emotional and physical settings are distinctly north Indian.

831 **The gift of a cow: a translation of the Hindi novel** *Godaan.*
Dhanpat Rai Srivastava, translated by Gordon C. Roadarmel.
Bloomington, Indiana: Indiana University Press, 1968. 442p.
A magnificent translation of a powerful novel about rural India. Srivasata (*pseud.* Premchand) depicts the oppression of the Indian peasantry by money-lenders and priests, and the all-pervasive spirit of resignation that permeates Hindu life. The author, torn between Gandhism and socialism, offers no solution. The lifestory of Premchand, north India's foremost Hindi-Urdu story-teller, is ably recounted in *Munshi Premchand: a literary biography* (New York: Asia, 1964. 462p.), by Gopal Madan.

832 **I won't let you go: selected poems.**
Rabindranath Tagore, translated by Ketaki Kushari Dyson.
Newcastle-upon-Tyne, England: Bloodaxe, 1991. 272p.
This anthology contains 140 poems. This represents a fraction of the upwards of 4,000 poems and lyrics written during the lifetime of Rabindranath Tagore (1861-1941), Bengal's Nobel laureate, but considerably more than the forty-eight which are included in the alternative *Selected Poems* (Harmondsworth, Middlesex: Penguin, 1985) translated by William Radice. Dyson includes an illustrated fifty-page introduction. This sets out Tagore's remarkable achievements and also brings out his continuing relevance, even going so far as to link Tagore with the contemporary 'Green' movement of ecological consciousness.

233

833 **Women writing in India.**
Compiled and edited by Susie Tharu, Ke Lalita. London: Pandora, 1991-93. 2 vols.
A collection of translated texts by women writers from ancient to modern times. Volume one, which covers the period between 600 BC, when *Therigatha* ('Songs of the Buddhist nuns') was written, to the early 20th century, includes selections from sixty-three authors. Volume two covers the 20th century and contains selections from seventy-three writers translated from thirteen regional languages.

Anglo-Indian literature

834 **More stories from the Raj and after: from Kipling to the present day.**
Edited by Saros Cowasjee. London: Grafton Books, 1986. 288p.
A sequel to *Stories from the Raj* (London: Grafton Books, 1982), this volume comprises a selection of short stories by Western and Indian writers on Indian themes written during the colonial and post-colonial eras. The Western writers include Rudyard Kipling, Ruth Prawer Jhabvala and Flora Annie Steel, and the Indian, Mulk Raj Anand, R. K. Narayan, Khushwant Singh, and Raja Rao.

835 **A passage to India.**
Edward Morgan Forster. Harmondsworth, England: Penguin, 1989. 363p.
A literary masterpiece by one of England's finest novelists. Forster (1879-1970) visited India for extended periods in 1912-13, 1921, and 1945. In *A passage to India*, first published in 1924, he brilliantly depicts the spiritual and subterranean political tensions of two clashing civilizations. The central plot concerns a mysterious incident which occurred in the Marabar caves and was to result in Adela Quested, newly arrived in India, accusing Dr. Aziz of rape. The work is subtle and complex in its structure, being based around the three Indian seasons: hot, rains and cold/winter.The great strength of the work is the insight the Cambridge-educated Forster provides into the mindset of India's colonial administrators. An excellent film of the novel was made in 1984 by the late David Lean. Forster's principal Indian writings, describing his fantastical sojourn in the tiny princely state of Dewas, have been collected together in a volume edited by Elizabeth Heine, *The hill of Devi and other Indian writings* (London: Edward Arnold, 1983. 419p.).

836 **Heat and dust.**
Ruth Prawer Jhabvala. New York: Harper, 1983. 181p.
Perhaps the best-known novel of a European expatriate in India, this won the Booker Prize in 1975 and inspired the Ismail Merchant and James Ivory film of the same name. Set in central India, it is the story of an Englishwoman who deserts her husband for inter-racial romantic love and the resulting agony. This episode is subsequently re-evaluated fifty years later by the woman's stepdaughter with a deeper understanding of what really happened to her stepmother.

837 **Plain tales from the hills.**
Rudyard Kipling, edited by H. R. Woudhuysen. Harmondsworth, England: Penguin, 1990. 295p.

A collection of short stories which were first published in 1888 when Kipling, the British Raj's most famous chronicler, was in his early twenties. Deriving from the author's observations while working as a journalist in northern India, these tales contain vivid insights into Anglo India at work and play. Kipling's also wrote a classic novel set in India, *Kim* (Harmondsworth, England: Penguin, 1989. 366p.), which was first published in 1901.

838 **Staying on.**
Paul Scott. London: Heinemann, 1977. 216p.

A revised version of the comedy of the White Man's Burden, this novel is set in the Indian hill station of Pankot in 1972. Here Col. 'Tusker' Smalley and his wife Lucy are living out their retirement after having chosen to 'stay on' in the subcontinent after Indian independence in 1947. The novel won the Booker Prize in 1977 and is the sequel to the author's acclaimed *Raj quartet* (London: Heinemann, 1976.), which, comprising *The jewel in the crown, The day of the scorpion, The towers of silence,* and *A division of the spoils,* was made into a hugely successful British television series in the early 1980s.

Indo-Anglian literature

839 **Coolie.**
Mulk Raj Anand. New Delhi: Arnold Heinemann, 1980. 320p.

The foremost Indian novelist of the 1930s and 1940s, Anand, along with R. K. Narayan and Raja Rao, established Indo-Anglian fiction (the term used to describe Indian fiction in English) as a respected and popular genre. Anand, a disciple of M. K. Gandhi and Nehru, chose the disadvantaged and the underprivilieged as his central characters. In *Coolie,* which was first published in 1936, we encounter a hill-boy who works at various menial jobs and dies of tuberculosis as a young rickshaw-puller in imperial Simla. Two other excellent novels by Anand are: *Two leaves and a bud* (New Delhi: Hind Pocket Books, 1972. 203p), which portrays a Punjabi worker destined to toil and murder in an Assam tea plantation during the colonial period; and *Untouchable* (Harmondsworth, England: Penguin, 1986. new ed. 156p), Anand's first novel, which was originally published in 1935. An excellent study of Anand's life and writings is *The wisdom of the heart: a study of the works of Mulk Raj Anand* (New Delhi: Sterling, 1985.), by Marlene Fisher.

840 **He who rides a tiger.**
Bhabani Bhattacharya. New Delhi: Arnold Heinemann, 1977. 245p.

Superstitions, urban vices, and caste tyranny by the rich are the themes of this poignant Indian novel, set during the Bengal famine of 1943. A village blacksmith fakes a miracle, becomes a holy man, secures wealth from his former oppressors and is detected as a fraud, but is still loved by his own low-caste people.

Literature. Indo-Anglian literature

841 English August: an Indian story.
Upamanyu Chatterjee. London: Faber & Faber, 1988. 304p.

An entertaining, wryly observed account of a bored young Indian civil servant newly posted to a small, dusty provincial town. The junior bureaucrat's lively imagination is dominated by thoughts of literature, women and soft drugs.

842 Cry, the peacock.
Anita Desai. New Delhi: Orient Paperbacks, 1980. 218p.

First published in the 1960s, this has been one of the most successful of the many novels written by Anita Desai. In *Cry*, Mrs. Desai portrays the breakdown of a wife who cannot cope with her husband's cold detachment. Another excellent Desai novel is *In custody* (Harmondsworth, England: Penguin, 1985. 203p.).

843 All about H. Hatterr.
Govindas Vishnoodas Desani. New York: Farrar, Straus, 1970. rev. ed. 287p.

Hailed by T. S. Eliot and others as a literary sensation, this novel's strength lies in the beauty of its language and a Joycean construction. A Eurasian ('I am fifty-fifty of the species') turns up on the shores of India, seeks the wisdom of its seven sages, and develops a comprehensive philosophy of life which is then told in this 'autobiography'.

844 Nectar in a sieve.
Kamala Markandaya. New York: John Day, 1955. 255p.

The great 'sob-story' of India, this masterfully portrays the tragic assault upon a traditional village by modern technology and industry. Rukmini, the heroine, is Mother India, whose virtues, stoic courage, and boundless capacity to endure suffering are characteristic of village India.

845 A river sutra.
Gita Mehta. London: Minerva, 1994. 292p.

At the centre of this hypnotic novel is the river Narmada, India's holiest waterway, mere sight of which is salvation. Written with seductive prose, Mehta tells the tale of a retired civil servant who has escaped the world to spend his twilight years running a guest house on the banks of the holy river.

846 The bachelor of arts.
Rasipuram Krishnaswami Iyer Narayan. London: Minerva,1993. new ed. 264p.

The Tamil-speaking R. K. Narayan, who chose English as his literary language, is perhaps the least didactic or political Indian novelist. *The bachelor of arts*, first published in 1937, is an amusing story of a college student, his desire to become a hermit, the recovery of love in an arranged marriage, and the powerful influence of a mother-in-law on a young bride. The novel is set in the enchanting, Madras and Mysore-inspired, timeless fictional territory of Malgudi, along with thirteen other Narayan 'classics' such as *The man-eater of Malgudi* (1961) and *The vendor of sweets* (1967). These works brilliantly relate the simple ironies of Indian life and are very Hindu in their themes. *A Malgudi omnibus* (London: Minerva, 1994. 474p.) contains Narayan's three best-loved Malgudi novels.

847 Kanthapura.
Raja Rao. New York: New Directions, 1967. 244p.
Raja Rao is India's foremost philosophical novelist writing in English. The reassertion of Indian traditions, the recovery of Hinduism, and the exploration of spiritual depths by an intellectual hero form the substance of both this and Rao's other major work, *The serpent and the rope* (1960). Published originally in 1938, *Kanthapura* examines the impact of Gandhi on Indian spiritual life. An excellent literary biography of Raja Rao is *Raja Rao* (New Delhi: Arnold Heinemann, 1973. 170p.), by C. D. Narasimhaiah.

848 Midnight's children.
Salman Rushdie. New York: Knopf, 1981. 445p.
An extraordinary, mythical novel of rare beauty that encapsulates the reality of modern India. The first thirty-one years of Indian independence (1947-78) are seen through the eyes of two persons, born in the first hour of India's independence, 15 August 1947, in a Bombay nursing home, and switched: one destined to an aristocratic Muslim home, and the other to a street-singer's family. Expected to be the nation's hope, the children grow up as mortal enemies and watch their country's loss of innocence. A *tour de force* which was justly awarded the Booker Prize in 1981. Rushdie's subsequent works have been less accessible and politically controversial. The author's 1988 novel, *The satanic verses*, viewed as blasphemous by Muslims, resulted in Iran's theocracy imposing in 1989 a *fatwa* calling for Rushdie's assassination and forcing the Bombay-born, but England-based, writer underground.

849 Rich like us.
Nayantara Sahgal. Sevenoaks, England: Sceptre, 1987. 268p.
The story of India during the mid-1970s Emergency when power became arbitrary, written by an author who was active in the civil liberties movement. The characters include Rose, a cockney *memsahib*, Ravi, a Marxist turned placeman, and Kishori Lal, an idealist who finds that citizens can be imprisoned for what they think.

850 A suitable boy.
Vikram Seth. New Delhi: Viking; London: Phoenix House, 1993. 1,347p.
This work has the distinction of being the longest English-language novel of the century. Notwithstanding its size, it became a bestseller in the West and in India and has received widespread critical acclaim. Originally conceived as five short stories, the novel, sprawling in scope, took eight years to write. Essentially a family saga set in India during the early 1950s, Seth wrestles with the tensions of caste/class, religion and changing values. Its central characters are Lata, a college student, and her sister, a newlywed. The running motif is the determination of Lata's mother to find 'a suitable boy' for her daughter to wed. However, there are numerous subplots involving local and national politics, Hinduism, Islam, agriculture, children, shoes, poetry, and music. Seth's style is engaging – vivid in its detail, never heavy and often funny.

851 **The great Indian novel.**
Shashi Tharoor. Harmondsworth, England: Penguin, 1990. 423p.
A novel which, as its title suggests, is based on the characters, events, and incidents of the great ancient epic, the *Mahabharata* (see item no. 822). However, the setting is the 20th century, with the author desrcribing the disintegration of the British Raj and the creation of an independent India. Personalities and episodes from the Sanskrit epic are interwoven in the narrative with consummate skill.

852 **Song of Anasuya: a novel.**
Uma Vasudev. New Delhi: Vikas, 1978. 174p.
The first novel by a distinguished political analyst, *Song of Anasuya* tells of the torment and rapture of a man who, after years of loveless sex, finds himself involved with two women. The characters of the tormented hero and his two women, one involved platonically and the other erotically, are drawn with subtle sensitivity. This is a well written book.

Literary biographies and memoirs

853 **Iqbal: poet-patriot of India.**
S. M. H. Burney. New Delhi: Vikas, 1987. 136p. bibliog.
Born in Sialkot, now in Pakistan, Sir Mohammad Iqbal (1875-1938) wrote poems in Urdu and Persian full of a compelling mysticism and nationalism. This is a fine short biography of a man regarded almost as a prophet by Muslims, who during his life advocated the establishment of a separate Muslim state in India.

854 **Autobiography of an unknown Indian.**
Nirad Chandra Chaudhuri. London: Hogarth, 1987. new ed. 506p.
The boyhood experiences and intellectual growth of a distinguished Bengali author. Autobiographical information is used to make some startling comments about India, its history and nationalism, and its culture. For instance, Chaudhuri dismisses as superannuated folly the notion that the Hindu civilization can be revived. Originally published in 1951. A broad-ranging follow-up volume of reminiscences bears the title, *Thy hand, great anarch ! : India 1921-1952* (London: Hogarth, 1990. new ed. 1,008p.).

855 **Kabir: the apostle of Hindu-Muslim unity; interaction of Hindu-Muslim ideas in the formation of the *bhakti* movement.**
Muhammad Hedayetullah. New Delhi: Motilal Banarsidass, 1977. 320p.
A biography of Kabir (1440-1518), one of the finest Hindi *bhakti* saint-poets of medieval India. Originally a poor Muslim weaver of Banaras, Kabir became a disciple of Ramananda, who appealed across caste and communal lines to commoners, and composed appealing rhymes and aphorisms. He taught that God was in everything and that no single religion had a monopoly of divine wisdom.

856 **Rabindranath Tagore: a biography.**
Krishna Kripalani.   Calcutta: Visva-Bharati, 1980. 491p. bibliog.

A fine, well-balanced biography of the extraordinary Bengali philosopher-poet Rabindranath Tagore (1861-1941) who won the Nobel Prize for Literature in 1913, the first Asian to do so. The son of a wealthy Hindu religious reformer, Tagore was a prolific and multi-talented artist – the author of sixty collections of poetry, an equal number of plays, a dozen novels, nearly a hundred short stories, sixty anthologies of essays, more than a dozen volumes of letters, seventy songbooks, and the national anthems of India and Bangladesh. Acknowledged as the literary guru of modern India, his own memoirs are available in *My Reminiscences* (London: Macmillan Papermac, 1991. 232p.), translated by Andrew Robinson. Kripalani's volume covers many facets of Tagore's engrossing life: his educational philosophy, his involvement in Indian politics, his search for a synthesis of East and West, and his loneliness both as a child and as India's senior statesman in his old age. Robinson, with Krishna Dutta, is author of the fine recent biography, *Rabindranath Tagore: the myriad-minded man* (London: Bloomsbury, 1995).

857 **Daddyji-Mamaji.**
Ved Mehta.   London: Pan Books, 1984. 346p.

A brilliant portrait of a north Indian family in the 1930s. The central characters are the author's physician father, a product of education in India and in Britain, and uncomfortable in both cultures, and his mother, who was married at the age of seventeen. The ambivalent impact of the West on India's cultural tradition is clearly indicated by the book's title – two English words each with an Indian suffix.

858 **My days: a memoir.**
Rasipuram Krishnaswami Iyer Narayan.   London: Chatto & Windus, 1975. 186p.

The autobiography of India's foremost story-teller is more a recollection of his Madras boyhood than a full-length account of his life. At the age of two he was plucked from his family and sent to live with his grandmother and uncle, where his best friends were a peacock and a monkey. Narayan (b. 1906) keeps his adult life private, but he does provide information about his excursions into the occult following the death of Rajam, his wife of four years, from typhoid in 1930. Well worth reading.

859 **The fiction of Ruth Prawer Jhabvala: the politics of passion.**
Laurie Sucher.   Basingstoke, England: Macmillan, 1989. 251p. bibliog.

A review of the life and literary works of the German-born novelist, brought up in England, who, after marrying an Indian architect, came to live in Delhi between 1951 and 1975 and has written a series of acclaimed novels set in India. These have included *Esmond in India* (1958) and *Heat and Dust* (1975).

Literary history and criticism, literary journals

860 **Righteous Rama: the evolution of an epic.**
John L. Brockington. New Delhi: Oxford University Press India, 1984. 363p. bibliog.

This book sets the epic *Ramayana* of Valmiki (see item no. 820) in context. The first section is devoted to a linguistic analysis of the text, while the second establishes a relative chronology of the different layers of its composition and uses this classification to better understand the material, social, religious, and cultural milieux of ancient Indian civilization. The author separates the text into three distinct strata, dating respectively from the 4th to the 5th centuries BC, the 3rd century BC to the 1st century AD, and the 1st to the 3rd centuries AD.

861 **A new history of Sanskrit literature.**
Krishna Chaitanya. New Delhi: Manohar, 1977. 2nd ed. 490p. bibliog.

This is the best short, but comprehensive, history of Sanskrit literature, which includes a discussion of epic poetry (*Ramayana* and *Mahabharata*) and also of epic legends (*Puranas*, Buddhist *Jatakas,* and Jain legends), often excluded in traditional histories.

862 **Inventing India: a history of India in English-language fiction.**
Ralph J. Crane. New York: St. Martin's Press; Basingstoke, England: Macmillan, 1992. 212p. bibliog.

An examination of how different phases of Indian history have been portrayed and imagined in novels written in English by British, Anglo-Indian, and Indian writers. The chapters are chonologically arranged, focusing on critical periods in Indian history. The author analyses the extent to which the novels surveyed are historically accurate and convey the 'feel of the age'. There are also plot summaries. Particularly interesting is chapter one, which compares depictions of the 1857 great revolt in the writings of J. G. Farrell (*The siege of Krishnapur*), M. M. Kaye (*Shadow of the moon*), John Masters (*Nightrunners of Bengal*), and Manohar Malgonkar (*The devil's wind*). A complementary work is, *After the Raj: British novels of India since 1947* (Hanover, New Hampshire: University Press of New England, 1986. 197p.), by David Rubin.

863 **Cool fire: culture specific themes in Tamil short stories.**
Gabriella Eichinger Ferro-Luzzi. Gottingen, Germany: Rader Verlag, 1983. 365p. bibliog. (Edition Herodot Monographica 3).

This book comprises a synopsis and analysis of the content of 560 Tamil short stories by fifty-two authors. The first eight chapters discuss social and worldly themes found in Tamil short fiction, such as traditional marriage rites and the Hindu *asrama* cycle. The closing chapters examine psychological and spiritual themes: magic and magical beings, *bhakti*, the sometimes erotic side of Hinduism, and death.

864 **International encyclopaedia of Indian literature.**
Ganga Ram Garg. New Delhi: Mittal Publication, 1987. 2nd ed.
Vol. 1. 660p.

A reference work encompassing creative writers in Sanskrit, Pali, Prakrit and Apabhramsa from ancient times to 1981. The volume, which is divided into two separately published parts, summaries the outstanding work of each writer and includes articles on the *Vedas, Brahmanas, Upanishads, Puranas, Ramayana* and *Mahabharata.* Though chiefly an encyclopaedia on literature, the volume also includes references to treatises on religion, philosophy, astronomy, mathematics and science.

865 **A history of Indian literature.**
Edited by Jan Gonda. Wiesbaden, Germany: Otto Harrassowitz,
1975- . in progress.

Under the editorship of Gonda, a distinguished European Indologist, a comprehensive survey of the history of Indian classical, medieval, and modern literatures has been undertaken. The following are the titles of each volume of the set: *Hindi literature in the twentieth century,* Hans Peter Theodor Gaeffke (188p.); *Kashmiri literature,* Braj B. Kachru (114p.); *Hindi literature from its beginnings to the nineteenth century* (239p.) and *Hindi literature of the nineteenth and early twentieth centuries* (60p.), both by Ronald Stuart McGregor; *Assamese literature,* Satyendra Nath Sarma (76p.); *Classical Urdu literature from the beginning to Iqbal* (139p.), *Islamic literatures of India* (60p.); *Sindhi literature* (41p.), all by Annemarie Schimmel; *Classical Marathi literature from the beginning to AD 1818,* Shankar Gopal Tulpule (160p.); *Bengali literature,* Dusan Zbavitel (188p.); *Tamil literature,* Kamil Veith Zvelebil (316p.). Each volume includes a bibliography. All these volumes are significant improvements on the histories of regional literature published by the Sahitya Akademi during the 1960s and 1970s. The series also includes volumes on Vedic literature, the *Puranas,* and Sanskrit-Pali-Prakrit classical poetry.

866 **The great encounter: a study of Indo-American literary and cultural relations.**
R. K. Gupta. Riverdale, Maryland: The Riverdale Co., 1987. 276p.

A study of Indo-American literary, academic and cultural relations during the last two centuries, including those in art, dance, music, and film. The final chapters, 'India in America' and 'America in India', demonstrate an unexpectedly broad array of contacts and reciprocal influences.

867 **The style of Bana: an introduction to Sanskrit prose poetry.**
Robert A. Hueckstedt. Lanham, Maryland: University Press of
America, 1985. 212p. bibliog.

A pioneering literary analysis of the syntactic and stylistic choices of the great Sanskrit prose author Bana, who was responsible for the masterpieces *Harsacarita* and the *Purvabhaga* of the *Kadambari* – Bana's son, Bhusanabhatta completed the second half. The work seeks to retrieve Bana's fine works from the low estimation they have received from many European Orientalist and Indian critics.

868 **Indian Literature.**
New Delhi: Sahitya Akademi, 1957- . quarterly.

This publication of India's national academy of letters provides English translations of poems and short stories and topical articles on Indian writers and regional literatures. Occasionally special issues on selected authors are included.

869 **Journal of South Asian Literature.**
East Lansing, Michigan: Asian Studies Center, Michigan State University, 1963- . biannual.

The only journal in the West devoted primarily to the literatures of South Asia. While north Indian literature is emphasized generally, there are occasional pieces on other regional literatures. Literary criticism, literary history, translations into English, and good book reviews are the standard fare. Between 1963 and 1972, it was known as *Mahfil: a quarterly magazine of South Asian literature.*

870 **Urdu literature.**
D. J. Matthew, Christopher Shackle, Shakrukh Husain.   London: Third World Foundation, 1985. 139p. bibliog.

A succinct survey of Urdu literature from its 17th- and 18th-century roots to the present day. The work is designed for the general reader and includes translations of poems and literary pieces.

871 **Realism and reality: the novel and society in India.**
Meenakshi Mukherjee.   New Delhi: Oxford University Press India, 1994. new ed. 232p. bibliog.

This study provides a commentary on the Indian regional novel and suggests a methodology by which other derivative literatures within the colonized world reconciled the demands of Western realism with the representation of indigenous realities.

872 **A history of Indian English literature.**
M. K. Naik.   New Delhi: Sahitya Akademi, 1982. 320p. bibliog.

An excellent, chronologically-based account of the development of Indian writing in English, from 1809, the year of the first significant composition, to 1980. Poetry, drama, fiction, prose, and short stories are all covered, along with brief accounts of the works of around a hundred writers.

873 **Marvelous encounters: folk romance in Urdu and Hindi.**
Frances W. Pritchett.   Riverdale, Maryland: The Riverdale Co., 1985. 220p. bibliog.

An introductory study of the *qissa,* the popular literary genre of folk romance which accounts for a large proportion of the printing market in Hindi- and Urdu-speaking regions of north India. Though the literature is more accessible, it has been neglected by Western and Indian scholars in favour of more élite, classical genres. It derives from the Persian *dastan* tradition.

874 **Laughing matters: comic tradition in India.**
Lee Siegel.   Chicago: University of Chicago Press, 1987. 497p.
bibliog.
An accessible, insightful work, designed for the general reader, which highlights a
neglected area of Indian literature, the comic tradition. The author demonstrates the
abundance of comedy in the ancient Indian literary tradition, including examples from
diverse sources, including the *Jatakas*, Sanskrit plays, and Jaina works. There are
sections on satire, humour in classical works, and contemporary humour. The
narration is light-hearted and anecdotal, in keeping with the subject matter.

875 **Ratnakara's *Haravijaya*: an introduction to the Sanskrit court
epic.**
David Smith.   New Delhi: Oxford University Press India, 1985. 330p.
An in-depth study of the Sanskrit court epic which focuses on the long-neglected
Haravijaya. Smith re-evaluates this classical Sanskrit epic poem.

876 **Studies in Indian literature and philosophy: collected articles of
J. A. B. Van Buitenen.**
Johannes Adrianus Bernardus Van Buitenen, edited by L. Rocher.
New Delhi: Motilal Banarsidass, 1988. 339p. bibliog.
A collection of twenty-seven articles by the great literary scholar and philologist
Johannes A. B. Van Buitenen written between 1955 and 1979, the year of his
premature death. The papers are testimony to the breadth and depth of the author's
learning in Vedic and Sanskrit literature. He was one of the most perceptive analysts
of India's epics, classical dramas, and story literature, and a skilled translator.

877 **A history of Indian literature.**
M. Winternitz, Vols. 1 and 2 translated by S. Ketkar, Vol. 3 translated
by Subhadra Jha.   Calcutta: University of Calcutta, Vols. 1 and 2,
1959-63. 2 vols. bibliog; New Delhi: Motilal Banarsidass, Vol. 3
(in 2 parts), 1963. 2 vols. bibliog.
Winternitz's history remains unsurpassed both in its scope and scholarship. The first
volume deals with early Vedic literature and the great epics; the second with Buddhist
and Jain legends; the third with ornate poetry, dramas, and other technical literatures.

The Arts

General

878 **Indian epigraphy and its bearing on the history of art.**
Edited by Frederick M. Asher, G. S. Gai. New Delhi: Oxford & IBH and American Institute of Indian Studies, 1985. 294p.

A collection of fifty scholarly papers which were presented in 1979 by art historians and epigraphers at a symposium held at Varanasi (Banaras), in north India. The work is divided into five chronological sections: the early Buddhist period; post-Gupta epigraphy; medieval north India; medieval south India; and Islamic inscriptions.

879 **The Raj: India and the British 1600-1947.**
Edited by Christopher Alan Bayly. London: National Portrait Gallery, 1990. 432p. maps. bibliog.

Published to coincide with a massive 1990-91 'Raj exhibition' at the National Portrait Gallery in London, this sumptuous work, available in paperback, includes reproductions of nearly all of the exhibits – paintings, photographs, cartoons. There are 630 annotated entries arranged in four chronological sections: Mughal India and the rise of the East India Company, ca. 1760-1800; Company supremacy and Indian resistance, 1800-1858; the Victorian Raj and the rise of nationalism, 1858-1914; and the road to partition and independence, 1914-47. The sections are subdivided into topics covering such themes as British landscape painting in India, colonial anthropology, photography in 19th-century India, and artistic responses to colonialism, each preceded by a brief overview written by an expert. An informative, beautifully illustrated work.

880 **Indian art : a concise history.**
Roy C. Craven. London: Thames & Hudson, 1976. 252p. bibliog.

A noted American museum director and professor of art history reviews, for non-specialists, the whole of the art of India from the 3rd millennium BC Harappan finds, through to the 18th-century miniature painting schools. By means of illustrations, which appear on almost every page of the book, and the text which interprets them, the author guides the reader through the main periods, major forms, and some outstanding examples of Indian art. An excellent survey for students and generalists, which, originally titled *A concise history of Indian art*, is available now in paperback.

881 **The gardens of Mughal India: a history and guide.**
Sylvia Crowe, Sheila Haywood, Susan Jellicoe, Gordon Patterson.
London: Thames & Hudson, 1972. 200p. maps. bibliog.

The formal gardens laid out by the Mughal rulers of India, with their interweaving of water, trees and flowers, formed an integral part of Indo-Muslim culture. This book, intended for a general audience, documents and illustrates the most famous royal gardens, including extensive quotes from Mughal emperors and European travellers, as well as many monochrome photographs and copies of miniatures.

882 **The art and architecture of the Indian subcontinent.**
James Coffin Harle. Harmondsworth, England: Penguin; New York: Viking, 1986. 597p. 2 maps. bibliog. (Pelican History of Art).

A most comprehensive and balanced work which, based on three decades of research, covers such topics as Harappan art and sculpture, Hindu temple structures, Mughal painting, and Indo-Islamic architecture. Unusual attention is given to the often neglected 550-950 AD post-Gupta period. An excellent textbook which includes many good quality photographic reproductions. A complementary work is, *The arts of India* (Oxford: Phaidon, 1981. 224p.), edited by Basil Gray, which includes eleven essays arranged in three sections: Buddhist, Hindu and Jain art; art in the Islamic period; and modern art.

883 **The art of ancient India: Buddhist, Hindu and Jain.**
Susan L. Huntington, with contributions by John C. Huntington.
New York, Tokyo: Weatherhill, 1985. 786p.

An authoritative overview of early Indian art which complements the works of Harle (see item no. 882) and Rowland (see item no. 888). A feature of the work is the comprehensive coverage which is given to art in the so-called 'classical age' of the Guptas. There are twenty-five regional chapters arranged chronologically in five parts, commencing with the prehistoric and protohistoric era and ending with the Vijayanagara period (1336-1565 AD). The fifty-four page bibliography is particularly useful and there are forty-seven colour plates.

884 **Lalit Kala Contemporary.**
New Delhi: Lalit Kala Akademi, 1962- . semi-annual.

This lavishly illustrated journal, published by India's National Academy of Fine Arts, is devoted exclusively to modern Indian art. Individual issues are mainly thematic and include articles, statements, and reviews by artists, critics and art historians.

885 **Marg: a magazine of the arts.**
Bombay: Marg Publications, 1946- . quarterly.

Long edited and published by Mulk Raj Anand, a well-known Indian literary figure,
this quarterly is devoted to the arts and crafts of South Asia. Well illustrated, each
issue is devoted to a single art form.

886 **The powers of art: patronage in Indian culture.**
Barbara Stöler Miller. New Delhi: Oxford University Press India,
1992. 338p.

This work, the product of a conference spawned by the 1985 Festival of India,
examines architectural, musical, artistic and literary patronage in India from ancient
to colonial times. There are four sections. In the first, essays by Romila Thapar,
Barbara Miller and Devangana Desai examine the patronage of Buddhist monuments,
coinage, the poetry of Kalidasa during Gupta times, and the Lakhshmanu temple at
Khajuraho. Section two includes pieces on literature, poetry, songs and architecture in
medieval south India. Section three focuses on Mughal and Rajput art patronage and
includes an important essay by Catherine Asher on 'sub-imperial' architecture.
Section four, 'Under British rule', includes a chapter by Partha Mitter on the training
of Indian artists in schools suported by the British Raj.

887 **Much maligned monsters: history of European reactions to Indian
art.**
Partha Mitter. Oxford: Clarendon Press, 1977. 351p. bibliog.

An engaging study of European reactions and changing interpretations of Hindu,
Buddhist and Jain painting, sculptures and monuments. The author notes that, while
Indo-Islamic architecture and painting was easily understood in the West and popular
from an early date, Hindu sculptures, with their multi-limbed gods and the eroticism
associated with certain cults, were not so easily comprehended and assimilated. Early
European travellers saw Hindu sacred images as depicting infernal and diabolic
monsters. Only much later, with the revolt against the classical tradition in the West
and the search for alternative values, was classical Indian art reinterpreted and praised
for its spirituality.

888 **The art and architecture of India: Buddhist, Hindu, Jain.**
Benjamin Rowland, revised and updated by James Coffin Harle.
Harmondsworth, England: Penguin, 1977. 1st integrated ed. 512p.
map. bibliog. (The Pelican History of Art).

An authoritative, lucid, and beautifully illustrated history of the Buddhist, Hindu, and
Jain art of India, the most satisfying single volume on the subject. It is a connected
narrative, not unduly burdened by archaeological and iconographical details. The
author includes the impact of Graeco-Roman art on the art of India and surveys the
influence of Indian art in Turkestan, Tibet, Nepal, Sri Lanka, Myanmar (Burma),
Cambodia, and Java.

889　Facets of Indian art.
　　Edited by Robert Skelton, Andrew Topsfield, Susan Stronge,
　　Rosemary Crill.　London: Victoria and Albert Museum, 1986. 269p.
A collection of papers presented at an international symposium held in 1982 at the
Victoria and Albert Museum, London, at the time of the Festival of India. The chief
subject is the decorative arts, with essays on classical Indian carpets, Mughal period
furniture, carpets, and costume pieces, and the art of Indian playing cards. There are
also two sections on 'Sculpture and architecture', and 'Painting', which examine
regional architectural and artistic styles. Contributors include Walter Spink, Wayne
Begley, and Simon Digby.

890　Essays on Gupta culture.
　　Edited by Bardwell Leith Smith.　New Delhi: Motilal Banarsidass,
　　1983. 360p.
This volume collects together papers from a US symposium on India's 'golden age'.
There are excellent contributions by A. L. Basham, Barbara Stöler Miller (drama),
Frederick M. Asher (art), and Walter M. Spink (the Elephanta cave), and two
bibliographic chapters on Gupta religion, art, literature, and history.

891　Classical Indian dance in literature and the arts.
　　Kapila Vatsyayan.　New Delhi: Sangeet Natak Akademi, 1977.
　　2nd ed. 431p. bibliog.
This very detailed, scholarly work on the place of dance in classical Sanskrit
literature and traditional sculpture is both analytical and evaluative. It deals also with
the subject of aesthetics as relevant to Indian dance and with the general theory and
technique of Indian classical dance. The photographs of sculptural representation give
a comprehensive picture of the dance as found in ornamental stone imagery and in
iconography. A smaller and simpler treatment of Indian dance is the author's
Classical Indian dance (Thompson, Connecticut: Inter Culture Associates, 1975.
153p.).

892　Myths and symbols in Indian art and civilization.
　　Heinrich Zimmer, edited by Joseph Campbell.　Princeton, New
　　Jersey: Princeton University Press, 1992. 248p.
A brilliant introduction to the Indian mythological tradition and its influence on the
development of Indian thought and aesthetics, which is now available in paperback.
Zimmer utilizes his vast knowledge of Sanskrit literary tradition to convey the
significance of Indian myths and symbols and their representations in Indian art. He is
author of the two volume, The art of Indian Asia: its mythology and transformations
(Princeton, New Jersey: Princeton University Press, 1968. 2nd ed.).

Painting

893 **India revealed: the art and adventures of James and William Fraser 1801-35.**
Mildred Archer, Toby Falk. London: Cassell, 1989. 144p.

Mildred Archer, widow of the late William G. Archer (1907-79), has written extensively on late-18th- and early-19th-century Indian art and on the sketches and paintings of visiting British artists. She has also been responsible for the publication of the invaluable catalogue, *The India Office collection of paintings and sculptures* (London: British Library, 1986. 168p.). In this volume, the paintings commissioned by two Scottish brothers, James Baillie Fraser (1783-1856) and William Fraser (1784-1835), who stayed in India between 1801 and 1835, are reproduced and their colourful life stories retold. The paintings include village landscapes and exquisitely detailed portraits of horse merchants, dancing girls and military recruits.

894 **Indian paintings from the Punjab hills: a survey and history of the Pahari miniature painting.**
William George Archer. London: Sotheby Parke-Bernet, 1973.
2 vols.

A catalogue of all Punjab hill paintings held principally in the Victoria and Albert Museum, London. There are over 900 small, clear monochromes in this volume, with descriptions of twenty-one distinctive major schools of the region, grouped by periods. A crowning achievement by a distinguished art historian and critic.

895 **Indian painting.**
Douglas Barrett, Basil Gray. London: Macmillan, 1978. new ed.
214p. maps. bibliog.

A survey of Indian art from wall paintings of the 2nd century to the 19th-century Rajasthan and Punjab hills schools. Intended for the general reader, the book includes more than eighty colour reproductions.

896 **Mughal and Rajput painting (Vol. I:3 in The New Cambridge History of India).**
Milo Cleveland Beach. Cambridge: Cambridge University Press, 1992. 252p. bibliog.

Covering the period between 1540 and 1858, this volume focuses on artistic works produced under court patronage, rather than on uncollected folk and village traditions. In particular, it examines the artistic systems which developed under the patronage of the Hindu Rajput rulers of northern and central India and under their Mughal overlords. Beach, a prolific writer on both Mughal and Rajput miniatures, reveals European artistic influences on Mughal painting. Rajput artistic styles are shown, in contrast, to have been more diverse, localized and personalized. There is also a useful background chapter on painting in north India before 1540. The book includes 16 colour plates and 179 black-and-white illustrations. Unfortunately many of the black-and-white reproductions are either too small or fuzzy to permit identification of component details. In this respect, the work falls short of the standard established in Barrett and Gray (see item no. 895).

897   **The making of a new 'Indian' art: artists, aesthetics and**
       nationalism in Bengal, c. 1850-1920.
       Tapati Guha-Thakurta.   Cambridge: Cambridge University Press,
       1992. 352p. bibliog. (Cambridge South Asian Studies, no. 52).
An exploration of the impact of colonialism and nationalism on Indian art and
aesthetic values. The focus is on Bengal from the mid-19th century to 1920. The
author analyses the shifting status of artisans and artists, the emergence of new
professional and commercial opportunities, and   the permeation of Western
techniques and standards that transformed popular commercial art in Calcutta and
created a new Indian 'high art'. Ninety-six monochrome illustrations accompany the
text. This work should be read alongside the more general, *Arts and nationalism in
colonial India: Occidental orientations* (Cambridge: Cambridge University Press,
1994. 400p.), by Partha Mitter.

898   **The emperors' album: images of Mughal India.**
       Stuart Cary Welch, Annemarie Schimmel, Marie L. Swietochowski,
       Wheeler M. Thackston.   New York: Metropolitan Museum of Art,
       1987. 318p. bibliog.
This volume was published in connection with an exhibition held in New York in
1987. It contains a detailed catalogue of the Kekorvian album whose highlights are
the miniatures which were painted for the emperors Jahangir and Shah Jahan. The
illustrations are well reproduced and there are introductory essays on various aspects
of Mughal painting. Welch is also author of *Imperial Mughal painting* (London:
Chatto & Windus, 1978. 119p.).

Architecture and sculpture

899   **Architecture of Mughal India (Vol. I:4 in The New Cambridge**
       History of India).
       Catherine B. Asher.   Cambridge: Cambridge University Press, 1992.
       368p. map. bibliog.
This volume considers the entire scope of architecture built by the imperial Mughals
and their subjects. Organized chronologically, it begins with a short chapter on the
Indian and Timurid precedents of the Mughal style. There then follow chapters on
architectural developments between 1526 and 1707 during the reigns of each of the
Great Mughal emperors from Babur to Aurangzeb. Asher shows that the evolution of
imperial Mughal architectural taste and idiom was directly related to political and
cultural ideology. Attention is also given to construction away from the centre by an
Indian nobility which built permanent edifices in the imperial Mughal style. The book
contains 226 monochrome plates and a closing chapter on 18th- and early-19th-
century architectural styles in the post-Mughal 'successor states' of northern and
central India.

900 **Taj Mahal: the illuminated tomb: an anthology of seventeenth century Mughal and European documentary sources.**
Edited by Wayne Edison Begley, Ziauddin Ahmed Desai. Seattle, Washington: University of Washington Press, 1990. 329p.

A beautifully printed reference volume on India's most famous architectural monument, providing material of interest to historians of art history and religion. The book contains excerpted translations from contemporary texts, an introductory essay on the construction of the Taj, translations of inscriptions and calligraphy, and many well-produced plates.

901 **The caves at Aurangabad: early Buddhist Tantric art in India.**
Carmel Berkson. Ahmedabad, India: Mapin, 1986. 238p.

A lavish, non-academic presentation of 220 exquisite photographs of the cave excavations at Aurangabad, one of India's architectural masterpieces, accompanied by an essay describing each cave and the social and aesthetic background of the world from which they originated. The earliest carvings at Aurangabad date from before the Christian era, but most were created between the late-5th and late-6th centuries and are dominated by Buddhist and Hindu iconography.

902 **Essays in early Indian architecture.**
Ananda Kentish Coomaraswamy, edited by Michael W. Meister.
New Delhi: Oxford University Press India, 1994. 180p. bibliog.

This volume brings together the major essays of Ananda Coomaraswamy, whose contribution to the history of architecture in India was limited but profound. In particular, he is remembered for his reconstruction from texts and reliefs of early wooden structures. The work also includes an analysis of architectural terms and accompanying drawings.

903 **Splendours of the Raj: British architecture in India, 1660 to 1947.**
Philip Davies. London: John Murray, 1985. 272p. bibliog.

An authoritative, well-researched study of the architectural achievements and legacy of India's British imperial rulers. The work can be read usefully alongside *Stones of empire: the buildings of the Raj*, by Jan Morris (Oxford; New York: Oxford University Press, 1983. 234p.). The volume by Davies has individual chapters devoted to the cities of Calcutta. Madras, Bombay, and New Delhi, which he describes as 'The Rome of Hindustan'. There are also chapters on cantonments, hill stations, and churches. The volume by Morris includes photographs by Simon Winchester and analysis of a more diverse range of constructions, including hotels, theatres, *golas* (grain storehouses), department stores, and private mansions.

904 **Hindu temple art of Orissa.**
Thomas E. Donaldson. Leiden, the Netherlands: E. J. Brill, 1985-87.
3 vols. maps. (Studies in South Asian Culture, vol. 12).

A detailed, encyclopedic catalogue of Orissan temple and detached sculpture dating from the 6th to 15th centuries. Volume one describes temples dating through the 12th century; volume two, the period to the 15th century and discusses 'Stylistic and iconographic peculiarities of select features and motifs'; and volume three concerns sculpture. The volumes contain more than 4,300 illustrations, including many of the magnificent monuments at Bhubaneswar.

905   **The architecture of India.**
      Satish Grover. New Delhi: Vikas, 1980-81. 2 vols.
A chronologically and regionally structured overview of architectural development in India. Volume one commences with the Indus Valley Civilization and surveys Buddhist and Hindu sculpture and constructions. It closes with the Vijayanagara era. Volume two describes Indian architecture during the period of Islamic dominance, 727-1707 AD.

906   **The 'Pala-Sena' schools of sculpture.**
      Susan L. Huntington. Leiden, the Netherlands: E. J. Brill, 1984.
      296p. maps.
A meticulous and comprehensive stylistic study, based on fifteen years of research, of the sculpture of Bengal and Bihar between the 9th and 13th centuries AD. Region by region, the author constructs a chronology of the Pala-Sena school stone and bronze images, analyses the different Buddhist and Brahminical sculpture styles encountered, and discusses the nature of artistic patronage.

907   **Encyclopedia of Indian temple architecture.**
      Edited by Michael W. Meister, M. A. Dhaky, Krishna Deva.   New
      Delhi: American Institute of Indian Studies; Princeton, New Jersey:
      Princeton University Press; Philadelphia: University of Philadelphia
      Press, 1983- . in progress.
An ambitious project, with twenty-two separate volumes envisaged, providing detailed descriptions of the major regional and dynastic traditions of Indian temple architecture constructed between ca. AD 400 and the 18th century. Volume one covers south India and will comprise five parts, two of which were published in 1983 and 1986. Each 'part' consists of text and plates which are bound separately. Volume two focuses on north Indian architectural styles, the first two parts of which were published between 1988 and 1992. Individual chapters are contributed by specialists and comprise a brief dynastic history, a survey of architectural features, and detailed technical descriptions of key temple examples. A monumental work.

908   **An imperial vision: Indian architecture and Britain's Raj.**
      Thomas R. Metcalf.   Berkeley, California: University of California
      Press, 1989. 302p. bibliog.
This book demonstrates the relation of culture and power as expressed in British Indian colonial architecture. The author, a historian (see item no. 190), argues that India's colonial administrators looked to ancient Rome as a precedent, using classicism, seen to embody eternal values of law, order and government, to give visible shape to the empire. There are chapters on the design of New Delhi, the relationship between Indian princes, their palaces and architectural design, and the transfer of the assumptions of the Arts and Crafts Movement to India.

909   *Haveli*: **wooden houses and mansions of Gujerat.**
      V. S. Pramar.   Seattle, Washington: University of Washington Press,
      1990. 240p.

A superbly illustrated and documented book on 'vernacular architecture' which is the
first in a projected series on 'Traditional Indian Architecture'. The author shows how
the choice of construction materials in Gujarat, west India, is influenced by climatic
and resource considerations, but also demonstrates the influence of other styles –
Mughal, Portuguese, and British – on Gujarati architecture. Distinctions are made
between architectural styles in north Gujarat, Saurashtra and the tribal villages of
south Gujarat. A complementary work is, *Indian mansions: a social history of the
haveli* (Cambridge: Oleander, 1994. 203p.), by Sarah Tillotson.

910   **Divine ecstasy: the story of Khajuraho.**
      Shobita Punja.   New Delhi: Viking, 1992. 297p. bibliog.

In this interesting and informative work, Shobita Punja, a young art historian,
presents a new thesis to explain why the famous temple complexes at Khajuraho were
constructed and what their erotic sculptures depict. The author suggests that the
monuments, built during the 10th and 11th centuries, had a single unifying purpose:
the celebration of the marriage of Shiva to Parvati as recounted in the *Shiv Purana*.
The conglomeration of temples were designed to represent the gods who were present
on this divine occasion. The iconography supports this imagery, in Punja's view, and
had little to do with esoteric Tantric cults or the moral decadence of the patrons, as
had been suggested by earlier scholars.

911   **The history of architecture in India: from the dawn of civilization
      to the end of the Raj.**
      Christopher Tadgell.   London: Phaidon, 1994. 408p. bibliog.

An excellent, accessible synthesis which draws together all the strands of India's
architectural history: from the Vedic and native traditions of early India, through
Hindu, Buddhist, Islamic and secular architecture, to the eclecticism of the British
Raj. Available in paperback, the volume is accompanied by 96 colour and 454
monochrome illustrations.

912   **The Rajput palaces: the development of an architectural style,
      1450-1750.**
      Giles Henry Rupert Tillotson.   New Haven, Connecticut; London:
      Yale University Press, 1987. 224p. map. bibliog.

An accessible and extensively illustrated work which, though based on a doctoral
dissertation, is aimed at the non-specialist and assumes no previous detailed
knowledge of Indian history and architecture. The opening two chapters set out the
political and architectural context of Rajput palace building, situating them within the
Hindu heritage but noting influences of Islamic neighbours. The remaining nine
chapters include analyses and descriptions of individual palaces, including those at
Amber, Bikaner, Chitor, Gwalior, Jaipur, Jodhpur, and Udaipur. Tillotson is also
author of a popular architectural guide for travellers to India, *Mughal India*
(Harmondsworth, England: Penguin, 1991. 150p.).

913   **The tradition of Indian architecture: continuity, controversy and
change since 1850.**
Giles Henry Rupert Tillotson.   New Haven, Connecticut: Yale
University Press, 1989. 166p. bibliog.

A study of the changes which occurred after 1850 in architectural tradition and Indian
taste in response to the influence of British architecture and imperial policies. There
are interesting chapters on classicism, Westernization and stylistic change, the
building of New Delhi, the revival in craft traditions, and post-independence
developments.

914   **Ajanta: its place in Buddhist art.**
Sheila L. Weiner.   Berkeley, California: University of California
Press, 1977. 202p. 2 maps. bibliog.

A scholarly study of the famous Buddhist cave-temples at Ajanta in the western
Ghats, Maharashtra. The author situates the painting and sculptured cult-images
within the developing Buddhist tradition and analyses iconographic and stylistic
trends. The text is complemented by 104 monochrome plates.

Decorative arts and crafts

915   **Handicrafts of India.**
Kamaladevi Chattopadhyaya.   New Delhi: Indian Council for
Cultural Relations, 1975. 146p. map.

Written by one of the leading experts on the traditional handicrafts of India, this book
provides a perceptive introduction to the following crafts: earthenware, woodwork,
stoneware, textiles, metalwork, jewellery, ivory, basketry and mat weaving, horn and
shola (carving) work, toys and dolls, leatherwork, glasswork, folk painting, and
theatre crafts. Chattopadhyaya is also author of an excellent concise introduction to
Indian carpet work: *Indian carpets and floor coverings* (New Delhi: All India
Handicrafts Board, 1974. 68p.).

916   **Handwoven fabrics of India.**
Edited by Jasleen Dhamija, Jyotindra Jain.   Seattle, Washington:
University of Washington Press, 1990. 168p.

This collection highlights India's long tradition of handweaving craftsmanship,
dyeing and textile embellishment: today four million handlooms are still operated. It
comprises articles written by ethnographers and textile historians, several specially
translated, and also the results of Jasleen Dhamija's survey of regional fabrics.
Particularly interesting are the pieces on weaving in Vedic India (Wilhelm Rau) and
state weaving in Mauryan India (Romila Thapar).

917 **The techniques of Indian embroidery.**
Ann Morrell. London: Batsford, 1994. 144p.

An accessible and well-illustrated introduction to the historical development of Indian textiles, including the influences of local and regional traditions. The chapters explore individual techniques such as quilting, counted-thread work, *shisha* (mirror) work, metal work, beading, appliqué and patchwork.

918 **Metalcraftsmen of India.**
Meera Mukherjee. Calcutta: Anthropological Survey of India, 1978. 461p.

A study of the traditional techniques employed by artisans in the preparation of brass, bell-metal, and bronzeware. The book is divided into three sections: the first deals with metalcraftsmen, their castes and their position in society; the second describes how the author located and interviewed artisans in different parts of India; the third gives information on the techniques used by these artisans.

919 **A golden treasury: jewellery from the Indian subcontinent.**
Susan Stronge, Nina Smith, James Coffin Harle. London: Victorian and Albert Museum, 1988. 144p. map.

A well-illustrated work providing examples of Indian jewellery. It should be read in conjunction with *Masterpieces of Indian jewellery* (Bombay: Taraporevala, 1979. 54p.), by Jamila Brijbhusan, a fascinating study of the history of Indian jewellery and techniques.

920 **Dress and undress in India: problem of what to wear in the late colonial and modern era.**
Emma Tarlo. London: C. Hurst, 1993. 352p. bibliog.

A fascinating account of how different individuals and groups have used clothes to assert power, challenge authority, define or conceal identity, and instigate or prevent social change at various levels of Indian society since late colonial times. The focus is on the problem of what to wear rather than on describing what is worn, but there are 120 accompanying illustrations. Covering a longer timespan, *Costumes of India and Pakistan: a historical cultural study* (Bombay: Taraporevala, 1969. 244p.), by Shiv Nath Dar, which analyses regional and communal variations in dress and changing sartorial styles from ancient times to the present, and *Indian dress: a brief history* (London: Sangam Books, 1994. 104p.), by Charles Louis Fabri, are interesting complementary works.

Performing arts

921 The theatre of the *Mahabharata*: *Terukkuttu* performances in south India.
Richard Armando Frasca. Honolulu, Hawaii: University of Hawaii Press, 1990. 286p. bibliog.

Based on fieldwork carried out between between 1977 and 1982, this book describes *Terukkuttu*, a village-based ritual theatre of Tamilnadu, focusing on its relationship to the regional cult of Draupadi, the central female character of the *Mahabharata* (see item no. 822). The author describes the background, troupe, literary corpus, performing techniques, make-up, religious context, and codes of communication.

922 Grounds for play: the *Nautanki* theatre of north India.
Kathryn G. Hansen. Berkeley, California: University of California Press, 1992. 367p. bibliog.

A study, based on extensive archival research and fieldwork, of north Indian *Nautanki* theatre, also known as *Swang*, and its musical tradition. The author examines the origin, development and decline of *Nautanki* and its manipulation of gender differences. There are textual and socio-cultural analyses of several *Nautanki* plays and in the appendixes there are lists of texts and recorded performances.

923 At play with Krishna: pilgrimage dramas from Brindavan.
John Stratton Hawley, in association with Shrivatsa Goswami. Princeton, New Jersey: Princeton University Press, 1981. 339p. bibliog.

A unified view of the myth of Lord Krishna in its living dramatic form. Hawley has chosen four texts from the *Raslila* genre of north Indian folk theatre, translated them, and linked them to reconstruct Krishna's life. An introductory essay deals with Brindavan as a pilgrimage centre.

924 The theatric universe: a study of the *Natyasastra*.
Pramod Kale. Bombay: Popular, 1974. 196p. bibliog.

The *Natyasastra* ('Study of Dramatic Arts'), dating from the 3rd century and attributed to Bharata, stands as the foundation of all modern speculation on the manner in which ancient Sanskrit plays were probably performed. In Sanskrit literature it occupies a position similar to Aristotle's *Poetics*. Kale provides a sensible and enlightening interpretation of its meaning, but unfortunately chose to exclude music and dance from his discussion, two essential ingredients necessary to a complete understanding of classical theatre practices.

925 Tradition of Indian classical dance.
Mohan Khokar. London: Peter Owen, 1980. 168p.

An elegantly produced volume by an acknowledged expert. The text, complemented by fifty-one photographs, covers history and aesthetics, as well as all genres and styles of Indian classical dance. Twenty-five distinct modes of classical dance, regionally grouped, are clearly and logically presented. *Classical and folk dances of*

India (Bombay: Marg Publications, 1963. 372p.), provides a comprehensive survey of dance forms across sixteen different regions of India.

926 **Indian theatre.**
Adya Rangacharya. New Delhi: National Book Trust, 1971. 163p.
A succinct and readable survey of the development of Indian theatre from classical times to the present. Rangacharya argues that although classical Sanskrit drama declined after the 10th century, it was replaced by regional folk dramas with their own lively traditions, and Indian drama did not go through a dark age as is popularly assumed. The author is at his best in describing and analysing Indian theatrical traditions of the 19th and 20th centuries. For more detailed accounts of classical and folk dramas, see: *The Indian drama: the Sanskrit drama* (Calcutta: General Printers and Publishers, 1969. 213p.), by Sten Konow; and *Folk theater of India* (Seattle, Washington: University of Washington Press, 1966. 217p.), by Balwant Gargi.

927 **Indian theatre: traditions of performance.**
Edited by Farley P. Richmond, Darius L. Swann, Phillip B. Zarrilli.
Honolulu, Hawaii: University of Hawaii Press, 1990. 504p.
A text designed for introductory use by Western theatre students, this work covers a representative sample of eleven Indian theatre genres, ranging from Sanskrit to modern, and including ritual (*Teyyam* and *Ayyapan Tiyatta*), devotional (*Ras* and *Ram Lila*), folk-popular (*Nautanki* and *Tamasha*), and dance-drama (*Kathakali* and *Chau*) forms. Each chapter includes sections on origins, performers, training, plays, context, costume and make-up, music, performance, the current state of the art, and a brief bibliography of English-language sources. There are many illustrations.

928 **Sangeet Natak.**
New Delhi: Sangeet Natak Akademi, 1965- . quarterly.
Published by India's National Academy of Music, Dance, and Drama, this quarterly carries articles on the classical forms of the performing arts. Occasionally includes illustrations and book reviews.

929 **Traditions of Indian folk dance.**
Kapila Vatsyayan. New Delhi: Clarion Books, 1987. 2nd ed. 400p. maps. bibliog.
A close look at tribal and traditional folk-dances in eight cultural regions of India. Vatsyayan classifies Indian folk dances in seven categories: hunt dances, devotional dances, functional-occupational dances of the peasants, dances of fertility rites and magic, dances that re-enact scenes from the epics, dances reflecting seasons and seasonal festivals of India, and dance-dramas found both in urban and rural India. An excellent work, accompanied with colour and monochrome illustrations.

Music

930 The music of the Bauls of Bengal.
Charles Capwell.   Kent, Ohio: The Kent State University Press, 1986. 242p.

A comprehensive study of the folk musical culture of a free-spirited Bengali cult, the Bauls, who perform their songs, accompanied by a string instrument, at household or neighbourhood celebrations and fairs and as mendicants. The book includes thirty-four transliterated and translated song texts, the musical transcription of one complete song and many excerpts, an analysis of the instruments used, biographical data, performance contexts, and numerous photographs. Cassette tapes of twenty-four performances are available from the publishers.

931 Musical instruments of India.
B. Chaitanya Deva.   Calcutta: Firma KLM, 1978. 306p. bibliog.

Art, literature, archaeology, ancient and modern literary references, and the musical traditions of neighbouring countries are combined to present comprehensive accounts of various instruments. Pre-Aryan, Aryan, Central and West Asian, Persian, and Arab musicological influences on the shaping of Indian instruments are carefully discussed and the eastward and westward spread of Indian music described. Over 200 photographs enhance the value of the book.

932 Chant the names of god: musical culture in Bhojpuri-speaking India.
Edward O. Henry.   San Diego, California: San Diego University Press, 1988. 318p. bibliog.

An excellent analysis of Indian folk music written by a musician and anthropologist. The Bhojpuri region, situated in north India, comprises western Bihar and eastern Uttar Pradesh. Henry divides the musical culture studied into two basic categories: participatory music, namely women's songs (of weddings, sons, dirges, and other genres), and men's group song; and the non-participatory music performed by unpaid specialists and Hindu and Muslim mendicants, and paid entertainment and processional music. Each musical genre is described, including information about performers, the social setting of performances, and translations of song lyrics.

933 The *ragas* of north India.
Walter Kaufmann.   Sittingbourne, England: Asia Publishing, 1993. reprint of 1968 ed. 640p. bibliog.

934 The *ragas* of south India: a catalogue of scalar material.
Walter Kaufmann.   Sittingbourne, England: Asia Publishing, 1991. reprint of 1976 ed. 723p. bibliog.

In the above two entries the author analyses hundreds of *ragas* of north and south India and gives their details in Western notation, making these books necessities for serious students of Indian music. The introduction to the first volume gives a concise explanation of the Indian musical system, with time-theory included. Ragamala paintings are used as illustrations. These are excellent reference volumes for libraries. An accessible alternative introductory work is Nazir A. Jairazbhoy *The ragas of north Indian music: their structure and evolution* (Middletown, Connecticut: Wesleyan University Press, 1971. 222p.), which is accompanied by a record of musical examples played by Vilayat Khan.

935 Music and its study.
Mobarak Hossain Khan. New Delhi: Sterling, 1988. 116p.

An accessible presentation of the terms, ideas and concepts of north Indian classical music presented by a long-term student of the tradition. There are chapters devoted to the theories of *raga* and *tala*, Bhatkhande's ten parent scales (*thats*), notation systems, musical intruments, classical and folk genres, and the leading names in the history of north Indian music.

936 The music of India.
Reginald Massey, Jamila Massey. London: Kahn & Averill, 1993. 189p. bibliog.

A very useful general introductory work designed for the general reader. The first eight chapters trace the historical evolution of music in India from Vedic to modern times, relating it to social, cultural, religious and political factors. There are two technical chapters which explain the *raga* and *tala* systems. Chapters are also devoted to the description of individual instruments, accompanied by line drawings, and to short biographies of established musicians, composers and musicologists. At the end there is a representative discography. A briefer guide, which includes two cassettes and is sponsored by the 'world music' Womad Foundation, is *Music of India* (Oxford: Heinemann Educational, 1994. 72p.), by Gerry Farrell.

937 *Sufi* music of India and Pakistan: sound, context and meaning in *Qawwali*.
Regula Burckhardt Qureshi. Cambridge: Cambridge University Press, 1986. 265p. bibliog. (Cambridge Studies in Ethnomusicology).

Qawwali is the musical genre associated with *sufi* religious practices performed at shrines throughout the subcontinent. This study, based on detailed fieldwork, looks at *qawwali* from an ethnomusicological perspective, treating the music both as music and as a performance in a religious context.

938 My music, my life.
Ravi Shankar. New York: Simon & Schuster, 1969. 160p. map.

This autobiographical account by India's best-known and universally acclaimed musician discusses his musical heritage and provides basic information about the history, theory, and instruments of Indian music. The description of Shankar's childhood in Banaras (Varanasi) and his utter devotion to his music teacher are delightful. A manual for sitar explains both the melodic and rhythmic systems for playing the instrument.

939 **Music in India: the classical traditions.**
Bonnie C. Wade. Englewood Cliffs, New Jersey: Prentice Hall,
1979. 252p. map. bibliog. (Prentice Hall History of Music Series).
An introductory text 'for the uninitiated Westerner' which discusses the melody and
metre of Indian music and its performance genres. The music is placed in its cultural
context and there is an annotated bibliography, a discography, and a filmography.
Wade is also author of an interesting scholarly work on *khyal*, a style of singing
which emerged in north India in the 18th century and is now the dominant classical
form: *Khyal: creativity within north India's classical musical tradition* (Cambridge:
Cambridge University Press, 1984. 314p.).

Photography

940 **Victorian India in focus: a selection of early photographs from the
collection of the India Office Library and Records.**
Ray Desmond. London: HMSO, 1982. 100p.
A selection of more than ninety pioneering monochrome photographs taking in India
during the mid- and later-19th-century. They reveal a variety of facets of Indian and
European life in Victorian India. Twelve pages of accompanying text details the early
development of photography in India from the 1840s and the encouragement given by
the Government of India which saw the value of the new technology in assisting
military, police, and engineering work. A companion volume is, *The last empire:
photography in British India, 1855-1911* (London: Fraser, 1976. 149p.), with text by
Clark Worswick and Ainslie T. Embree, which contains 150 photographs.

941 **Delhi.**
Photographs by Raghu Rai, text by Pavan K. Varma. New Delhi:
Harper Collins India, 1994. 127p.
A collection of images of India's fast changing capital city taken by Raghu Rai, the
country's best-known photographer. Black-and-white photographs depict both the
early work of Rai and a city of grace. The more recent colour photographs capture the
degenerating condition of such historical monuments as the Red Fort, today's
teeming, smoke-clogged, congested streets, and the lives of street dwellers.

942 **The Ganges.**
Photographs by Raghubir Singh. New York: Thames & Hudson,
1993. 190p.
This visually striking book contains beautifully reproduced pictures of scenery and
activities along the sacred Ganges river and is accompanied by engaging and
illuminating text. Raghubir Singh, whose work has been included in many museum
collections and has appeared in *LIFE* and *National Geographic,* is considered one of
the world's finest photographers, The pictures here are suffused with an exquisite
light and visual purity which give them a timeless quality. Singh has also produced
similarly arresting volumes on *Rajasthan, Kashmir, Banaras* and *Calcutta.*

943   **Princely India: photographs by Raja Deen Dayal.**
      Edited by Clark Worswick.   New York: Knopf, 1980. 151p. bibliog.

Clark Worswick has selected and reproduced 123 photographs from the huge
collection by Raja Deen Dayal, a court photographer for the Nizam of Hyderabad in
the late 19th century. Topics covered by the photographs include upper-class British
and Indian society, military operations, religious ceremonies, and royal hunts.

Folk Culture and Traditions

Folklore

944 **Folktales of India.**
Edited by Brenda E. F. Beck, Peter J. Claus, Praphulladatta Goswami, Jawaharlal Handoo. Chicago: University of Chicago Press, 1987. 357p. map. (Folktales of the World, no. 13).
A goldmine for folklorists, this excellent volume collects together ninety-nine vernacular oral folktales from every major region of India. The tales are arranged in three groups: stories which centre on family relationships; tales that reveal cultural and personal values and stereotypes; and 'origin tales'. The editors provide a thematic introduction at the start of each section and an interpretive introduction before each story. The effect of the collection is to provide a cumulative collage of folk attitudes, mores and life in India. There are detailed end-notes on the occasion and setting of each tale and story, tale-type, and motif indexes.

945 **The *Katha sarit sagara*: or ocean of the streams of story.**
Somadeva Bhatta, translated from the 11th-century original Sanskrit by C. H. Tawney. New Delhi: Munshiram Manoharlal, 1968. 2nd ed. 2 vols.
The earliest and largest collection of stories extant in the world, and the source of many tales in *The thousand nights and a night*, and by Boccacio, Chaucer, La Fontaine, and others in the West. Somadeva's introduction gives an account of the work's contents, an outline of various chapters, and the origin of the tales.

946 **Another harmony: new essays on the folklore of India.**
Edited by Stuart H. Blackburn, Attipat Krishnaswami Ramanujan.
Berkeley, California: University of California Press, 1986. 387p.
bibliog.

A rich and stimulating collection of essays in which, largely Dravidian, materials on Indian folklore are studied from new perspectives, focusing on relationships and social and performative contexts. Contributors, in addition to the two editors, include Susan S. Wadley, David Schulman, George Hart, Peter J. Claus, Brenda E. F. Beck, Margaret Egnor, and V. Narayana Rao. A related work is, *Oral epics in India* (Berkeley, California: University of California Press, 1989. 290p.), edited by Stuart H. Blackburn, Peter J. Claus, and Susan S. Wadley, which analyses folk poetry with epic features.

947 **Myths of Middle India.**
Verrier Elwin. New Delhi: Oxford University Press India, 1991.
new ed. 532p. bibliog.

Verrier Elwin (see item no. 317) devoted his adult life to the study of Indian folk traditions and tribal life, publishing over 2,500 folk-tales. In this representative volume, first published in 1991, Elwin reproduces many collected tales derived from his study of the Muria Gond tribe of central India.

948 **A bibliography of Indian folklore and related subjects.**
Sankar Sen Gupta, Shyam Parmar. Calcutta: Indian Publications,
1967. 196p. (Indian Folklore Series, no. 11).

About 5,000 entries, mostly articles, in the English language on various aspects of Indian folklore. The book is divided into seventeen sections, including: general folklore; prose narratives; folk music; dance, and drama; arts, crafts, and architecture; proverbs, parables, and epigrams; totems, taboos, and superstitions; and material culture.

949 **Ancient Indian magic and folklore: an introduction.**
Margaret Stutley. Boulder, Colorado: Great Eastern, 1980. 190p.
bibliog.

Based mainly on the *Atharva Veda*, a classical magico-religious text compiled about 1400 BC, the book describes charms relating to women, priests, demons, and sorcerers, as well as charms for prosperity, harmony, healing, longevity and war. Stutley argues that the wearing of lucky charms and talismans; the belief in lucky and unlucky days, birds, and animals; and the fear of demonic possession or curses are common in both European and Indian folklore.

950 **Studies in Indian folk traditions.**
Ved Prakash Vatuk. New Delhi: Manohar, 1979. 221p. bibliog.

Nine essays analysing the content and significance of various folklore genres. Almost all the essays deal with north Indian folk literature and art. Vatuk covers several areas such as opera, riddles, hymns, songs, private sayings, and the character of the stepmother in Indian folk traditions.

Festivals

951 **Festivals of India.**
Brijendra Nath Sharma. New Delhi: Abhinav, 1978. 156p. bibliog.
This well-illustrated book provides a panoramic view of Indian festivals of all faiths. Its first part describes forty-four festivals of ancient India and the second part has information on 185 modern festivals. Dr. Sharma has also included the principal sites of these festivals such as Sivaratri at Varanasi (Banaras), Holi at Mathura, Baisakhi at Amritsar, Id ud-Zuha at Delhi and Lucknow, Christmas at Goa, and Parsee Navroz at Bombay. Each description has a brief history of the festival and its approximate date according to the local calendar.

Social customs and superstitions

952 **Hindu omens.**
C. D. Bijalwan. New Delhi: Sanskriti, with Arnold Heinemann, 1977. 176p. bibliog.
A large part of this book is a translation from *Shakunauti*, an 18th-century compilation of omens, and from *Basantarajashakunodaya*, a pre-12th-century text. Twelve chapters include omens based on animals, throbbing limbs, and sneezing; augurs related to prominent religious characters; and omens based upon astrological indications. The author includes traditional amulets used by the superstitious to ward off bad omens.

953 **Popular religion and folklore in northern India.**
William Crooke. New Delhi: Munshiram Manoharlal, 1968. reprint of 1896 ed. 2 vols.
An encyclopedic collection of information on folk customs, proverbs and religious practices in the Ganges Valley (Uttar Pradesh) region of north India by a colonial official. Crooke, a part-time ethnographer with a great interest in and sympathy for rural India, received much of this data from informants.

954 *Sati*: **a historical, social and philosophical enquiry into the Hindu rite of widow burning.**
Vishwa Nath Datta. New Delhi: Manohar; London: Sangam Books, 1988. 279p. bibliog.
The Hindu practice of *sati* (the burning of a widow on the funeral pyre of her husband) was legally banned in 1829 by governor-general Lord William Bentinck (see item no. 245) and stringent anti-*sati* measures were enforced during the mid-19th century administration of Lord Dalhousie. These were largely successful, but *sati* did not fully disappear: in September 1987 there was a highly publicized case at Deorala in Rajasthan. This book explains the origins of and rationale for *sati* and, concentrating on the period between the mid-18th and mid-19th centuries, reviews

British policy towards its suppression and the views of reformist Hindu thinkers, notably Ram Mohan Roy. It can be read alongside a recent collection of scholarly essays on the phenomenon, *Sati, the blessing and the curse: the burning of wives in India* (New York: Oxford University Press USA, 1994. 256p.), edited by John Stratton Hawley.

955 **Hindu manners, customs and ceremonies.**
Jean Antoine Dubois, translated by Henry K. Beauchamp. Oxford: Clarendon Press, 1968. 3rd ed. 741p. bibliog.
Though written with the bias of a Catholic priest towards Hindu heathens, this is perhaps the most informative book on early-19th-century socio-religious customs. Dubois himself observed most of these customs in south India, but his information on north India is from other informants. Practices such as *sati* have now been banned, but Dubois provides an eyewitness account of many of them.

956 **Hindu predictive astrology.**
Gopesh Kumar Ojha. Bombay: Taraporevala, 1972. 347p. bibliog.
In no country of the world is astrology as popular and taken as seriously as in India. Even the exact time of the transfer of British power to Indians in 1947 was determined astrologically. Ojha's beautifully written book is an authoritative introduction to this occult science. The author rejects the unequal house division system now being popularized by some south Indian astrologers.

957 **Cults, customs and superstitions of India.**
John Campbell Oman. New York: AMS, 1975. reprint of 1908 ed. 336p. bibliog.
A reprint of the original 1908 edition, this book contains material that has, in part, been updated by other scholars. Oman reports in detail on fairs and festivals, domestic relations, witchcraft, superstitions, and fortune telling. The book's strength lies in its reporting Hindu customs at the turn of the century, long before reform movements began making their mark on Indian life.

Cookery

958 **The Raj at table: a culinary history of the British in India.**
David Burton. London: Faber & Faber, 1993. 240p.
A fascinating account of the curious, unique cuisine which the British developed during their period in India. Drawing on first-hand accounts, the author describes the culinary balance achieved in Anglo-Indian cooking and reproduces more than sixty recipes. Covering a longer timespan, *Indian food: a historical companion* (New Delhi: Oxford University Press India, 1994. 322p.), by Kongandra Thammu Achaya, is an interesting account of changing Indian diets.

959 **Lord Krishna's cuisine: the art of Indian vegetarian cooking.**
Yamuna Devi. London: Century Hutchinson, 1990. new ed. 799p.
A compendium of 520 vegetarian recipes, covering rice, dals, breads, salads, chutneys, sauces, light meals and savouries, snacks, sweets and beverages, and accompanied by background information on the history of dishes and regional specialities. An A-Z of general information includes a glossary and guide to ingredients and techniques. The author is an American who, in 1967, became a disciple of and personal cook for A. C. Bhaktivedanta Swami Prabhupada (1896-1977), founder of the International Society for Krishna Consciousness.

960 **A taste of India.**
Madhur Jaffrey. London: Pan Books, 1987. 213p.
Written by a leading radio, television, and film personality of India especially for foreigners, this book provides recipes for more than a hundred different regional dishes. The work can be complemented by Jaffrey's earlier *An invitation to Indian cooking* (New York: Knopf, 1978. 285p.), which provides recipes for appetizers, breads, salads, soups, *pilafs* (rice dishes), relishes and desserts, as well as information on how to obtain spices. A similar work, but which also provides useful background information on ingredients to buy, utensils, and cooking methods, is, *The complete book of Indian cookery* (Slough, England: Foulsham, 1994. 288p.), by Premila Lal.

961 **The Hindu hearth and home.**
Ravindra S. Khare. New Delhi: Vikas, 1976. 315p. bibliog.
An ethnographic account of contemporary ways of handling food in north India. Khare examines Hindu culinary and gastronomic traditions as practiced in everyday life and on ceremonial occasions. A concluding chapter examines how the theory and practice of commensality has changed in the recent past.

962 **Cooking delights of the Maharajahs.**
Digvijaya Singh. Bombay: Vakils, 1982. 192p.
Written by the former ruler of a princely state in Madhya Pradesh, central India, this book contains 164 recipes for dishes, ranging from snacks through entrées to desserts, that once supposedly graced the tables of India's princely rulers. Many of the recipes, especially those dealing with game, are not found in other Indian cookery books. Attractively designed with many photographs.

Sports

963 **The wrestler's body: identity and ideology in north India.**
Joseph S. Alter. Berkeley, California: University of California Press,
1992. 305p. bibliog.

Wrestling is believed to have flourished in India as early as 1500 BC and is
mentioned in classical epics such as the *Rigveda* and *Mahabharata* (see item no. 822).
The Mughals later sponsored regular wrestling competitions and during the 19th
century wrestlers such as Sadika, champion in 1840, acquired great fame. This book
is a study of wrestling culture in contemporary north India, where each day men
spend several hours in the early morning and evening at an *akhara* (health spa-cum-
gymnasium), lifting huge clubs and stones, receiving oil massages, bathing, offering
prayers to the monkey god Hanuman, and grappling under the eyes of gurus. Alter
provides details of a wrestler's diet and physical regimen and notes the links between
wrestling and Hindu nationalism.

964 **A *maidan* view: the magic of Indian cricket.**
Mihir Bose. London: George Allen & Unwin, 1986. 179p.

An entertaining and perceptive personal account of the place of cricket in modern
India by the cricket correspondent of the London *Sunday Times*. For Bose, the roots
of cricket remain much shallower in India than in England, Australia or the West
Indies. Indeed, since June 1932, when India made her Test debut, almost two-thirds of
her Test players have been drawn from just three states: Maharashtra, Gujarat and
Punjab. Moreover, unlike in England, where it is essentially rural and village-rooted,
Indian cricket is urban, played on the broad patches of green, called the *maidan*, and
the gully. However, if cricket itself has weak roots, Test cricket is hugely popular for
its *tamasha* (glamour and excitement) and its modern day stars, such as Gavaskar,
Vishwanath, Kapil Dev, Azharuddin, and Tendulkar, heroes comparable to the Hindi
film stars.

965   **Patrons, players and the crowd: the phenomenon of Indian cricket.**

Richard Cashman.   New Delhi: Orient Longman, 1980. 194p. bibliog.

An excellent socio-economic survey of cricket in India by an Australian historian. The first three chapters deal with the promotion of cricket, first by British officials in India, later by India's princes, and now by industrial houses and government agencies. Subsequent chapters deal with Test players, the crowd, and cricket commentators and writers. Several statistical appendixes describe the socio-economic characteristics of both the patrons and the players.

966   **History of Indian cricket.**

Edward Docker.   New Delhi: The Macmillan Company of India, 1976. 288p.

A short, but detailed, historical survey of the origin and development of cricket as an Indian sport. Played originally, using limited or primitive equipment, on public *maidans*, not until 1926, and the MCC tour of India, did India begin to compete on the international stage. This work charts the development of Indian cricket over the subsequent half century, embracing the inception of the Ranji trophy zonal tournament in 1934 and the development of regional rivalries. The focus is on Test series and leading personalities. For latest information, consult the *Indian Cricket Field Annual* (1962/63-) which contains a who's-who in Indian cricket. The detailed, *A history of Indian cricket* (London: Deutsch, 1990. 571p.), by Mihir Bose, is another useful work.

967   **Indian hockey: extra time or sudden death?**

Sunil Gujral.   New Delhi: Vikas, 1978. 128p.

Believed to be the oldest stick-and-ball game, field hockey has the distinction of being the national game of India, and the India team has been a dominant force in Olympic competition. Hockey was introduced and popularized by the British Army and was first played by Indians who maintained close contact with the British, notably Indian Christians and Eurasian railway-workers. Gujral's book highlights Indian achievements and the sport's recent decline in India.

968   *Kabaddi*: **native Indian sport.**

C. V. Rao.   Patiala, India: National Institute of Sports, 1971. 72p.

A game of tag between two teams of seven persons each, played on a court 13x10 metres divided into two halves (one for each team), and composed of two twenty-minute innings. The game of *kabaddi* is essentially of Indian origin, and is one of the most popular of India's outdoor sports. In the West it was first exhibited, but not included, in the 1936 Olympics, and in India it has been included in annual sports competitions since 1950. Rao's short book traces the growth of this sport, its popularity in India, Pakistan, Sri Lanka, Myanmar (Burma), Nepal and Malaysia, and recent efforts to standardize its rules.

Sports

969   **Ranji: a genius rich and strange.**
Simon Wilde.   London: The Kingswood Press, 1990. 257p. bibliog.
This, the fourth biography, of Kumar Shri Ranjitsinhji (1872-1933), popularly known
as 'Ranji', gives a full picture of the personal and sporting life of one of the great
cricketers and the first non-white sportsman to win international renown. Prince
Ranji's turbulent life is ably recounted. As a cricketer he was without equal during
what has been termed the 'golden age' of cricket. Between 1893 and 1920, playing
for Sussex, he scored almost 25,000 first class runs, retiring with an average of fifty-
six per innings, equalled only by Geoffrey Boycott in 1986. The swashbuckling Ranji
also played fifteen Test matches for England. However, Ranji was often in financial
straits and his succession to the throne of the Nawanagar Princely State in western
India was disputed.

Mass Media

Film, radio and television

970 **Indian film.**
Erik Barnouw, S. Krishnaswamy. New York: Oxford University
Press USA, 1980. 2nd. ed. 327p. bibliog.
A magisterial historical analysis of Indian cinema from its 1896 origins to
contemporary times. The book explains the extraordinary apotheosis of Indian film
stars in a land with a penchant for deification. The interplay between cinema and
politics is examined, as is the twin role of Indian film makers as reinforcers and
destroyers of tradition. Government censorship policy is also discussed. All of this is
interspersed with a first-rate critical evaluation of India's greatest films and film
makers, including the post-Satyajit Ray generation. Exhaustively researched and
lucidly written.

971 **Broadcasting in India.**
P. C. Chatterji. New Delhi: Sage Publications, 1991. 2nd ed. 228p.
map.
An account of the evolution of broadcasting in India, the system today, and its future.
Regular radio broadcasting commenced in 1927, with All India Radio being formed
in 1935. Television transmissions started experimentally in 1959, being known as
Doordarshan ('distant vision') since its inception. By 1990 there were an estimated
twenty-eight million television sets in India and, with the use of satellite links, TV
sets had spread deep into rural areas. The *Ramayana* (see item no. 820) and
Mahabharata (see item no. 822) serials, in particular, attracted massive national
audiences. Chatterji discusses ably these developments, as well as state regulation and
broadcasting policy. He also notes the recent competition introduced by cable
television networks, able to distribute foreign programmes.

972   **Mass media and village life: an Indian study.**
Paul Hartmann, Bhivarao Rajdhar Patil, Anita Dighe.   New Delhi:
Sage Publications, 1989. 280p. maps. bibliog. (Communication and
Human Values).

An assessment of the actual and potential contribution of the mass communications
media to the process of development and promotion of desirable social changes in
India. The book includes anthropological studies of five villages in the states of
Andhra Pradesh, Kerala, and West Bengal which lead to the conclusion that, so far,
the impact of mass communications has been limited.

973   **Encyclopaedia of Indian cinema.**
Ashish Rajadhyaksha, Paul Willemen.   London: British Film
Institute, 1994. 544p.

An invaluable reference work, this volume contains 700 entries on the leading
directors, stars, studios and genres in Indian cinema. There are also comprehensive
filmographies and 1,500 entries on key films from all periods and regions, including
cast and credits and critical evaluations.

974   **70 years of Indian cinema (1913-1983).**
Edited by T. M. Ramachandran and S. Rukmini.   Bombay: Cinema
India-International, 1985. 649p.

This encyclopedic volume, edited by the editor of the film magazine *CINEMA India-
International,* was produced to commemorate seventy years of Indian cinema – the
first silent feature film, Dadasaheb Phalke's *Raja Harishchandra* was screened in
May 1913. There are sixty-six chapters arranged in three broad sections. The first is
devoted to analytical studies of the pioneers of Indian cinema and includes articles on
the impact of the video and Indian film song. The second comprises historical surveys
of the fourteen principal regional cinemas, plus a chapter which reviews films
produced in fourteen minority languages and dialects. The third section, 'Government
at work', includes essays on film censorship in India, television, and international film
festivals. There is a chronological listing of 'Milestones in Indian cinema' and a
precis of key facts and figures about an industry with a current annual output of 700
feature films and average weekly audiences which exceed seventy million.

975   **Satyajit Ray: the inner eye.**
Andrew Robinson.   London: André Deutsch; Berkeley, California:
University of California Press, 1989. 412p. bibliog.

A comprehensive biography of India's foremost film director, dubbed 'India's
Kurosawa'. Written with Ray's cooperation and published just three years before his
death, this fascinating account sets Ray's development as a syncretic artist, blending
Western and Indian cinematic traditions, within his family and Bengali context. Ray's
grandfather was a pioneer of half-tone printing and a composer. His father, Sukomar,
was a writer and illustrator of innovative nonsense verse. Both were friends of
Rabindranath Tagore. Following the success at the Cannes film festival of *Pather
Panchali* (see item no. 824: Song of the Road: 1956), Satyajit became a full-time
director, making over thirty films, predominantly neo-realist in style.

976　**The moving image: a study of Indian cinema.**
Kishore Valicha.　London: Sangam Books; Bombay: Orient
Longman, 1988. 136p. bibliog.

A study of both the popular and serious Hindi and Bengali cinema, examining the role and place of film in modern Indian society and cinematic meaning (semiotics). Valicha analyses the popular Hindi 'mass film' genre, which he views as having reworked Hollywood within strongly Indian social and moral conventions so as to express Indian preoccupations. He notes the diverse influences on this genre, some traceable to Sanskrit drama and to venerable folk traditions – puppet shows, *tamasha* (street theatre), dance drama. There is also an analysis of the so-called 'parallel' or serious cinema, associated with such directors as Satyajit Ray, Shyam Benegal, Mrinal Sen and Mani Kaul, and concerned with neo-realist themes.

Publishing and journalism

977　**Romance of Indian journalism.**
Jitendra Nath Basu.　Calcutta: Calcutta University, 1979. 617p.
bibliog.

A detailed history of the growth of Indian journalism from the late-18th century to 1947. Basu divides the press in India into three broad categories: Anglo-Indian (controlled by Europeans resident in India), Indo-Anglian (English-language publications controlled by Indians), and vernacular. In addition to tracing the evolution of Indian journalism, the author provides sketches of leading journalists, Indian and foreign, who have made their mark on Indian journalism. The book has good sections on the efforts of the government to control the nationalist press.

978　**Book publishing in India.**
Kartar Singh Duggal.　New Delhi: Marwah, 1980. 267p.

An insider's story of book publishing in India, by a leading Indian man of letters, publisher, and former director of the National Book Trust of India. The book has fifty short articles covering almost all aspects of publishing, from the author-publisher relationship to the import and export of all kinds of books. Included in the collection are profiles of sixteen publishers covering a wide range from speciality publishers to those for the mass market.

979　**Communications and power: propaganda and the press in the Indian nationalist struggle.**
Milton Israel.　Cambridge: Cambridge University Press, 1994. 336p.

A scholarly analysis of the Indian press in the 19th and early 20th centuries, its role in helping to promote the nationalist message and British colonial attempts to control its output via censorship.

980 **A history of the press in India.**
Swaminath Natarajan. London: Asia, 1962. 425p. bibliog.

A well-written and analytical history of the press in India from its 18th-century beginnings to the report of the Press Commission of India in 1953. The author laments the departure of British journalists following Indian independence and readily admits that, whatever their personal political persuasions, these journalists had very high professional standards which were lacking in the Indian-controlled press of the 1950s. Natarajan does an excellent job of analysing press-related legislation introduced by the Indian government through the 1950s.

981 **The Emergency, censorship and the press in India, 1975-77.**
Soli J. Sorabjee. London: Writers & Educational Trust, 1977. 61p.

A judicious account of how Indira Gandhi harassed, subdued, and substantially tamed the Indian press in 1975. Until that time the Indian press were regarded as the freest in Asia. Sorabjee, a distinguished attorney, analyses Mrs. Gandhi's attempts under the Maintenance of Internal Security Act (MISA) to impose precensorship and other repressive measures on the Indian press.

Newspapers and magazines

982 **The Economic Times.**
Bombay: Times of India Group, 1961- . daily.

India's equivalent of the *Wall Street Journal*, with excellent coverage of the Indian economy. *Economic Times* is published simultaneously from Bombay, Ahmedabad, Calcutta, Bangalore and New Delhi and has a combined circulation of 190,000 copies. Since 1972, *Economic Times* has issued the *Economic Times Annual*, a comprehensive survey of Indian finance, economy, and trade.

983 **The Hindu.**
Madras: National Press, 1878- . daily.

This highly respected English-language conservative daily has been known for its balanced editorial policy and extensive coverage of both national and international events. Its interpretive articles are widely quoted and its background annual surveys of Indian agriculture, industry and the environment are kept for reference. As well as from Madras, it is published simultaneously from Coimbatore, Bangalore, Hyderabad, Madurai, Gurgaon and Visakhapatnam. The only major newspaper with in-depth coverage of local south Indian events. An abbreviated overseas weekly edition is also published for foreign readers. Circulation, 450,000 copies.

984 **The Hindustan Times.**
New Delhi: Hindustan Times Group, 1923- . daily.

A popular English-language daily (circulation 300,000 copies) published simultaneously in Delhi and Patna. Coverage of north Indian affairs is particularly strong. The pro-Congress K. K. Birla family controls the newspaper group.

985   **Illustrated Weekly of India.**
Bombay: Times of India Group, 1880- . weekly.
A popular general interest weekly akin to *Life* magazine. Each issue contains one or more feature articles dealing with Indian life and culture, short stories, film and society news, one or more photo-essays, and book reviews. Circulation, 50,000.

986   **India Today: the Fortnightly Newsmagazine.**
New Delhi: Thomson Living Media, 1975- . fortnightly.
Comparable in contents, style, and length to *Time* and *Newsweek*, this excellent newsmagazine has increased its circulation substantially in recent years to 350,000 copies. Investigative reporting is combined with a sensational style to enhance the magazine's importance. Coverage of national and state politics is its strength, but there are also fine business and arts sections. Hindi and Tamil editions are also produced with a combined circulation of 450,000 copies.

987   **Indian Express.**
Bombay: Indian Express Newspapers, 1953- . daily.
This daily, published simultaneously from sixteen major cities of India, has the second largest combined circulation (over 550,000 copies) among Indian English-language newspapers. Good coverage of political events in India, Pakistan, Nepal, and Sri Lanka. The proprietors are the Ramnath Goenka family.

988   **Link: Indian News Magazine.**
New Delhi: United India Periodicals, 1959- . weekly.
Produced in the style of *Time* and *Newsweek*, this is a left-leaning lively, informative, weekly news magazine. Though generally critical of Western powers and capitalism, it provides useful, but opinionated, surveys of the economic and political situation in India and of events elsewhere which it considers relevant to India. Circulation, 11,000 copies.

989   **Mainstream.**
New Delhi: Perspective Publications, 1963- . weekly.
Patterned after *Time* and *Newsweek*, this popular weekly strives to provide analysis of political and economic events, especially in India, from an independent-leftist perspective.

990   **Modern Review.**
Calcutta: Prabasi Press, 1907- . monthly.
One of the oldest general interest monthlies of India, in which articles by almost all the prominent public figures of 20th-century India have been published. It includes short essays on political, economic, literary, and cultural topics.

991   **Onlooker.**
Bombay: Onlooker Publications, 1939- . monthly.
This glossy coffee-table magazine was originally designed to reflect the 'Westernized' bourgeois culture and values of India's metropolitan centres. Though the outlook of *Onlooker* has now become more Indian, its style still strongly reflects an upper-class affluent modern lifestyle. Circulation, 60,000 copies.

992   **The Statesman.**
       Calcutta: Stateman's Press, 1875- . daily.

The *Statesman* is published simultaneously from Calcutta and New Delhi. Before independence, it was the voice of the British community. Today it remains somewhat élitist, but its coverage is reliable and especially strong of local events in east India. For overseas clientele it publishes a weekly digest, the *Statesman Overseas Weekly*. Circulation, 150,000 copies.

993   **The Times of India.**
       Bombay: Times of India Group, 1838- . daily.

Times of India, the oldest major English-language newspaper, is published simultaneously from Bombay, New Delhi, Jaipur, Bangalore, Patna, Lucknow, and Ahmedabad. Typographically it is one of the best laid out and designed of Indian newspapers. Its Sunday edition, following the tradition of the London *Sunday Times*, carries a well-edited supplement and reviews of books and the arts. Circulation, 600,000 copies. The Ashok Jain family controls the newspaper group.

News digests

994   **Asian Recorder.**
       New Delhi: Recorder Press, 1955- . weekly.

A weekly digest of Asian events modelled after *Keesing's Contemporary Archives*. The *Recorder* is indexed quarterly and has annual and triennial cumulations. The arrangement is by country and, within country, alphabetically by subject. Entries are numbered serially with references given to previous entries on topics. Very handy for current Indian events.

995   **Data India.**
       New Delhi: Press Institute of India, 1974- . weekly.

Published by the Press Institute of India, this weekly covers important regional and national Indian events. Information is culled from newspapers, government reports, research papers, and trade and commerce bulletins. Sources of information are cited. Quarterly subject indexes with annual cumulations are issued. *Data India's* coverage is broader than that provided by the *Indian Economic Diary* (see item no. 997).

996   **The Far East and Australasia.**
       London: Europa Publications, 1969- . annual. bibliog.

India is represented in this standard yearbook by up-to-date articles on its geography, history/political developments, and economy, and a statistical survey and directory giving details of the country's major institutions. Each annual entry is around sixty pages in length and is more detailed than the Indian entry in *Asia Yearbook* (Hong Kong: Far Eastern Economic Review, 1959- . annual).

997 **Indian Economic Diary: a Weekly Digest of Indian Economic Events with Index.**
New Delhi: H. S. Chhabra, 1970- . weekly.
Provides a weekly digest of economic events in India. Information for the diary is obtained primarily from English-language Indian newspapers. Coverage usually includes national and local events, foreign trade, and Indian foreign economic affairs. Includes a quarterly subject index with annual cumulation. An alternative current source of economic data is *Economic Intelligence Service*, which comprises ongoing statistical analyses and assorted special studies published by the Centre for Monitoring the Indian Economy, Bombay.

Professional Periodicals

998 **Asian Affairs.**
London: Royal Society for Asian Affairs, 1914- . thrice yearly.
The Royal Central Asian Society began publishing the *Royal Central Asian Journal* in 1914. In the 1970s both the name of the society and the title of the journal were changed to reflect more accurately the widening interests of the society. Interdisciplinary in nature, every issue of the journal carries one or two articles on India and a good book review section on South Asia.

999 **Asian Survey.**
Berkeley, California: University of California Press, 1961- .
monthly.
This American monthly superseded the *Far Eastern Survey*. Most of its articles deal with contemporary political and social developments and are based upon reports, interviews, and field research rather than standard documentary sources. Every year the first two issues survey major trends in Asian countries.

1000 **India Quarterly: a Journal of International Affairs.**
New Delhi: Indian Council of World Affairs, 1945- . quarterly.
India Quarterly offers both scholarly and general interest articles, almost all representing the point of view of the non-aligned nations, in general, and of India in particular. A substantial number of book reviews and occasionally a select bibliography of Indian publications on political, economic, and social issues are included.

1001 **Journal of Asian and African Studies.**
Leiden, the Netherlands: E. J. Brill, 1966- . quarterly.
An interdisciplinary journal, published under the editorship of an international board of Asian and Western scholars. The emphasis is on sociology, anthropology, and political and economic history. A good book review section is included.

1002　**Journal of Asian Studies.**
Ann Arbor, Michigan: Association for Asian Studies, 1941- .
quarterly.
The major US scholarly journal on Asian studies. A good number of articles deal with India. The emphasis is on the modern period, with articles on historical, political, anthropological and literary topics: articles on Indology are not included. It carries an extensive review of books. A separate *Bibliography of Asian Studies* (see item no. 1020) is produced annually by the Association for Asian Studies, along with *Doctoral Dissertations on Asia*. Until 1956 the journal was titled the *Far Eastern Quarterly*.

1003　**Journal of the Royal Asiatic Society.**
Cambridge: Cambridge University Press for the Royal Asiatic Society, 1834- . thrice yearly.
Contains accessible, scholarly articles on archaeology, art, history, language, literature, beliefs and customs of the Indian subcontinent and other parts of Asia. Nearly half the journal's pages are devoted to articles reviewing key publications or groups of publications. Triannual since 1991.

1004　**Modern Asian Studies.**
Cambridge: Cambridge University Press, 1967- . quarterly.
The British equivalent of the *Journal of Asian Studies* (see item no. 1002). It comprises research articles by international scholars on various aspects of the history, geography, politics, sociology, literature, economics, social anthropology and culture of Asia. There are fewer book reviews than its American counterpart.

1005　**New Quest.**
Poona, India: Indian Association for Cultural Freedom, 1977- .
bimonthly.
This bimonthly, published by the Indian Association for Cultural Freedom, carries a wide range of scholarly articles on literary and political topics with India as its main emphasis. Original poems and short stories are included occasionally, and there is a book review section. It is libertarian in outlook and similar to *Encounter*.

1006　**Pacific Affairs.**
Vancouver, Canada: University of British Columbia Press, 1928- .
quarterly.
The emphasis in this valuable and lively quarterly is substantial treatment of contemporary topics relating to Asian and Pacific countries. Contributions are from the United States, Canada, and other Commonwealth countries. There is an excellent book review section.

1007　**Seminar: the Monthly Symposium.**
New Delhi: Seminar Publications, 1959- . monthly.
Each issue is devoted entirely to a lively intellectual symposium on a single topic. Economic, political, and social issues are emphasized. At the end of the issue significant books on the topic under consideration are reviewed and a select bibliography is provided.

1008 **South Asia: Journal of South Asian Studies.**
Armidale, Australia: South Asian Studies Association, 1971- .
biannual.

This interdisciplinary journal, which emphasizes modern history and social sciences, is the best scholarly serial publication from the South Pacific.

1009 **South Asian Research.**
London: School of Oriental and African Studies, Centre for South Asian Studies, 1981- . biannual.

An interdisciplinary journal which includes articles on all aspects of South Asia by both young research students and established scholars and provides reports of research in progress and a cumulative index of research work. Review articles and book reviews are included. The journal is produced with the support of the British Association of South Asian Scholars. A quarterly *Bulletin of the School of Oriental and African Studies* (London: School of Oriental and African Studies, 1917-) is also produced which contains scholarly articles on India and excellent book reviews.

Libraries, Museums and Archives

1010   **Brief directory of museums of India.**
Compiled by Usha Agrawal.   New Delhi: Museum Association of India, 1980. 3rd. ed. 148p.

Entries are arranged alphabetically under state (or Union territory), and within state by cities. Each entry provides the name of the city; the museum's name and address; opening hours; types of collections; publications, if any; and availability of guide services.

1011   **Directory of research and special libraries in India and Sri Lanka.**
Niharkanti Chatterjee.   Calcutta: Information Research Academy, 1979-80. 2 vols.

This two-volume directory provides information on 463 research and special libraries in India and Sri Lanka. Each entry contains the address, phone number, year of establishment, subject of specialization, total number of volumes, annual budget, the name of the head librarian, number of staff, branch libraries, and publications, if any. More concise, covering 105 institutions, including universities, state archives and museums associated with historical and Indological studies, is *Historical and Indological institutions in India* (New Delhi: S. S. Publishers, 1987. 216p.), by P. N. Sahay.

1012   **Handbook of libraries, archives and information sources in India.**
Edited by B. M. Gupta.   New Delhi: Aditya Prakashan, 1991- . 12 vols.

This series comprises a comprehensive survey of India's libraries and information services. There are articles on separate institutions and on the history of Indian library development and annotated bibliographies. This reference work can be usefully complemented by two books discussing the evolution of and future prospects for

India's library services: *Library development in India* (New Delhi: Vikas, 1986. 568p.), by G. Kumar; and *Indian libraries: trends and perspectives* (New Delhi: Sangam Books, 1985. 244p.), edited by K. M. George.

1013 **Government archives in South Asia: a guide to national and state archives in Ceylon, India and Pakistan.**
Edited by Donald Anthony Low, J. C. Iltis, Mary Doreen Wainwright. London: Cambridge University Press, 1969. 355p. bibliog.

Over 300 pages are devoted to India in this comprehensive guide to South Asian archives. The guide covers only the national and state or provincial archives. District and subdistrict records, High Court records, private archival collections and most of the holdings on microfilms are excluded. Each sketch provides a brief history of the archive, access regulations, the nature and extent of holdings, and bibliographic references.

1014 **A general guide to the India Office Records.**
Martin Moir. London: British Library, 1988. 331p.

An invaluable handbook designed to assist scholars exploring the mass of records held at the India Office in London. Part one provides historical background information and descriptions of the East India Company and India Office. Part two is a descriptive inventory of materials held at the India Office Records and Library. These include original correspondence and files, minutes of committees, establishment lists, formal legal documents, ships' logs, accounting records, reports, statistical data, diaries, journals, maps, press cuttings, and official publications for the period between 1600 and 1947. This is complemented by *Guide to the Oriental and India Office collections of the British Library* (London: British Library, 1993.), by Anthony J. Farrington and Graham W. Shaw.

1015 **South Asian library resources in North America: a survey prepared for the Boston conference, 1974.**
Edited by Maureen L. Patterson. Zug, Switzerland: Inter Documentation Co., 1975. 223p. (Bibliotheca Asiatica, no. 12).

In-depth profiles of forty-three libraries, ranging from the Library of Congress to several small colleges with special holdings on South Asia, based on responses recieved to a questionnaire circulated by the Association for Asian Studies. Each response includes a short history and current status report on the South Asian programme; a summary of library holdings, special strengths, and languages represented; and the library's use of the Library of Congress's acquisition programmes in South Asia.

1016 **A guide to manuscripts and documents in the British Isles relating to South and South East Asia: a supplement.**
James Douglas Pearson. London: Mansell, 1989-90. 2 vols.

This volume updates and supplements the important guide produced by Mary D. Wainwright and Noel Matthews in 1965 (see item no. 1018).

1017 **Cambridge South Asian archive: records of the British period in South Asia relating to India, Pakistan, Ceylon, Burma, Nepal, and Afghanistan held in the Centre of South Asian Studies, University of Cambridge.**
Compiled and edited by Mary Thatcher. London: Mansell, 1973. 346p.

Details the collections of private papers held at Cambridge University's Centre of South Asian Studies which have been left by colonial officers, traders, engineers, and soldiers who served in South Asia. This is available on a 1980 microfiche. A short supplement is also available, *Brief guide to original memoirs held in the Cambridge South Asian Archive* (Cambridge: Centre of South Asian Studies, 1989. 24p.), by Lionel Carter.

1018 **A guide to Western manuscripts and documents in the British Isles relating to South and South East Asia.**
Mary Doreen Wainwright, Noel Matthews. London: Oxford University Press, 1965. 532p.

This comprehensive guide covers both official archives and private papers in all the main British and Irish centres, including record offices, libraries, and learned institutions dealing with South and Southeast Asian countries. India Office Library manuscripts are excluded on the assumption that research students of modern South Asia would begin their studies in that library, which has its own extensive guides (see item no. 1014). Entries are arranged chronologically under individual depositories and are quite often remarkably full and detailed, extending to individual items. While holdings of the Public Record Office are covered in a general way, Cabinet Office records are not included.

Bibliographies, Abstracts and Indexes

Bibliographies

1019 **BEPI: a bibliography of English publications in India.**
New Delhi: D. K. F. Trust, 1976- . annual.
This annual bibliography lists 'scholarly' and 'significant' English-language publications from India. The main section of the work, providing the fullest bibliographic information, is the author section, comprising around 10,000 entries. There are also title and subject entries.

1020 **Bibliography of Asian Studies.**
Ann Arbor, Michigan: Association for Asian Studies, 1980- . annual.
Issued before 1980 as part of the *Journal of Asian Studies* (see item no. 1002), this annual bibliography attempts to list all publications on Asian countries judged to be of scholarly interest. A *Cumulative Bibliography of Asian Studies* (Boston, Massachusetts: G. K. Hall, 1969-73. 14 vols.) is available which lists books and periodical articles on South Asia published between 1955 and 1970.

1021 **South Asian history, 1750-1950: a guide to periodicals, dissertations, and newspapers.**
Margaret H. Case. Princeton, New Jersey: Princeton University Press, 1968. 561p.
The guide includes 5,431 items selected from 351 periodicals published between 1800 and 1965, and twenty-six composite works. Items are mostly in English and more than half of them are briefly annotated. Entries are divided into six sections: areas not primarily under British control; areas primarily under British control; nationalism and politics; economic history; social history; and cultural history. Also listed are 650 dissertations and a significant number of newspapers (341 English and bilingual and 251 Indian-language) published in South Asia, and the newspaper holdings and locations of various South Asian and Western libraries.

1022 **Catalogue of European printed books [of] the India Office Library.**
Boston, Massachusetts: G. K. Hall, 1964. 10 vols.
Volumes one to six contains entries for about 90,000 books in European languages held in the India Office Library in 1963. Volumes seven to nine are a subject index to volumes three to six, and volume ten notes the periodicals held by the library. Between 1867 and 1947 the India Office Library was a depository for all books and pamphlets published in India, thus this catalogue is an important reference tool for research in Indian studies.

1023 **A select bibliography of periodical literature on India and Pakistan, 1947-70.**
Compiled by Pervaiz Iqbal Cheema. Islamabad: National Commission on Historical and Cultural Research, 1976-84. 3 vols.
A compilation of more than 5,000 unannotated entries drawn from 575 magazines and journals. The topics covered range widely – including sports, cookery, forestry, education, economics, and foreign affairs. All sources are in English. Volume two, published in 1979, covers India; volume three, India and Pakistan; and volume one, Pakistan.

1024 **Annotated bibliography on the economic history of India, 1500 A.D. to 1947 A.D.**
V. D. Divekar (chief editor). Poona, India: Gokhale Institute of Politics and Economics; New Delhi: Indian Council of Social Science Research, 1977-80. 4 vols. in 5. bibliog.
Prepared by the Gokhale Institute of Politics and Economics with financial assistance from the Indian Council of Social Science Research, this annotated bibliography, containing 31,484 items, is the most comprehensive source for the economic and social history of India, Pakistan, and Bangladesh. Coverage includes selections from records, survey and settlement reports, gazetteers, acts and regulations, British parliamentary papers, reports of various committees and commissions, census reports, serials, books, periodical articles, and theses. Briefly annotated entries highlight the parameters of statistical information – its nature and the area and period covered. Coverage is limited to English-language printed material. A monumental work for the specialist.

1025 **India in English fiction, 1800-1970: an annotated bibliography.**
Brijen K. Gupta. Metuchen, New Jersey: Scarecrow Press, 1973. 296p.
This comprehensive annotated bibliography consists of 2,272 titles and covers English novels, tales, and short stories about India originally written in English or translated into English. For the convenience of the user, title and theme indexes are provided. Very useful for studying Indian fiction in English as well as the influence of Indian culture on Western novels.

1026 **Painting in South Asia: a bibliography.**
      Ratan Pribhdas Hingorani. New Delhi: Bharatiya, 1976. 253p.
About 1,500 books and articles published up to 1972 dealing with South Asian
paintings are indexed here. Titles are arranged under author index, anonymous works
index, subject index, manuscript titles index, dated painting index, artists' index,
index of patrons, sites' index, and collections' index.

1027 **Indian National Bibliography.**
      Calcutta: Central Reference Library, 1958- . annual.
This annual cumulative bibliography includes all books in English and other major
languages published in India and required by law to be deposited in the National
Library of India. Maps, music scores, periodicals, and newspapers (except for the first
issue under a new title) are excluded. Author and subject indexes are provided.

1028 **Indiana: a bibliography of bibliographical sources.**
      M. K. Jain. New Delhi: Concept, 1989. 292p. (Concepts in
      Communication Informatics & Librarianship – 4).
This work lists 1,827 specialist bibliographies, abstracts, indexes, library catalogues,
dissertation lists and bulletins. Entries are arranged by subject. A useful reference
source for researchers, librarians and information scientists.

1029 **Library of Congress Accessions List – South Asia.**
      New Delhi: US Library of Congress, New Delhi Office, 1981- . monthly.
Lists publications purchased by the Library of Congress on its own behalf and for
other US institutions. Entries are arranged by country of publication and there are
divisions by language of publication. Part three of each December issue contains
cumulative author/title and subject indexes. The South Asia list is the successor to
separate country lists, which were issued before 1981. An excellent source for current
Indian scholarly publications.

1030 **Guide to selected reference tools and Indological source
      materials: classified and annotated.**
      A. K. Mukherjee. Calcutta: The World Press, 1979. 267p.
An accessible work which includes a useful historical background on the evolution of
Indian reference tools. There are 851 entries, including bibliographies, yearbooks,
directories, encyclopaedias, guides, and indexes. A complementary work is
Benoyendra Sengupta, *Indian reference and information sources: an annotated
bibliography of select reference and representative books and periodicals on different
aspects of Indian life and culture* (Calcutta: The World Press, 1981. 406p.).

1031 **South Asian civilizations: a bibliographical synthesis.**
      Maureen L. Patterson, in collaboration with William J. Alspaugh.
      Chicago: University of Chicago Press, 1981. 853p. 2 maps.
The focus of this indispensable bibliography is the Indian subcontinent plus the
adjacent islands, and Indian civilization, including its extensions into Southeast Asia
and beyond. The bibliography is limited to Western-language works, principally
English, but excluding Russian and other Slavic materials. This is a select

bibliography of about 28,000 books and articles, arranged in a well-designed mix of chronology, topics, and regions. The outline of headings alone occupies eighty-three pages, indicating the comprehensiveness of the bibliography. The author index runs to over a hundred pages, and the subject index, based on key words from headings, is forty-five pages in length.

1032 **South Asian bibliography: a handbook and guide.**
James Douglas Pearson (general editor). Atlantic Highlands, New Jersey: Humanities, 1979. 381p.

A guide in two parts to works of reference providing information on Afghanistan, Bangladesh, Myanmar (Burma), the Himalayas, India, Maldives, Pakistan, and Sri Lanka. In the first part, eight bibliographical essays examine the importance of manuscripts and other unpublished materials in major libraries and archives of South Asia, Europe, and North America. In the second part, twenty-nine essays survey printed books, periodicals, newspapers, maps, and government publications by subject and by country. The guide lacks uniformity of style. Scholars have contributed bibliographical essays; librarians have generally provided lists of titles, annotated or not.

1033 **Indian reference sources: an annotated guide to Indian reference material.**
Hari Dev Sharma, assisted by L. M. P. Singh, Ramji Singh, G. C. Kendadanath. Varanasi, India: Indian Bibliographic Centre, 1988-89. 2nd ed. 2 vols.

A comprehensive guide to Indian reference sources which are either in print or are readily available in libraries. Volume one, *Generalia and humanities*, contains around 2,500 entries and volume two, *Social sciences, pure and applied sciences*, around 3,000. The cut-off date for the inclusion of items is 1985. More comprehensive, but dated, containing 20,000 annotated entries and covering materials in many languages is, *A guide to reference materials on India* (Jaipur, India: Saraswati, 1974. 2 vols.), compiled and edited by N. N. Gidwani and K. Navalani.

1034 **Indian Books in Print.**
Compiled by Sher Singh. New Delhi: Indian Bibliographies Bureau, 1969- . irregular. 3 vols.

Patterned on *Books in Print* and *British Books in Print*, this valuable publication first appeared in 1969 and new volumes have been produced on a roughly triennial basis. The first edition, published in 1969, covered nearly 25,000 books in English published in India during 1955-67. More recent editions have included nearly 100,000 titles. Each edition is divided into three volumes – authors, titles, and subject guides. At the end of the third volume a list of publishers and their addresses is provided.

1035 **South Asia: a systematic geographic bibliography.**
B. L. Sukhwal. Metuchen, New Jersey: Scarecrow Press, 1974. 824p.

10,346 books, articles and dissertations without annotations are arranged by country and subject matter. The emphasis is on geography. Tibet is included with India, Bangladesh, Pakistan, Sri Lanka, and Nepal. There is a separate author index.

Abstracts and indexes

1036 **Guide to Indian Periodical Literature: Social Sciences and Humanities.**
Gurgaon, India: Indian Documentation Centre- . 1964. quarterly.

This guide, modelled after the *Social Sciences and Humanities Index*, is published quarterly with an annual cumulation. It is a subject-author index to articles in the social sciences and humanities from selected English-language periodicals published in India. A retrospective indexing plan is under way. A very useful source for current periodical literature.

1037 **Index India: a quarterly documentation list on India of material in English, combining, in one sequence, Indian newspaper index, index to Indian periodicals, index to composite publications, index to biographical profiles, index to book reviews, index to theses and dissertations, with separate author and subject indexes.**
Jaipur, India: Rajasthan University Library, 1967- . quarterly.

The descriptive title indicates the broad scope of this comprehensive index. Over 1,000 periodicals and newspapers, as well as some composite works, are indexed. The book review index is quite substantial. Though listed as a quarterly, many issues appear on a half-yearly basis. The usefulness of *Index India* is reduced by the publication time lag, which is about four years.

1038 **Indian Dissertation Abstracts.**
New Delhi: Indian Council of Social Science Research, 1973- . quarterly.

This quarterly journal is jointly sponsored by the Indian Council of Social Science Research and the Association of Indian Universities. The main emphasis of the coverage is social sciences: economics, education, management, political science, psychology, public administration, sociology, social anthropology, and demography.

1039 **Indian Press Index.**
New Delhi: Delhi Library Association, 1968- . monthly.

A monthly index to about twenty-five English-language Indian newspapers including *The Hindu* (see item no. 983), *Hindustan Times* (see item no. 984), *Indian Express* (see item no. 987), *The Statesman* (see item no. 992), and *The Times of India* (see item no. 993). All the signed and unsigned articles, special write-ups, editorials and important letters to the editor are indexed. Contains author and geographic entries. A quarterly supplement, *Book Review Supplement*, gives all the book reviews published in the indexed newspapers.

Indexes

There follow three separate indexes: authors (personal and corporate); titles; and subjects. Title entries are italicized and refer either to the main titles, or to other works cited in the annotations. The numbers refer to bibliographical entry rather than page numbers. Individual index entries are arranged in alphabetical sequence. Compound names have been indexed under the last element, e.g. Roy, Ram Mohan.

Index of Authors

N

Nadkarni, M. V. 80
Naik, M. K. 872
Naipaul, V. S. 14
Nair, K. 753
Nakamura, H. 374
Nanavutty, P. 452
Nanda, B. R. 255, 264, 653
Nandi, P. 827
Nandi, R. N. 410
Nandy, A. 10
Naqvi, H. K. 302
Narain, A. K. 294
Narain, J. 620
Narasimhaiah, C. D. 847
Narayan, K. L. 285
Narayan, R. K. 820, 834, 846, 858
Natarajan, S. 980
Nautiyal, K. P. 98
Navalani, K. 1033
Nayar, B. R. 579
Nayyar, D. 327, 716, 730
Nehru, J. 114, 257
Neill, S. 382
Newby, E. 59
Newman, R. 784
Nice, R. 395
Nikitin, A. 133
Nimbkar, J. 338
Nizami, K. A. 160, 220
Nock, O. S. 777
Norden, D. 69
Nossiter, T. J. 601
Nugent, N. 265
Nyrop, R. F. 15

O

Oberai, A. S. 283, 284
Oberoi, H. 447
Oberst, R. C. 543
Oddie, G. A. 367
Odyssey 74
O'Flaherty, W. D. 411
O'Hanlon, R. 499
Ojha, G. K. 956
Oldenburg, P. K. 544
Oman, J. C. 957
Omissi, D. 627

Omvedt, G. 10, 557
Orans, M. 319
Ostor, A. 486
Overstreet, G. D. 587
Owens, W. 774

P

Pachauri, R. K. 779
Padhi, S. 662, 757
Page, D. 178
Page, J. M. 736
Pal, R. N. 611
Palling, B. 60
Palmer, N. D. 588
Pande, B. N. 195
Pandey, G. 179, 205, 388
Pandeya, B. K. 149
Pandharipande, R. 337
Pandian, M. S. S. 754
Panikar, P. G. K. 514
Panikkar, K. M. 27
Panikkar, K. N. 172, 388
Papanek, G. F. 659
Papanek, H. 537
Parmar, S. 948
Parry, J. P. 363, 443, 500
Parthasarathy, R. 825
Parthasarathy, V. S. 503
Pasha, S. A. 80
Patankar, A. 167
Patel, P. 407
Patil, B. R. 972
Patkar, M. 81
Patnaik, J. M. 355
Patnaik, U. 755, 760, 789
Patterson, G. 881
Patterson, M. L. 1015, 1031
Paul, S. 593
Pavlov, V. I. 723
Peach, C. 325
Pearson, J. D. 1016, 1032
Pearson, M. N. 161, 714
Pelsaert, F. 137
Pentham, T. 551
Perlin, F. 708
Phadnis, U. 309, 567
Philips, C. H. 180, 221
Phillott, D. C. 121
Phul, R. K. 630
Pillai, T. S. 828

Piramal, G. 738
Pischel, R. 346
Platts, J. T. 356
Pliny 134
Pocock, D. 366
Podger, H. 46
Polunin, O. 73
Possehl, G. L. 96, 99
Potter, D. C. 612
Potter, K. H. 468
Pottinger, G. 244
Prabhakar, E. R. 690
Prabhakar, L. S. 80
Prakash, G. 791
Prakash, O. 708, 713, 714
Pramar, V. S. 909
Prasad, B. 266
Prasad, K. 303
Prasad, Kamta 567
Prasad, P. H. 284
Prasad, R. 113
Premchand, Munshi (see Srivastava, D. R.)
Premi, M. K. 285
Presler, F. A. 444
Priaulx 134
Pritam, A. 827
Pritchett, F. W. 873
Ptolemy 134
Pugh, J. F. 505
Punja, S. 910
Puri, B. N. 613
Puri, R. C. 234
Pylee, M. V. 623

Q

Qaisar, A. J. 714, 802
Quamruzzaman, M. 353
Qureshi, I. H. 429
Qureshi, R. B. 937

R

Radhakrishnan, S. 450, 469, 470
Radice, W. 832
Raheja, G. G. 525
Rahman, A. 794
Rahula, W. 375
Rai, A. 339

Tillotson, S. 909
Timberg, T. A. 384, 725
Times of India 22
Tindall, G. 308
Tinker, H. 119, 325, 329
Tisdell, C. A. 693
Tod, J. 140
Tolley, G. S. 762
Tomlinson, B. R. 677
Toomey, P. 408
Topsfield, A. 889
Toye, J. 691, 696
Tripathi, D. 702, 721, 726
Tripathi, L. K. 535
Troll, C. W. 251, 433
Tully, M. 23, 569
Tulpule, S. G. 865
Twaddle, M. 325
Tyabji, N. 737
Tyner, W. E. 781

U

Uberoi, P. 485
Uppal. J. S. 661

V

Vaghani, Y. 66
Vaid, K. B. 825
Vajpeyi, D. K. 563
Vakil, C. N. 703
Valicha, K. 976
Valmiki 820
Vanaik, A. 570
Van Buitenen, J. A. B.
   821, 822, 876
Van der Veer, P. 390, 445
Van Dijck, P. 716
Van Nooten, B. A. 336
Van Schendel, W. 791
Van Skyhawk, H. 310
Varady, R. G. 443
Varma, H. O. 680
Varma, L. B. 311
Varma, P. K. 941
Vasudev, U. 852
Vatsyayan, K. 891, 929
Vatuk, S. 483
Vatuk, V. P. 950
Veena, D. R. 782

Venkataraman, R. 268
Venkataramani, R. 734
Venkatasubbiah, H. 741
Vepa, R. K. 737
Verma, P. 792
Verma, S. 299
Vertovec, S. 325
Vidyarthi, L. P. 321
Vincent, R. 208
Vishakadatta 817, 821
Visram, R. 330
Visvanathan, S. 797
Viswanathan, S. 378
Vivekananda, Swami 462
Vohra, A. 467
Von Böhtlingk, O. 360
Von Fürer-Haimendorf, C.
   322
Von Fürer-Haimendorf, E.
   482
Vyasa, K. D. 822

W

Wade, B. C. 939
Wade, R. 766
Wadhwa, D. C. 780
Wadley, S. S. 528, 946
Wainwright, M. D. 180,
   1013, 1018
Walker, A. R. 323
Walker, J. 773
Wallace, P. 387
Wanmali, S. 719, 762
Warder, A. K. 357, 377
Washbrook, D. A. 207
Watters, T. 141
Wavell, Earl A. P. 247
Weber, M. 492
Weightman, S. C. R. 345
Weiler, J. 804
Weiner, M. 286, 585, 594,
   808
Weiner, S. L. 914
Welch, S. C. 898
Werner, K. 414, 473
Westwood, J. N. 777
Wheeler, M. 99, 117
Wheeler, T. 46
White, B. S. 325
Whittaker, W. 45
Wickwire, F. 248

Wickwire, M. 248
Wignaraja, P. 542
Wilde, S. 969
Wilkinson, T. 209
Willemen, P. 973
Williams, G. J. 46
Williams, M. M. 360
Williams, R. B. 418
Williamson, J. G. 299
Winchester, S. 903
Windmiller, M. 587
Wink, A. 166
Winslow, M. 361
Winternitz, M. 877
Wiser, C. M. 529
Wiser, W. H. 529
Withington, N. 127
Wolpert, S. A. 120, 205,
   269, 270
Wood, H. 530
Wood, J. R. 605
Woodcock, M. 74
Woodruff, P. 241
Worswick, C. 940, 943
Woudhuysen, H. R. 837
Wujastyk, D. 513
Wulff, D. M. 396

Y

Yadav, Y. 345
Yadava, B. N. S. 145
Yang, A. A. 210, 624, 759
Yapp, M. E. 654
Yorke, M. 322
Younger, C. 312
Yule, H. 351

Z

Zacharias, T. 340
Zaidi, A. M. 571, 595
Zaidi, S. 595
Zarrilli, P. B. 927
Zbavitel, D. 865
Zelliot, E. 419
Ziegler, P. 249
Zimmer, H. 892
Zograph, G. A. 333
Zvelebil, K. V. 809, 865
Zysk, K. G. 392, 515

Index of Titles

Family affair: India under three prime ministers 565

Family, kinship and marriage in India 485

Famine in South Asia: political economy of mass starvation 767

Famines in India: a study in some aspects of the economic history of India with special reference to food problems, 1860-1990 768

Far East and Australasia 996

Far Eastern Economic Review 681

Far Eastern Quarterly 1002

Far Eastern Survey 999

Fatal friendship: the Nawabs, the British and the city of Lucknow 298

Fatehpur Sikri 295

Festivals of India 951

Feudal social formation in early India 145

Fiction of Ruth Prawer Jhabvala: the politics of passion 859

Field guide to the common trees of India 66

Financial development of India, 1860-1977 706

Fissured land: an ecological history of India 78

Flowers of the Himalaya 73

Fluid signs: being a person the Tamil way 475

Fodor's India: the complete guide to the subcontinent with expanded coverage of Nepal 44

Folk theater of India 926

Folktales of India 944

Food and poverty: India's half won battle 750

Food policy in India: a survey 769

Food, society and culture: aspects in South Asian food systems 770

Foreign trade regimes and economic development: India 712

Forests in India: environmental and production frontiers 62

Formation of the Mughal empire 165

Foundations of Indian political economy: towards an agenda for the 1990s 698

Foundations of Indian political thought: an interpretation (from Manu to the present day) 551

Freedom at midnight 173

French in India: from diamond traders to Sanskrit scholars 208

Freshwater fishes of India, Pakistan, Bangladesh, Burma and Sri Lanka: a handbook 72

Friends, brothers and informants: fieldwork memories of Banaras 480

Frogs in a well: Indian women in purdah 537

From Akbar to Aurangzeb: a study in Indian economic history 672

From hierarchy to stratification: changing patterns of social inequality in a north Indian village 526

From isolation to mainstream: higher education in India 805

From lineage to state: social formation in the mid-first millennium BC in the Ganga valley 106

From Raj to Rajiv: 40 years of Indian independence 569

Frontiers of the Indus civilization 94

Fruitful journeys: the ways of Rajasthan pilgrims 442

Fully annotated atlas of South Asia 34

Fundamentalism, revivalists and violence in India 387

G

Gandhi: against the tide 253

Gandhi and his critics 255

Gandhi, Nehru, and J. P.: studies in leadership 266

Gandhi: prisoner of hope 252

Ganesa: lord of obstacles, lord of beginnings 396

Ganges 942

Ganges civilization (a critical archaeological study of the Painted Grey Ware and Northern Black Polished Ware periods of the Ganga plains of India) 102

Ganges in myth and history 24

Gardens of Mughal India: a history and guide 881

Gazetteer of India: Indian Union 35

General guide to the India Office Records 1014

Geographical factors in Indian history 27

Gift of a cow: a translation of the Hindi novel Godaan 831

Glimpses of India: an annotated bibliography of published personal writings by Englishmen, 1583-1947 138

311

322

Index of Subjects

A

Abstracts
  dissertations 1038
  economy 682
Abu'l Fazl Allami 121,
  220
  political ideas 551
Ad Dharm 495
Adi Granth 448-49
Adivasis (tribals) 493,
  695
Administration
  ancient 132, 134, 148,
    613
  Delhi Sultanate 154,
    613
  district 603
  Gupta 147, 613
  Indian Administrative
    Service (IAS) 552,
    612
  Indian Civil Service
    (ICS) 192, 237, 239,
    241, 459, 552, 610,
    612
  Mauryan 144, 613
  medieval 163
  Mughal 123, 613
  Panchayati Raj 602
  state 596
Advaita-Vedanta 414, 468
Aesthetics 891-92, 925
Afghanistan 244, 654
Afghans 155, 163
Agarwal community 739
Agency Houses 701, 720
Agra 47, 129, 389, 391
  village life near 528-29
  under Mughals 137, 295
Agrarian relations and
    social structure 744,
    746, 749, 755, 760-61
  mode of production
    debate 760
Agrarian struggles 174,
  557

Agrarian system (*see also*
    Economic history)
  Delhi Sultanate 154
  Mughal India 159-60,
    671-72
Agriculture 4, 655, 661,
    680, 742-71
  atlas 38
  commercialization of
    744, 757
  cropping patterns 31,
    666, 743, 758, 761
  development 684, 687,
    689, 694-95
  droughts' impact on 769
  grain cultivation 518
  green revolution 6, 10,
    526, 599, 689, 694,
    746, 758, 762
  history of 758, 798
  implements 747, 758
  in Andhra Pradesh 750,
    757
  in Bengal 217, 743-45
  in Bihar 750, 753, 759
  in Haryana 755
  in Punjab 666, 746, 748,
    753, 757
  in Tamil Nadu 216, 662,
    750, 752, 754
  in Uttar Pradesh 750,
    757, 761
  in western India 666-67,
    771
  labour 744, 791
  land control and tenures
    5, 177, 751-52, 759
  land reform 187, 689,
    751
  milk cooperatives 695
  output trends 703, 743
  policy 768
  productivity 743, 749
  programmes 692
  Review of 679
  rice cultivation 752,
    754

sayings 747
sugar production 742,
  749
technology and
  technical change 667,
  758, 761-62
tobacco production 757
tractorization 694
Ahmedabad 137, 300, 541
Aid (*see* Foreign aid)
Ai' n-i Akbari 121, 219,
  671-72
Ajanta caves 914
Akali Dal party 600
Akbar, Emperor 114, 127,
  158, 165
  and arts 231
  and Islam 433
  biography and official
    memoirs 121, 231
  poetry under 812
Akharas 963
Al-Biruni (Alberuni) 110,
  124
Alchemy 803
Alexander the Great 631
Ali, Amir 427, 432
Ali, Sher 244
Aligarh
  Muslim Anglo-Oriental
    college 263, 428
Allahabad 129, 287
  Kumbh Mela 23, 521
  village life near 521
Ambedkar, B. R. 261, 495
Amber 912
Amritsar
  Baisakhi festival 951
  massacre (1919) 627
  storming of Golden
    Temple in 1984 569,
    600
Anand, Mulk Raj 827,
  834, 885
  biography and works of
    839
Andaman Islands 244

Andhra Pradesh
  agriculture 750, 757
  history 223
  irrigation 766
  Naxalites 554
  state politics 554
Anekanta-vada 437
Anglo-Indians and
    Eurasians
  community, development
    of 198, 311-12
  cookery 958
  dictionary 351
  in fiction 843
Animals (*see* Fauna)
  fables 819
Ansari, M. A. 259
Anthropology 5, 9, 480
  and archaeology 84, 96,
    99
  atlas 42
  bibliography 482
  under British Raj 879
Anthropometry 17, 42
Arab music 931
Arab travellers' accounts
  11th century 124
  14th century 130
  15th century 133
Arab world
  Indian migration to 325
  relations with India 653
Arabs 163
Archaeology 83-106
  anthropological
    approaches 84, 96, 99
  Aryans 85, 92, 292, 497
  bibliographies 89, 482
  central India 97, 104
  climate 86, 104
  copper hoard culture 103
  domestication of
    animals 86
  early coinage 105
  early population growth
    95
  early trade and trade
    routes 93-94, 99, 134,
    715, 717
  early urbanization 85,
    94-95, 98-99, 101,
    107, 292, 303, 307,
    799

eastern Punjab 92, 106
encyclopaedia of 91
Ganges valley
  civilization 85, 87,
    95, 98, 102, 106
Harappan (Indus Valley)
    Civilization 16,
    83-85, 87-90, 92-94,
    96, 98-99, 103, 111
  history of 83, 87-88
  iron, use of 84, 98,
    102-03
  journals 100
Lord Curzon and 240
north-eastern India 105
pottery 91, 97, 799, 803
Son valley 104
Architecture 44, 802
  Ajanta 914
  ancient 880, 882-83,
    888, 901-02, 905,
    911
  British India 903, 908,
    911
  Buddhist 878, 882-83,
    886, 888-89, 901,
    911, 914-15
  Delhi Sultanate 154
  18th century 899
  folk and tribal 909, 948
  Gupta 883, 890
  Harappan 882, 905
  havelis (houses and
    mansions) 903, 909
  history 880, 882, 902,
    905, 911, 913
  Islamic 878, 882, 905,
    911
  Jain 882-83, 888
  journals 884-85
  Khajuraho 910
  modern 913
  Mughal 158, 899, 912
  railway 776
  Rajput 912
  regional styles 889
  Taj Mahal 131, 233,
    900
  temple 882, 890, 904,
    907, 910
  theatre 903
  Vedic 911
  Vijayanagara 883, 905

Archives 1011-18, 1032
  (*see also* Libraries)
  British 1014, 1016-18
  Cambridge South Asian
    archive 1017
  India Office Library and
    Records 1014
  Library of Congress
    1015
  national 1013
  North American 1015
  Public Record Office
    1018
  state and regional 1013
Arcot, battle of (1751)
  238
Aristotle 924
Arjuna 456
Armed forces (*see also*
    Defence)
  ancient period 134, 631
  British Raj 192, 626-27,
    629
  during the World Wars
    627, 629
  early medieval 163
  history 631
  mansabdari system 152,
    165, 630
  Maratha 213, 631
  Mughal period 123, 165,
    231, 630
  navy 630, 634
  nuclear arms 625, 632,
    634, 639
  organization 627, 631
  Rajput 628
  recruitment 627-628
  recruits in paintings 893
  sepoys 627-28
  since independence 626
  technology and
    equipment 627, 631
Arrian 134
Art 12, 43, 44, 878-914
  bibliography 482
  British India 879
  Buddhist 878, 882-83,
    886-88
  European reactions to
    887
  folk 948
  Gupta 147, 883, 890

327

337

338

Puranas 115, 396, 411, 861, 864-65
Ramayana 52, 342, 405, 412, 820, 860-61, 864, 971
reform and revivalist movements 179, 188, 362, 365, 404, 406, 499
religious literature 398, 405
Saivism 405, 407, 410
sants 400-01
Swaminarayan movement 418
temples 58, 149, 363, 400, 718, 882, 889, 904, 907, 910
Vaisnavism 405, 410, 413, 418, 501
Vedas 2, 398, 435, 455, 458, 468-70, 865, 877
Virasaivism 310, 410, 809
History
general 4, 6, 18, 44, 47, 107-20
agriculture, of 758, 798
ancient 83-106, 115, 142-44, 146-48, 150
archaeology, of 83, 87-88
architecture, of 880, 882, 902, 905, 911, 913
armed forces, of 631
art 24, 107, 880, 882-83, 888
atlases 36, 41
bibliographies 112, 210, 223
British period 113, 118, 120, 153, 167-210 (*see also* British Raj)
Buddhist era 115, 369, 372, 376-77
Cholas 149, 215
Christianity in India, of 382
cinema, of 970, 974
cricket, of 966

cultural 107, 113
Delhi Sultanate 113, 128, 130, 154, 163
dictionaries of 109, 189
diplomatic 645
early medieval 113, 124, 141, 142, 145, 149, 153, 166
economic 662-77 (*see also* Economic history)
18th century 151, 155-57, 166
essays 108, 110
famines, of 768
feudalism 108, 145, 215
food 958
Guptas 126, 141, 147, 890
historiography 9, 220-23, 664, 674-75
ideas 143, 171
Islam, of 422, 425, 431-32
Jainism, of 435-36
journals 224-27
literature 107, 143, 861, 865, 872, 877
Mauryas 118, 132, 144, 236, 613, 916
medicine, of 513, 515, 798, 801
military 123, 134, 163, 165, 192, 213, 231, 626-31
Mughals 5, 113, 118, 120, 121-23, 127, 131, 135-37, 139, 151-52, 155-63, 165, 478, 613, 671-73
music, of 936, 938
nationalist movement 170, 172, 175, 181, 183-84, 186-88, 195, 201-03, 205, 207, 250-53, 255, 257-58, 264, 270, 665
official manuals 121-22, 128, 131-32
painting, of 880, 882, 895

partition and transfer of power 54, 60, 120, 172-73, 180, 182, 192-93, 200, 204, 249, 260
police 613-14
press, of the 977, 979-80
railway 776-77
Rajput 153, 212, 613, 628
rebellion of 1857 10, 60, 110, 172, 190, 206, 218, 237, 263, 381, 739
regional history 149, 151, 153-54, 157, 159, 164, 176, 178, 185, 196-97, 199, 202, 207, 210-18
science and technology 798-803
Sikhism 211, 214, 446, 448
social history 167-68, 171, 179, 183, 186, 198, 200, 209
south India 164. 207, 215-16, 223, 256, 476
Subaltern school 179, 614, 742
sufism, of 430
theatre 926
trade unions, of 788, 790
travellers' accounts 123-27, 129-30, 133-41
tribals, of 318
Vijayanagara empire 164, 215, 883
Hockey 967
Holy places (*see* Sacred places)
Homeopathy 508
Hong Kong
Indian migration to 325
Hotels 44-46
Household (*see* Family)
Houses (*havelis*) 909
rural 39
Hsuan Tsang (Yuan Chwang) 141

fundamentalism 387
history of 422, 425,
  431-32
Khilafat movement 191
literature 853, 865
reform and revivalist
  movements 178, 432
seminaries *(madrasas)*
  428, 433
sharia (Islamic law) 421
Shia sect 423
shrines 433
spread to Bengal 420
sufism (Islamic
  mysticism) 401, 420,
  430, 448, 512
thought 427, 433
ulama (Islamic doctors
  of law) 420, 428
waqfs (endowments)
  425
Ismay, Lord 182

J

Jagirdars 154, 165
Jainism 310
  Anekanta-vada 437
  Architecture and art
    882-83, 887-88
  At Mathura 307
  Digambara and
    Svetambara sects
    435-36
  history of 435-36
  influence on
    Swaminarayan
    movement 418
  literature 861, 875, 877
  Mahavira, life of 436
  philosophy of 437, 463,
    470
  social aspects 434
Jahangir, Emperor 137,
  158
  biography 233
  painting under 898
Jaipur 47, 912
  19th century princely
    state 153, 196
Jajmani system 479, 519,
  522, 529

Jammu and Kashmir 223
Jana Sangh 386, 576,
  583
Janata Party 550
  1977-80 coalition
    government 565, 578,
    611, 650
Jang, Salar 196
Jatis 475, 700
Jats, in 18th century
  155-56
Jayadeva 814
Jayarasi 457
Jewellery 915, 919
Jews 166
  Baghdadi Jews 383-84
  Bene Israel of Bombay
    383-84
  Calcutta Jewish
    community 384
  Cochin Jews, social
    stratification 384
  Malabar Jews 384
Jhabvala, Ruth Prawer
  834, 836, 859
Jharkhand, tribals 320
Jinnah, M. A. 10, 180,
  193, 204, 259
  biographies 260, 269
Jodhpur 912
Jones, Sir William 243
Joshi, Arun 825
Journalism 977, 979-81
  (*see also* Newspapers)
Journals (*see* Periodicals)
Judicial system
  ancient 620
  judicial review 616
  redistributive justice
    620
  Supreme Court 616

K

Kabaddi 968
Kabir 401, 855
Kalhana 221
Kalidasa 815-17
Kama 411
Kanauj
  early medieval 113
  5th century 126

Kannada
  community of New
    York 335
  dictionaries 352
  grammars 337
  literature 809
Kanpur 95, 300, 389
  caste in 491
  19th century 125
Kapilvastu, 5th century
  126
Karnataka
  bilingualism in 335
  forests 76
  history 223
  migration 285
  politics 605
  12th century 809
  village life in 527
Karma 393, 403, 478
Kashmir
  feudalism 145
  history 223
  Indo-Pakistan dispute
    over 644
  photography of 942
  politics 554
Kashmiri
  grammars 343
  literature 343, 865
  pandits 486
Kautilya 132, 665
  political ideas 661
Kaye, Molly M. 862
Kekorvian album 898
Kerala
  Christianity in 378
  health care in 514
  in fiction 828
  land reform 751
  migration 284
  politics 597-98, 601,
    605
Khajuraho 886, 910
Khan, Sadat 176
Khan, Sir Sayyid Ahmad
  427, 432
  and Aligarh Muslim
    Anglo-Oriental
    College 428
  biography 263
Khasis 320
Khilafat movement 191

341

O

Occult 858, 956
Official publications 1014,
  1024, 1032
Oil and petroleum 778-79,
  781
Omens 952
Orissa
  19th century 237
  temple art 904
  village life 520, 522
Oriya
  dictionaries and
    grammars 355
Oudh (*see* Awadh)

P

Padma river
  in fiction 823
Painting 44, 889
  Bengal 897
  bibliography
    history 880, 882, 895
  journals 884-885
  landscape, of British
    India 879, 893
  miniature 894, 896,
    898
  Mughal 880, 896, 898
  Pahari 894
  patronage 886, 896
  Punjab hills 894-95
  Rajput and Rajasthan
    212, 895-96
  wall 895
Pakistan 1, 6, 18, 29, 31,
  45, 61
  archaeology 85, 92 (*see
    also* Harappan
    Civilization)
  archives 1013
  bibliographies 1024,
    1032, 1035
  biographies 230
  birds 63
  demand for creation of
    178, 193, 204
  economic development
    689
  fishes 72

foreign relations with
  India 638-39, 641-44,
  651-53
history 119
Indo-Pakistan wars 262,
  639, 642, 644
Islam in 431
land reform 751
migration from 329
nuclear policy 632, 634
periodical literature
  1023
purdah in 537
sufi music 937
Western economists and
  692
women's political
  participation in 539
Pala-Sena sculpture 906
Pali
  Buddhism 373, 377
  dictionaries and
    grammars 357
  literature 864-65
Paltu, Sahib 401
Panchayati Raj 602
Pandharpur pilgrimage
  419, 442
Panipat, battle of (1526)
  118
Parliament (*see Lok
  Sabha*)
Parsees 166, 362, 451-52
  (*see also*
  Zoroastrianism)
Parthasarathy, Rajagopal
  825
Partition and transfer of
  power (1947) 54, 120,
  172-73, 180, 182,
  192-93, 200, 204,
  249, 260
  in fiction 848
  in travellers' accounts
    60
Parvati 910
Patel, Vallabhbhai 267,
  566
Patna, 5th century 126
Peasant resistance and
  movements 1, 172,
  174, 179, 744
People of India project 42

Pepper 713
Performing arts 921-29
  (*see also* Dance and
  Theatre)
Periodic markets 719
Periodicals (*see also*
  Magazines)
  anthropology 1001-02,
    1004
  bibliographies 1020-21,
    1023-24, 1032
  economic developments
    1000, 1004, 1007
  economic history 1001
  foreign relations 1000,
    1006
  geography 1004
  history 1001-04, 1008
  literary 1002, 1004-05
  politics 999, 1000-02,
    1004-05, 1007-08
  social developments
    999, 1007
  sociology 1001, 1004
Persian 245, 356
Peshawar, 5th century 126
Philosophy 864
  Advaita-Vedanta 414,
    468
  Aurobindo Ghose 362,
    453, 459, 465, 470-71
  Bhagavad Gita 392,
    415, 456, 465, 470
  Buddhist 369, 372-75,
    377, 457, 463-64, 470
  Carvakas 470
  concepts 12
  early period 142-43,
    148, 458, 463-64, 468
  11th century 124
  encyclopaedia of 468
  Gandhism 362, 453,
    460, 471
  Grammarians 468
  Guru Nanak 449
  Hindu 393, 395, 397,
    405, 417
  illusion 464
  Indian renaissance 453
  Islamic 427, 433
  Jain 437, 463, 470
  journals 461
  karma 393, 403, 478

R

Radha 396, 814
Radhakrishnan, Sarvepalli
    362, 414, 450, 453,
    469-71
  biography 467
Radhasoamis 391, 401,
    495
Radio 971-72
  All India Radio 971
Ragas 933-36
Rai, Raghu 941
Railways 189, 241
  Bengali villagers' tour
    of 530
  contemporary travel 48,
    61
  environmental impact
    443
  fares and timetables
    47
  history 196, 776-77,
    800
  impact on famine 771
  locomotive types 48,
    776
  stations 776
Rajagopalachari, C. 253
Rajasthan 47
  cultural history and
    geography 212
  early 19th century 140
  history 153, 222-23
  joint family in 483
  painting 212, 895-96
  photography of 942
  pilgrimages 416, 442
  population growth 279
  sati 954
  17th century and 18th
    century 159
  tribals 559
  village life 155
Rajputs 153, 212, 613,
    628, 912
Rajya Sabha 606
Ram, Mangoo 495
Ram Mohan Roy (*see*
    Roy, Ram Mohan)
Rama 52, 412, 445, 820,
    860-61, 864
Ramakrishna 416

Ramakrishna Mission 324,
    462
Ramakrishna Movement
    362
Ramananda 855
Ramanuja 458, 470
Ramayana 52, 342, 405,
    412, 820, 860-61, 864
  television broadcasts
    971
Ranade, M. G. 665
Rao, Gundu 605
Rao, Raja 834, 839, 847
Rashtriya Swayamsevak
    Sangh (RSS) 386-87,
    572, 583
Ratnakara 875
Ravidas 496
Ray, Satyajit 824, 970,
    976
  biography 975
Razzak, Abdul 133
Rebellion of 1857 10, 110,
    172, 190, 206, 218,
    237, 263, 739
  and Christian
    missionaries 381
  in fiction 862
  in travellers' accounts
    60
Reference
  annual 8
  guides 1028, 1030,
    1033
Religion 362-452 (*see also*
    Buddhism,
    Christianity,
    Hinduism, Jainism,
    Islam, Jews, Muslims,
    Parsees, Sikhism, and
    Zoroastrianism)
  general 15, 18, 39, 47,
    362-67, 864
  ancient 134
  and nationalism 364
  and peasant society 493
  atlas 39
  conversion 367
  Delhi Sultanate 154
  11th century 124
  Gupta 890
  Harappan 890
  in Bengal 217

  in travellers' accounts
    60
  popular in north India
    953
  revival movements 362,
    365, 367
  16th century 136
  thinkers 362
  village 493, 524, 527
Remittances 283, 327,
    660, 716
  impact on villages 522
Renu, P. N. 829
Reptiles 67, 71
Research institutes 228
Research work
  index 1009
Reservation policies 10
Residents, in princely
    states 167, 176, 196
Rice cultivation 752, 754
Rig Veda 2 (*see also*
    Vedas)
Ripon, Lord 242
Rivers
  boats 59, 764, 802
  commerce 24
  Ganges 24, 50-51, 59,
    772, 942
  Narmada 50, 845
  Padma 823
  steamboats on 772
  travels along seven 50
Roads
  ancient routes 93
  engineering 773
  pre-rail transport on
    773
Roberts, Lord 629
Rohillas, 18th century
    156
Rowlatt Satyagraha 183
Roy, M. N. 453
  political ideas 551
Roy, Ram Mohan 362
  biography 406
  ideas of 453
  opposition to sati 954
Rural (*see* Agriculture,
    and Village life)
Rushdie, Salman 848
Ryotwari settlement 189,
    246

S

Sacred places (*tirthas*)
  Buddhist
    distribution of 438
  Hindu 400, 417, 438-45
  Muslim 433
Sadhus 445
Sahgal, N. 849
Saikia, B. N. 825
Sailors (*lascars*) 330
Saivite philosophy 405,
    454
Salt transport 773
Samkhya philosophy 457,
    468
Sankara 468-70
Sanskrit 245
  dictionaries 360
  drama 924, 926-27
  grammars 342, 356
  influence on Hindi 348
  literature 24, 336, 535,
    810-11, 814-17,
    820-22, 861, 864-65,
    867, 874-76
  studies 336
Sanskritization 491, 502
Santals 316, 319
Santo Stefano, H. 133
Sarais (resthouses) 773
Saran district, Bihar
  19th century agrarian
    relations 210
Sati (widow burning) 189,
    245, 954-55
  in 14th century 130
Saurashtra 909
Science and technology 8
  agricultural 667, 758,
    761-62
  ancient 99, 101, 801
  appropriate technologies
    793-94
  astronomy 124, 798-99,
    801, 864
  botany 798
  chemistry 798, 803
  chronometry 802
  computer industry 796
  11th century 124
  European and colonial
    impact 800, 802

Harappan 99
  history of 798-803
  impact on society 795
  in ancient India 799,
    801, 803
  journals 795
  mathematics 124,
    798-99, 801, 864
  military 627, 631
  policy 793
  reference sources 1033
  research and
    development 793,
    797, 805
  technical education
    800
  under Indira Gandhi
    563
Scientists, biographies
    228
Sculpture (*see also*
    Architecture)
  Ajanta 914
  Aurangabad 901
  bronze 906
  dance in 891
  erotic 887, 910
  Khajuraho 886, 910
  Pala-Sena school of 906
  regional styles 889
  stone 906
Seafaring, ancient 87
Self-employed Women's
    Association 541
Sepoys 627-28
Seringapatam 246
Servants 330
Seth, Vikram 850
Settlement patterns 28
Sexual relationships 12,
    475
Shah Jahan, Emperor 123,
    136, 152, 158
  biography and court
    history 131, 233
  painting under 898
Shahjahanabad 131 (*see
    also* Delhi)
Shakas, trade 715
Shamans 512
Shastri, Lal Bahadur 262,
    625
Shekhar, Chandra 268

Shipbuilding industry 800,
    802
Shipping
  Harappan 717
  16th and 17th century
    714
  steam 800
Shiv Sena 14, 580
Shramik Sanghatana
    movement 554
Shri Ram, Lala 739
Shivaji 234
Sikh
  administration 613
  fundamentalism 387,
    600
  politics 599-600
  terrorism 14
Sikhism 310
  gurus 214, 446, 448-49
  history 211, 214, 446,
    448
  in Britain 324
  in 18th century 155
  in North America 326
  influence of *bhakti* and
    sufism 448
  sacred writings 448-50
  Singh Sabhas 362
  teachings of Guru
    Nanak 449
Sikkim, history 223
Silk 713
Simla 288, 839
Sindhi literature 865
Singapore
  Indian migration to 310
Singh, Duleep 330
Singh, Guru Gobind 214,
    448
Singh, Khushwant 448,
    827, 834
Singh, Raghubir 942
Singh, V. P. 268
Sitar 938
Siva 396, 407, 411, 815,
    910
Slavery 789
Slim, Sir William 629
Smallpox 505, 513
Social
  atlas 38
  development 30

353

sanitation 800
town plans 36, 46
urban systems 304-05
women 538, 540
Urbanization
ancient 85, 94-95, 98,
101, 108, 292, 307,
799
early medieval 306
Harappan 99
late medieval and
Mughal 294-95, 302
modern 39, 289-90, 299,
304-05, 662, 671
under Kusanas 303
Vijayanagara 164
Urdu
development of 339,
348
dictionaries 356
grammars 339, 345
literature 865, 870, 873
phrasebook 46
spread of 334
USA (*see* United States of
America)
USSR (*see* Soviet Union)
Usury, in ancient India
674
Uttar Pradesh
history 181, 231
irrigation 766
kinship organization
486
land reform 187, 751
migration 284
politics 605
population growth 279
village life 245, 518,
520, 525-26, 528-29
zamindari abolition
187

V

Vaid, K. B. 825
Vaisali, 5th century 126
Vaishesika philosophy 468
Vaisnavism 405, 410, 413,
418, 501
Valmiki 412, 820, 860
political ideas 551

Valmiki Sabha 495
Van Buitenen, J. A. 876
Varna system 497
Vasudev, Uma 852
Vedantic philosophy 455,
458, 465, 469-70
Vedas 2, 398, 435, 455,
458, 468-70, 865,
876-88
Vedic India
architecture 911
cosmology in 455
hand weaving 916
myths 418
ritual 478
Vellore massacre 245
Venkataraman,
Ramaswami 268
Viceroys of British Raj
238 (*see also*
individual viceroys)
Vidyasagar, I. C. 453
Vijayanagara 164, 215,
883, 905
Village life 5, 41, 481
agriculture 518,
527-28
bibliographies 523
caste 475, 498, 516-17,
524-27
central India 520
class stratification 526
commerce 521
crime 524
diachronic studies 522,
528
dreams of villagers 475
ecology 527
education 528
family relations 524,
527-28
festivals 521, 524
food 524
green revolution impact
526
Himalaya 516
impact of mass media
972
in fiction 826, 828-29,
831, 844
in 19th century
Rajasthan 155
in paintings 893

in travellers' accounts
60
kinship and marriage
516, 525, 527
labour relations and
jajmani system 479,
519, 522, 528-29
land control 5, 177, 518,
751-52, 759
medicines and drugs
524
north India 479, 518,
520-22, 525-26,
528-29
Orissa 520, 524
outmigration impact
280, 282-83, 520, 522
plague and 759
politics and elections
524
population growth 522
poverty 519, 687, 695,
747
religion 493, 524, 527
rituals 521, 525
sexuality 475
shamanism 479
south India 475, 517,
520, 527
superstitions 530
theatre 921
untouchables (*harijans*)
524
western India 519-20
women, position of 524,
528
Virasaivas 310, 410, 809
Vishakadatta 817, 821
Vishwa Hindu Parishad
(VHP) 386, 572
Vivekananda, Swami 362,
414, 462
Vyasa 822
political ideas 551

W

Wage trends 791
Wall paiting 895
Water control (*see*
Irrigation)
Water resources 26, 31

Map of India

This map shows the more important towns and other features

ALSO FROM CLIO PRESS

INTERNATIONAL ORGANIZATIONS SERIES

Each volume in the International Organizations Series is either devoted to one specific organization, or to a number of different organizations operating in a particular region, or engaged in a specific field of activity. The scope of the series is wide-ranging and includes intergovernmental organizations, international non-governmental organizations, and national bodies dealing with international issues. The series is aimed mainly at the English-speaker and each volume provides a selective, annotated, critical bibliography of the organization, or organizations, concerned. The bibliographies cover books, articles, pamphlets, directories, databases and theses and, wherever possible, attention is focused on material about the organizations rather than on the organizations' own publications. Notwithstanding this, the most important official publications, and guides to those publications, will be included. The views expressed in individual volumes, however, are not necessarily those of the publishers.

VOLUMES IN THE SERIES

1 *European Communities*, John Paxton
2 *Arab Regional Organizations*, Frank A. Clements
3 *Comecon: The Rise and Fall of an International Socialist Organization*, Jenny Brine
4 *International Monetary Fund*, Anne C. M. Salda
5 *The Commonwealth*, Patricia M. Larby and Harry Hannam

6 *The French Secret Services*, Martyn Cornick and Peter Morris
7 *Organization of African Unity*, Gordon Harris
8 *North Atlantic Treaty Organization*, Phil Williams
9 *World Bank*, Anne C. M. Salda
10 *United Nations System*, Joseph P. Baratta

TITLES IN PREPARATION

British Secret Services, Philip H. J. Davies
Israeli Secret Services, Frank A. Clements

Organization of American States, David Sheinin